Chalice Worship

For David,
with prayers for
your continuing
ministry!
Cricket Harrison

Compiled and Edited

by

Colbert S. Cartwright

and

O. I. Cricket Harrison

Chalice Press
ST. LOUIS, MISSOURI

10 9 8 7 6 5 4 3 2   98 99 00 01 02

Library of Congress Cataloging–in–Publication Data

Cartwright, Colbert S., 1924-1996
    Chalice worship / Colbert S. Cartwright and O. I. Cricket Harrison.
       p. cm.
    ISBN—Hardcover 0-8272-0465-5
       Leather: 0-8272-0470-1
    1. Public worship—Handbooks, manuals, etc. I. Harrison, O. I. Cricket
(Ola Irene Cricket), 1955-   . II. Title.
BV25.C37   1997   95-48142
264—dc20   CIP

Printed in the United States of America

$\mathcal{C}$ONTENTS

I. $\mathcal{G}$ENERAL SERVICES OF WORSHIP

II. $\mathcal{E}$CUMENICAL SERVICES OF WORSHIP

III. *Worship Services for the Christian Year*

IV. *Worship on Special Sundays*

V. *SPECIAL WORSHIP OCCASIONS IN THE LIFE OF THE CHURCH*

VI. *WORSHIP RESOURCES*

*C*NDEXES

Introduction

Public worship is a gift of God's grace to the church. It is the means by which God's people join together to glorify God through adoration and praise. In return, God pours out the richness of bounteous grace to strengthen and nurture those who worship.

Worship is not so much a performance before God as it is an intimate sharing of joyous fellowship with the one who creates, redeems, and sustains us. The spirit of worship is a celebration of the special relationship God has with all who name Jesus Christ as Lord and seek to follow him.

Centering upon the Christ who presides at the Lord's table, the whole atmosphere of worship is colored by the conviction that Christ is in the midst of God's people. Thus, worship is a time of close communion of believers with the Christ who is friend of all. In this spirit worship is a glad celebrative mixture of sharing with God in Christ our deepest devotion and attentive listening for God's word for our lives. Worship is dialogical in nature. This dialogue is actually a conversation extending in many directions. We attend to God's word and worshipfully respond to God's presence. But we are called also to listen for and respond to the needs of those with whom we worship and of the wider community. Worship is worldmaking. That is to say, worship equips and empowers us to act as agents of God's transformation.

Because in worship God and believers meet at the depths of their being, we have sought to find the ways and words to express that authenticity. We have carefully searched out from around the world worship materials that speak to today's people. In addition, we have composed original materials geared to the contemporary mind.

These materials have been compiled with the conviction that words do matter. Finding the right words to give voice to particular human experiences is an ongoing challenge in our dialogue with God. Generally we have sought to eliminate archaic language so as to make our words to God more like contemporary speech. We have been conscious of the injustices perpetrated upon women and other oppressed groups by the overuse of masculine and hierarchical terms and other hurtful images, such as the identification of darkness with sinfulness. At the same time, we have struggled with

xi

the reality that such language is deeply embedded in our faith tradition, as well as in the spiritual experiences of many individuals and congregations. Rather than purge liturgical language of problematic terms, we have sought to expand the vocabulary of praise, proclamation, and prayer. Words and the images they convey shape the spiritual possibilities of a worshiping people. It is our fervent hope that these resources will enrich and enliven worship through the use of familiar and unfamiliar, perhaps even challenging, images.

These materials are intended to assist worship leaders in preparing for the various worship occasions of the people of God. Although they are carefully crafted, they should be adapted to meet the special needs of specific congregations. In some instances, the materials may serve as a model to stimulate the user to develop original material that speaks more directly to a specific people.

Many of the prayers and litanies can deeply enrich the life of public worship. Pastors may also use them as resources for developing their own pastoral prayers. Adaptation is fully appropriate.

The arrangement of the materials has proved to be difficult. Each user has a distinct way of approaching a resource book such as this. We have tried to develop a sequence that will generally be useful. The first five sections contain special services and resources for special occasions in the life of the church. The final section, which comprises the second half of the book, supplies specific materials for various parts of a worship service. Instead of attempting to collect all the materials relating to the church year in one section, we have placed these materials under the various types of worship usage.

Specific hymns are recommended in appropriate places throughout the first half of the book. These are identified with their location in *Chalice Hymnal (CH)*, though many of them can be found in other widely used hymnals as well.

We wish to acknowledge with gratitude those who have especially assisted in the production of this book. We are grateful to David Polk of Chalice Press, who conceived of this project. We have been generously assisted by a research grant from Quentin and Stella Mae Barber, Emil and Peggy D'Acosta, and Dwain and Jane McDonald of South Hills Christian Church, Fort Worth. Without their monetary assistance and friendly encouragement, this book would not have come to completion. We are also indebted to the Mary Couts Burnett Library of Texas Christian University, whose personnel have gone out of their way to search out printed worship resources from across the nation.

We are conscious of being heir to those Disciples who have pioneered in developing worship resources. The first and last complete book of worship resources was edited by G. Edwin Osborn in 1953 under the title *Christian Worship: A Service Book*. It set a benchmark for any who would come after him in similar labors. In our own time, a book edited by Keith Watkins titled *Thankful Praise* has pioneered in fresh expressions of worship.

Although influenced by its efforts, the editors have chosen, due to the limitations of space, not to replicate materials found in this most helpful book, which is still in print. The editors also recommend the use of worship materials in *Chalice Hymnal* and have generally not replicated them in the present collection.

Finally, we are grateful for one another as we have collaborated in an effort to express both feminine and masculine viewpoints, as well as the perspectives of our differing ages and concerns. We celebrate our association together and gladly offer the results of our labor to the church we love, the Christian Church (Disciples of Christ), and to all others who find this volume useful.

Colbert S. Cartwright

O. I. Harrison

A CODA TO THE INTRODUCTION

As Colbert Cartwright and I began this voyage of discovery, seeking to craft a worship resource that would serve the Christian Church (Disciples of Christ) well into the twenty-first century, he spoke candidly and often of the fragile nature of his health. It is a testament to his indomitable spirit and his deep, abiding, and amazingly clear-sighted love for the church that Bert completed his work on *Chalice Hymnal* and the *Chalice Hymnal Worship Leader's Companion*, as well as crafting this present volume into final manuscript form. I pray that all those who use these resources will thank God for the many gifts of this servant of the gospel of Jesus Christ. It was my honor, joy, and pleasure to work with Bert on *Chalice Worship*.

There are also two others with whom it was my honor, joy, and pleasure to work. When it fell to me to chase down incomplete copyright information, Ann Cartwright opened her home to me and made it possible for me to sift through the stacks and stacks of material in Bert's study to locate the pertinent information. Her gifts of hospitality and encouragement in the completion of this project have been invaluable.

The second of these trusted companions is David P. Polk, editor of Chalice Press and truly the unnamed third editor of this work. Without his tireless devotion to this project, *Chalice Worship* quite simply would not exist.

He has been a partner with Bert and me since he first invited us to undertake this formidable task. He has been cheerleader, guide, and goad in the months following Bert's death. Among other things, David worked out the basic design, cleaned up the overall structure, saw holes that needed filling, eliminated all unintended repetitions, and built the three indexes.

For the gifts of these two friends and companions, as well as the prayers of a multitude of friends and colleagues, I give thanks. To the memory of Colbert S. Cartwright, God's indefatigable servant, I wish this book to be dedicated.

With humility and gratitude, I pray that *Chalice Worship* will serve to enliven and inspire the worship life of the church.

O. I. Cricket Harrison

I

GENERAL
SERVICES
OF

*T*HE LORD'S DAY SERVICE
AMONG DISCIPLES CONGREGATIONS

Disciples understand the purpose of worship as being for the Christian community to glorify God in such a way that God's grace is manifested to all who participate. Responding to God's self-revelation in the life, death, and resurrection of Jesus Christ, the community attends to God in love and devotion. In return the community receives God's renewal and benediction. At heart worship consists of communion with God and with one another in the power of the Holy Spirit. Worship is completed as those who worship move out in daily service to God and neighbor.

Most Disciples recognize corporate worship as being essentially a community of faith gathering with grateful hearts to share in the Lord's supper. God is known and worshiped by remembering the gift of salvation through words, symbols, and actions that dramatize Christ's self-sacrifice on behalf of a sinful world. The whole of worship is a celebration of the good news of God's saving action in history.

The predominant mood of worship, therefore, is one of festivity. This is not to say that the community does not respond to moments of trouble and sorrow, but that we are able, in the midst of those dark times, to recognize and celebrate God's abiding presence with us. The service is characterized by a symbolic meal where bread and wine are gladly shared in joyous remembrance of a living Savior who through death has been made alive to commune friend-to-friend with his followers. The remembrance of Christ's death on a cross keeps the occasion from being frivolous. The awareness that Christ is alive among his people in power and love engenders joy.

This centering upon Lord's Day worship as being essentially a feast to celebrate the glad good news of God's saving work in Jesus Christ does not diminish the importance of any of the various elements of worship. Rather, it sets the tone for all that takes place. Sunday worship overall is a joyous occasion for marking Christ's resurrection and to commune in holy fellowship with the Giver of Life. The gospel is good news and Christians are impelled to celebrate it so as to live it out in acts of service.

Within this context of table fellowship Disciples share in a myriad of activities fitting to the occasion. Each element has its own function in contributing to the fullness of worship. God's grace is made manifest through calls to worship, prayer, song, scripture; through proclaiming good news; and through celebrating life together in communion through bread and cup. All contribute to the glory of God and the nourishment of God's people.

Therefore it is inappropriate to summarize Disciples worship as a service of word and sacrament. To do so would be to ignore the complexity of celebrative activities through which the gathered faithful meet the risen Christ. The church is the body of Christ and its worship has many valued parts. Every action is a part of the organic whole of worship—each with its own unique means of imparting God's grace. Some aspects may be regarded as more vital than others, but all contribute to the full expression of worship. Disciples meeting to feast with their Lord delight in these abundant ways to celebrate.

With this holistic understanding of worship Disciples have not emphasized a uniformity in the ordering of worship. The very abundance of the ways God graces worship suggests variety rather than a fixed pattern. Recognizing the variety of ways worship is expressed in the New Testament, Disciples have felt free to let culture, tradition, and "consecrated common sense" determine its specific shape. There has never been one order of worship for Disciples.

At the same time Disciples have always regarded the ordering of worship seriously. Disciples forebear Alexander Campbell set forth, in his *Christian System*, a model of worship for a church that conducted worship without a preaching elder. The early evangelist Walter Scott printed a model order of worship in the hymnbook he produced. The emphasis was always upon a congregation's acting responsibly in conducting its worship rather than upon observing a proper form. So it has been throughout Disciples history.

Of particular concern to Disciples has been the location of the partaking of the Lord's supper within the service of worship. Although there has never been unanimity in this regard, the predominant early practice among Disciples was to close the service with communion. As revival movements swept the American church with an emphasis upon preaching, many congregations moved the Lord's supper to an earlier position. Recent times have witnessed a recovery of the early Disciples tradition, regarding the partaking of the meal as the climax to the service.

Currently several models are being suggested. Generally they have been informed by studies of how the church in the first four centuries struggled to deal with the new aspects of worship that varied from Hebrew heritage. They reflect what appears to be a growing convergence of understanding among Christians around the world as to the shape of worship. The order generally follows the pattern set forth by Justin Martyr:

> Readings from the Gospels
> Sermon by the president
> Prayers by all the people
> Bread, wine, and water are brought
> Extempore prayer of thanksgiving
> People's response: Amen
> Distribution and reception of elements

Disciples, whose polar star is that of Christian unity, have been influenced by this ecumenical convergence in regard to the nature and ordering of worship. From their beginning Disciples have recognized the way the Lord's supper characterizes the church and its life and have been eager to learn from those who are also freshly centering upon this insight.

At the same time Disciples, like those of other church traditions, recognize that convergence does not mean uniformity. The various church bodies live out of a unique heritage that influences the way they give specific form to the converging shape. Even acknowledging a common shape, some communions emphasize some aspects of worship more than others. Such differences are to be celebrated—not lamented.

Individual congregations within a church heritage express their worship uniquely as well. The manner in which each congregation worships has grown through shaping and reshaping as circumstances have shifted. Established congregations seldom decide to abandon their old worship for an entirely different form. Changes are made as a congregation deems them fitting.

Two contemporary Disciples models of worship influenced by recent ecumenical studies of early Christian worship are presented here. They express different ways of reflecting Disciples heritage within this common understanding. Their suggestions may stimulate an individual congregation to renew its worship within its own unique heritage to the end that God may be glorified and God's people respond in faithful service.

A third Lord's Day service is also given, which has been designed by the Consultation on Church Union for ecumenical or general use. It carefully expresses the elements regarded by many Christian traditions to be fully expressive and essential to the meaning of the sacrament of the Lord's supper. This service is presented in Part II, "Ecumenical Services of Worship."

☿ LORD'S DAY SERVICE I

This order of worship was developed by Colbert S. Cartwright in a book entitled Candles of Grace: Disciples Heritage in Perspective *(St. Louis: Chalice Press, 1992). Cartwright emphasizes that the Lord's supper is the constituting factor in Disciples worship, shaping all of its life. All parts of a worship service, including the hearing and proclaiming of the word of God, are expressions of the one purpose for communal gathering.*

Candles of Grace *entertains a dialogue between early Disciples heritage and contemporary issues of liturgical reform. It seeks to respect what is familiar in Disciples tradition, at the same time ordering the service to express our distinctive heritage with greater clarity and force.*

The service is designed to emphasize worship as an act of praise and response to God by the people of God. The community itself is crucial to its worship. The service moves from gathering as a community of concern to the hearing and proclaiming of God's word. The community, in response, communes with Christ in grateful remembrance through bread and wine, and quickly disperses into ministry.

This summary is intended to outline how the service is developed, giving minimal commentary. The subheadings are given so as to clarify the intention and movement of worship, but should not be emphasized in a printed order of worship to the point of suggesting distinctive breaks in worship.

A fuller explanation of this order of worship, along with an interpretation of how it relates to Disciples heritage, may be found in the book from which it has been abstracted (pp. 40–54).

ORDER OF WORSHIP

THE COMMUNITY GATHERS BEFORE GOD

MUSICAL VOLUNTARY

> *The music may be of a festive nature expressing the joy of a community gathering after a time of absence.*

SHARING WITHIN THE COMMUNITY

> *The leader informally gains the congregation's attention, announcing matters relating to the life of the community, and inviting expressions of joy and concern from the people.*

> *The leader concludes the informal period by calling upon the community to prepare for the worship of God.*

MUSICAL VOLUNTARY

> *The music, necessarily brief, expresses a meditative mood that engenders quiet centering upon God.*

LIGHTING OF THE CANDLES

> *One or two persons approach the Lord's table during the musical voluntary to light the candles on the table.*

CHORAL INTROIT

> *The choral introit serves to call the community to participate in worship.*

CALL TO WORSHIP

> *Quite specifically the leader through scripture or other words calls upon the people to worship God. It is important that the reason for gathering in worship be clearly stated.*

HYMN

PRAISE, AFFIRMATION, AND/OR PRAYER

The community may actively participate in a variety of expressions through-
out the year, either responsively or in unison:

  1. Act of Praise
  2. Confession of Sins and Assurance of Pardon
  3. Opening Prayer
  4. Affirmation of Faith

CHORUS OF ACCLAMATION OR PRAISE

This may take the form of a trinitarian gloria doxology, a familiar hymn re-
frain, or a chorus.

CALL TO PRAYER

The Lord be with you.
And also with you.

PASTORAL PRAYER

The pastor as representative minister gathers together the affirmations, joys,
and concerns of the community and lifts them to God in praise, thanksgiving,
confession, petition , and intercession. The pastoral prayer is the grand culmi-
nation of this opening section of worship in which the community is gathered
before God.

Upon occasion the prayer may take the form of a litany, a bidding, or guided
meditation. Whatever form it takes, this prayer is representative of the
community's life engaged with God.

THE COMMUNITY HEARS AND PROCLAIMS GOD'S WORD

Although early Disciples generally ordered the Lord's supper as the climax of
worship, some congregations have always felt free to place it earlier in the
service. This custom may be accommodated by reversing the order of this and
the next section, adjusting the singing of hymns to make a smooth transition.

READING FROM HEBREW SCRIPTURE

Communities following the Revised Common Lectionary will find three scrip-
ture readings plus a psalm assigned for each Sunday. Some communities read
fewer scripture passages. By referring to this first reading as Hebrew scrip-
ture the community recognizes its roots in the Judaic tradition.

PSALM

READING FROM THE EPISTLES

MUSICAL RESPONSE

This may be a vocal solo, an anthem, instrumental music, or dance. It is representative in nature, enhancing the worship expression of the community.

READING FROM THE GOSPELS

There is an ancient Christian tradition that the community stands in reverent attention to the word of God in Christ while the Gospel lesson is read. When the sermon immediately follows the Gospel lesson, the linkage between hearing and proclaiming God's word is maintained. It is appropriate that a hymn or chorus be sung, at which time children may depart for children's church.

SERMON

INVITATION TO CHURCH MEMBERSHIP

This invitation may appropriately find its place before the closing hymn. Placed after the sermon, the invitation emphasizes response of individuals to the hearing and proclaiming of God's word. This placement also highlights receiving the new members into communion. The latter position has the advantage of not interfering with the flow of moving directly from sermon to sacrament and gives less emphasis upon responding to a specific sermon. The choice will directly affect how the sermon is presented and perceived.

Various actions may be included at this point in response to the hearing of the Word. Among them may be the reception of new members, baptism, prayers for healing, installations, dedication of church buildings or furnishings, and commissioning to service. An affirmation of faith by the congregation may also be made at this time.

HYMN

Participating elders may come forward at the hymn's beginning in readiness to greet any new members and to take their positions at the table. At the close of the hymn new members are incorporated into the community.

THE COMMUNITY SHARES IN CHRIST'S LIFE

INVITATION TO THE LORD'S TABLE

It is appropriate to conduct this whole portion of the service from behind the Lord's table. In a few sentences the purpose of gathering is given and a welcome extended.

HYMN

The Lord's supper consists of four actions expressed in the words of institution:

1. *TAKE (Offering): The offering of bread, cup, and money placed upon the table as an act of self-giving by the members of the community.*
2. *BLESS (Prayers): An act of thankful remembering of God's saving acts, calling upon the Holy Spirit to show forth the presence of Christ in the life of the community.*
3. *BREAK (Words of Institution): As the words of institution are spoken, the bread is broken and the wine poured, so as graphically to convey the gift of Christ's brokenness for the world's salvation.*
4. *GIVE (Partaking): The bread and cup are shared in holy communion.*

OFFERTORY SENTENCE

OFFERING

Members of the diaconate move from the back of the sanctuary directly to their assigned positions in the aisles and proceed with the collection of the offering.

OFFERTORY RESPONSE

During the singing of this response, the offering of bread, cup, and money is brought forward to be placed upon the table.

TABLE PRAYERS

There is no necessity for a separate offertory prayer. The communion prayers may include reference to the gifts brought forward. These are prayers of grateful remembrance for God's saving act in Jesus Christ, whose effective presence is made known within the community through the power of the Holy Spirit. The prayers are offered in an act of self-giving on behalf of the community that it and the world may be blessed.

WORDS OF INSTITUTION

The one loaf may be broken and proffered toward the people. The wine may be poured from a pitcher into a cup or chalice that is lifted toward the people. There is dramatic symbolism in doing this even when individual cups are used. The symbolism is strengthened when the one loaf is actually distributed to the people. Disciples heritage emphasizes the communal sharing of one loaf of common bread as an act of Christian unity, symbolizing participation in the one body of Christ—the church.

THE LORD'S PRAYER

From earliest times the Lord's Prayer has been prayed in conjunction with the partaking of the Lord's supper as an earnest and exacting prayer before receiving Christ anew.

PARTAKING OF BREAD AND CUP

The elders and deacons having been served, the one presiding may declare to the people, either in its entirety or as a responsive reading, some such words as these adapted from 1 Corinthians 10:

The bread which we break,
Is it not a means of sharing in the body of Christ?
The cup of blessing which we bless,
Is it not a means of sharing in the blood of Christ?
Because there is one bread, we who are many are one body,
For we all partake of the one bread.

The congregation is served.
There is no need for the trays to be brought back to the table.

CLOSING COMMUNION PRAYER OF THANKSGIVING

This may be a brief unison prayer that sums up the meaning of the Lord's supper and looks forward to service in daily discipleship.

THE COMMUNITY DEPARTS FOR MINISTRY

HYMN

SENDING FORTH WITH BENEDICTION

CONGREGATIONAL OR CHORAL RESPONSE

CARRYING THE LIGHT TO THE WORLD

One or two persons light hand-held tapers from the candles on the Lord's table, then extinguish the lighted candles. With lighted tapers they lead participating leaders to the sanctuary doors.

MUSICAL VOLUNTARY

🍷 *LORD'S DAY SERVICE II*

This order for the Sunday service, along with commentary and model worship resources, was published under the title Thankful Praise *and edited by Keith Watkins (St. Louis: Chalice Press, 1987). A team effort of Disciples funded in part by the Division of Homeland Ministries and published by CBP Press, its central purpose was "to strengthen Christian public worship and especially the celebration of the Lord's Supper." Dissatisfied with the general tenor of much Disciples worship, this book declared that "the time has come for reclaiming the authentic Disciples tradition, for cutting away its limiting features, and for presenting a strong case for reform." To this end the team was guided by five stated principles:*

1. To connect Disciples worship more firmly with the great tradition of Christian worship stemming from the time of the apostles and from the church of the first centuries after the resurrection of Christ.

2. To be responsive to the search for Christian unity and to the agreements on liturgy growing out of ecumenical convergence and consensus statements.

3. To be faithful to the crucial features of traditional Disciples worship, including the important role of lay leadership, prayer that is created for each new celebration, and to the preeminent place of the Lord's Supper.

4. To be sensitive to essential lessons from contemporary life, including the growing awareness of social injustice around the world and of the church's responsibility for addressing it; especially in regard to anti-Jewish and sexist expressions.

5. To enhance the beauty and diversity of worship in the Disciples of Christ by striving for language that is vivid, biblical, and felicitous; and by encouraging variety in the ordering of the service (8–9).

Intended to be both provocative and persuasive, the book requires a thorough reading in its entirety. This summary is intended to emphasize its suggested structuring of worship, with minimal summation of its commentary. Its fuller rationale, along with model resources, is delineated in the book. A study guide, suitable for use with congregational leaders, is also available.

ORDER OF WORSHIP

THE COMMUNITY COMES TOGETHER TO SERVE GOD IN WORSHIP

GATHERING OF THE COMMUNITY

The community reestablishes its identity and through an informal moment is oriented to the service and shares in announcements relating to its life. Members may be called upon to greet one another. Unless this is clearly understood as an act of reconciliation it should not be regarded as a passing of the peace.

OPENING MUSIC

This music, an integral part of worship, marks the boundary of sacred time, inviting the congregation to enter into thankful praise to God in Christ.

GREETING

This salutation to God, as among friends, may be a call to worship addressed to the people or an ascription of praise directed to God.

HYMN

OPENING PRAYER(S)

This first of several prayers in the service may take the form of an openness to God's presence or a prayer of confession followed by words of assurance.

THE COMMUNITY PROCLAIMS THE WORD OF GOD

PRAYER FOR ILLUMINATION

The proclamation of the word of God may begin with a prayer for illumination.

FIRST READING FROM THE BIBLE

The first reading is from Hebrew scriptures, rooting the community in its Jewish heritage. When only two readings are given, one should be from Hebrew scripture.

PSALM OR OTHER RESPONSE

A children's sermon, if used, may be given at this point.

SECOND READING FROM THE BIBLE

ANTHEM OR OTHER RESPONSE

READING FROM THE GOSPEL

SERMON

THE COMMUNITY RESPONDS TO THE WORD OF GOD

CALL TO DISCIPLESHIP

This is an invitation to respond to the word of God through incorporation into the life of the church or by rededication.

HYMN

AFFIRMATION OF FAITH

By making an affirmation of faith, believers confess God as the fundamental reality of their lives and acknowledge that the triune God is the source of their salvation and of their unity as followers of Christ.

PRAYERS OF THE PEOPLE

This period of prayer may take one of several forms:
1. *Pastoral prayer*
2. *Short prayers delivered by different members*
3. *Bidding prayer*
4. *Guided meditation*
5. *Responsive prayer*

Whatever the form, the prayers would be characterized by such elements as praise, adoration, confession, thanksgiving, intercession, petition, and submission.

THE COMMUNITY COMES TOGETHER
AROUND THE LORD'S TABLE

THE INVITATION TO COMMUNION

The invitation to commune is extended upon Christ's behalf for all baptized believers to partake. It includes an expression of the meaning of communion. It may conclude with a summons to offer gifts of praise and thanksgiving.

OFFERING

The offering is both an act of dedication in response to the word of God and a preparation for the Lord's supper. It is appropriate for the elements of communion to be carried to the Lord's table with the offering of money.

PRAYERS AT THE TABLE

The prayers are introduced by an opening dialogue:

The Lord be with you.
And also with you.
Lift up your hearts.
We lift them to the Lord.
Let us give thanks to the Lord our God.
It is right to give our thanks and praise.

Following the prayers offered by elders, the pastor and congregation engage in a responsive prayer designed to clarify and strengthen the theological meaning of the service and to express the congregation's role as co-celebrants of communion. This could take such a form as this:

Almighty and loving God,
you have created and redeemed us,
and through the presence of your Holy Spirit
you sustain us in daily life.

**Now let this same Spirit descend upon these gifts
that in the breaking of the bread and the sharing of this cup
we may know the living presence of Jesus
who gave his body and blood for all.**

May your Spirit fill us with a longing for a deeper unity
in Christ's body, the church,
and with commitment to greater service
in Christ's name in the world.

**Give us an unshakable hope
in the holy commonwealth which is to come.
For we pray through Jesus Christ,
with you and the Holy Spirit
one God, now and forever. Amen.**

The dramatic breaking of the bread may be done as the words of institution are spoken or may be done silently as a separate act.

LORD'S PRAYER

This greatest of all Christian prayers is a fitting climax to the other prayers, reinforcing the anticipation of the fulfillment of God's purpose for the world.

PEACE

This symbol of reconciliation may fittingly be expressed through a visible greeting, a handshake, an embrace. This passing of the peace could take place earlier in the service following the assurance of pardon or as a climax to the partaking of communion.

COMMUNION

PRAYER AFTER COMMUNION

This is a prayer of thankful response reminding the community of the intimate bond between worship and mission.

THE COMMUNITY GOES FORTH
TO SERVE GOD IN MISSION

HYMN

CLOSING WORDS

This properly is a declaration of the favor of God addressed to the congregation. It may take the form of a benediction or blessing in the name of God. This is often combined with a commission to go forth to do God's work.

CLOSING MUSIC

*D*AILY MORNING WORSHIP

*This service is intended for various occasions when Christians gather at the begin-
ning of the day to join together to center life in God. It may be freely adapted to
circumstance, but should not lose its focus upon the dedication of the day to God
in the context of praise.*

STATEMENT OF PURPOSE

We gather this morning as a community of God's people
   to offer ourselves afresh in adoration to God,
   to conform our minds more nearly to the mind of Christ,
   to receive the renewing gift of the Holy Spirit.
We unite as God's people in the company of Christ
   to hear and proclaim God's holy word,
   to pray for ourselves and the whole world,
   to dedicate this day and all we are to the glory and service of God;
   through Jesus Christ who is our peace.

CALL TO WORSHIP

One or more of these scripture sentences, or other similar ones, may be read.

O Lord, open my lips,
And my mouth shall proclaim your praise.
I pray to you, O Lord;
you hear my voice in the morning;
at sunrise I offer my prayer
and wait for your answer.

Or:

This is the day that the LORD has made;
   let us rejoice and be glad in it.   (PSALM 118:24)

Or:

Lord, I will sing of your might;
   I will sing aloud of your steadfast love in the morning.
For you have been a fortress for me
   and a refuge in the day of my distress.
O my strength, I will sing praises to you,
   for you, O God, are my fortress,
   the God who shows me steadfast love.   (PSALM 59:16–17)

Or:

O God, satisfy us in the morning with your steadfast love,
   so that we may rejoice and be glad all our days.   (PSALM 90:14)

Or:

O God, let me hear of your steadfast love in the morning,
    for in you I put my trust.
Teach me the way I should go,
    for to you I lift up my soul.   (PSALM 143:8)

HYMN

PSALM

Such psalms as these may be read:

Psalm 8—The majesty of God's name
Psalm 19—The heavens are telling God's glory
Psalm 27—The Lord is my light
Psalm 39—Let me know my end
Psalm 46—God is our refuge
Psalm 103—Bless the Lord, O my soul
Psalm 116—God has heard my voice
Psalm 121—I will lift up my eyes

SCRIPTURE READING

*Scriptures are read that encourage the community in its praise, prayer, and
meditation. Examples of such passages are:*

Deuteronomy 6:4–7—God is one
Isaiah 55:1–3—Listen to God
Matthew 6:25–34—Do not worry about our life
John 4:1–26—Jesus and the woman of Samaria
Romans 6:1–14—Dying and rising with Christ
2 Corinthians 4:1–15—Treasure in clay jars
Ephesians 6:10–20—The whole armor of God

SILENCE

*The silence may be closed by a brief prayer. If the occasion requires it, a spoken
meditation may be given at this point.*

HYMN/SPIRITUAL/CHORUS/CANTICLE

INVITATION TO PRAYER

The Lord is near; have no anxiety,
but in everything make your requests known to God
in prayer and petition with thanksgiving.
Then the peace of God,
which is beyond our utmost understanding,
will keep guard over your hearts and your thoughts,
in Christ Jesus.   (PHILIPPIANS 4:6–7, NEB)

PRAYERS OF THANKSGIVING AND INTERCESSION

> *A prayer may be freely given by an individual, either on behalf of the worshipers or as a bidding prayer. Equally appropriate would be the solicitation of prayers from the worshipers. After each prayer, the leader may conclude:* Lord, in your mercy, *and all may respond:* **Hear our prayer.**

> *An individual may give the following or a similar prayer:*

Eternal God, we rejoice this morning in the gift of life, which we have received by your grace, and the new life you give in Jesus Christ. Especially we thank you for
> the love of our families…
> the affection of our friends…
> strength and abilities to serve your purpose today…
> this community of which we are a part…
> opportunities to give as we have received…

God of grace, we offer our prayers for the needs of others and commit ourselves to serve them even as we have been served in Jesus Christ. Especially we pray for
> those closest to us, families, friends, neighbors…
> refugees and homeless men, women, and children…
> the outcast and persecuted…
> those from whom we are estranged…

Hear us now, O God, as we commit our deepest concerns to you:

> *Here other petitions may be made either by the leader or voluntarily by worshipers.*

Before we know what to ask, O God,
you are fashioning out of your love everything we can need.
Today give us courage
to witness to your wondrous love
and to share in your work
which you have given us as disciples of Jesus Christ,
our Servant Lord. **Amen.**

THE LORD'S PRAYER

HYMN/SONG/SPIRITUAL/CHORUS

DISMISSAL WITH BLESSING

> Grow in the grace and knowledge of our Lord and Savior Jesus
>   Christ.   (2 PETER 3:18)

> May the God of hope fill you with all joy and peace in believing, so
> that you may abound in hope by the power of the Holy Spirit.
>   (ROMANS 15:13)

DAILY EVENING WORSHIP

This service is designed for use at the close of an evening in which Christians have been engaged in a common endeavor. It may be adapted for a variety of circumstances, but should not lose its focus upon presenting the day to God in the context of grateful confidence in God's abiding presence.

STATEMENT OF PURPOSE

We gather this evening as a community of Christ's people
to draw near to one another in fellowship with God;
to praise the One who has cared for us this day;
to feed upon God's word, our sustenance for life.
We present ourselves and this day into God's keeping,
asking God to accept and use all our endeavors;
seeking God's forgiveness as we forgive the wrongs of others;
committing ourselves and the world to God's safekeeping;
through Jesus Christ who is our peace.

CALL TO WORSHIP

One or more scriptural sentences such as these may be given:

Jesus Christ is the light of the world,
the light no darkness can overcome.
Stay with us, Lord, for it is evening,
and the day is almost over.
Let your light scatter the darkness
and illumine your church.
Or:
If I ascend to heaven, you are there;
if I make my bed in Sheol, you are there.
If I take the wings of the morning
and settle at the farthest limits of the sea,
even there your hand shall lead me,
and your right hand shall hold me fast.
If I say, "Surely the darkness shall cover me,
and the light around me become night,"
even the darkness is not dark to you;
the night is as bright as the day,
for darkness is as light to you.   (PSALM 139:8–12)
Or:
This is the message we have heard from Christ and proclaim to you, that God is light and in God there is no darkness at all. If we walk in the light as God is truly in the light, we have fellowship with one another, and the blood of Jesus the Son cleanses us from all sin.

(1 JOHN 1:5, 7, ALT.)

LIGHTING OF CANDLE

A single white candle is lighted to signify the light of God's presence.

HYMN

OPENING PRAYER

We praise and thank you, O God,
    for you are without beginning and without end.
Through Christ, you created the whole world;
    through Christ, you preserve it.
You made the day for the works of light
    and the night for the refreshment of our minds and bodies.
Keep us now in Christ; grant us a peaceful evening,
    a night free from sin; and bring us at last to eternal life.
Through Christ and in the Holy Spirit,
    we offer you all glory, honor, and worship,
    now and forever. **Amen.**

PSALM

Such psalms as these may be read:

Psalm 4—Answer me when I call
Psalm 33—Rejoice in the Lord
Psalm 34—Bless the Lord at all times
Psalm 91—The shelter of the Most High
Psalm 134—Come, bless the Lord
Psalm 136—God's steadfast love endures forever
Psalm 139:1–12—Where can I go from your spirit?

SCRIPTURE READING

Scriptures are read that encourage the community in its praise, prayer, and meditation. Examples of such passages are:

Genesis 1:1–5, 14–19—In the beginning God
Exodus 13:21–22—The pillars of cloud and fire
Isaiah 40:1–8—O comfort my people
Matthew 25:1–13—Ten bridesmaids and their lamps
John 14:15–27—I am coming to you
Philippians 4:4–9—Rejoice in the Lord always

SILENCE

The silence may be closed by a brief prayer. If the occasion requires it, a spoken meditation may be given at this point.

HYMN/SPIRITUAL/CHORUS

PRAYER OF COMMENDATION

Grant, O eternal God,
    that we may lie down in peace,
    and raise us up, O Sovereign, to life renewed.
Spread over us the shelter of your peace;
    guide us with your good counsel;
    and for your name's sake, be our Help.
Shield us from hatred and plague;
    keep us from war and famine and anguish;
    subdue our inclination to evil.
O God our Guardian and Helper,
    our gracious and merciful Ruler,
    give us refuge in the shadow of your wings.
O guard our coming and our going,
    that now and always we have life and peace.
Blessed is the Lord, Guardian of the people Israel forever. **Amen.**

CANTICLE

*If desired, the traditional Song of Simeon, the Nunc Dimittis (CH 156), may
be sung or read responsively.*

BLESSING

Lord, fill this night with your radiance.
May we sleep in peace and rise with joy
to welcome the light of a new day in your name.
We ask this through Christ our Lord. Amen.

PASSING THE PEACE

Signs of peace may be exchanged with a familiarity appropriate to the occasion.

ADDITIONAL RESOURCES

The following response may be read or sung. The tune is found in Canticles and
Gathering Prayers *by John P. Mossi and Suzanne Toolan (Winona, Minnesota:
Saint Mary's Press, 1989), p. 90.*

**R: God of healing, God of rest, gather us in peace.
Be our night of healing rest.**

God of healing and rest, at this day's end we come to you.
Lift us from the burdens of this day.

Your world is magnificent,
    yet we forget to acknowledge your beauty
    and the mystery of your inner workings.
Help us now to thank you in the midst of our evening cares.   R

Make us again receivers of your life, sharers of your gifts,
    servants of you and one another,
    and seekers of your wisdom.   R

Help us at this evening hour from diminishing energy,
    from petty grievances, from hopelessness,
    from resentments, and from our fears and jealousies.
Enable us again to seek you
    in the beauty of our journey and our world.   R

Grant us wisdom to listen to your voice in our needed rest and dreams.
Give us courage to face you in the quiet and stillness of the dark.
For you are as present in the night as in the day.   R

As evening falls, enshrine your hope and love
    like a light within our heart.
As we patiently await your day of Final Coming,
    be our Light unending and night of healing rest.   R

+ + +

Watch, dear Lord, with those who wake, or watch, or weep tonight,
    and give your angels charge over those who sleep.
Tend your sick ones, O Lord Christ, rest your weary ones.
    Bless your dying ones. Soothe your suffering ones.
Pity your afflicted ones. Shield your joyous ones.
    and all for your love's sake. **Amen.**

+ + +

O God, before we sleep,
    we remember before you all the people we love,
    and now in the silence we say their names to you.
All the people who are sad and lonely, old and forgotten,
    poor and hungry and cold,
    in pain of body and in distress of mind.
Bless all who specially need your blessing,
    and bless us as well,
    and make this a good night for each of us.
This we ask for your love's sake.

+ + +

Creator God:
>It was in the cool of the day that you came to Adam and Eve,
>>and in the evening that they confessed their sin;
>It was at evening that the dove returned to Noah
>>with the olive leaf that was your sign
>>of new hope and a fresh beginning;
>It was toward evening that Jesus completed his suffering
>>for our redemption,
>and as darkness came that his risen presence
>>and his peace dispelled his disciples' fear.

Loving Savior:
>At the end of the day
>>may we be overjoyed that you are among us,
>>and be strengthened now by your Holy Spirit to serve you
>>as you will send us in your name.

 # ℬLESSING OF SMALL CHILDREN

The purpose of this portion of Sunday worship is to welcome with thanksgiving infants or small children into the church's nurturing life and care, anticipating a later point in their lives when they will confess Christ and be baptized. It is an occasion for both parents and congregation to enter into a covenant of responsibility on behalf of its children.

This blessing of small children is designed to be incorporated into the congregation's usual service of Sunday worship whenever it is needed. It may take place early in the worship or following the sermon.

The parents and children join the minister in the chancel.

GREETING AND STATEMENT OF PURPOSE

>As the family of God we rejoice in God's good gift of life through the miracle of birth. We join with these parents in embracing these children with open arms, even as Jesus welcomed little children and their mothers with words of blessing. We acknowledge God's abounding love already at work in these children, and come to pledge ourselves in covenant to nurture them into fullness of life.

HYMN   Filled with the Joy and Gladness (*CH* 362)

READING OF SCRIPTURE

One or both of the following printed scripture passages may be read that emphasize the ongoing covenant work of nurturing. In addition, other scriptures may be read, such as: 1 Samuel 1:9–11, 20–28; 2:26; Psalm 8; Matthew 18:1–4; Mark 10:13–16; Luke 2:22–32, 52.

Give ear, O my people, to my teaching;
    incline your ears to the words of my mouth.
I will open my mouth in a parable;
    I will utter dark sayings from of old,
things that we have heard and known,
    that our ancestors have told us.
We will not hide them from their children;
    we will tell to the coming generation
the glorious deeds of the LORD, and his might,
    and the wonders that he has done.
He established a decree in Jacob,
    and appointed a law in Israel,
which he commanded our ancestors
    to teach to their children;
that the next generation might know them,
    the children yet unborn,
and rise up and tell them to their children,
    so that they should set their hope in God,
and not forget the works of God,
    but keep his commandments.   (PSALM 78:1–7)

Or:

Hear, O Israel: The LORD is our God, the LORD alone. You shall love the LORD your God with all your heart, and with all your soul, and with all your might. Keep these words that I am commanding you today in your heart. Recite them to your children and talk about them when you are at home and when you are away, when you lie down and when you rise.   (DEUTERONOMY 6:4–7)

COVENANT

You parents now are to recall your own baptism and, seeking to fulfill its promises, give yourselves in covenant to lead your children toward full discipleship in Christ.

With gratitude to God:
Do you receive this child as a precious gift of God, and seek God's grace and this community's support in nurturing and caring for this child?
Do you covenant to remain faithful in love to your child, whatever the future may bring?

Do you promise before God and this community so to fashion your lives that your child may come to know Jesus Christ as Lord and Savior?

I do, God helping me.

The church, as a family of God, gladly joins you in holy covenant for the care and nurture of these children.
The congregation stands.

Do you promise as a community of faith:
> to surround each of these families with your love
>> for the strengthening of their life together;
> to be for these parents and children a family in Christ
>> whose love for them cannot be broken;
> to accept these children into your loving care
>> for shared responsibility in their growth
>> toward fullness of life in Christ;
> to tell these children the good news of Christ,
>> to help them learn Christ's ways
>> and to lead them in service to God and neighbor?

We do, God helping us.

The congregation may be seated.

The minister either receives each child or touches each one, speaking the name of the parents and the name of the child, saying:

Name, may the peace of God be always with you.

The children may be carried into the aisles as an act of welcome, their names being spoken in introduction. A rosebud and/or certificate may be presented to the parents.

PRAYER

O God of everlasting covenant, we rejoice in every gift of life.
Be present always to strengthen and guide these your children
> that they may increase in wisdom and in years,
> and in divine and human favor.
Bind us in covenant that we, your people,
> may be faithful in keeping the vows we have made.
We look to you for strength in the knowledge that you will fulfill
> by your power every good resolve and work of faith
> through Christ Jesus our Lord. Amen.

ADDITIONAL RESOURCES

CONGREGATIONAL COVENANTS

The church is the family of Christ,
the community in which we grow in faith and commitment.

We rejoice to take *Name* under our care.
We seek God's grace to be a community
in which the gospel is truly proclaimed to all.
We will support you and minister with you
as workers together in Christ Jesus
and heirs of his promise.

+ + +

To be spoken in unison.

With God as our witness
we covenant with these parents and children
to surround them with your love
for the strengthening of their life together;
to be for them a family in Christ
whose love for them cannot be broken;
to accept these children into our loving care
for shared responsibility in their growth
toward fullness of life in Christ;
to tell these children the good news of Christ
that they may know themselves loved of God
and freely give of themselves in love to others.

+ + +

From CH 364:

O God, as a mother comforts her children,
you strengthen, sustain, and provide for us.
We come before you with gratitude
for the gift of this child,
for the joy that has come into this family,
and for the grace with which you surround them and all of us.
As a father cares for his children,
so you continually look upon us with compassion and goodness.
Pour out your spirit.
Enable your servants to abound in love,
and establish our homes in holiness;
through Jesus Christ our Lord. Amen.

CHRISTIAN BAPTISM

Persons become disciples of Christ as they are moved by God's spirit
>*to turn away from sin and evil,*
>*make a profession of faith,*
>*receive God's renewing grace through baptism,*
>*and thereby become one with the whole people of God.*

Although these steps may be separated in time, they are one action. This unity is most fully expressed when they follow one another in the same service of worship. However, in keeping with many local traditions, the first two actions may take place at one service and the latter two in another.

Normatively baptism takes place within a congregation's regular Sunday worship service following a sermon relating to the baptismal theme. Baptism is followed by sharing in the Lord's supper with the new members. Baptisms also may be conducted as a part of an Easter Vigil or in a separate service. The material that follows may be adapted to these various circumstances.

Since baptism receives persons into the universal church, the service is designed to be sensitive to the larger church's understanding of how baptism is properly administered. The ecumenical convergence statement on baptism found in Baptism, Eucharist and Ministry *states: "Within any comprehensive order of baptism at least the following elements should find a place:*
>*the proclamation of the scriptures referring to baptism;*
>*an invocation of the Holy Spirit;*
>*a renunciation of evil;*
>*a profession of faith in Christ and the Holy Trinity;*
>*the use of water;*
>*a declaration that the persons baptized have acquired a new*
>>*identity as sons and daughters of God;*
>*and, as members of the church, called to be witnesses of the Gospel."*

(BEM 4.1)

Although Disciples make a point that no creedal statement should stand between the believer and Christ as a test of fellowship, the church has always baptized persons in the name of the Father and the Son and the Holy Spirit. Thus, it is appropriate to ask the candidates to affirm these words of baptism in a noncreedal way. Although God transcends all names and forms, the use of the word Father *for God is normative in all churches to this date. Alternative wording is provided for making this affirmation.*

BAPTISMAL COLLECT

Creator Spirit,
>who in the beginning hovered over the waters,
>who at Jesus' baptism descended in the form of a dove,
>who at Pentecost was poured out under the signs of fire and wind,

come to us, open our hearts and minds,
 so that we may hear the life-giving word
 and be renewed by your power
in the unity of the Father and the Son, now and forever. **Amen.**

RENUNCIATION OF EVIL AND CONFESSION OF FAITH

The renunciation of evil and confession of faith may take place either as persons come forward at the invitation, or in the baptistry prior to the act of baptism.

Name(s) come/comes before God and this congregation today to confess Jesus Christ as Lord and Savior.

Name, I now ask you:
Do you renounce evil, repent of your sins, and turn to Christ?

I do.

Do you confess that Jesus is the Christ, the Son of the living God, and do you accept and proclaim him to be Lord and Savior of the world?

I do.

Looking to your baptism
in the name of the Father, Son, and Holy Spirit,
do you, in the company of all Christians,
believe and trust in God the Father, who made the world;
and in his Son Jesus Christ, who redeemed humankind;
and in the Holy Spirit, who gives life to the people of God?

I do so believe and trust.

Or:

Recalling that Jesus told us, "Go, therefore and make disciples of all nations, baptizing them in the name of the Father and of the Son and of the Holy Spirit," I ask you:

Do you believe in God the Source, the fountain of life;
and in Christ, the offspring of God,
embodied in Jesus of Nazareth and in the church;
and in the liberating Spirit of God, the wellspring of new life?

I believe.

Look with joy to your baptism.

SCRIPTURE SENTENCES

Hear these words from holy scripture:

A selection may be made among these or other appropriate scripture passages.

In those days John the Baptist appeared in the wilderness of Judea, proclaiming, "Repent, for the kingdom of heaven has come near." Then

Jesus came from Galilee to John at the Jordan, to be baptized by him. John would have prevented him, saying, "I need to be baptized by you, and do you come to me?" But Jesus answered him, "Let it be so now; for it is proper for us in this way to fulfill all righteousness." Then he consented. And when Jesus had been baptized, just as he came up from the water, suddenly the heavens were opened to him and he saw the Spirit of God descending like a dove and alighting on him. And a voice from heaven said, "This is my Son, the Beloved, with whom I am well pleased."

(MATTHEW 3:1–2; 13–17)

Now the eleven disciples went to Galilee, to the mountain to which Jesus had directed them. When they saw him, they worshiped him; but some doubted. And Jesus came and said to them, "All authority in heaven and on earth has been given to me. Go therefore and make disciples of all nations, baptizing them in the name of the Father and of the Son and of the Holy Spirit, and teaching them to obey everything that I have commanded you. And remember, I am with you always, to the end of the age."

(MATTHEW 28:16–20)

Peter said to them, "Repent, and be baptized every one of you in the name of Jesus Christ so that your sins may be forgiven; and you will receive the gift of the Holy Spirit. For the promise is for you, for your children, and for all who are far away, everyone whom the Lord our God calls to him." And he testified with many other arguments and exhorted them, saying, "Save yourselves from this corrupt generation." So those who welcomed his message were baptized, and that day about three thousand persons were added. They devoted themselves to the apostles' teaching and fellowship, to the breaking of bread and the prayers.

(ACTS 2:38–42)

Do you not know that all of us who have been baptized into Christ Jesus were baptized into his death? Therefore we have been buried with him by baptism into death, so that, just as Christ was raised from the dead by the glory of the Father, so we too might walk in newness of life. For if we have been united with him in a death like his, we will certainly be united with him in a resurrection like his.   (ROMANS 6:3–5)

If you confess with your lips that Jesus is Lord and believe in your heart that God raised him from the dead, you will be saved. For one believes with the heart and so is justified, and one confesses with the mouth and so is saved. The scripture says, "No one who believes in him will be put to shame."

(ROMANS 10:9–11)

In Christ Jesus you are all children of God through faith. As many of you as were baptized into Christ have clothed yourselves with Christ. There is no longer Jew or Greek, there is no longer slave or free, there is no longer male and female; for all of you are one in Christ Jesus.

(GALATIANS 3:26–28)

STATEMENT OF PURPOSE

The statement may be read solely by the celebrant, or responsively by the celebrant and congregation.

From apostolic times persons have become disciples of Christ by confessing that Jesus is God's Messiah—the Lord and Savior of the world. In obedience to Christ's command and in likeness to Christ's example, they have been baptized.

Today we joyously receive new disciples into Christ's one, holy, apostolic, and universal church.

Through baptism we are brought into union with Christ, with each other, and with the church of every time and place.

Through baptism we are buried with Christ, that we like him, may be raised from the dead to walk in newness of life.

Through baptism into Christ God graces us with the gift of the Holy Spirit to forgive our sins, to cleanse us from all wrongs, to clothe us with God's own righteousness, and to strengthen us all our days.

Through baptism into Christ we gain a new identity as sons and daughters of God, and receive a new life-purpose of christlike ministry by word and deed.

Let us each remember and rejoice in our own baptism as we join in receiving these new disciples into Christ and Christ's church.

PRAYER

Gracious God, we thank you that in every age
    you have made water a sign of your presence.
In the beginning your Spirit brooded over the waters
    and they became the source of all creation.
You led your people Israel through the waters of the Red Sea
    to their new land of freedom and hope.
In the waters of the Jordan, your Son was baptized by John
    and anointed with your Spirit for his ministry of reconciliation.
May this same Spirit bless the water we use today,
    that it may be a fountain of deliverance and new creation.
Wash away the sins of those who enter it.
Embrace them in the arms of your church.
Pour out your Spirit on them
    that they may be agents of reconciling love.
Make them one with Christ,
    buried and raised in the power of his resurrection,
    in whose name we pray. **Amen.**

If the candidate has not already made a confession of faith, it appropriately may be done at this point, followed directly by the act of baptism.

BAPTISM

The celebrant leads each candidate into the baptistry and lowers her or him into the water. This descent into the waters may be made either backward, forward, or by use of a chair upon which to sit as water is poured over the head.

By the authority of Jesus Christ, I baptize you, *Name*,
in the name of the Father and of the Son and the of the Holy Spirit.
Amen.

Or:

Name, by the authority of Jesus Christ, you are baptized in the name of
the Father and of the Son and of the Holy Spirit. Amen.

Immediately after the administration of the water, as hands are placed on the head of each person, the celebrant says to each:

The Holy Spirit abide with you,
the Spirit of wisdom and understanding;
the Spirit of counsel and inward strength;
the Spirit of knowledge and true godliness;
the Spirit of joy and hope.

Or:

The Holy Spirit be at work in you
to do far more than you dare ask or imagine,
keeping you in the knowledge of Christ's love,
too wonderful to be measured.

POST BAPTISMAL PRAYER

We give you thanks, O Holy One,
mother and father of all the faithful,
for *this your child/these your children*
and for the grace acknowledged here today
in water and the Holy Spirit.
Embrace us all as daughters and sons
in the one household of your love.
Grant us grace to receive, nurture, and befriend
this new member/these new members
of the body of Christ. **Amen.**

Give to the newly baptized:
strength for life's journey,
courage in time of suffering,
the joy of faith,
the freedom of love,

and the hope of new life;
through Jesus Christ who makes us one. Amen.

Or:

Merciful God, you call us by name
and promise to each of us your constant love.
Watch over your servants, *Names.*
Deepen *their* understanding of the gospel,
strengthen *their* commitment to follow the way of Christ,
and keep *them* in the faith and communion of your church.
Increase *their* compassion for others,
send *them* into the world in witness to your love,
and bring *them* to the fullness of your peace and glory,
through Jesus Christ our Lord. **Amen.**

As the newly baptized dress, the congregation may celebrate the occasion in a number of ways:

1. A member of the congregation may read scripture passages designed to assist the worshipers to meditate upon and recall the significance of their own baptism. Readings may include: Jeremiah 31:31–34; Mark 1:14–20; Matthew 16:24–27; John 14:15–18; John 15:1–11; 1 Peter 2:4–10; Romans 8:11–17.

2. The congregation may sing hymns expressing its commitment to Christ.

3. The choir may sing an anthem of praise and devotion to Christ.

WELCOME

When all are dressed, the celebrant enters the chancel, moves behind the Lord's table, followed by the newly baptized who gather facing the table in front. They carry small, unlighted white candles. Taking a lighted candle (either from the table, or using a Paschal candle), the celebrant says such words as these:

Jesus said: "I am the light of the world. Whoever follows me will never walk in darkness but will have the light of life" (John 8:12). Receive this light. Shine as a light in the world to the glory of God.

After all candles are lighted, each newly baptized person places the lighted candle on the Lord's table in an act of consecration. Having the new members turn toward the congregation, the celebrant may lead the congregation in welcoming the new members, using these or similar words:

Name(s), God has blessed you with the Spirit
and received you by baptism
into the one, holy, catholic, and apostolic church.

With joy and thanksgiving, we welcome you into Christ's church,
joined together with all those who in every place
call on the name of our Lord Jesus Christ.
Together let us encourage one another,
building up each other within Christ's body.
Together let us esteem one another in love,

**praying without ceasing for every good grace
to grow into the full likeness of Christ.**

*Each person may be seated in a specially reserved section for receiving holy
communion or anywhere within the congregation. The service may proceed by
sharing in the Lord's supper.*

 # $\mathcal{S}$ERVICE OF CONFIRMATION

*This service is intended for those baptized at some time in the past who come to
make their own confession of Christian faith and enter into the full privileges and
responsibilities of membership in Christ's church.*

INTRODUCTION

In the name of the Lord Jesus Christ, the only head of the church, we
seek now the gift of the Holy Spirit in confirming and strengthening
the faith of *Name.*

In baptism we are welcomed into the family and household of God,
raised to new life in Christ, and nurtured in the Holy Spirit. In response
to the call of Christ and the leading of the Holy Spirit, *Name* comes
now to make *her/his* own profession of Christian faith and to accept the
responsibilities and privileges of membership.

RENEWAL OF BAPTISMAL PROMISES

Name *will now make* her/his *own the promises declared when* she was/he
was/they were *baptized. The congregation may be invited to share in making the promises as an act of renewal.*

Do you believe and trust in one God, Father, Son, and Holy Spirit, maker
of heaven and earth, redeemer of the world, giver of life?

I do.

Do you, trusting in God's grace, repent of your sins, renounce evil, and
turn to Christ?

I do.

Do you promise, trusting in God's grace, to be faithful in public and
private worship, to live in the fellowship of the church, to share in its
witness?

I do.

Do you promise, by that same grace, to follow Christ and to seek to do and bear his will all the days of your life?

I do.

And do you trust in his mercy alone to bring you into the fullness of the life of the world to come?

I do.

CONFIRMATION

Almighty and ever-living God, by baptism you have delivered *Name(s)* from the domain of darkness and brought *her/him/them* into the kingdom of your beloved Son, in whom our release is secured and our sins forgiven.

Send your Holy Spirit upon *him/her/them*: the spirit of wisdom and understanding; the spirit of counsel and power; the spirit of knowledge and the fear of the Lord.

The minister lays hands on each candidate, saying:

By your Holy Spirit confirm and strengthen, O God, your servant *Name.* **Amen.**

Or:

The God of all grace, who has called you to Christian faith and service, confirm and strengthen you with the Holy Spirit and keep you faithful to Christ all your days. **Amen.**

Peace be with you.

Candidate(s): **And also with you.**

Gracious God, keep *this servant/these servants* within your heavenly grace, that *she/he/they* may continue to be yours for ever, bearing in life the fruits of the Spirit and growing into the full stature of Christ.

Candidate(s): **Amen.**

WELCOME

In the name of the Lord Jesus Christ, I welcome you to the full privileges and responsibilities of membership of the one, holy, catholic, and apostolic church, and in particular to the life of this congregation of Christ's people.

The minister and one or more of the elders give to the member(s) a sign of welcome (e.g. the kiss of peace or the right hand of fellowship). A Bible may be presented.

In the name of Christ we welcome you. May we grow together in unity, and be built up into the body of Christ in love, to the glory of God, now and forever. **Amen.**

CHRISTIAN MARRIAGE I

ENTRANCE

As the people gather, music appropriate to the praise of God may be offered. At the appointed time the bride, groom, and other members of the wedding party present themselves and stand before the minister. The families of the bride and groom may stand with the couple.

During the entrance of the wedding party, the people may stand and sing a psalm, hymn, or spiritual. Or an anthem may be sung, or instrumental music may be played.

SENTENCES OF SCRIPTURE

The minister calls the people to worship, either before or after the entrance, using one of the following, or another appropriate verse from scripture:

God is love, and those who abide in love
abide in God, and God abides in them.   (1 JOHN 4:16)

Or:

This is the day that the LORD has made;
    let us rejoice and be glad in it.   (PSALM 118:24)

Or:

O give thanks, for the LORD is good.
    God's love endures forever.   (PSALM 106:1, ALT.)

The minister says:

We gather in the presence of God
to give thanks for the gift of marriage,
to witness the joining together of *Name* and *Name*,
to surround them with our prayers,
and to ask God's blessing upon them,
so that they may be strengthened for their life together
and nurtured in their love for God.

God created us male and female,
and gave us marriage
so that husband and wife may help and comfort each other,
living faithfully together in plenty and in want,
in joy and in sorrow, in sickness and in health,
throughout all their days.

God gave us marriage
for the full expression of the love between a man and a woman.
In marriage a woman and a man belong to each other,

and with affection and tenderness
freely give themselves to each other.

God gave us marriage
for the well-being of human society,
for the ordering of family life,
and for the birth and nurture of children.

God gave us marriage as a holy mystery
in which a man and a woman are joined together,
and become one, just as Christ is one with the church.

In marriage, husband and wife are called to a new way of life,
created, ordered, and blessed by God.
This way of life must not be entered into carelessly,
or from selfish motives,
but responsibly, and prayerfully.

We rejoice that marriage is given by God,
blessed by our Lord Jesus Christ,
and sustained by the Holy Spirit.
Therefore, let marriage be held in honor among all.

PRAYER

The minister says:

Let us pray:

Gracious God, you are always faithful in your love for us.
Look mercifully upon *Name* and *Name*,
who have come seeking your blessing.
Let your Holy Spirit rest upon them
so that with steadfast love
they may honor the promises they make this day,
through Jesus Christ our Savior. Amen.

The congregation may be seated.

DECLARATION OF INTENT

*The minister addresses the bride and groom individually, using either one of
the following:*

Name, understanding that God has created, ordered, and blessed the
covenant of marriage, do you affirm your desire and intention to enter
this covenant?

I do.

Or:

If both are baptized, the following may be used.

Name, in your baptism
you have been called to union with Christ and the church.

Do you intend to honor this calling
through the covenant of marriage?

I do.

AFFIRMATION OF CHILDREN

*If children will share in the new family, they may either stand in their places
or move near the couple. The minister addresses each child by name:*

Name(s), you are entering a new family.
Will you give to this new family your trust, love, and affection?

Each child: **I will, with the help of God.**

The minister addresses the bride and groom:

Name and *Name,*
will you be faithful and loving parents to *Name(s)*?

The couple: **We will, with the help of God.**

AFFIRMATIONS OF THE FAMILIES

The minister may address the families of the bride and groom:

Name and *Name,*
do you give your blessing to *Name* and *Name,*
and promise to do everything in your power
to uphold them in their marriage?

The families of the bride and groom answer either:

**We /I give *our/my* blessing
and promise *our/my* loving support.**

Or:

We /I do.

The families of the bride and groom may be seated.

AFFIRMATION OF THE CONGREGATION

The minister may address the congregation, saying:

Will all of you witnessing these vows do everything in your power
to uphold *Name* and *Name* in their marriage?

We will.

A psalm, hymn, spiritual, or anthem may be sung.

READING FROM SCRIPTURE

The following, or a similar prayer for illumination, may be said.

God of mercy, your faithfulness to your covenant
frees us to live together in the security of your powerful love.
Amid all the changing words of our generation,
speak your eternal Word that does not change.

Then may we respond to your gracious promises
by living in faith and obedience;
through our Lord Jesus Christ. Amen.

One or more scripture passages are read.

SERMON

After the scriptures are read, a brief sermon may be given.

A psalm, hymn, spiritual, or other music may follow.

VOWS

The people may stand.

The minister addresses the couple:

Name and *Name*, since it is your intention to marry,
join your right hands, and with your promises
bind yourselves to each other as husband and wife.

*The bride and groom face each other and join right hands.
They in turn then make their vows to each other.*

A
The man says:

I, *Name*, take you, *Name*, to be my wife;
and I promise, before God and these witnesses,
to be your loving and faithful husband;
in plenty and in want;
in joy and in sorrow;
in sickness and in health;
as long as we both shall live.

The woman says:

I, *Name*, take you, *Name*, to be my husband;
and I promise, before God and these witnesses,
to be your loving and faithful wife;
in plenty and in want;
in joy and in sorrow;
in sickness and in health;
as long as we both shall live.

B
The man says:

Before God and these witnesses,
I, *Name*, take you, *Name*, to be my wife,
and I promise to love you,
and to be faithful to you
as long as we both shall live.

The woman says:

Before God and these witnesses,
I, *Name*, take you, *Name*, to be my husband.
and I promise to love you,
and to be faithful to you,
as long as we both shall live.

EXCHANGE OF RINGS (OR OTHER SYMBOLS)

If rings are to be exchanged, the minister may say to the couple:

What do you bring as the sign of your promise?

When the rings are presented the minister may say the following prayer:

By your blessing, O God,
may these rings be to *Name* and *Name*
symbols of unending love and faithfulness,
reminding them of the covenant they have made this day,
through Jesus Christ our Lord. Amen.

The bride and groom exchange rings using A or B or other appropriate words. The traditional trinitarian formula should be omitted for both the bride and groom if one of the marriage partners is not a professing Christian.

A

The one giving the ring says:

Name, I give you this ring as a sign of our covenant,
in the name of the Father, and of the Son, and of the Holy Spirit.

The one receiving the ring says:

I receive this ring, as a sign of our covenant,
in the name of the Father, and of the Son, and of the Holy Spirit.

B

As each ring is given, the one giving the ring says:

This ring I give you,
as a sign of our constant faith and abiding love,
in the name of the Father, and of the Son, and of the Holy Spirit.

PRAYER

The couple may kneel.

One of the following prayers, or a similar prayer, is said:

1

Let us pray:

Eternal God, creator and preserver of all life,
author of salvation, and giver of all grace:

look with favor upon the world you have made and redeemed,
and especially upon *Name* and *Name*.

Give them wisdom and devotion in their common life,
that each may be to the other a strength in need,
a counselor in perplexity, a comfort in sorrow,
and a companion in joy.

Grant that their wills may be so knit together in your will,
and their spirits in your Spirit,
that they may grow in love and peace
with you and each other, all the days of their life.

Give them the grace, when they hurt each other,
to recognize and confess their fault,
and to seek each other's forgiveness and yours.

Make their life together a sign of Christ's love
to this sinful and broken world,
that unity may overcome estrangement,
forgiveness heal guilt, and joy conquer despair.

Give them such fulfillment of their mutual love
that they may reach out in concern for others.

[Give them, if it is your will, the gift of children,
and the wisdom to bring them up to know you,
to love you, and to serve you.]

Grant that all who have witnessed these vows today
may find their lives strengthened,
and that all who are married
may depart with their own promises renewed.

Enrich with your grace all husbands and wives, parents and children,
that, loving and supporting one another,
they may serve those in need as a sign of your reign.

Grant that the bonds by which all your children
are united to one another
may be so transformed by your Spirit
that your peace and justice may fill the earth,
through Jesus Christ our Lord. Amen.

2
Eternal God, without your grace no promise is sure.
Strengthen *Name* and *Name*
with patience, kindness, gentleness,
and all other gifts of your Spirit,
so that they may fulfill the vows they have made.

Keep them faithful to each other and to you.
Fill them with such love and joy
that they may build a home of peace and welcome.
Guide them by your Word to serve you all their days.

Help us all, O God,
to do your will in each of our homes and lives.
Enrich us with your grace
so that, encouraging and supporting one another,
we may serve those in need
and hasten the coming of peace, love, and justice on earth,
through Jesus Christ our Lord. Amen.

LORD'S PRAYER

The minister invites all present to sing or say the Lord's Prayer.

CANDLELIGHTING

If a unity candelabra consisting of three candles is used, the outer candles representing husband and wife are lighted first. The center candle, representing the united couple, is lighted without extinguishing the other candles. Thus, the preeminent candle represents the oneness of the couple with the other candles signifying their individuality. However, if local custom dictates the extinguishing of the two smaller candles, it would be appropriate to interpret that action as a reminder of the "two becoming one."

ANNOUNCEMENT OF MARRIAGE

The minister addresses the congregation, using the optional phrases only if appropriate:

Before God and in the presence of this congregation,
Name and *Name* have made their solemn vows to each other.
They have confirmed their promises by the joining of hands
[and by the giving and receiving of rings].
Therefore, I proclaim that they are now husband and wife.
[Blessed be the Father and the Son and the Holy Spirit
   now and forever.]

The minister joins the couple's right hands. The congregation may join the minister saying:

**Those whom God has joined together
let no one separate.**

CHARGE

The minister addresses the couple, using one of the following:

1

As God's own,
clothe yourselves with compassion, kindness, and patience,
forgiving each other as the Lord has forgiven you,
and crown all these things with love,
which binds everything together in perfect harmony.

(COLOSSIANS 3:12–14, ALT.)

2

Whatever you do, in word or deed,
do everything in the name of the Lord Jesus,
giving thanks to God through him.   (COLOSSIANS 3:17, ALT.)

BLESSING

The minister gives God's blessing to the couple and the congregation, using one of the following:

1

The Lord bless you and keep you.
The Lord be kind and gracious to you.
The Lord look upon you with favor
and give you peace. Amen.

2

The grace of Christ attend you,
the love of God surround you.
The Lord look upon you with favor
and give you peace. Amen.

A psalm, hymn, spiritual, or anthem may be sung, or instrumental music may be played, as the wedding party leaves.

HOLY COMMUNION

If the service is to conclude with partaking of holy communion, the bride and groom may bring bread and wine forward as the minister steps behind the table. Since the Lord's supper is an action of the church, all Christians present are served. The partaking may begin with the couple serving one another.

BENEDICTION

The minister addresses the couple and the congregation:

The Lord bless you and keep you.
The Lord be kind and gracious to you.
The Lord look upon you with favor
and give you peace. Amen.

Or:

The grace of Christ attend you,
the love of God surround you,
the Holy Spirit keep you,
that you may live in faith,
abound in hope, and grow in love,
both now and forevermore. Amen.

A psalm, hymn, spiritual, or anthem may be sung, or instrumental music may be played as the wedding party leaves.

CHRISTIAN MARRIAGE II

THE GATHERING OF THE COMMUNITY

Guests are invited to gather informally in a designated location. The gathering is to be informal, allowing the guests to become acquainted with one another. This is a way to celebrate all relationships among the people of God, with one another and with God. The call to worship is given in the gathering place. The congregation processes together, into the worship area, led by the families of the bride and groom as they sing the hymn of praise.

RESPONSIVE CALL TO WORSHIP

We have come to worship God.

**We are grateful to be created male and female,
in the image of God.**

We have come to celebrate our relationship
with God and one another.

We praise God for creating us to love.

HYMN OF PRAISE

OPENING STATEMENT

Name and *Name*, we gather as family and friends to worship God and to acknowledge God as the source of love. We are here to celebrate with you what already exists—the living love of two who have found joy and meaning together. Marriage is a great adventure. It becomes a daily broadening of one's horizon, a continuing opportunity to learn something new about life, about human existence, and about God. It is an act of faith that reflects God's love.

The gospel tells us that it is God's intent that we have loving, supportive relationships with one another. These relationships exist within community and especially the community of faith. It is appropriate in this time of worship to acknowledge the commitment of love that *Name* and *Name* have made to each other. We join with them in committing to seek the blessing of God and of the community of faith for their marriage.

The wedding party may be seated with the congregation prior to beginning this next section.

The Celebration of the Word

Scripture Reading
Genesis 2:4b–9, 15–24 *(or other appropriate scripture)*

Musical Response
This may take the form of a hymn, anthem, or solo.

Homily
The wedding party rises and returns to their places in the front of the worship space.

The Covenant of Marriage

Covenant of the Couple
Marriage is a sacrament of God's grace, a spiritual bond, created and sustained by God. In its mutuality marriage envisions God's gracious vision of fullness of life and acknowledges the Spirit of God in all relationships. *Name* and *Name*, this celebration of your marriage is itself a symbol of your awareness of this spiritual bond that exists between you, and your commitment to live toward God's Shalom, God's Vision. Signifying your covenant to continue to live in faithfulness to God and one another, join hands now and make your vows to each other.

These printed vows, or others made in consultation with the minister, are spoken, first by the bride and then by the groom.

Name, in the sight of God and in the presence of our loved ones, I choose you to be my life's partner. I promise to love you, to honor you and to care for you tenderly through all the varying experiences of our life together.

COVENANT OF THE FAMILIES

Name and *Name* have made a covenant before you to live in faithfulness to God and one another, as husband and wife. Will you support and strengthen their marriage, and will you give them the love and freedom that will enable them to grow together as they establish a new life? We invite you, their family members, to covenant with them.

Family Members:

We celebrate the union of *Name* and *Name* in marriage, and pray God's blessing upon them. We commit ourselves to support and care for them as individuals, and together as a couple. We, as their family, will work with them to create a life among us that is loving and healthy, being ever mindful that God must always be our center.

VOW BY THE COMMUNITY

We celebrate the union of *Name* and *Name* in marriage, and pray God's blessing upon them. We commit ourselves to support and care for them as individuals, and together as a couple. We, as the community of faith, will work with them to create a life among us that is loving and healthy, being ever mindful that God must be at our center.

SYMBOLS OF COVENANT

As symbols of your vows you have brought rings to give and receive. May they always be reminders of this day and the covenant you have made with one another, with this community, and with God. *Name,* as you place the ring on *Name's* finger, I invite you to say these words: "I give this ring as a token of my love for you and of my faithfulness to our holy covenant." *[Repeat]*

PRAYER

Gentle and loving God, may these two people, now married, keep this covenant they have made. May they be a blessing and comfort to each other, sharing each other's joys, consoling one another in sorrow, helping each other in all the changes of life. May they encourage each other in whatever they set out to achieve. May they, trusting each other, trust life, and not be afraid. We pray for them happiness...not freedom from life's struggles, but the knowing awareness that they are not alone. May they continue to love one another forever. Amen.

ANNOUNCEMENT OF MARRIAGE

Name and *Name,* you have expressed your deep love for each other; you have vowed to be always loving and loyal toward each other; and you have exchanged rings to symbolize your love, thus formalizing in our presence the existence of the loving bond between you. On behalf of your family, friends, and the whole human community, I pronounce you husband and wife.

CELEBRATION OF COMMUNION

INVITATION TO COMMUNION

WORDS OF INSTITUTION

DISTRIBUTION OF EMBLEMS

PRAYER OF THANKSGIVING

O loving and creating God, we give thanks for your gift of grace in the sharing of this bread and cup, providing nourishment and renewal for our spirits. You touch our deepest needs as you call us to a life of hope. Through Christ you give us courage and strength as we discern your will for us in response to your loving invitation to live in relationship with you. We are grateful, Source of Life, for the many blessings that we have received. In the joy of this hour we give you glory and praise. Amen.

HYMN OF DEDICATION

RESPONSIVE PRAYER OF BLESSING

Loving God, hear us as we ask your blessings on *Name* and *Name* as they make their covenant of marriage this day.

Awaken in each the gifts of your caring. Let them be strength and solace for each other. Help them to listen well, to look first to you for guidance, wisdom, and comfort. Let your Spirit overflow their home with joy and laughter.

Grant that their relationship may grow deeper in intimacy, love, and mutual respect. Teach them to care for their relationship of love as the living, growing, life-giving possibility it can be.

May their forgiveness for one another be quick and their fault-finding slow. Polish their life together that it will become a reflection of your abiding concern and ready forgiveness for your broken and hurting world.

Let this time of celebration be a source of strength to all persons who are married here. Strengthen all those relationships and renew their bonds of loyalty.

May all who are alone be bound up in your community of care as we share this time of joy together.

Grace us with your Loving Spirit that we might be messengers of love as we leave this place of hope and love and celebration.

POSTLUDE

Wedding Anniversary

A Litany

The following response may be read or sung. The tune is found in Canticles and Gathering Prayers *by John P. Mossi and Suzanne Toolan (Winona, Minnesota: Saint Mary's Press, 1989), p. 86.*

R   Come, eat rich food and drink sweet wine.
Today is holy to our God.

Loving and gracious God, over and over again
    you show us that you are a God of love.
At all times, you are friend and companion to us;
    your joy is ever with us.
In your generosity you invite us to partake in the banquet of life,
    to dance, to laugh, to eat the best of foods,
    and to celebrate your Spirit and kindness.
Today you are present with us
    as we celebrate this wedding anniversary.
The sacred stories of our tradition
    show your abiding interest and concern
    in the human experience of marriage.
You made Eve and Adam to companion one another
    and blessed them with all the good gifts of your creation.
You blessed Abram and Sarah with the promise
    of a child and a nation in their old age.   **R**

Marriage, with its celebration and feasts,
    continually reminds us of the joy to which you invite us
    when we live in harmony with one another and with you.   **R**

In Cana many years ago,
    your Anointed One graced the wedding of a poor couple.
Jesus showed himself to be at home at parties
    and to cherish human joys and distresses.
The wine supply ran out,
    and Jesus changed water into delicious wine.
Jesus performed this first of his signs at Cana;
    he revealed his power and love,
    and his disciples believed in him.   **R**

Gracious God, even as we celebrate your glory among us,
    we ask you to bless this gathering of friends and family.
When we are reminded that life is short,
    we desire even more that we may gain
    wisdom of heart through the experiences life gives us.

Balance our afflictions with joy;
    when you fill us with love through one another,
    we shall celebrate all our days.   **R**

Today, especially bless *Name* and *Name*
    as they celebrate their (___) wedding anniversary.
They have known the gift
    of a good and happy marriage.
[They enjoy the affection of their children
    and continually praise you for your goodness.]
Their lives have been rich,
    full of good works and friendship.
During these mature years of their marriage,
    bless them with health
    and enable them to provide for all their needs.
May they enjoy many more years of each other's companionship
    and may they know the fullness of your love for them.   **R**

Finally, we ask you to bless all here present
    who share in this celebration.
May all of us find our way to you
    in the fullness of love and friendship.
Bless this food that we enjoy from your bounty
    and make us always mindful
    of the needs of those who are poorer than we
    in food and in friendship.   **R**

BLESSING OF FRIENDSHIP

One of the gifts God gives is the gift of friendship. This blessing may be included in a regular service of worship. It may be occasioned by a time of stress, such as when one friend is moving away.

STATEMENT OF PURPOSE

    We gather today to celebrate the special friendship that *Name* and *Name* enjoy. Friendship is a gift from God. From the book of Ecclesiasticus we read: "A faithful friend is a sure shelter, whoever finds one has a rare treasure." Jesus said, "There is no greater love than this, that one will lay down one's life for one's friends."

The two friends who come for blessing may tell something of the character of the friendship.

BLESSING

God our fortress, our guardian, our guide, our friend—we ask your blessing on this friendship. Strengthen *Name* and *Name* that they might listen with care, respond to the other's needs with empathy, and treasure the other with understanding. Let the light of humor sparkle in their hearts. Let your holy laughter cleanse the wounds between them. Grant that the bonds of friendship they have forged will become stronger with time. Help them to be quick to forgive and ready to embrace the other when difficult times arise. Let their mutual respect, love, and caring inspire us all to plumb the holy mysteries of friendship. Help us all to discover Christ's face looking at us through human eyes. Amen.

If desired, small mementos of the occasion may be exchanged.

If one friend is moving, a farewell litany or prayer may follow, such as:

BLESSING OVER A FRIENDSHIP

Gracious God,
    we thank you for the delicate weaving of these two lives,
    shared moments spun of fragile energy.
We rejoice in the bold colors of strength,
    the whispered encouragements, the honesty of tears.
Bless this friendship as a tapestry to last beyond time,
    beyond miles, defying the bounds of separation.
Grant that these friends will continue
    to call out the best in one another,
    to empower each other for service.
Give them strength to walk, together or apart,
    as children of God. Amen.

PRAYER SERVICE FOR HEALING

This service of healing is intended for use sometime other than the Lord's Day service. In some churches it is the custom to hold a prayer service for healing regularly on a weekday. This service includes provision for the laying on of hands with prayer and the anointing with oil. These aspects are optional, and may be used privately under other circumstances. The whole service may be adapted to specific needs of a congregation.

See Chalice Hymnal 501–512 for hymns that specifically relate to the theme of healing and wholeness.

WELCOME AND STATEMENT OF PURPOSE

Greetings in the name of our Savior and Friend, Jesus Christ.
We are the body of Christ and individually members of it.
    If one member suffers, all suffer its pain.
    If one member is honored, all share its joy.
We gather as a community of love to bring ourselves and others
    to Jesus the Great Physician,
    whose gift is wholeness.
We ask for God's blessing in body, mind, and spirit.
We open ourselves to the healing ministry of God
    through Jesus Christ,
    in the power of the Holy Spirit.

SCRIPTURE SENTENCES

One or more of these may be said:

The Lord is near; have no anxiety, but in everything make your requests known to God in prayer and petition with thanksgiving. Then the peace of God, which is beyond understanding, will keep guard over your hearts and your thoughts, in Christ Jesus.   (PHILIPPIANS 4:6–7, NEB)

Or:

Jesus answered them, "Have faith in God. Truly I tell you, if you say to this mountain, 'Be taken up and thrown into the sea,' and if you do not doubt in your heart, but believe that what you say will come to pass, it will be done for you. So I tell you, whatever you ask for in prayer, believe that you are receiving it, and it will be yours. Whenever you stand praying, forgive, if you have anything against anyone; so that your Father in heaven may also forgive you your trespasses."

(MARK 11:22–25)

Or:

Our help is in the name of the LORD,
    who made heaven and earth.   (PSALM 124:8)

HYMN

CONFESSION OF SIN

The people are called to confession with these or other sentences of scripture that promise God's forgiveness.

Jesus said: Ask, and it will be given you;
search, and you will find;
knock, and the door will be opened for you.

**For everyone who asks, receives; and everyone who searches, finds;
and for everyone who knocks, the door will be opened.**

Friends in Christ, God knows our needs before we ask
and in our asking prepares us to receive the gift of grace.
Let us open our lives to God's healing presence
and forsake all that separates us from God and neighbor.
Let us be mindful not only of personal evil
but also of our communal sins of family, class, race, and nation.
Let us confess to God
whatever has wounded us or brought injury to others,
that we may receive mercy
and become for each other ministers of God's grace.

Silence may be observed for examination of conscience.

Let us confess our sins together.

**Merciful God, we confess that we have sinned against you
in thought, word, and deed,
by what we have done, and by what we have left undone.
We have not loved you
with our whole heart and mind and strength;
we have not loved our neighbors as ourselves.
In your mercy, forgive what we have been,
help us amend what we are, and direct what we shall be,
so that we may delight in your will and walk in your ways,
to the glory of your holy name. Amen.**
Or:
**Eternal God, in whom we live and move and have our being,
your face is hidden from us by our sins,
and we forget your mercy in the blindness of our hearts.
Cleanse us from all our offenses
and deliver us from proud thoughts and vain desires.
In reverence and humility may we draw near to you,
confessing our faults, confiding in your grace,
and finding in you our refuge and our strength;
through Jesus Christ your Son. Amen.**

Assurance of God's forgiving grace is declared by the minister. These or other words may be used:

The mercy of the Lord is from everlasting to everlasting.
I declare to you, in the name of Jesus Christ,
 you/we are forgiven.

May the God of mercy, who forgives *you/us* all *your/our* sins,
 strengthen *you/us* in all goodness
 and by the power of the Holy Spirit
 keep *you/us* in eternal life. Amen.

Or:

Hear the good news!
 Who is in a position to condemn?
Only Christ, and Christ died for us,
 Christ rose for us,
 Christ reigns in power for us,
 Christ prays for us.
Anyone who is in Christ is a new creation.
 The old life has gone; a new life has begun.
Friends, believe the gospel.
 In Jesus Christ, we are forgiven.

Thanks be to God.

A joyful response is sung or said.

SCRIPTURE READING

Among many appropriate scriptures are these:

Psalm 23—The Lord is my shepherd
Psalm 42:1–5—My soul thirsts for God
Psalm 121—I will lift my eyes to the hills
Psalm 139:1–18, 23–24—Lord, you have searched me
Isaiah 35—The compassion and care of God
Isaiah 40:28–31—God gives strength to the weak
Isaiah 61:1–4—The Lord anoints for service
Matthew 11:2–5—Go and tell John what you hear and see
Matthew 11:28–30—Come unto me all who labor
Luke 4:40—Jesus laid his hands upon them
Luke 5:12–16—A leper is cleansed
Luke 8:43–48—A woman is healed
John 14:1–6, 25–27—Let not your hearts be troubled
Acts 3:1–10—The lame man at the temple gate
Romans 5:1–11—Hope does not disappoint

Romans 8:26–28—The Spirit helps in our weakness
Romans 8:31–39—God is for us
Philippians 4:4, 6–9—Have no anxiety
Hebrews 4:14–16; 5:7–9—Learning obedience through suffering
James 5:13–16—Any among you who are suffering
1 Peter 1:3–9—A new birth into a living hope

MEDITATION ON THE SCRIPTURE

OFFERTORY

It is appropriate to receive an offering contributing to reconciliation, justice, compassion, and peace. This may also serve as an occasion for persons to place cards of intercessory concern in the trays for public note at the time of intercessions.

DOXOLOGY

CALL TO PRAYER

Come to the Lord our God, who forgives all our offenses,
 cures all our diseases, redeems our lives from the abyss,
 and crowns us with faithful love and tenderness.
Come now to receive the laying on of hands:
 for assurance of forgiveness;
 commitment to Christ;
 healing of the body, mind, and spirit;
 help for yourselves or for others in facing personal problems.

HYMN

INTERCESSIONS

A general prayer of intercession may be given with particular references to the concerns expressed on cards or by those gathered. Following the intercessory prayer any who have come forward for the laying on of hands with prayer may be ministered to individually. This or a similar prayer may be given:

Giver of Life, your will for all people is health and salvation.

We praise you and thank you, O Lord.

God the Son, you came that we might have life, and might have it more abundantly.

We praise you and thank you, O Lord.

God the Holy Spirit, you make our bodies the temple of your presence.

We praise you and thank you, O Lord.

Grant now your healing grace to all who are sick, injured, or disabled, that they may be made whole.

Hear us, O Lord of life.

Grant to all who seek your guidance, and to all who are lonely, anxious, or despondent, a knowledge of your will and an awareness of your presence.

Hear us, O Lord of life.

Mend broken relationships, and restore those in emotional distress to soundness of mind and serenity of spirit.

Hear us, O Lord of life.

Especially, O God, do we pray for *Name*, that....

Here may be offered petitions for those who have requested prayers, making reference to particular circumstances.

Attend to each one, O God, out of your boundless love.
Bless physicians, nurses, and all others who minister to the suffering, granting them wisdom and skill, sympathy and patience.

Hear us, O Lord of life.

Grant to the dying peace and a holy death, and uphold by the grace and consolation of your Holy Spirit those who are bereaved.

Hear us, O Lord of life.

Restore to wholeness whatever is broken by human sin, in our lives, in our nation, and in the world.

Hear us, O Lord of life.

You are the Lord who does wonders.

You have declared your power among the peoples.

With you, O Lord, is the well of life:

And in your light we see light.

Hear us, O Lord of life:

Heal us, and make us whole.

Let us pray.

A period of silence follows.

Heavenly Father, you have promised to hear what we ask in the name of your Son: Accept and fulfill our petitions, we pray, not as we ask in our ignorance, nor as we deserve in our sinfulness, but as you know and love us in your Son Jesus Christ our Lord. Amen.

THE INVITATION

> In the name of the Lord Jesus who sent forth his disciples to preach the kingdom of God and to heal, we invite you who wish to receive the laying on of hands and the anointing with oil to come forward or summon us to come to your side.

> We invite all here present to participate in this act of faith through the offering of silent prayers for those who seek Christian healing.

LAYING ON OF HANDS WITH PRAYER

> *Since healing is a ministry of the church it is appropriate that the minister be joined by one or two elders, or such persons as the elders may designate, for the laying on of hands. The minister or an elder may also anoint the worshiper with oil following the blessing.*

> Holy scripture teaches us that in acts of healing and restoration our Lord Jesus and his disciples laid hands upon the sick (and anointed them). By so doing they made known the healing power and presence of God. Pray that as we follow our Lord's example, you may know his unfailing love.

> *A prayer is offered as hands are laid upon each recipient's head. This may be extempore or one of the following.*

> *Name*, may the Lord Christ grant you the healing and renewal for which you pray, according to God's perfect will. Go in peace. Amen.

> *Or:*

> *Name*, I/we lay *my/our* hands upon you
> in the name of our Sovereign and Savior Jesus Christ,
> calling upon Christ to uphold you and fill you with grace,
> that you may know the healing power of God's love. Amen.

> *Or:*

> *Name*, receive now the healing presence of God for you *and those dear to you*. May the God of hope fill you with all joy and peace in believing, so that you may abound in hope by the power of the Holy Spirit. Amen.

ANOINTING WITH OIL

> *If the passage from James 5:14–15 has not been previously read, it may be spoken at this point:*

> Are any among you sick? They should call for the elders of the church and have them pray over them, anointing them with oil in the name of the Lord. The prayer of faith will save the sick, and the Lord will raise them up; and anyone who has committed sins will be forgiven.

(JAMES 5:14–15)

Using the thumb, anoint with olive oil each person with the sign of the cross on the forehead, saying these or similar words.

Name, as you are anointed with this oil,
so may God grant you the anointing of the Holy Spirit.

Or:

Name, as you are outwardly anointed with this oil,
God grant that you may inwardly be anointed
by the good grace of the Holy Spirit,
restoring you to wholeness and strength.

PRAYER OF THANKSGIVING

Let us pray.

**We give praise and thanks to you, O God.
In Jesus Christ, you have given us life;
    brought ministry, forgiveness, healing, and peace;
    commanded the disciples to heal the sick;
    and continued the healing ministry among us to this day.
Keep us mindful of your love and mercy
    that we may be faithful throughout all our days,
    in the name of Jesus Christ. Amen.**

LORD'S PRAYER

HYMN

DISMISSAL AND BENEDICTION

Go in peace to love and serve God.
May God bless you and keep you.
May God's face shine upon you and be gracious to you.
May God look upon you with kindness and give you peace. Amen.

(NUMBERS 6:24–26, ALT.)

ADDITIONAL RESOURCE

Happy are those whose transgression is forgiven,
    whose sin is covered.
While I kept silence, my body wasted away
    through my groaning all day long.
Then I acknowledged my sin to you,
    and I did not hide my iniquity;
I said, "I will confess my transgressions to the LORD,"
    and you forgave the guilt of my sin.

(PSALM 32:1, 3, 5)

Let us confess our sin to almighty God. Let us pray.

Have mercy on us, O God,
 according to your steadfast love;
according to your abundant mercy,
 blot out our transgressions.
Wash us thoroughly from our iniquity,
 and cleanse us from our sin.
Create in us a clean heart, O God,
 and put a new and right spirit within us.
Do not cast us away from your presence,
 and do not take your holy spirit from us.
Restore to us the joy of your salvation,
 and sustain in us a willing spirit;
 through Jesus Christ our Lord. **Amen.**   (PSALM 51:1–2,10–12, ALT.)

PRAYER FOR CHRISTIAN HEALING IN HOME OR HOSPITAL

Ministers, elders, deacons, or other visitors should use this service with sensitivity to the specific needs of the person(s) being visited and after ascertaining their willingness to participate in this act of faith. It would be most appropriate to use this service after a preliminary conversation and expression of pastoral concern.

GREETING

Grace and peace to you from God our Father and Christ Jesus our Lord. We are here in the name of the Lord Jesus whose ministry to God's people was one of healing power and saving grace. He promised those who believe in him that he would be with them always, and his promise is true. He is present among us still to heal and to make whole.

CONFESSION OF SIN

Now in the presence of the Lord, let us confess our sins. Let us pray.

Silence may be kept, after which one of the visitors may offer the following, or another, prayer.

O God, who hears our prayers before we speak them, who knows our needs before we raise them up; you have heard the confession of our hearts. Now grant us your mercy and forgiveness through Jesus Christ our Lord, who came into the world to rescue us from sin and bring us to life in him. Amen.

ASSURANCE OF PARDON

The following, or another scriptural assurance, may be offered.

With everlasting love I will have compassion on you, says the LORD your Redeemer. I, I am the one who blots out your transgressions for my own sake, and I will not remember your sins. Return to me, for I have redeemed you. (ISAIAH 54:8; 43:25; 44:22; ALT.)

PRAYERS OF INTERCESSION

Prayers may be offered for the person being visited asking for God's healing love and tender care to be granted in Christ's name. The prayers may be concluded with the following petition:

O God, who in Jesus Christ called us out of the darkness into your marvelous light; enable us always to declare your wonderful deeds, thank you for your steadfast love, and praise you with heart, soul, mind, and strength, now and forever. Amen.

SCRIPTURE READING

One or more brief passages of scripture may be read. See listing provided under "Prayer Service of Healing" above.

LAYING ON OF HANDS AND ANOINTING WITH OIL

Are any among you suffering? They should pray. Are any cheerful? They should sing songs of praise. Are any among you sick? They should call for the elders of the church and have them pray over them, anointing them with oil in the name of the Lord. The prayer of faith will save the sick, and the Lord will raise them up; and anyone who has committed sins will be forgiven. (JAMES 5:13–15)

The pastoral visitors shall lay hands on the head of the sick person. One of them may say one of the following after which the sick person may be anointed with oil. Olive oil may be used, applying it to the forehead with the thumb, making the sign of the cross.

May the hands of the Great Physician, Jesus Christ, rest upon you now in divine blessing and healing. May the cleansing power of his pure life fill your whole being, body, mind, and spirit, to strengthen and heal you. Amen.

Or:

Eternal God, for Jesus' sake, send your Holy Spirit upon your servant *Name:* drive away all sickness of body and spirit; make whole that which is broken. Grant deliverance from the power of evil, and true faith in Jesus Christ our Lord, who suffered on our behalf but also rose from death so that we, too, could live. In his name we pray. Amen.

A brief silence may be kept, after the sick person has been anointed.

PRAYER OF THANKSGIVING

Most gracious God, source of all healing; we give thanks to you for all your gifts but most of all for the gift of your Son, through whom you gave and still give health and salvation to all who believe. As we wait in expectation for the coming of that day when suffering and pain shall be no more, help us by your Holy Spirit to be assured of your power in our lives and to trust in your eternal love, through Jesus Christ our Lord. Amen.

BENEDICTION

THE FUNERAL: A SERVICE OF MEMORY AND HOPE

The universality of death means that a funeral may take place under a wide variety of circumstances. The deceased may have been a devoted Christian, a member of another religious community, or one who never confessed any specific beliefs. Those who gather may be a close fellowship of believers or a diverse spectrum of contemporary society. There are those for whom death is the end of personal existence; and others for whom death is the gateway to eternal life with God. Burial customs vary from place to place.

The minister, as representative of Christ and the church, must sensitively respond to each circumstance with compassion and integrity. Each funeral service is a unique occasion to witness to the gospel and to minister in Christ's name upon behalf of the whole people of God.

Presented here is a model designed to be adapted to the specific needs of each situation. It is designed to allow for the growing desire to conduct the service of committal first, to be followed by a service of grateful memory. Yet it is easily adaptable to reversing the two services.

When the committal service is conducted first, it is usually held at the cemetery chapel or crematorium as an intimate gathering of relatives and close friends. The service may be less formal and more expressive of personal feeling. An opportunity may be given for personal words of gratitude and love. When the committal service is held following the service of grateful memory, it tends to make the occasion more formal and less responsive to feeling. The memoriam is usually brief, having been given in the public service.

The service of grateful memory appropriately is held in a church and is conducted as a service of worship in which all participate. The sharing in the Lord's supper may be especially meaningful when the assembly is predominantly composed of a congregation's members. When the service is held in a funeral home, it is still a Christian service of worship shaped by the church's understanding of life and death in Christ.

Materials relating to distinctive occasions such as the death of a child or sudden tragedy are found at the end of this section.

� THE COMMITTAL

CALL TO WORSHIP

> God is our refuge and strength,
>> a very present help in trouble.   (PSALM 46:1)

> The eternal God is our refuge, and underneath are the everlasting arms.
>> (DEUTERONOMY 33:27, KJV)

> Lord Jesus, to whom shall we go? You have the words of eternal life.
>> (JOHN 6:68, ALT.)

> Christ has promised: "I will not leave you comfortless: I will come to you."   (JOHN 14:18, KJV)

PURPOSE

> In the stillness of this place we turn to God who is our beginning and our end. From dust we have been made and to dust we return. With reverence we gather to thank God for the gift of *Name* to us, and to commit *his/her* earthly body to the *ground/elements* with the confidence that neither life nor death can separate any of us from the love of God we know in Christ Jesus.

PRAYER

> God of heaven and earth, in your Son Jesus Christ
> you have given us a true faith and a sure hope.
> Strengthen this faith and hope in us all our days,
> that we may live as those who believe in
>> the communion of the saints,
>> the forgiveness of sins,
>> and the resurrection to eternal life;
> through your Son Jesus Christ our Lord. Amen.

MEMORIAM

We hold in grateful memory this one who is now separated from us by death. Though we cannot recall *him/her* to life, we can remember *him/her* and fix *his/her* memory within our hearts for as long as we shall live. We can celebrate the fullness of *his/her* life, with all its strengths, foibles, goodness, and weaknesses; and rejoice in the ties that bind us one to another.

In this spirit listen to these words of holy scripture that bespeak something of our loved one's faith and life. Recall the uniqueness of this one whom we honor, and, at the close of our reading, let us share with one another grateful memories we associate with *him/her*.

Here may be read brief scripture passages specifically appropriate to the person held in memory. They may be accompanied by brief comments by the reader as to why they are particularly fitting. At the conclusion of the reading:

STATEMENTS OF LIFE

If you would care to express words of gratitude for the character and contributions of this one whom we treasure in our hearts, do so now. As each thought is expressed, I shall say, "Hear our prayer, O God." You will respond: "O God, we give you thanks."

When those who care to speak have done so, conclude with this:

Loving God, gather together all our gifts of gratitude, spoken and unspoken, and treasure them in your eternal mind where nothing is ever forgotten. We thank you for all the goodness and loving-kindness you have bestowed upon *Name* in this earthly life, and pray that now beyond the bounds of death you will bless *him/her* with the gift of eternal fellowship with you and all your saints; through Christ, who lives and reigns with you and the Holy Spirit now and always. Amen.

COMMITTAL

Having commended *Name*, our companion on life's journey, into the hands of God, we now commit *his/her* body to the *ground/elements*; confident that the one who has made us shall not leave us in the dust, but in Christ give us the victory of eternal life. We look to the final day when, as the scriptures promise, God "will wipe every tear from their eyes. There shall be an end to death, and to mourning and crying and pain, for the old order has passed away."   (REVELATION 21:4, NEB)

CLOSING PRAYER

God of all life, we thank you for the life we remember here today.
We ask that you be with us in the days ahead
    as sorrow and loneliness weave their shadows around us.

Through the power of Christ's resurrection
>   restore our hope and give us strength to carry on with our lives.
We pray that your grace and love will be an abiding presence
>   in this time of need.
Fill our spirits with the truth of life. Grant us your peace. Amen.
Or:
O Lord, support us all the day long,
until the shadows lengthen and the evening comes,
and the busy world is hushed,
the fever of life is over and our work done.
Then, Lord, in your mercy grant us safe lodging,
a holy rest, and peace at the last;
through Jesus Christ our Lord. Amen.
Or:
God grant:
Deep peace of the Running Wave to you,
deep peace of the Flowing Air to you,
deep peace of the Quiet Earth to you,
deep peace of the Shining Stars to you,
deep peace of the Son of Peace to you.
Or:
May God bless you and keep you.
May God's face shine upon you and be gracious to you.
May God look upon you with kindness and give you peace. Amen.

(NUMBERS 6:24–26, ALT.)

Or:
Keep us ever in your love, O God.
Support us and strengthen us that we might be
Support and strength for those who need us. Amen.

☻ *SERVICE OF GRATEFUL MEMORY*

CALL TO WORSHIP
>   Gathered in Christ's name, let us praise God
>   >   who is our certain hope in all life's varied circumstances.
>   In the face of death believe the good news the scriptures proclaim:
>   As a mother comforts her child, so I will comfort you.   (ISAIAH 66:13)

>   As a father has compassion for his children,
>   >   so the LORD has compassion for those who fear him.   (PSALM 103:13)

"Blessed are those who mourn, for they will be comforted."

(MATTHEW 5:4)

"I am the resurrection and the life," says the Lord.
"Those who believe in me, even though they die, will live,
and everyone who lives and believes in me will never die."

(JOHN 11:25–26)

MUSIC

The congregation may sing a hymn. Vocal or instrumental music may be substituted.

GREETING

We have come together within the strengthening fellowship
of friends and family:
>to praise God for the life of *Name;*
>to share our grief with God and with one another;
>to reaffirm our faith in God's unfailing goodness;
>to hear again God's promise of resurrection;
>and to commend *Name* to God's everlasting care.

An obituary, or brief recounting of the deceased's life, may be presented as a means of acquainting those present with the relationships of the one held in memory.

OPENING PRAYER

Gracious God, your steadfast love endures forever,
>your faithfulness to all generations.

Trustworthy in all your words, and gracious in all your deeds,
>minister now to us in our grief.

Speak to our hearts your word of comfort.
Touch us into hope through the promises of holy scripture.
Enfold us within the fellowship of all who share our sorrow.
Fill us with the joy and peace that comes from above.
In quietness and peace we wait upon you.
Silence
 Amen.

Or:

Almighty God, source of all mercy and giver of comfort:
Deal graciously we pray, with those who mourn;
>that casting all their sorrow on you,
>they may know the consolation of your love;
>through your Son, Jesus Christ our Lord. Amen.

Or:

O gracious Lord, enable us to listen lovingly to your word.
May we console each other with the message you proclaim,
>so finding light in darkness and faith in the midst of doubt;
>through Jesus Christ our Lord. Amen.

Or:

O God of grace and glory, we remember before you this day
>our *brother/sister Name.*
We thank you for giving *him/her* to us,
>*his/her* family and friends,
>to know and to love as a companion on our earthly pilgrimage.
In your boundless compassion, console us who mourn.
Give us faith to see in death the gate of eternal life,
>so that in quiet confidence we may continue our course on earth,
>until, by your call,
>we are reunited with those who have gone before;
>through Jesus Christ our Lord. Amen.

The Lord's Prayer, spoken in unison, may be prayed.

PRAYER OF ILLUMINATION

Let us pray:
Eternal God, our refuge and our strength, console and support those who are sorrowful through the comfort of your Word, so we might be confident in this and every time of need, trusting in your love; through Jesus Christ our Lord. Amen.

Or:

Almighty God, whose love never fails, and who can turn the shadow of death into the light of life, illumine us through your Word; so that hearing your promises, we may be lifted out of darkness and distress into the light and peace of your presence, through Jesus Christ our Lord. Amen.

Or:

Holy One, in our sorrow we seek the comfort of your presence.
Let your Word be a lamp to our weary feet, and a light to our path.
Holy Wisdom, enter our troubled hearts this hour.
Grant that your Word might shine brightly therein,
that we might discover the fullness of new life's promises. Amen.

READING OF SCRIPTURE

It is appropriate that some of the scripture passages be read by relatives or close friends of the deceased. There is strength in reading the scriptures directly from the Bible which declares the word of God. Printed below are a few familiar passages that have been shortened by selection of appropriate verses.

The Psalms

Lord, you have been our dwelling place
    in all generations.
Before the mountains were brought forth,
        or ever you had formed the earth and the world,
        from everlasting to everlasting you are God.
You turn us back to dust,
        and say, "Turn back, you mortals."
For a thousand years in your sight
        are like yesterday when it is past,
        or like a watch in the night.
You sweep them away; they are like a dream,
        like grass that is renewed in the morning;
in the morning it flourishes and is renewed;
        in the evening it fades and withers.
The days of our life are seventy years,
        or perhaps eighty, if we are strong.
So teach us to count our days
        that we may gain a wise heart.   (PSALM 90:1–6, 10, 12)

Other appropriate psalms:

Psalm 23—The Divine Shepherd
Psalm 42:1–8—Longing for God and help in distress
Psalm 46—God is with us
Psalm 121—Assurance of God's protection
Psalm 130—Hope in God
Psalm 139—God's eternal presence

Hebrew Scriptures

But now thus says the LORD,
        he who created you, O Jacob,
        he who formed you, O Israel:
Do not fear, for I have redeemed you;
        I have called you by name, you are mine.
When you pass through the waters, I will be with you;
        and through the rivers, they shall not overwhelm you;
when you walk through fire you shall not be burned,
        and the flame shall not consume you.
For I am the LORD your God,
        the Holy One of Israel, your Savior.
Do not fear, for I am with you;
        I will bring your offspring from the east,
        and from the west I will gather you;
I will say to the north, "Give them up,"
        and to the south, "Do not withhold;

bring my sons from far away
and my daughters from the end of the earth—
everyone who is called by my name,
whom I created for my glory,
whom I formed and made."
I am God, and also henceforth I am He;
there is no one who can deliver from my hand;
I work and who can hinder it?
I am the LORD, your Holy One, the Creator of Israel, your King.
Do not remember the former things,
or consider the things of old.
I am about to do a new thing;
now it springs forth, do you not perceive it?
I will make a way in the wilderness
and rivers in the desert.
I, I am He
who blots out your transgressions for my own sake,
and I will not remember your sins.
Thus says the LORD, the King of Israel,
and his Redeemer, the LORD of hosts:
I am the first and I am the last;
besides me there is no god.
Do not fear, or be afraid;
have I not told you from of old and declared it?
You are my witnesses!   (ISAIAH 43:1–3A, 5–7, 13, 15, 18–19, 25; 44:6, 8A)

Other appropriate passages from Hebrew scripture:

Isaiah 40:1–8—The comfort of God
Isaiah 40:28–31—Power to the faint
Lamentations 3:22–26; 31–33—God is good

New Testament Readings
Now I would remind you, brothers and sisters,
of the good news that I proclaimed to you,
which you in turn received, in which also you stand,
through which also you are being saved.
Now if Christ is proclaimed as raised from the dead,
how can some of you say there is no resurrection of the dead?
For if the dead are not raised, then Christ has not been raised.
If Christ has not been raised,
your faith is futile and you are still in your sins.
Then those also who have died in Christ have perished.
But in fact Christ has been raised from the dead,
the first fruits of those who have died.
But someone will ask, "How are the dead raised?
With what kind of body do they come?"

Fool! What you sow does not come to life unless it dies.
And as for what you sow, you do not sow the body that is to be,
    but a bare seed, perhaps of wheat or of some other grain.
But God gives it a body as God has chosen.
What is sown is perishable, what is raised is imperishable.
    It is sown in dishonor, it is raised in glory.
    It is sown in weakness, it is raised in power.
    It is sown a physical body, it is raised a spiritual body.
If there is a physical body, there is also a spiritual body.
When this perishable body puts on imperishability,
    and this mortal body puts on immortality,
    then the saying that is written will be fulfilled:
"Death has been swallowed up in victory."
    "Where, O death, is your victory?
    Where, O death, is your sting?"
But thanks be to God, who gives us the victory
    through our Lord Jesus Christ.

(1 Corinthians 15:1–2a, 12, 16–18, 20, 35–38a, 42b–44, 54–55, 57)

There is therefore now no condemnation
    for those who are in Christ Jesus.
For the law of the Spirit of life in Christ Jesus
    has set you free from the law of sin and of death.
If the Spirit of him who raised Jesus from the dead dwells in you,
    he who raised Christ from the dead
    will give life to your mortal bodies also
    through his Spirit that dwells in you.
For all who are led by the Spirit of God are children of God.
    and if children, then heirs,
    heirs of God and joint heirs with Christ—
    if, in fact, we suffer with him
    so that we may also be glorified with him.
I consider that the sufferings of this present time
    are not worth comparing with the glory about to be revealed to us.
We know that all things work together for good
    for those who love God,
    who are called according to his purpose.
What then are we to say about these things?
If God is for us, who is against us?
He who did not withhold his own Son, but gave him up for all of us,
    will he not with him also give us everything else?
Who will separate us from the love of Christ?
Will hardship, or distress, or persecution,
    or famine, or nakedness, or peril, or sword?
As it is written, "For your sake we are being killed all day long;
    we are accounted as sheep to be slaughtered."

No, in all these things we are more than conquerors
    through him who loved us.
For I am convinced that neither death, nor life,
    nor angels, nor rulers, nor things present, nor things to come,
    nor powers, nor height, nor depth, nor anything else in all creation,
    will be able to separate us from the love of God
        in Christ Jesus our Lord.

(ROMANS 8:1–2, 11, 14, 17–18, 28, 31–32, 35–39)

Other appropriate New Testament passages include:

2 Corinthians 4:5–18—The unseen is eternal
1 Peter 1:3–9, 13, 21–25—A living hope
1 John 3:1–2—We will be like God
Revelation 7:9–17—The multitude of the redeemed
Revelation 21:1–7—The home of God

The Gospel Reading

Hear these words from Jesus:
"Do not let your hearts be troubled.
Believe in God, believe also in me.
In my Father's house there are many dwelling places.
If it were not so,
    would I have told you that I go to prepare a place for you?
And if I go and prepare a place for you,
    I will come again and will take you to myself,
    so that where I am, there you may be also.
And you know the way to the place where I am going.
I will not leave you orphaned; I am coming to you.
In a little while the world will no longer see me,
    but you will see me;
    because I live, you also will live.
I have said these things to you while I am still with you.
But the Advocate, the Holy Spirit,
    whom the Father will send in my name,
    will teach you everything,
    and remind you of all that I have said to you.
Peace I leave with you; my peace I give to you.
I do not give to you as the world gives.
Do not let your hearts be troubled, and do not let them be afraid."

(JOHN 14:1–4, 18–19, 25–27)

Other appropriate Gospel passages include:

Matthew 5:1–10, 13–16, 6:19–21, 7:24–27—The counsel of Christ
John 5:24–27—Passing from death to life
John 10:11–16—The Good Shepherd
John 11:21–27—The resurrection and the life

MESSAGE

MUSIC

The congregation may sing a hymn. Vocal or instrumental music may be sub-stituted. If the Lord's supper is to be observed, deacons and elders may come forward during the singing of the hymn. The usual aspects of the Lord's supper may be observed. A communion invitation should be extended that makes clear to visitors the meal's essential meaning and who may appropriately partake.

STATEMENTS OF LIFE

The minister or any others may gratefully express the ways in which the de-ceased has graced their lives and the lives of others. If desired, any present may be invited to join in the statements of life.

GENERAL PRAYER

O God, our Strength and our Redeemer, Giver of life, and Conqueror of death, we open our hearts to you just as we are. We celebrate your gift of life freely given, but are grieved by a sense of loss in the face of death. The love which binds us to one another leaves us aching as ties are broken. Accept our tears as emblems of devotion, and transform them into waters of life to nourish us in the days ahead.

We trust you. We love you. We know in Christ that your love is ever-lasting. Nothing can separate any of us from your abiding care. With you is eternal life.

Remind us of our baptism in which we were baptized into Christ's death that we might rise to newness of life. United with him in a death like his, we will certainly be united with him in a resurrection like his. Together we are the body of Christ and individually members. Within the fellowship of the saints we join ourselves together with the great host of all times and places who celebrate your eternal love. We add our voices to theirs in giving you unbroken praise.

We thank you especially for your gift of *Name* into the lives of those who have known and loved *him/her.*

Here may be offered special thanksgivings for the one held in memory.

With confidence we now entrust *Name* to your unfailing love and over-flowing goodness. Through the power that raised Christ from the dead to live eternally with you, lift up this, your servant, to life fulfilled be-yond our imagining. We give you but your own. Accept *him/her* as he is with all *his/her* frailties as well as *his/her* strengths. Enfold *him/her* in your everlasting arms. Embrace *him/her* as your friend.

Now strengthen us, through the gift of your Spirit, to face into the fu-ture with confidence that you stand with us. Grant that the changes of life may leave us stronger as we journey through life.

Reassured of your abiding presence, help us to knit more firmly the ties that bind us one to another. Renewed by your love, help us to love in ever larger circles so as to embrace your people everywhere till at last we are all united eternally through Christ, who lives and reigns with you and the Holy Spirit, one God, now and forever. Amen.

PARTAKING OF THE LORD'S SUPPER

If the Lord's supper is observed, an emphasis may be made upon communion with the host of Christian believers of all times and places. The invitation should make clear the Lord's supper's meaning and that participation is open to all Christ's followers.

MUSIC

The congregation may sing a hymn—a recessional hymn if appropriate. Vocal or instrumental music may be substituted.

DISMISSAL WITH BLESSING

Take courage. Go in the knowledge that the loving God
    is your eternal friend and companion.

And may the God of peace,
    who brought back from the dead our Lord Jesus,
    the great shepherd of the sheep,
    by the blood of the eternal covenant,
make you complete in everything good so that you may do God's will,
    working in you that which is pleasing in God's sight,
    through Jesus Christ, to whom be the glory forever and ever. Amen.

(HEBREWS 13:20–21, ALT.)

Or:

And may the peace of God which is beyond our understanding guard your hearts and your thoughts in Christ Jesus. Amen.

(PHILIPPIANS 4:7, ALT.)

ADDITIONAL RESOURCES

GREETINGS AND CALLS TO WORSHIP

If your love mourns, come, and God shall hold you.
We will not be alone in the pain of our loss.

If your heart grieves, come, and God's arms shall enfold you.
Our tears of sorrow will mingle with God's.

We will trust in our Keeper and not be afraid.
Our God has seen, and shall not turn away.
Our God has seen and shall always remain.

+ + +

Hear the promises of our God:
God hears the silent grief of our hearts.
Yet God takes joy, as do we, in the gifts that were and are life.
God is faithful and will abide as Light and Love for us all,
    even as our grieving hearts are silent.

PRAYER

Are we to mourn our dead, or beloved, as ones that have no hope?
O God, you are not the God of the dead, but of the living.
    In your resurrection, O Christ, we celebrate ours.
The gift of your life, O Holy Spirit, is not for a season, but forever.
As long as you are with your servants, your children,
    they are with you; they lose nothing by dying.
They depart out of the world, but not out of your family.
They vanish from our sight, but not from your care.
    One sun has set upon them, but a greater is risen.
They are not dead; no, it is death that has died in them.
They leave behind the mortal, to put on immortality;
    theirs is entrance into healing, into rest, into glory.

Lord, you have made, endowed, redeemed, employed your children;
    you cannot desert or annihilate them,
    cannot but be gracious eternally.
You reward the benefactors we never knew.
You, the one who holds worlds in life, hold them.

O Father, O Savior, O Giver of Life,
    by your mercy, your unalterable love,
gather your sons and daughters together unto yourself,
    those who have taken you for their strength,
    those who have served you with sacrifice,
    those who have offered you thanks and praise.
May they rejoice in the Jerusalem of grace and peace,
    and praise you among the choirs of the blessed, in joy without end.

Ⓨ *FOR A STILLBORN OR NEWLY BORN CHILD*

*This is truly a child of God who has been affirmed in love by a caring family and
who is commended to God's everlasting love. The deliberate use of the child's name
in the service gives expression to this loved one's individuality and uniqueness.*

After reading several scriptural sentences of comfort, reference may be made to the circumstances by saying:

GREETING

> Friends, we have gathered to worship God
> > and to witness to our faith,
> even as we mourn the death of this infant, *Name,*
> > the child of *Name* and *Name.*
> We come together in grief, acknowledging our human loss.
> May God search our hearts, that in pain we may find comfort,
> > in sorrow hope, in death resurrection.

SCRIPTURE READINGS

> Psalm 23   John 1:1–5
> Psalm 139:1–3, 7–18   Ephesians 3:14–19
> Mark 10:13–16

PRAYER

> O God of life, in whom we live and move and have our being,
> > be present now to this mother in her emptiness,
> > to this father in his desolation,
> > to this family,
> > and to all of us who stand with them stricken with grief.
> Joy has been turned to mourning; celebration into lament.
> We are left bewildered and perplexed before the mystery of death.
> > Let us not be dismayed.
> Help us to trust you as a father who yearns for his child;
> > as a mother who gives comfort to the fruit of her womb.
> In your good time dispel our darkness and brighten our lives
> > with fresh hope.

> Accept now our hopes and dreams
> > which cannot now be fulfilled on this earth,
> and bless *Name* with the fullness and wholeness of life
> > lived out eternally in your loving presence.
> In the knowledge that it is not your will
> > that the least of your children should perish,
> > we entrust *Name* to your tender care.
> Take our love and add it to yours
> > that *he/she* may be richly blessed.

> O God, good creator of life, all that you bring forth is good.
> > Nothing is created in vain. We give you back your own.
> And as we commend *Name* to your keeping,
> > we pray your blessing upon these parents in their sorrow.

Console and comfort them in the knowledge that
    you accompany them in the days ahead as a near friend,
    wise counselor, strengthening companion.
You are our trust. Your love never fails.
We pray in the name of Jesus Christ our Lord and Savior. Amen.

 *FOR A CHILD*

God's love embraces all God's children. This is particularly important for any children who are present at this service to understand. Scriptures read from such translations as "The Bible for Today's Family" (Contemporary English Version) or "Today's English Version" may assist communication. Following the reading of appropriate scripture sentences, reference may be made to the particular circumstances:

STATEMENT OF PURPOSE

We gather before God in grief at the death of this child of God, *Name*, the *son/daughter* of *Name* and *Name*. We come to praise God for life in the midst of death; for God's good understanding in the face of bewildering sorrow; for the sharing of comfort with one another; and to affirm our trust in the everlasting love of God. We cling to the promise of God in Jesus Christ: "Blessed are those who mourn, for they shall be comforted."

SCRIPTURE READINGS

Psalm 23—The Shepherd God
Matthew 18:1–5, 10–14—The greatest in God's realm
Mark 10:13–16—Let the children come
2 Corinthians 1:1–4—The consolation of God
Revelation 7:17—God wipes away every tear

PRAYER

God of all hopefulness, we gather with *Name* and *Name*
    mourning the loss of their *daughter/son*, *Name*.
They shared with us such hopes for this child.
They dreamed such big dreams. Their plans were wonderful.
All of us took much joy in the promises of life to come—
    promises that can never be.

Loving God, do not abandon us to our hopelessness.
    Do not leave us to our tormented questioning.
    Do not take your holy light from us.
Help of the helpless, we give *Name* into your hands.
    Hold *her/him* close to your heart.
    Wrap *her/him* round in your love and care.

God of all hopefulness, through the power of Christ within us,
    bind us all closer to one another and to you. Amen.

Or:

Caring God, our everlasting friend, we know you
    as one who calls children to you with outstretched arms.
We do not understand what has happened,
    and can only feel grief-stricken that *Name* is no longer with us.
But we know Jesus and the great love he has
    for every man, woman, and child—a love of self-giving for others
    that they may live eternally with you.

We entrust *Name* to your loving care,
    for we know your love for *him/her* is greater than our own.
Look after *him/her* and bring *his/her* life to wholeness
    within the fellowship of those who love you.
We thank you for the joy that was *his/hers*
    and the pleasure *he/she* brought to those who knew *him/her*.
There were good times and there were bad times,
    but they all come together as precious moments
    as we gratefully recall all that is special about *Name's* life.

Here gratitude may be expressed for the characteristics of this child.

Meet us in our loneliness. Accept our brokenness.
Strengthen our ties with one another in the days ahead.
Help us to celebrate the goodness of life—
    whether it spans many days or only a few.
Guide us as we pick up our lives and move into your future,
    that we may rejoice in what you have made
    and find eternal gladness, through Jesus Christ our Lord. Amen.

COMMITTAL

Loving God, give us faith to believe,
though this child has died, that you welcome *him/her*
and will care for *him/her*, until, by your mercy,
we are together again in the joy of your promised kingdom;
through Jesus Christ our Lord.

 AFTER A SUICIDE

Being sensitive to the circumstances, the emphasis of the service should be upon the valued gifts of this person, rather than upon how the life has ended. At the same time, the troubled feelings of those who have come to mourn must be taken into account. Within this context such prayers as these may be offered:

PRAYER

Lord, we do not understand what has happened.
There seems to be no sense in the ending of this life
    and we are puzzled and distressed.
In the crucifixion of Jesus you have shown us
    that your love is alongside us even when we feel abandoned.
As we remember *Name* and think of the despair
    that must have engulfed *him/her* at the end,
    help us to realize that there is nothing more powerful than your
    love.

We thank you for the good things in *Name's* life
    and ask forgiveness for those times when we let *him/her* down.
Forgive our sins and heal our guilt, we pray.
Redeemer God, take what has happened and somehow weave it
    into your loving purpose,
    so that *Name* may not have lived or died in vain.
This we ask in the name of Jesus our Savior. Amen.

Or:

Lord Jesus Christ,
    you spoke of your Father's love for all people;
help us to know that your love
    will never be withdrawn from *Name* or from us.
Lord Jesus Christ,
    you wrestled with questions of life and death in Gethsemane;
help us to know that you understand
    and are present where there is anguish of mind. Amen.

☧ *IN THE FACE OF SUDDEN TRAGEDY*

When death comes under tragic circumstances, it is important to acknowledge the sense of shock and disbelief that is being experienced, and then move on toward expressions of acceptance in the context of Christian affirmation.

OPENING SENTENCES

Out of the depths we cry to you, O Lord.
    Hear our voice!
Let your ears be attentive
    to the voice of our supplications!
We wait for the LORD,
    and in God's word we hope.
For with the LORD there is steadfast love,
    and with the LORD is great power to redeem.

(PSALM 130:1–2, 5, 7, ALT.)

OPENING PRAYER

Our Father, God, we are in your hands;
   we want to open ourselves to your perspective,
   your grace and light.
And yet our feelings lock us into the present.
   We offer them to you now:
Our shock at the news of *Name's* sudden death,
   the numbness—it still doesn't seem real.
Our sadness at losing a friend,
   the pain as our hearts ask: 'Why?'
Lord, these are some of the thing we feel,
   the questions that force their way into our consciousness.
We offer them to you, and ask you to comfort us and lead us into truth.

We thank you that *Name's* trust was in you,
   that faith was lived out in *him/her*,
   that *his/her* life was grounded in your love.
Make us aware of that deep faith now
   and help us to ground our lives on you,
   so that in our turmoil we will still have you as our foundation;
   in suffering we will know your presence:
   know that it is in suffering that you show yourself as God-with-us.
Meet us in this service, through your Word spoken to us
   and demonstrated in *Name's* life.
May we know healing in our grief,
   peace in confusion,
   your strength in our frailty. Amen.

SCRIPTURE READINGS

Psalm 22:19–27—The comfort of the afflicted
Psalm 103:1–5, 10–18—Forget not God's benefits
Lamentations 3:19–26, 31–33—Hope in God's mercies
John 6:35–40—God's will that nothing be lost

COMMITTAL PRAYER

God of us all, we thank you for Christ's grace,
   through which we pray to you in this dark hour.
A life we love has been torn from us.
Expectations the years once held have vanished.
   The mystery of death has stricken us.
O God, you know the lives we live and the deaths we die—
   woven so strangely of purpose and of chance,
   of reason and of the irrational,
   of strength and of frailty,
   of happiness and of pain.

Into your hands we commend the soul of *Name*.
No mortal life you have made is without eternal meaning.
No earthly fate is beyond your redeeming.
Through your grace
    that can do far more than we can think or imagine,
    fulfill in *Name* your purpose that reaches beyond time and death.
Lead *her/him* from strength to strength,
    and fit *her/him* for love and service in your kingdom.

Into your hands also we commit our lives.
You alone, God, make us to dwell in safety.
Whom, finally, have we on earth or in heaven but you?
Help us to know the measure of our days, and how frail we are.
Save our minds from despair and our hearts from fear,
    and guard and guide us with your peace. Amen.

II

ECUMENICAL
SERVICES
OF

Service for the Sacrament of the Lord's Supper

This service was prepared by the Commission on Worship of the Consultation on Church Union and published with the approval of its executive committee. It may appropriately be used upon ecumenical occasions when several denominations participate, or as a variation for any Sunday worship service.

The member churches of the Consultation on Church Union are: African Methodist Episcopal Church, African Methodist Episcopal Zion Church, Christian Church (Disciples of Christ), Christian Methodist Episcopal Church, Episcopal Church, International Council of Community Churches, Presbyterian Church (U.S.A.), United Church of Christ, and United Methodist Church.

GATHERING

OPENING SENTENCES

The grace, mercy and peace of Jesus Christ be with you.
And also with you.

Or:

Alleluia, Christ is risen.
The Lord is risen indeed. Alleluia.

Or other scriptural sentences of greeting may be used.

HYMN OF PRAISE

PRAYER *(In unison)*

**Almighty God: you are the infinite, eternal, and unchangeable,
    glorious in holiness, full of love and compassion,
    abundant in grace and truth.
All your works praise you in all places of your dominion,
    and your glory is revealed in Christ, our Savior.
Therefore we praise you, Blessed and Holy Trinity,
    One God, forever and ever.**

Or:

**Almighty God, to you all hearts are open,
    all desires known, and from you no secrets are hid:
Cleanse the thoughts of our hearts
    by the inspiration of your Holy Spirit,
    that we may perfectly love you,
    and worthily magnify your holy Name;
    through Christ our Lord. Amen.**

PROCLAMATION AND RESPONSE

FIRST LESSON

ACT OF PRAISE *(A psalm, canticle, or hymn may follow the reading)*

SECOND LESSON

ACT OF PRAISE

LESSON FROM THE GOSPELS

SERMON

RESPONSES

There may occur in response to proclamation any of the following: an altar call or invitation to Christian discipleship, the reception of new members, the ordination and installation of church officers, the sacrament of baptism, a call to action, or the reciting of a creed. An act of confession and reconciliation such as the following may be used in response to the proclamation.

We confess that often we have failed to be an obedient church.
> **We have not done your will,**
> **we have broken your law,**
> **we have rebelled against your love,**
> **we have not loved our neighbors,**
> **and we have not heard the cry of the needy.**
Forgive us, we pray. Free us for joyful obedience,
through Jesus Christ our Lord. Amen.

DECLARATION OF PARDON

> Anyone in Christ becomes a new person altogether;
> > the past is finished and gone,
> > everything has become fresh and new.
> Friends, believe the good news of the gospel:
> **In Jesus Christ, we are forgiven.**

CONCERNS AND PRAYERS OF THE CHURCH

The people are encouraged to express their own concerns, whether by stating them personally or communicating them to the leader before the service. The intercessions may take the form of one continuous prayer by the leader, biddings, or a litany.

SERVICE OF THE TABLE

THE PEACE

> The peace of Christ be with you.
> **And also with you.**

The ministers and people may stand and exchange signs and words of God's peace.

PRESENTING THE GIFTS

GREAT THANKSGIVING

Lift up your hearts.
We lift them to the Lord.
Let us give thanks to the Lord our God.
It is right to give God thanks and praise.

It is right and good to give you thanks, Almighty God, for you are the source of light and life. You made us in your image and called us to new life in Jesus Christ. In all times and places your people proclaim your glory in unending praise:

The preceding paragraph is known as "the Preface." Local congregations and eucharistic communities are encouraged to make their own decisions about the content and style of the preface, focusing on general themes stressing the creation, the season or day in the church year, or a local occasion. Proper prefaces for seasons of the church year are found at the conclusion of this service.

Holy, holy, holy Lord, God of power and might,
    heaven and earth are full of your glory.
Hosanna in the highest.
Blessed is the one who comes in the name of the Lord.
Hosanna in the highest.

We remember with joy the grace by which you created all things
    and made us in your own image.
We rejoice that you called a people in covenant
    to be a light to the nations.
Yet we rebelled against your will.
In spite of the prophets and pastors sent forth to us,
    we continued to break your covenant.
In the fullness of time, you sent your only son to save us.
Incarnate by the Holy Spirit, born of your favored one, Mary,
    sharing our life, he reconciled us to your love.
At the Jordan your Spirit descended upon him,
    anointing him to preach the good news of your reign.
He healed the sick and fed the hungry,
    manifesting the power of your compassion.
He sought out the lost and broke bread with sinners,
    witnessing the fullness of your grace.
We beheld his glory.

On the night before he died for us, Jesus took bread;
    giving thanks to you, he broke the bread
    and offered it to his disciples, saying:

"Take this and eat; this is my body which is given for you,
    do this in remembrance of me."
Taking a cup, again he gave thanks to you,
    shared the cup with his disciples and said:
"This is the cup of the new covenant in my blood.
    Drink from this, all of you.
This is poured out for you and for many,
    for the forgiveness of sins."

After the meal our Lord was arrested,
    abandoned by his followers and beaten.
He stood trial and was put to death on a cross.
Having emptied himself in the form of a servant,
    and being obedient even to death,
    he was raised from the dead
    and exalted as Lord of heaven and earth.
Through him you bestow the gift of your Spirit,
    uniting your church, empowering its mission,
    and leading us into the new creation you have promised.
Gracious God, we celebrate with joy
    the redemption won for us in Jesus Christ.
Grant that in praise and thanksgiving
    we may be a living sacrifice,
    holy and acceptable in your sight,
    that our lives may proclaim the mystery of faith:

Christ has died,
Christ is risen,
Christ will come again.

Loving God, pour out your Holy Spirit upon us and upon these gifts,
    that they may be for us
    the body and blood of our Savior Jesus Christ.
Grant that we may be for the world the body of Christ,
    redeemed through his blood,
    serving and reconciling all people to you.
Remember your church, scattered upon the face of the earth;
    gather it in unity and preserve it in truth.
Remember the saints who have gone before us
    especially *Name* and *Name.*

    Here may occur special names.

In communion with them and with all creation,
    we worship and glorify you always:
Through your Son Jesus Christ
with the Holy Spirit in your holy church,
all glory and honor is yours, Almighty God,
now and forever. Amen.

THE LORD'S PRAYER

BREAKING OF THE BREAD

The minister breaks the bread in silence or while saying:

The bread which we break, is it not a sharing in the body of Christ?
Because there is one bread, we who are many are one body,
for we all partake of the one bread.

The wine which we drink, is it not a sharing in the blood of Christ?
The cup which we bless is the communion in the blood of Christ.

SHARING OF THE BREAD AND THE CUP

CLOSING

PRAYER

Bountiful God, we give thanks that you have refreshed us at your table
by granting us the presence of Christ. Strengthen our faith, increase
our love for one another, and send us forth into the world in courage
and peace, rejoicing in the power of the Holy Spirit. Amen.

Or:

God our help, we thank you for this supper shared in the Spirit with
your servant Jesus, who makes us new and strong, who brings life eternal. We praise you for giving us all good gifts, and pledge ourselves to
serve you, even as in Christ you have served us. Amen.

HYMN

DISMISSAL

The grace of the Lord Jesus Christ and the love of God
    and the communion of the Holy Spirit be with you all. Amen.

A deacon or layperson may dismiss the people with these words:

Go out into the world in peace,
    have courage; hold on to what is good;
    return no one evil for evil; strengthen the fainthearted;
    support the weak; help the suffering;
    honor everyone; love and serve God,
        rejoicing in the power of the Holy Spirit.

THE PROPER PREFACES FOR SEASONAL USE

ADVENT: It is right and good to give you thanks, Almighty God. You sent
your servant John the Baptist to preach repentance and to prepare the way
of our Lord Jesus Christ. Therefore, in all times and places your people
proclaim your glory in unending praise:

CHRISTMAS: It is right and good to give you thanks, Almighty God. You gave us the gift of your Son Jesus, who is the light in this dark world and our only Savior. Therefore, in all times and places your people proclaim your glory in unending praise:

EPIPHANY: It is right and good to give you thanks, Almighty God. You have given us the Word made flesh, and through our baptism we are blessed to share in the healing and reconciling love of Christ. Therefore, in all times and places your people proclaim your glory in unending praise:

LENT: It is right and good to give you thanks, Almighty God. You call us to cleanse our hearts and prepare with joy for the victory of the Lamb who is slain. Therefore, in all times and places your people proclaim your glory in unending praise:

EASTER: It is right and good to give you thanks, Almighty God. You have brought forth our Lord Jesus from the grave. By his death he has destroyed death, and by his rising to life again he has won for us everlasting life. Therefore, in all times and places your people proclaim your glory in unending praise:

PENTECOST: It is right and good to give you thanks, Almighty God. You poured out the Holy Spirit upon the disciples, teaching them the truth of your Son Jesus, empowering your church for its service, and uniting us as your holy people. Therefore, in all times and places your people proclaim your glory in unending praise:

 # MARTIN LUTHER KING, JR., DAY

Observed on the third Monday in January, this day celebrates the life, ministry, and vision of Martin Luther King, Jr. (1929–1968). An American Baptist minister and civil rights leader, he was awarded the Nobel Peace Prize in 1964 and died by an assassin's bullet.

The service is designed for ecumenical participation, but is adaptable for use within a Sunday service preceding the holiday.

GREETING

We have gathered here to celebrate the life
   and prophetic legacy of Dr. Martin Luther King, Jr.,
   who, in Christ's holy name,
   called us to a ministry of witness and reconciliation.
But we have much to confess, even as we give thanks for that life.

The tools of science we have created
    bring both medical miracles and the devastation of war.
The pleasures we chase often end up leaving us empty.

Our love of money too often crowds out
    those loving relationships that would fill our hearts
    with the joy and peace for which we long.
Have faith! God is able to grant us new life.

Even death itself can cause us no harm.
Nothing is impossible for God.

No loss or disappointment can break us if we put our trust in God.
**Nothing in all creation can separate us from the love of God
    in Christ Jesus, our Lord!**

HYMN

PRAYER
    O God, who has made all races to dwell upon the earth as one family:
    Break down the barriers of fear and suspicion that divide us.
    Build bridges of love and justice which lead us
        to greet one another as brothers and sisters
        and to embrace one another in reconciling fellowship.
    Gathering us hand to hand, lead us to join with you
        to make this earth fair and life a blessing to all;
        that in everything your name may be praised. Amen.

STATEMENT OF PURPOSE
    We gather to remember Martin Luther King, Jr.:
    to recall a person who had a dream
        to bring all peoples together in mutual respect and love;
    to remember the life he lived of unmerited suffering
        that others may be free;
    to engrave on our hearts the good news he proclaimed
        that through the power of God love can conquer hatred;
    to capture his spirit and to know the strength to love
        in the face of every inequity.

MUSIC   *This may be a hymn, anthem, or solo.*

SPECIAL PRESENTATION
    *A person from the community who exemplifies the spirit and commitment of
    Martin Luther King, Jr., may be honored.*

READING FROM HEBREW SCRIPTURE
    One or more of the following may be read:
        Deuteronomy 8:11–20

Isaiah 11:1–9
Isaiah 51:1–12
Isaiah 61:1–4

ANTHEM OR HYMN

READING FROM THE NEW TESTAMENT

One or more of the following may be read:
Luke 4:16–21
Matthew 5:38–48
2 Corinthians 5:11–21

SERMON

INTERCESSIONS

*The worship leader may offer prayers in the spirit of Martin Luther King, Jr.,
such as the one found in* The United Methodist Book of Worship, #435.

HYMN   Lift Every Voice and Sing (*CH* 125)

BENEDICTION

And now unto the One who is able to keep us from falling
and lift us from the dark valley of despair
   to the bright mountain of hope,
from the midnight of desperation
   to the daybreak of joy:
to God be power and authority, forever and ever. Amen.

ℰCUMENICAL
CELEBRATION OF THANKSGIVING

*Thanksgiving Day is a national holiday in which persons from many religious
traditions may join as one in acts of gratitude to God. This service, designed to
express festive gratitude, seeks to be inclusive of various traditions, affirming what
all may affirm.*

INSTRUMENTAL VOLUNTARY

INSTRUMENTAL CALL TO WORSHIP

A conch shell or ram's horn may be blown to signal the beginning of the service.

DECLARATION OF PURPOSE

Earth is crammed with the glory of God.
Let us lift hearts and hands and voices
to praise our Earthmaker and Lord of Creation,
the one who blesses us with the grandeur of life.

HYMN

This may be a processional hymn at which time supplies collected for distribution to the needy may be brought forward.

CALL TO WORSHIP

Worship the Lord in gladness,
    come before him with joy.
Enter his gates with thanksgiving,
    with gratitude sing out his praise.
**The Lord, creator of the heavens and the earth,
    provides food for the hungry with mercy.**

Praise the Creator who works great wonders,
    who ennobles us from birth, who treats us with compassion.
How shall we thank God for our blessings?

Let us share our bread with the hungry;
    let us not turn away from the needy.
**Clothe the naked and shelter the homeless,
    help those who have no help.**

Sing a new song for the Lord.
Where the faithful gather, let God be praised.

OPENING PRAYER

This or a similar prayer may be given. Note that this one includes a dedication of an offering presented in the processional.

Almighty and ever-living God,
    you have richly blessed this land
    with the bounteous goodness from your hand.
Accept these expressions of our caring
    as tokens of our abiding concern for others.
With gratitude we count and celebrate life's blessings.
We rejoice in your everlasting love
    which draws us together despite cherished differences.
Grant that we may draw together in praise
    and go forth with compassion to serve. Amen.

READING OF THANKSGIVING PROCLAMATION

HYMN/ANTHEM/SOLO

READINGS

Several readings may be given representing differing traditions. Appropriate biblical passages include:

Leviticus 19:1–2, 15–18   Matthew 5:1–10
Exodus 22:20–23   1 Thessalonians 1:2; 3:9, 12
Deuteronomy 6:5–8

Here are some other possibilities.

Whereas it is the duty of all nations to acknowledge the providence of almighty God, to obey his will, to be grateful for his benefits, and humbly to implore his protection and favor: And whereas both Houses of Congress have, by their joint committee, requested me to recommend to the people of the United States, a day of public thanksgiving and prayer, to be observed by acknowledging with grateful hearts the many and signal favors of almighty God, especially by affording them an opportunity peaceably to establish a form of government for their safety and happiness...Now therefore, I do recommend...that we may then all unite in rendering unto him our sincere and humble thanks for his kind care and protection of the people of this country.

(George Washington's Proclamation Establishing a day of Thanksgiving, October 3, 1789)

+ + +

O Great Spirit, whose voice I hear in the winds,
    and whose breath gives life to all the world,
    hear me.
I am small and weak. I need your strength and wisdom.
Let me walk in beauty and make my eyes ever behold
    the red and purple sunset.
Make my hands respect the things you have made.
Make my ears sharp to hear your voice.
Make me wise so that I may understand
    the things you have taught your people.
Let me learn the lessons you have hidden in every leaf and rock.
I seek strength, not to be greater than my brother,
    but to fight my greatest enemy—myself.
Make me always ready to come to you
    with clean hands and straight eyes.
So when life fades, as the fading sunset,
    my spirit may come to you without shame.

(Prayer of a Native American)

+ + +

The time for reciting the morning prayers almost had past and still the Rabbi of Apt had not yet appeared at the synagogue. His disciples sought him out, and found him in his study, smoking his pipe, lost in thought. "Master, the time for reciting the morning prayers is almost past," they said, breaking his intense concentration. "I know," he said. "Early this morning, I arose and I began to recite the prayer 'I offer thanks to you...' and since then I have been thinking one thought: Who am I that I deign to offer thanks to you?"

(ABRAHAM HESCHEL, THE RABBI'S PRAYERS)

+ + +

Most high, almighty, good Lord God,
>   to you belong praise, glory, honor and all blessing.
Praised be my Lord God, with all your creatures,
>   and especially our brother the sun,
>   who brings us the day and who brings us the light:
>   fair is he, and he shines with a very great splendor.
>   O Lord, he signifies you to us.
Praised be my Lord for our sister the moon, and for the stars,
>   which you have set clear and lovely in the heaven.
Praised be my Lord for our brother the wind,
>   and for air and clouds, calms and all weather,
>   by which you uphold life and all creatures.
Praised be my Lord for our sister water, who is very serviceable to us,
>   and humble and precious and clean.
Praised be my Lord for our brother fire,
>   through whom you give us light in the darkness;
>   he is bright and pleasant and mighty and strong.
Praised be my Lord for our mother the earth,
>   which sustains and keeps us and brings forth all kinds of fruits
>   and flowers of many colors and the grass.
Praised be my Lord for all those
>   who pardon one another for love's sake,
>   and who endure weakness and tribulation.
Blessed are they who peacefully shall endure,
>   for you, O Most High, will give them a crown.
Praised be my Lord for our sister, the death of the body,
>   from which no one escapes.
>   Blessed are those who die in your most holy will.
Praise and bless the Lord and give thanks to God
>   and serve God with great humility.

(FRANCIS OF ASSISI, "CANTICLE TO GOD'S CREATURES")

PSALM 107:1–9 OR 148

RESPONSIVE PRAYER

>   Praised are you, Lord our God, ruler of the universe,
>   for granting us life, for sustaining us,
>   and for causing us to reach this day.

We give thanks to you, God, we give thanks to you,
    as we call upon your name, as we recount your wondrous deeds.

Praised are you, Lord our God, ruler of the universe,
    who has withheld nothing from your world
    and has created beautiful creatures and beautiful trees
        for mortals to enjoy.
We give thanks to you, God, we give thanks to you,
    as we call upon your name, as we recount your wondrous deeds.

Praised are you, Lord, God of all creation,
    for you feed the whole world with your goodness,
    with grace, with loving-kindness and tender mercy.
You give food to all creatures,
    and your loving-kindness endures forever and ever.
We give thanks to you, God, we give thanks to you,
    as we call upon your name, as we recount your wondrous deeds.

Praised are you, Lord our God, ruler of the universe
    who with wisdom fashioned the human body,
    creating openings, arteries, glands and organs,
    marvelous in structure, intricate in design.
Should but one of them, by being blocked or opened, fail to function,
    it would be impossible to exist.
Praised are you, Lord,
    healer of all flesh who sustains our bodies in wondrous ways.
We give thanks to you, God, we give thanks to you,
    as we call upon your name, as we recount your wondrous deeds.

Praised are you, Lord our God, ruler of the universe,
    who graciously bestows favor upon the undeserving,
    even as you have bestowed favor upon us.
We give thanks to you, God, we give thanks to you,
    as we call upon your name, as we recount your wondrous deeds.

HYMN

BENEDICTION

    May God bless you and keep you.
    May God's face shine upon you and be gracious to you.
    May God look upon you with kindness and give you peace. Amen.

                              (NUMBERS 6:24–26, ALT.)

III

SERVICES
FOR THE
CHRISTIAN YEAR

LIGHTING THE CANDLES OF ADVENT

"The people who walked in darkness have seen a great light." The prophet Isaiah (9:2b) sang these words long ago. They resonate in our lives even now. The four candles of Advent stand as stubborn reminders that the deepest darkness of our world will not overcome the light of God's loving grace.

The suggested sung responses are optional. Some of the lines chosen sound unfinished musically. Given the anticipatory nature of Advent this is appropriate. Sing the response thoughtfully and let the ending ring in the air. Do not try to close the cadences. God's promise has yet to be fulfilled.

FIRST SUNDAY IN ADVENT: AWAKE! WAIT! WATCH!

RESPONSE *(cantor of choir or congregation) CH 119*

Rejoice! Rejoice! Immanuel shall come to thee, O Israel!

The darkness has long been upon us.
We long for the light—the fulfillment of God's promise of salvation.
The people who walked in darkness have seen a great light!

The light has not yet come.
We wait and watch for the dawning of God's glory.
This one candle casts its light into the darkness.
It reminds us to stay awake and watchful,
for the Promised One will come to us at an unexpected hour!
Light the first candle.

PRAYER

How we long for the Light of your presence, Holy God!
Guide us from the night of our hopelessness
and lead us with joy toward the dawning of your New Day. Amen. **R**

SECOND SUNDAY IN ADVENT: PREPARE THE WAY!

RESPONSE *(cantor of choir or congregation) CH 121*

Prepare the way of the Lord.
Prepare the way of the Lord.

We have heard the promise.
God's chosen One will soon be among us. We must make ready.
"Prepare the way of the Lord, make his paths straight."

The wilderness places of our lives may threaten to overwhelm us.
We easily lose our way. But a second candle adds its light.
The candle of wisdom and preparation
joins the candle of watchful waiting.

Light two candles.

PRAYER

Send your Spirit to the wild corners of our hearts.
Grant us wisdom and understanding that we will prepare well
for the coming of your promised counselor. Amen.   R

THIRD SUNDAY IN ADVENT: PROCLAIM CHRIST'S COMING!

RESPONSE *(cantor of choir or congregation) CH 167*

**Go tell it on the mountains,
over the hills and everywhere...**

"There was a man sent from God, whose name was John...."
He came to witness to the Light and we are called to do the same.

Christ is coming! We gain confidence from that assurance.
And look! Our hope grows even stronger
for three lights are burning where there was darkness!

Light three candles.

PRAYER

Holy God, help us give voice to the wonderful news:
you, yourself are coming to dwell among us!
Quicken our imaginations to find new and creative ways
to proclaim Christ's coming. Amen.   R

FOURTH SUNDAY IN ADVENT: REJOICE AND BELIEVE!

RESPONSE *(cantor of choir or congregation) CH 125*

**Come, O long-expected Jesus, born to set your people free.
From our fears and sins release us; Christ, in whom our rest shall be.**

Long ago the people were given a sign of God's presence.
**"Look, the virgin shall conceive and bear a son, and
they shall name him Emmanuel," which means "God is with us."**

God's promise to us remains sure and true.
God's Anointed One will soon walk among us, to lighten our darkness,
to restore the joy of our salvation, to save us from our sins.
Four lights now shine in spite of our despair. Jesus is coming soon!

Light four candles.

PRAYER

God of mystery,
help us accept your gifts of grace that we cannot begin to understand.

Plant a stubborn hope deep in our hearts as we will be able to embrace
the Christ-child when Jesus is birthed anew in our lives.
Teach us your ways of joy. Amen.   **R**

CHRISTMAS EVE: "LET US GO OVER TO BETHLEHEM"
RESPONSE *(cantor of choir or congregation) CH* 155, st. 1

Angels we have heard on high, sweetly singing o'er the plains,
and the mountains in reply echoing the joyous strains.
"Gloria in excelsis Deo! Gloria in excelsis Deo!"

Can you imagine the shepherds' surprise at seeing
a choir of angels singing with joy the news of Christ's birth?
Can you sense the wonder? Do you share perhaps their fear?

Joy and fear join hands this night.
Hope and despair are well known to us.
But we have heard the news—Christ is born!
And after weeks of waiting and watching, we are ready to celebrate!
We are ready to worship the Holy Child.
We are ready to welcome Christ into our hearts.

The Gospel of Luke reads that the shepherds heard the news
and then went off to Bethlehem to find the newborn babe,
the hope of the ages, God's Promised One!
These four familiar flames, now familiar to us,
will light our way to the Christ child's side.

Light the four outer candles.

RESPONSE *(cantor of choir or congregation) CH* 155, st. 2

Shepherds, why this jubilee? Why your joyous strains prolong?
What the gladsome tidings be which inspire your heav'nly song?
Gloria in excelsis Deo! Gloria in excelsis Deo!

People of God, your waiting in darkness is over.
The Light of God's promise has dawned.
Even now Christ the Child, Christ the Savior,
seeks entrance into our hearts.

Light the Christ candle.

PRAYER

God of joy and jubilee, fill our hearts with the light of your promise.
Enter our lives as softly and quietly as a child
so we might learn to love you in simplicity and purity of heart.

Come into our hearts with power and compassion, that we might
always draw strength from your abiding presence in our lives.
Thank you, holy God, for your gift of love, born to us this night. Amen.

RESPONSE *(cantor of choir or congregation) CH 155, st. 3*

**Come to Bethlehem and see Christ, who comes in lowly birth.
Come adore on bended knee Jesus, joy of heav'n and earth.
Gloria in excelsis Deo! Gloria in excelsis Deo!**

 # HANGING OF THE GREENS

This service may take place at any time during Advent. It may be used on a Sunday morning during the Entrance or as a Response to the Word, or it may be used as an evening service. During the singing of "Come, Thou Long-Expected Jesus," greens may be brought in and, if appropriate, the Advent candle(s) lighted.

Each lesson should, if possible, be read by a different reader. The content of the lessons may be enhanced by each reader's announcing the lesson by the descriptive title preceding it. At the end of the lesson, the reader or another person reads the narrative.

INTRODUCTION

How shall we prepare this house
    for the coming of God's Royal Son?
With branches of cedar, the tree of royalty.

How shall we prepare this house
    for the coming of the eternal Christ?
**With garlands of pine and fir,
    whose leaves are ever living, ever green.**

How shall we prepare this house
    for the coming of our Savior?
**With wreaths of holly and ivy,
telling of his passion, death, and resurrection.**

How shall we prepare our hearts
    for the coming of the Son of God?
**By hearing again the words of the prophets,
who foretold the saving work of God.**

For God did not send the Son into the world to condemn the world,
    but that the world through him might be saved.
Glory to God in the highest!

GOD WILL SEND A RIGHTEOUS KING: Jeremiah 23:5–6

> In ancient times the cedar was revered as the tree of royalty.
> It also signified immortality and was used for purification.
> We place this cedar branch as a sign of Christ,
> > who reigns as King for ever,
> > and whose coming, in justice and righteousness,
> > will purify our hearts.

HYMN   Come, O Long-expected Jesus (*CH* 125)

THE PROPHET DECLARES A CHILD WILL BE BORN: Isaiah 9:2, 6–7

> Because the needles of pine and fir trees
> > remain green from season to season,
> > the ancients saw them as signs of things that last forever.
> Isaiah tells us that there will be no end to the reign of the Messiah.
> Therefore, we hang this wreath of evergreens shaped in a circle,
> > which itself has no end,
> > to signify the eternal reign of Jesus, the Christ.

HYMN   O Come, O Come, Emmanuel (*CH* 119)

THE FOURTH SERVANT SONG: Isaiah 53:1–6

> For Christians, this passage from Isaiah
> > reflects the sufferings of Jesus,
> > who saved us from our sins by his death on the cross,
> > and by his resurrection from the dead.
> In ancient times, holly and ivy
> > were considered signs of Christ's passion.
> Their prickly leaves suggested the crown of thorns,
> > the red berries the blood of the Savior,
> > and the bitter bark the drink offered to Jesus on the cross.
> As we hang the holly and ivy,
> > let us rejoice in the coming of Jesus, our Savior.

HYMN   Let All Mortal Flesh Keep Silence, st. 1, 2 (*CH* 124)

THE MYSTERY OF THE INCARNATION: John 1:1–5, 9–14

> As we prepare for the coming of Jesus, the Light of the World,
> > we light the *Christmas/Chrismon* tree.
> During this Advent, wherever you see a lighted Christmas tree,
> > let it call to mind the One who brings light to our darkness,
> > healing to our brokenness, and peace to all who receive him.

The tree is now lighted.

BENEDICTION

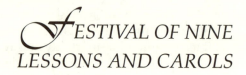

FESTIVAL OF NINE LESSONS AND CAROLS

This service, shaped by English tradition, consists of a series of scripture lessons ordered so as to proclaim the significance of the coming of Jesus Christ into the world. Interspersed with prayers and carols, it affords the worshipers a festive celebration of Christ's advent. Each lesson may be read by a different person.

The service is easily adapted to fit into the various Christmas celebrations conducted by a congregation or community. It may take place within a Sunday morning worship service during Advent and may include the Lord's supper. It may serve as a Christmas Eve family celebration. The full use of choir, soloists, and musical instruments strengthens participation in a festive spirit.

INSTRUMENTAL VOLUNTARY

HYMN   People, Look East (*CH* 142)

STATEMENT OF PURPOSE

Beloved in Christ,
      with delight we prepare ourselves
      to hear again the message of the angels,
      and go in heart and mind to Bethlehem
      to see Mary and Joseph with Jesus in a manger.
Let us listen to the story of God's loving purpose
      which traces God's saving acts from humanity's first disobedience
      down to the glorious redemption brought to all by this Holy Child.
And let us make these hallowed walls reverberate
      with the glad tidings of great joy which is to all the people.

BIDDING PRAYER

In preparation for the festival
      let us pray for the needs of God's whole world:
In a world fragmented by warring factions and rampant injustice,
      we pray for peace and goodwill over all the earth.
Hear us, O God, in the silence of our hearts.

We pray for reconciling love and unity
      within the church Christ formed to be his continuing body
      to minister to the world.
Hear us, O God, from the depths of our spirits.

We pray for the poor, the helpless, the cold,
    the hungry, and the oppressed;
    the sick and those who mourn; the lonely and the unloved.
Hear us, O God, as we seek your strength.

We pray for those who do not know the Lord Jesus,
    or who do not love him,
    or who by sin have grieved his heart of love.
Hear us, O God, as we yearn to tell your good news.

We pray for the great cloud of witnesses of all times and places
    whose hope is in the Word made flesh,
    and whose home is with you forever.
Hear us, O God, as we join with them to give you praise.

GLORIA PATRI: (*CH* 35, 36, *or* 37)

FIRST LESSON: Genesis 3:8–15

CAROL   Come, O Long-expected Jesus (*CH* 125)

SECOND LESSON: Isaiah 9:1–7

CAROL   O Come, O Come, Emmanuel (*CH* 119)

THIRD LESSON: Isaiah 11:1–9

CAROL   Lo, How a Rose E'er Blooming (*CH* 160)

FOURTH LESSON: Micah 5:2–4a

CAROL   O Little Town of Bethlehem (*CH* 144)

FIFTH LESSON: Luke 1:26–35, 38

CAROL   My Soul Gives Glory to My God (*CH* 130)

SIXTH LESSON: Matthew 1:18–21

CAROL   The First Noel (*CH* 151)

SEVENTH LESSON: Luke 2:8–20

CAROL   Infant Holy, Infant Lowly (*CH* 163)

EIGHTH LESSON: Matthew 2:1–11

CAROL   O Morning Star (*CH* 105)

NINTH LESSON: John 1:1–14

CAROL   O Come, All Ye Faithful (*CH* 148)

MEDITATION
    The partaking of the Lord's supper may take place at this point in the service.

HYMN: Silent Night, Holy Night (*CH* 145)

DISMISSAL WITH BLESSING

> Welcome the coming of Christ with gladness.
> Make room for the Savior in your lives.
> Embrace Christ as your Friend.
> Accompany him in his ministry.
>
> And may God's hope fill you with all joy and peace in believing,
> so that you may abound in hope by the power of the Holy Spirit.

(ROMANS 15:13, ALT.)

A CELEBRATION OF CANDLELIGHT COMMUNION ON CHRISTMAS EVE

This service begins with the sanctuary containing only enough light for persons to be seated safely. The chancel candelabra are unlit. If possible, candleholders may be stationed along the pews. The candles of the Advent wreath remain unlit until designated times in the service.

PRELUDE

PROCESSION OF LIGHTS

> Hymn: O Come, O Come Emmanuel (*CH* 119)
>
> *Acolytes bring the light into the sanctuary and light the candles in the chancel.*

CALL TO WORSHIP

> Tonight old dreams die and new dreams come to life.
>> The promise is fulfilled!
>
> **Glory to God in the highest, and on earth, peace.**
>
> Hope gives way to joy and prayer to proclamation.
> **Glory to God in the highest, and on earth, peace.**
>
> Our candles illuminate our story. Dawn invades midnight.
>> The Light of the World has come.
>
> **Glory to God in the highest, and on earth, peace.**
>
> And this light is a light for all; igniting a flame in the soul,
>> warming us from within, radiating love, lighting our lives

with the presence of God-come-alive in human flesh
within us and among us now and always.
Glory to God in the highest, and on earth, peace, goodwill to all.

PROCESSIONAL HYMN O Come, All Ye Faithful (*CH* 148)

MEDITATION: The Lights of Christmas
Preferably the following readings should be given by persons of differing voices. The readings should be well rehearsed but not presented in an affected manner. After completing the reading each reader goes to the Advent wreath and lights one of the Advent candles.

THE LIGHT OF HOPE: Isaiah 35:1–10

HYMN OR ANTHEM (*Optional*)

THE LIGHT OF PEACE: Isaiah 9:2, 6–7

HYMN OR ANTHEM (*Optional*)

THE LIGHT OF JOY: A Litany of Glad Tidings
Blessed are you, Sun of righteousness,
    shining forth from the heavens
    and enlightening the whole universe.
Let heaven and earth rejoice!

Blessed are you, Lord Jesus Christ,
    reigning with the Creator and Holy Spirit above the cherubim;
    worshiped by the seraphim.
Let heaven and earth rejoice!

Blessed are you, born as a little child and laid in a manger.
Let heaven and earth rejoice!

Blessed are you, humble offspring of a virgin, yet truly God.
Let heaven and earth rejoice!

Blessed are you, Sovereign of Glory,
    graciously coming to dwell among us.
Let heaven and earth rejoice!

Blessed are you, giving us all we possess,
    yet accepting the gifts of the visitors from the East.
Let heaven and earth rejoice!

Blessed are you, our Bread of Life,
    giving eternal life to our souls.
Let heaven and earth rejoice!

With the angelic host and all the heavenly powers,
    let us proclaim and celebrate our Savior's birth.
Let heaven and earth rejoice!

With the spirits of the just made perfect,
    let us magnify and bless the Lord to all eternity.
Let heaven and earth rejoice! Amen.

HYMN   Joy to the World (CH 143)

THE LIGHT OF LOVE: Luke 2:1–20

HYMN   O Little Town of Bethlehem (CH 144)

THE LIGHT OF THE WORD: John 1:1–14

THE LIGHTING OF THE CHRIST CANDLE
    The reader says these words before lighting the Christ candle.

We have celebrated God's gifts of hope, peace, joy and love.
Jesus coming to us
    was the Gift that made all those other gifts real in our lives.
We celebrate God coming to us in human form,
    bringing light to all the world.
May every knee bow before the newborn Savior;
    with the angels, may every tongue sing
    "Glory to God in the highest."

The Christ candle is lit.

HYMN   Angels We Have Heard on High (CH 155)

SERVICE OF COMMUNION

CALL TO CONFESSION:
    Out of the darkness of our world, we have seen a great light.
    The birth of the Christ Child calls us to something special.
    Let our confession be our new beginning.

UNISON PRAYER OF CONFESSION:
    **Light of the World: you gave us the transforming birth of the child
    Jesus as a light for our path. Yet we confess that we shut our eyes to
    the light. We admit that we do not want to see the gift you have given
    us. We acknowledge our reluctance to see and share our gifts with
    our sisters and brothers. We are often dazzled by the glitter and tin-
    sel the world has made of Christ's birth. We ask that your Spirit be
    lit within us, that the light of peace and justice may shine through
    us. We seek to receive, and to share the gift of Christ's birth and death,
    again and again. Amen.**

WORDS OF ASSURANCE

God comes to us now in this busy Christmas season to make all things new. God makes room for us even when there is no room at the inn. Where we are too busy, God brings peace; where we are lost, salvation; where we are sad, joy; where we are bitter, God gives us courage to love again. Rejoice, Christ has come to us bringing us all these gifts of God. In Christ, we are forgiven!

LITANY OF REMEMBRANCE AND CONSECRATION

God of light, in whom there is no shadow, your gifts to us are from the very beginning of time.

They begin with creation, when your Spirit gave form to the chaos of energy and matter, and when your Word brought forth light on the face of the earth.

They continued with our ancient ancestors, like Noah, whom you blessed with the colorful promise of the rainbow.

And like Sarah and Abraham, whom you blessed with a child whose descendants, as many as the stars of the sky, were to be a light to the nations.

In the desert, you gave the gifts of manna and of living water to the weary pilgrims whom you led by a cloud by day and a pillar of fire by night.

At last, you sent your light into the world in the form of a tiny child, fragile and vulnerable, who grew to be the very Light of Light, full of grace and truth, revealing your glory on earth.

We thank you, O God, that you have sent Jesus Christ to bring life and immortality to light. Help us to receive your gifts with joy and humility: as we receive this bread and wine, may we open our hearts to receive your love and grace in Jesus Christ, and receive the love and support of one another. Be born among us, that we may give Christ's love to the world, through the presence and the power of the Holy Spirit. Amen.

WORDS OF INSTITUTION

DISTRIBUTION OF THE ELEMENTS

UNISON PRAYER OF THANKSGIVING

We give you thanks, O God, that you have come to us through Jesus Christ, both in the midst of time and history in the city of Bethlehem, and in the timeless presence of Christ's Spirit as we receive the gifts of bread and wine. Send us out into the world rejoicing, ready to share your love with the people we meet; through the grace of Jesus Christ. Amen.

SERVICE OF CANDLELIGHTING

Small congregations may choose to make a circle around the sanctuary. Other congregations may prefer to remain standing in the pews. Still other congregations may leave the sanctuary and light their candles outside. In any case, water should be available in a number of locations. Children must be well supervised.

CHARGE FOR BEARERS OF THE LIGHT

Jesus said he was the Light of the World. Now he sends us out to be light to the world, sharing the gifts of God's love to all people. "Let your light shine before all people that they will glorify God in heaven."

The following hymn may be sung as light is brought from the Christ candle to the congregation.

HYMN   Silent Night (CH 145)

BENEDICTION

God is light! Let us walk in the light as God is in the light.
Go in peace. God is with you. **Amen.**

Epiphany is the celebration of the manifestation of the divine nature of Jesus Christ to the Gentiles as represented by the Magi. Although Epiphany is traditionally observed on the fixed date of January 6, it is more commonly celebrated on the first Sunday in January. The Epiphany service of worship usually adheres to a congregation's regular pattern of worship.

The materials below are intended for possible use at various points within the congregation's familiar pattern of worship. Additional resources may be found in this book under the heading of Worship Resources. There each aspect of worship includes resources for special days of the Christian year. Since some congregations observe a season of Epiphany from January 6 to the beginning of Lent, resource materials for those Sundays are also included within the Worship Resources under this subheading.

CALL TO WORSHIP

God was making friends of all people through Christ.
God did not keep an account of their sins against them,
and God has given us the message how to make them friends.

(2 CORINTHIANS 5:19, ADAPT., TEV)

Or:

Blessings to God, who gives hope in the darkness of our lives.
Blessings to Jesus Christ, who reveals God's love unto the world.

Blessings to the Holy Spirit, who empowers us to be a light for others.
Blessings, honor, and glory to God, today and forever. Amen.

OPENING PRAYER

Lord God of the nations,
    we have seen the star of your glory rising in splendor.
The radiance of your incarnate Word
    pierces the night that covers the earth
    and signals the dawn of justice and peace.
May his brightness illumine our lives
    and beckon all nations to walk as one in your light.
We ask this through Jesus Christ your Word made flesh,
    who lives and reigns with you and the Holy Spirit,
    in the splendor of eternal light, God forever and ever. Amen.

Or:

Almighty God, as your Son our Savior was born of a Hebrew mother,
but rejoiced in the faith of a Syrian woman and of a Roman soldier,
    welcomed the Greeks who sought him,
    and suffered a man from Africa to carry his cross;
so teach us to regard the members of all races
    as fellow heirs of the kingdom of Jesus Christ our Lord. Amen.

CONFESSION OF SIN

God's ways are not our ways. God's thoughts are not our own.
God watches over us far beyond the powers of human reasoning.
God searches for us,
yet we will find God hidden deep in our hearts.
Let us turn away from evil
and God will have mercy on us.

INTERCESSION FOR CHURCH AND WORLD

Let us pray for the church: *(Silence for prayer)*

God, whose promise is for all nations,
sustain the Christmas glory still.
May the Lord shine upon us.
By the Holy Spirit, reveal your plan.
We pray to our God:
May your love be near.

Let us pray for God's light: *(Silence for prayer)*

May the nations walk by your light
and kings and queens by your shining radiance.
Let all search together for profound peace.
We pray to our God:
May your love be near.

Let us pray for those without strength: *(Silence for prayer)*

Save the lives of the poor.
Rescue them when they cry out.
Govern your people with justice
and your afflicted ones with careful judgment.
We pray to our God:
May your love be near.

Let us pray for unity among all believers: *(Silence for prayer)*

Bring the new epiphany
where all will share the promise and rise in splendor.
In the Spirit, all are called to love.
We pray to our God:
May your love be near.

OFFERTORY PRAYER

Loving and receptive God,
creator of a Bethlehem birth
and sustainer of the whole human family,
we come to you seeking to be wise women and wise men.
Like the gifts of those travelers long ago,
may our gifts be a sign that wisdom is marked
by an offering of self and substance to the Christ,
in whose name we pray. Amen.

BLESSING

May Christ the Son of God be manifest to you
that your lives may be a light to the world;
and the blessing of the almighty God,
creator, redeemer, and sustainer, be with you all. Amen.

$\mathcal{A}$SH WEDNESDAY

Ash Wednesday is the first day of Lent. It takes its name from the ceremonial imposition of ashes on the foreheads of worshipers as a sign of human sin and mortality. This ancient tradition, going back at least to the tenth century, communicates the human condition before God by solemn word and sign.

The ashes take on added significance if they are made from burning the branches carried the previous Palm Sunday. They should be dark in color and may need to be pulverized. A small amount of oil may be added for readily marking each forehead with the sign of the cross. A towel should be provided for cleansing the leaders' hands.

The service may be conducted early in the morning, at noon, or in early evening. Since this is a distinctly Lenten service, not held on a Sunday, the Lord's supper is inappropriate. The elements of the service may be adjusted according to time constraints.

CALL TO WORSHIP

> Yet even now, says the Holy One, return to me with all your heart,
>> with fasting, with weeping, and with mourning;
>> rend your hearts and not your clothing.
> Return to the Lord, your God, who is gracious and merciful,
>> slow to anger, and abounding in steadfast love,
>> and relents from punishing.   (JOEL 2:12–13, ALT.)

HYMN   Lord, Who Throughout These Forty Days (CH 180) *NCH 211*

PRAYER

> Almighty and everlasting God,
>> you hate nothing that you have made
>> and forgive the sins of all those who are penitent.
> Create and make in us new and contrite hearts, that,
>> lamenting our sins and acknowledging our wretchedness,
>> we may receive from you, the God of all mercy,
>> perfect forgiveness and peace;
>> through Jesus Christ our Lord. Amen.

STATEMENT OF PURPOSE

> Friends in Christ, we begin today a forty-day journey toward Easter.
> We enter the Lenten season to prepare ourselves to welcome
>> the risen Christ with lives renewed by the breath of his spirit.
> We assume a discipline of self-examination,
>> confession, and penitence.

We dedicate ourselves to meditate upon the scriptures
and to converse with God in prayer.
We seek to be more faithful disciples of Christ
whose lives are shaped by the one
whom we confess to be Lord and Savior of the world.
To this end let us worship God.

non trad. service - but silence in lieu of scream

FIRST SCRIPTURE READING: Isaiah 58:1–12

Or, if not used earlier: Joel 2:1–2, 12–17

silence

SECOND SCRIPTURE READING: 2 Corinthians 5:20B—6:10

silence

ANTHEM

GOSPEL READING: Matthew 6:1–6, 16–21

silence

SERMON

THE SIGN OF ASHES

From ancient times Christians have on this day
searched their hearts and sought to be cleansed from sin.
They have sought reconciliation with God and with one another.
They have received ashes marked on their foreheads
as a sign of sin's disfigurement and of their own mortality.

Explain source

PRAYER OVER THE ASHES

Almighty God, you have created us out of the dust of the earth,
May these ashes be to us a sign of our mortality and penitence,
so that we may remember that only by your gracious gift
are we given everlasting life;
through Jesus Christ our Savior. Amen.

IMPOSITION OF ASHES

The leader, with those assisting, holds the ashes before the congregation, invit-ing the community by word or gesture to come forward. A thumb is dipped in the ashes to make a cross on the forehead of each person with these words spoken:

Remember that you are dust, and to dust you shall return.

And/or:

Repent, and believe the gospel.

ACT OF PENITENCE AND RECONCILIATION

In fear, but also in hope, we come together with ashes on our heads.
The planet is dying in our hands; people turn to each other for food
and strength only to be shoved away. Each day we deal in death, yet
pretend that we are good. Let us take forty days to look hard at our so-
called goodness and see what it covers up. Then, we will join together

in taking up the cross of living in the world as it is, for there is only one earth, and, as far as we know, only one human race. Join me in prayer by responding to each spoken petition with the words: "Hear our prayer, O God." Let us pray:

That as disciples of Christ we might start using our hands, feet, money, time, and energy for the good of the poor, let us pray to the God of mercy.
Hear our prayer, O God.

That citizens everywhere may realize that care for their neighbor consists of more than the mere giving of money, let us pray to the God of mercy.
Hear our prayer, O God.

For the needy, that they may not have to remain despondent and alone, let us pray to the God of mercy.
Hear our prayer, O God.

For all of us here that we may be honest enough to admit what we are selfish about, and what we can do to remedy our lack of love, let us pray to the God of mercy.
Hear our prayer, O God.

For those who share Christ's charity toward sinners, let us pray to the God of mercy.
Hear our prayer, O God.

Merciful God, the ashes are our pledge to take up the cross of life. We came from the earth and we will go back to it. In the meantime, beginning these forty days, we will try to live here and make it a better home for everybody. Through Christ our Lord. **Amen.**

THE DECLARATION OF GOD'S MERCY

Hear the good news of God's reconciling love toward all, and believe: Through Christ God chose to reconcile the whole universe, making peace through the shedding of Christ's blood upon the cross—to reconcile all things, whether on earth or in heaven, through Christ alone.

(COLOSSIANS 1:20, NEB, ALT.)

PASSING OF THE PEACE

HYMN

BENEDICTION

Holy God, through the discipline of these forty days,
    make your Spirit's cleansing fire burn within us.
Lift us from the dying embers of our inattention.
Mark us with the sign of your holy passion.
Make us ready to respond to the call of Jesus Christ. Amen.

*Ⅾ*AILY LENTEN SERVICES

The days of Lent afford Christians the opportunity to assume a spiritual discipline that includes gathering for services of praise, prayer, and meditation in preparation for the celebration of Easter. These services, generally brief, may be held at early morning, at noon, or early evening. They may be held each day or less frequently. One possibility is to conduct one service at midweek until Holy Week, when services are then held each day.

Here an outline for Lenten services is given, with suggested resources for Holy Week. Tradition fixes no set scriptures for these days. Several Gospel passages are suggested for each day of Holy Week, from which a single selection may be made.

AN ORDER OF WORSHIP

GREETING/CALL TO WORSHIP

HYMN

PSALM

SCRIPTURE

MEDITATION

PRAYER

HYMN

DISMISSAL WITH BENEDICTION

May grace and peace be yours in abundance
in the knowledge of God and of Jesus our Lord.   (2 PETER 1:2)

ADDITIONAL RESOURCES

LENTEN PRAYERS

winter's robe lies heavily upon my frozen heart
dare I pray for spring?
dare I ask for new life—
beyond my dreams, beyond all hope?
I see the signs, the willful green nudging into view
budding limbs, barely patient
awaiting release from winter's dark pregnancy
I feel the signs within me, too
I fear these the most, God
I fear this new life you call me to explore

I fear the pain of growth
I cannot embrace your gift of resurrection
for I cannot risk the loss of myself
my hands can carry no nailprints, my forehead no scars
new life carries too high a price
the ice-fortress holds fast
I dare not cry

yet I feel your tears
gently, indomitably
the gift is given to us all
and
new
life is…

such love breaks my heart

yours was broken for all your children

I taste my own tears

dear God,
dare I pray for spring?

+ + +

Almighty God, we pray that through this season of Lent, by prayer and study and self-giving, we may penetrate more deeply into the mystery of Christ's sufferings; that following in the way of his cross and passion we may come to share in the glory and triumph of his resurrection; through the same Jesus Christ our Lord. Amen.

+ + +

Eternal God, we pray that you will change the grief of our guilt into the joy of forgiveness, that we may be delivered from sin and set free to serve Jesus Christ, our crucified and risen Lord. Amen.

 # PASSION/PALM SUNDAY

The observance of Holy Week commemorates the mighty acts of Christ from his entry into Jerusalem till, put to death on a cross, his body was laid to rest in a tomb. The risen Christ calls the Christian community to remember these sacred events and to renew itself to be more fully the body of Christ. The church has developed many traditional services to accomplish this work of sacred memory. As a congregation develops its own ways of observing Holy Week it will want to afford its people a full participation in the varied aspects of the week leading to Easter.

Since many worshipers attend only Sunday services, the Sunday before Easter needs to emphasize the whole of Christ's passion. The church in celebrating Palm Sunday needs to include the story of the cross. Otherwise many worshipers miss the profound meaning of Easter's good news of Christ's being raised from the dead. The other services during Holy Week spin out of Palm Sunday's passion story.

The service of Palm/Passion Sunday is similar to that of any other Sunday, except for a Palm Sunday gathering with processional and the full reading of the passion story from one of the Gospels. This longer Gospel reading may be presented as a dramatic reading by multiple voices. Due to its length, the sermon may either be shortened or displaced by the scripture. The gospel dramatically read becomes the gospel proclaimed. The service is festive in nature. It begins in high spirits as Palm Sunday is remembered. It becomes more contemplative as attention is centered upon Christ's passion.

To heighten the drama of the day the congregation may gather at a place outside the sanctuary. At the appointed time the minister calls the people to worship, gives brief instructions, offers a prayer, and leads a procession into the sanctuary. Each participant is given a palm branch as the line proceeds. All go forward to place palm branches on the floor of the chancel to place them on the chancel floor or as other decoration, and move to their seats. If this procession is not feasible, children and the choir may carry the palm branches in a processional.

CALL TO WORSHIP

Hosanna!
Hosanna in the highest!
Blessed is the one who comes in the name of the Lord!
Hosanna in the highest heaven!

PURPOSE OF GATHERING

Friends in Christ, we gather with Christians around the world to celebrate the holiest of all weeks in the church's life. It is the week in which Christ entered in triumph into his own city to complete his work as God's Messiah—to suffer, to die, and to rise again. Let us remember with devotion this entry which began his saving work and follow him with a lively faith. United with him in his suffering on the cross, may we share his resurrection and new life.

PALM SUNDAY SCRIPTURE READING

Year A: Matthew 21:1–11
Year B: Mark 11:1–11 *or* John 12:12–16
Year C: Luke 19:28–40

PRAYER

Triumphant God, who comes to us as one who seeks and serves,
　　lead us through the events of this Holy Week,
　　that we may receive Christ afresh into our lives,
　　and embody Christ's spirit into the world.

Fill now our hearts with gospel joy,
      as with anticipation we enter the sanctuary.
Bless us and these branches we bring,
      that our very being shall cry aloud,
"Hosanna! Hosanna in the highest heaven!" Amen.

PROCESSION

The minister(s) and choir are first in the procession so that upon entering the sanctuary they may lead the people in singing as they enter.

HYMN   All Glory, Laud, and Honor (CH 192)

The hymn begins when the choir has entered the sanctuary and does not conclude until all have taken their places.

The service proceeds with the usual order.

ADDITIONAL RESOURCES

Lord Jesus, could anyone but you,
who carried the cross to Calvary,
maintain that life's burden is light?

To all who are crushed, and all who tend to live frivolously,
grant the strength of your love,
and make us attentive to all who suffer
on their own way of the cross:
      the sick,
      the prisoners,
      the refugees,
      the lonely,
      the unloved,
      the despised,
      the misunderstood…
Teach us to discover your cross in our crosses.

+ + +

O God, we pray that you enter into our worship and into our lives as you did into Jerusalem on that Palm Sunday long ago. Be our gentle conqueror. On this first day of the week that is called "Holy Week," enable us to offer a disciple's praise whenever we meet Jesus Christ along our way. Teach us to heed Christ's bidding even when the requests seem strange or the teachings reach beyond our ability to understand. Strengthen us to stand by Christ and to accept risk as an element of faithfulness. Confront us with our capacity to deny and to crucify. As this week passes, speak to us through its events, reminding us of your constant love, surprising grace, and caring power. In the name of Jesus Christ, Amen.

MONDAY OF HOLY WEEK
ENTRY INTO JERUSALEM

GREETING/CALL TO WORSHIP

Bless the Lord, your inmost self!
Everything in you, bless God's holy name.
Bless the Lord, your inmost self.
Do not forget what God has done—
pardoning all your sin,
healing your every disease,
redeeming your life from the grave,
crowning your head with constant compassion.

(PSALM 103:1–4, CHAMBERLAIN)

PSALM 51:1–18

GOSPEL LESSONS

Matthew 26:1–30/Mark 14:1–26/Luke 22:1–34;/John 12:9–19

PRAYER

Create in us clean hearts, O God.
Help us to recognize Love's costly gifts poured out on our behalf.
Watch over us in your abundant mercy
as we follow your Son to the cross. Amen.

TUESDAY OF HOLY WEEK
PRAYING IN GETHSEMANE

GREETING/CALL TO WORSHIP

Come, let us kneel and worship the LORD;
Let us bow before God our maker.
Today God will be our God—
who chooses a people and tends them,
whose hand will guide us like sheep—
if we will only heed God's voice.

(PSALM 95:6–7, CHAMBERLAIN)

PSALM 102:1–12

GOSPEL LESSONS
   Matthew 26:31–56/Mark14:27–52/Luke 22:35–53

PRAYER
   Listening God, we know you hear the prayers that stay as unspoken sighs. Watch over us as we struggle to walk the way of the cross. Do not let us escape the pain of your son's holy passion, but grant that your life and peace may find new expressions in all we do and say. Amen.

WEDNESDAY OF HOLY WEEK
JESUS' TRIAL AND DENIAL

GREETING/CALL TO WORSHIP
   Let us give praise to our God!
   Let us praise the Most High as long as we live;
      let us sing praise to our God while we have being.
   Put no trust in sovereigns,
      in mortal flesh in whom there is no help.
   Our help is in the Most High,
      who alone made heaven and earth,
   who keeps faith forever;
      who executes justice for the oppressed.
   The Most High will reign forever and ever,
      through all generations.   (PSALM 146:1–3, 5B–7A, 10, ADAPT.)

PSALM 55

GOSPEL LESSONS
   Matthew 26:57–75/Mark 14:53–72/Luke 22:54–71

PRAYER
   All-seeing God, we are troubled by this story of your Son's betrayal. As Jesus was beaten and abused, one of his closest friends denied him. Help us, when confronted with the truth, to stand boldly with our Redeemer. For it is in Christ's name we pray. Amen.

THURSDAY OF HOLY WEEK
THE UPPER ROOM

GREETING/CALL TO WORSHIP

> Praise the LORD!
> You, the LORD's servants, praise,
> > praise the name of the LORD.
> Let the LORD's name be blessed
> > from now on, and forever.
> Wherever the sun shines, from dawn until dusk,
> > let the LORD's name be praised.   (PSALM 113:1–3, CHAMBERLAIN)

PSALM 43

GOSPEL LESSONS

> Matthew 26:20–30/Mark 14:12–25/Luke 22:14–27/John 13:1–15

PRAYER

> God of grace and compassion, we confess we do not always want to follow Jesus. Humility is not our choice. Lowliness is not our desire. Forgive us when our drive for control blocks us from dealing with others in love. Invite us once more to our Lord's table so that we may be served in order to serve. Amen.

FRIDAY OF HOLY WEEK
CHRIST IS NAILED TO THE CROSS

GREETING/CALL TO WORSHIP

> Praise the LORD, all nations.
> > All peoples, glorify God,
> whose grace, like a wave, surges over us,
> > whose faithfulness lasts for all time.
> Praise the LORD!   (PSALM 117, CHAMBERLAIN)

PSALM 22

GOSPEL LESSONS

> Matthew 27:32–54/Mark 15:21–39/Luke23:26–47/John19:16–30

PRAYER

> Our redeemer God, we bless you for meeting us in Jesus Christ, who for our salvation humbled himself to die for us.

We bless you for all the burdens Christ has borne,
    for all the tears he has wept,
    for all the pains he has suffered,
    for every word of comfort he spoke on the cross,
    for every conflict with the powers of darkness,
    and for his eternal victory over the terrors of death.
Lead us through the valley of the shadow of death,
    that we may fear no evil, for you are eternally with us;
    through Jesus Christ, our Lord. Amen.

SATURDAY OF HOLY WEEK
CHRIST'S BURIAL

The church has had various thoughts about the appropriate observance of Holy Saturday. To emphasize the reality of Christ's death no service may be held, or, if held, the scriptures read leave the reader at the Cross. Sometimes, to emphasize the hopelessness, the stark tragedy of Christ's death, no Gospel is read, but another New Testament passage is substituted. Another tradition completes the passion story with Christ's burial.

GREETING/CALL TO WORSHIP
    Praise the LORD, who is good;
        God will be faithful forever.
    Now declare this, Israel:
        "God will be faithful forever."
    The LORD is our strength and power,
        and has become a savior to us.
    God will be faithful forever.   (PSALM 118:1–2, 14, 29B, CHAMBERLAIN)

PSALM 88:1–12

GOSPEL LESSONS
    Matthew 27:57–61/Mark 15:42–47/Luke 23:50–56/John 19:38–42

    If the Gospel reading is omitted, Romans 8:1–11 may be read.

PRAYER
    All merciful and eternal God, Creator of heaven and earth,
        we are struck with awesome wonder that
        our Savior was scorned, crucified, and left for dead.
    Grant that we may be faithful even when hope is dimmed,
        in the knowledge that your power is greater than death,
        your love stronger than all that would destroy it. Amen.

*H*OLY THURSDAY WITH TENEBRAE

Christians meet on Thursday evening of Holy Week to remember Christ's gather-
ing his disciples in an upper room for a special meal before moving toward the
events culminating in his crucifixion. It was upon this occasion that Jesus took
bread and wine and identified them with himself as a means for remembering him
always. This service is designed to draw Christians back in time to recall and ex-
perience the significance of that night in the light of their present knowledge of the
risen Christ.

The central focus of the service is upon the Lord's table. First, the community
recalls Christ's institution of the Lord's supper and partakes. Then the community
devoutly remembers the events that transpired leading to Christ's betrayal, denial,
and death. The distinguishing feature of the service is the symbolic extinguishing
of lighted candles, signifying the approach of Jesus' death. When only the Christ
candle remains, it, too, is extinguished as a symbol of Christ's crucifixion. After a
period of complete darkness, the Christ candle is re-lit in anticipation of the resur-
rection.

This extinguishing of lights in memory of Christ's passion is called the Office of
Tenebrae (Shadows) and dates back to the fourth century. Originally intended for
use on Good Friday, it has been adapted through the years in a variety of ways.
This Maundy Thursday service utilizes eight black (or dark purple) candles spaced
across a large table so that readers can sit behind each candle. At the center is a
large white Christ candle behind which the one presiding sits. Upon the reading of
each scripture passage, the reader extinguishes the appropriate candle and takes a
seat in the congregation. With the extinguishing of each candle the sanctuary lights
are dimmed by degrees till at the end there is complete darkness. At the close of the
service only enough light should be provided for persons safely to exit in silence.

The gradual extinguishing of lights is symbolic of the flight of the disciples, the
approach of the enemies, and the suffering of Jesus. The total darkness recalls the
days Christ was in the tomb. Readers do not represent Jesus and his disciples, but
the whole of humanity, which shares in causing Christ to suffer.

If desired, the Tenebrae portion of this service may be used separately in a Good
Friday service.

FELLOWSHIP OF THE UPPER ROOM

INSTRUMENTAL VOLUNTARY

INTROIT

CALL TO WORSHIP
>   Let us hold fast to the faith we confess.
>   For we have a great high priest
>   who has gone into the very presence of God—Jesus, the Son of God.

Our high priest is not one
>who cannot feel sympathy with our weaknesses.
On the contrary, we have a high priest
>who was tempted in every way that we are, but did not sin.
Let us be brave, then,
>and come forward to God's throne, where there is grace.
There we will receive mercy and find grace to help us
>just when we need it.   (HEBREWS 4:14–16, TEV)

HYMN   An Upper Room with Evening Lamps Ashine, st. 1–3 (*CH* 428)

OPENING PRAYER AND THE LORD'S PRAYER

Eternal God of mercy, we gather in awesome wonder to behold your loving gift of Jesus Christ, who, coming to bring the world to wholeness, was broken by it. Yet by his death we live and know your unbreakable love. As we gather to remember Christ's gift of fellowship at table, and to recall our frail failings of devotion, pierce our hearts with a conviction of our own betrayals, reassure us of your abiding presence, and transform us by the Spirit of Christ, who teaches us to pray, saying, Our Father...

NEW TESTAMENT LESSON

Appropriate scriptures include:

John 13:1–15—The Washing of Feet
John 13:31–35—The New Commandment

>*or any portion of the Passion story*

INVITATION TO COMMUNE

This invitation should be preceded by a few paragraphs that proclaim the gospel prior to partaking of communion.

HYMN

WORDS OF INSTITUTION

PRAYERS OF ELDERS

PARTAKING OF BREAD AND WINE

>*Music, instrumental or vocal*

OFFICE OF TENEBRAE

ANTHEM OR HYMN

SHADOW OF BETRAYAL   Matthew 26:20–25

SHADOW OF DESERTION   Matthew 26:31–35

ANTHEM OR HYMN

SHADOW OF LETHARGY   Mark 14:32–41

SHADOW OF VIOLENCE   Matthew 26:47–52

ANTHEM OR HYMN

SHADOW OF DENIAL   Luke 22:54–62

SHADOW OF CYNICISM   John 18:33–38a

ANTHEM, SOLO, OR HYMN

SHADOW OF IRRESPONSIBILITY   Matthew 27:20–26

SHADOW OF MOCKERY   Mark 15:16–20

THE EXTINGUISHING OF THE CHRIST CANDLE

HYMN *(In darkness)*   When I Survey the Wondrous Cross, st.1 *(CH 195)*
   This hymn, or another musical selection, may be sung only by a choir, possibly gathered in the narthex.

PROPHECY OF RESURRECTION   Mark 8:31

RELIGHTING CHRIST CANDLE

PRAYER OF CONSECRATION
   Loving Creator, we thank you for the gift of Jesus Christ to be the Savior of the world. We thank you for the mystery of your love as revealed to us in the cross. We cannot understand all that the cross may mean, but we feel your hand upon us and we would give ourselves afresh to you. Love so amazing, so divine, demands our lives, our souls, our all. Take our lives, use them in your ministry of reconciliation to a world deeply in need of love and mercy and justice and righteousness. Lord, here we are as your disciples. Send us out to do your work. In Christ's name we pray. Amen.

BENEDICTION
   Now may the God of peace,
       who brought back from the dead our Lord Jesus,
       the great shepherd of the sheep,
       by the blood of the eternal covenant,
   make you complete in everything good so that you may do God's will,
       working in you that which is pleasing in God's sight,
       through Jesus Christ, to whom be the glory forever and ever. Amen.
                                              (HEBREWS 13:20–21, ALT.)

CHORAL RESPONSE

> Love so amazing, so divine,
> demands my soul, my life, my all. (*CH* 195)

COMMENTARY

The communion table may need to be extended to accommodate the nine people gathered around its three sides. The chairs and unlit black or purple candles, along with the communion elements, may be positioned before the service. During the opening anthem of the Tenebrae service those participating at the table take their places. The one presiding lights all the candles. There should be no other candles used in the service other than the specific ones for the readings.

Usually, even though the sanctuary lights are dimmed the readers can obtain sufficient light from the candles to read. The prophecy (Mark 8:31) is given from memory in the dark. The choir will require some light for participation. Memorization of the final anthem and choral response so as to require no light increases the effectiveness of the service. The sanctuary lights are dimmed as to coincide with the extinguishing of the second candle in each pair of readings. At the close of the service the one presiding may leave the table as a signal that the congregation may depart.

All participants need carefully prepared written instructions. Since scripture readers sometimes forget to extinguish the candle following their reading, this aspect should be emphasized. The congregation is assisted in participation by the inclusion of a few paragraphs of interpretation and description in an order of worship regarding the service and its origins.

HOLY THURSDAY: REMEMBERING THE UPPER ROOM

If the full Passion narrative was read on Passion/Palm Sunday, a service on Maundy Thursday that does not include the Tenebrae office may be preferred. The emphasis of this service is upon Christ's gift of a new commandment and the institution of the Lord's supper. An insert in the order of worship describing the service and its significance may assist the worshipers to enter more fully into the spiritual significance of the service.

GREETING

> This is the day
> that Christ the Lamb of God
> gave himself into the hands of those who would slay him.

This is the day
> that Christ gathered with his disciples in the upper room.

This is the day
> that Christ took a towel and washed the disciples' feet,
> giving us an example that we should do to others
> as he has done to us.

This is the day
> that Christ our God gave us this holy feast,
> that we who eat this bread and drink this cup
> may here proclaim his holy sacrifice
> and be partakers of his resurrection
> and at the last day may reign with him in heaven.

HYMN

RESPONSIVE CALL TO WORSHIP

Where charity and love are, there is God.
The Love of Christ has gathered us as one.
> Let us rejoice and be glad in him.
Let us fear and love the living God
> and in purity of heart let us love one another.

Where charity and love are, there is God.
When therefore we are gathered together
> let us not be divided in spirit.
Let bitter strife and discord cease between us;
> let Christ our God be present in our midst.

Where charity and love are, there is God.
With all the blessed may we see for ever
> thy face in glory, Jesus Christ our God.
Joy that is infinite and undefiled
> for all the ages of eternity.

PRAYER

ANTHEM

INVITATION TO REMEMBER THE UPPER ROOM

Let us go back in time to relive the night in Jesus' life when he gathered his disciples in an upper room to celebrate the Passover and to share a meal of remembrance. Recalling that night from scripture, let us join with those first disciples and the church of all times and places to know Christ anew in the breaking of the bread.

HYMN   An Upper Room Did Our Lord Prepare, st. 1–3 (CH 385)

As this hymn is sung, a minister and twelve persons gather around three sides of an extended communion table covered by a white cloth. The table is set with two Passover candles and enough chalices of wine and empty plates to serve communion to the congregation. Since this is not a reenactment of an actual meal, there is no need to have a setting in front of each person. In prominent view there is a separate stand upon which is placed a basin, a pitcher of water, a sponge, and a towel. The participants do not need to be robed as disciples and may be male or female. What follows is a dramatized reading from the Bible. The participants may use open Bibles from which to read their lines. As they gather, one person lights the candles. They remain standing until after the opening psalm.

DRAMATIZED READING

JESUS: Praised are you, Lord our God, Ruler of the universe, who has sanctified us by your commandments and commanded us to kindle the lights of the Passover festival. *(He lights the two candles and then continues.)* I pray that the brightness of these lights may shine in our darkness to give us a certain hope that our Liberator still acts to save as in the days when our forebears were slaves in Egypt. Amen.

Let us praise God with a psalm as we recall God's deliverance from Egyptian bondage. *(Beckons them to stand.)*

JESUS AND DISCIPLES : Psalm 114

(This traditional Passover psalm may be read in unison or responsively with possibly a sung response. If desired, the congregation may be invited to join in the reading.)

When all are seated, Jesus looks about the table, rises, takes off a jacket, and ties a towel about him. He pours water into a basin. After washing the feet of two disciples, he comes to Peter.

PETER: Lord, are you going to wash my feet?

JESUS: You do not know now what I am doing, but later you will understand.

PETER: You will never wash my feet.

JESUS: Unless I wash you, you have no share with me.

PETER: Lord, not my feet only but also my hands and my head!

JESUS: One who has bathed does not need to wash, except for the feet, but is entirely clean. And you are clean, though not all of you.

Jesus washes Peter's feet and then returns to his place, puts on his jacket and speaks.

JESUS: Do you know what I have done to you? You call me Teacher and Lord—and you are right, for that is what I am. So if I, your Lord and Teacher, have washed your feet, you also ought to wash one another's feet. Very truly, I tell you, servants are not greater than their master, nor are messengers greater than the one who sent them. If you know these things, you are blessed if you do them. *(Pausing, troubled.)* Very truly, I tell you, one of you will betray me.

The disciples look at one another, uncertain of whom he is speaking. Peter motions to the Beloved Disciple to ask Jesus who the betrayer will be.

BELOVED DISCIPLE: Lord, who is it?

JESUS: It is the one to whom I give this piece of bread when I have dipped it in the dish. *(Jesus dips the bread in a cup and hands it to Judas.)* Do quickly what you are going to do.

Judas gets up and leaves. Lights dim.

JESUS: Now the Son of Man has been glorified, and God has been glorified in him. If God has been glorified in him, God will also glorify him in himself and will glorify him at once. Little children, I am with you only a little longer. I give you a new commandment, that you love one another. Just as I have loved you, you also should love one another. By this everyone will know that you are my disciples, if you have love for one another. *(Jesus deliberates, stands. He takes unleavened bread, holds it up, and prays.)* Let us pray: Blessed are you, Lord our God, Ruler of the Universe, who brings forth bread from the earth; who sanctifies us with your commandments; who has commanded us to eat unleavened bread. *(Jesus breaks the bread, passing it to a nearby disciple who does not partake.)* This is my body, which is given for you. Do this in remembrance of me. *(Jesus lifts a cup and prays.)* Let us pray: Blessed are you, Lord our God, Ruler of the universe, creator of the fruit of the vine. *(Then)* Drink from it, all of you; for this is my blood of the covenant, which is poured out for many for the forgiveness of sins. I tell you, I will never again drink of this fruit of the vine until that day when I drink it new with you in my Father's kingdom. *(Jesus passes the cup to a nearby disciple who receives it but does not partake. Jesus beckons the disciples and the congregation to rise.)*

COMMUNION PRAYER(S)

This may be prayed in unison by the congregation, or given in the usual manner by one or more elders.

MEDITATION AND INVITATION TO PARTAKE

This should consist of a few brief paragraphs of a meditative nature, serving as the proclaiming of the gospel prior to partaking of communion.

HYMN

The congregation may stand to sing. As the hymn is sung, Jesus breaks the bread into pieces, placing them on the bread plates for the congregation. Assigned persons move to stations where the members of the congregation may come forward to partake of the emblems by breaking the bread and dipping it into the cup.

JESUS: The table of the Lord is spread.
Come, for all things are now ready.

PARTAKING

> *Those who are unable to come forward should be sought out and served where they are. Those holding the elements then return to the table to serve the one presiding and one another.*

POST-COMMUNION PRAYER

HYMN

SENDING FORTH AND BLESSING

ADDITIONAL RESOURCE

God, we witness unheard of things.
You, God, have given power to Jesus of Nazareth,
    whom we recognize as one of us,
    to be merciful to others and to forgive them.
We ask you, God, for this power, this freedom
    to be a healing grace to all those who live with us in this world,
    as a sign that you are the forgiveness of sins.
God, we break bread for one another
    and receive the body of Jesus Christ, your Son.
We ask you that, strengthened by him,
    we may live in love and peace,
    so that he may be present wherever we speak words,
    and may become his body in this world, forever. Amen.

The Good Friday service may take place in the midday or at night. Its purpose is to recall the nailing of Jesus to a cross and its significance for believers. This is an appropriate service for the beginning of a twenty-four hour prayer vigil by individual members. The material that follows may be adapted to any of these or other circumstances. If desired, a large plain cross may be the focus of attention, either put in place before the service, or brought in procession during the opening hymn.

CALL TO WORSHIP

We gather to remember the one who was
 wounded for our transgressions,
 crushed for our iniquities;
upon him was the punishment that made us whole,
and by his bruises we are healed.   (ISAIAH 53:5, ALT.)

Christ himself bore our sins in his body on the tree,
 that we might die to sin and live to righteousness.

OPENING PRAYER

STATEMENT OF PURPOSE

HYMN   Were You There When They Crucified My Lord? (*CH* 198)

PROCLAIMING AND HEARING GOD'S WORD

I. LUKE 23:32–34

NARRATOR: Now two others, both criminals, were led away with Jesus to be crucified. When they came to the place called Skull, they crucified him and the criminals there, one on his right, the other on his left. Then Jesus said:

ALL: **"Father, forgive them, for they know not what they do."**

Silent prayer or meditative comment or prepared prayer may follow.

MINISTER: Have mercy on us, O Lord.

ALL: **Jesus, we believe in you, we hope in you, we love you.**
Through your cross you brought us the hope of resurrection.

HYMN OR ANTHEM

II. LUKE 23:39–43

NARRATOR: Now one of the criminals hanging there reviled Jesus, saying:

SPEAKER: "Are you not the Messiah? Save yourself and us."

NARRATOR: The other, however, rebuking him, said in reply:

SPEAKER: "Have you no fear of God, for you are subject to the same condemnation? And indeed, we have been condemned justly, for the sentence we received corresponds to our crimes, but this man has done nothing criminal."

NARRATOR: Then he said,

SPEAKER: "Jesus, remember me when you come into your kingdom."

NARRATOR: Jesus replied to him,

ALL: **"Amen, I say to you, today you will be with me in Paradise."**

Silent prayer or meditative comment or prepared prayer may follow.

MINISTER: Have mercy on us, O Lord.

ALL: **Jesus, we believe in you, we hope in you, we love you.**
Through your cross you brought us the hope of resurrection.

HYMN

III. JOHN 19:25–27

NARRATOR: Standing by the cross of Jesus were his mother, his mother's sister, Mary the wife of Clopas, and Mary of Magdala. When Jesus saw his mother and the disciple there whom he loved, he said to his mother,

ALL: **"Woman, behold your son."**

NARRATOR: Then he said to the disciple,

ALL: **"Behold, your mother."**

Silent prayer or meditative comment or prepared prayer may follow.

MINISTER: Have mercy on us, O Lord.

ALL: **Jesus, we believe in you, we hope in you, we love you.**
Through your cross you brought us the hope of resurrection.

HYMN OR ANTHEM

IV. MATTHEW 27:45–46

NARRATOR: From noon onward, darkness came over the whole land until three in the afternoon. And about three o'clock, Jesus cried out in a loud voice,

ALL: **"My God, my God, why have you forsaken me?"**

Silent prayer or meditative comment or prepared prayer may follow.

MINISTER: Have mercy on us, O Lord.

ALL: **Jesus, we believe in you, we hope in you, we love you.**
Through your cross you brought us the hope of resurrection.

HYMN OR ANTHEM

V. JOHN 19:28

NARRATOR: Aware that everything was now finished, in order that Scripture might be fulfilled, Jesus said,

ALL: **"I thirst."**

Silent prayer or meditative comment or prepared prayer may follow.

MINISTER: Have mercy on us, O Lord.

ALL: **Jesus, we believe in you, we hope in you, we love you. Through your cross you brought us the hope of resurrection.**

HYMN OR ANTHEM

VI. JOHN 19:30

NARRATOR: There was a vessel filled with common wine. So they put a sponge soaked in wine on a sprig of hyssop and put it up to Jesus' mouth. When Jesus had taken the wine, he said,

ALL: **"It is finished."**

Silent prayer or meditative comment or prepared prayer may follow.

MINISTER: Have mercy on us, O Lord.

ALL: **Jesus, we believe in you, we hope in you, we love you. Through your cross you brought us the hope of resurrection.**

HYMN OR ANTHEM

VII. LUKE 23:44–46

NARRATOR: It was now about noon and darkness came over the whole land until three in the afternoon because of an eclipse of the sun. Then the veil of the temple was torn down the middle. Jesus cried out in a loud voice,

ALL: **"Father, into your hands I commend my spirit."**

Silent prayer or meditative comment or prepared prayer may follow.

MINISTER: Have mercy on us, O Lord.

ALL: **Jesus, we believe in you, we hope in you, we love you. Through your cross you brought us the hope of resurrection.**

HYMN OR ANTHEM

RESPONDING IN CONTRITION AND PENITENCE

MEDITATION

Briefly the gospel is proclaimed relating to Christ's death, making a transition to the traditional reproaches of God to the church.

THE REPROACHES

O my people, O my church,
what have I done to you,
or in what have I offended you?
Answer me.
I led you forth from the land of Egypt
and delivered you by the waters of baptism,
but you have prepared a cross for your Savior.
Holy God, have mercy upon us.

I led you through the desert forty years,
and fed you with manna:
I brought you through tribulation and penitence,
and gave you my body, the bread of heaven,
but you have prepared a cross for your Savior.
Holy God, have mercy upon us.

My peace I gave, which the world cannot give,
and washed your feet as a sign of my love,
but you draw the sword to strike in my name
and seek high places in my kingdom.
I offered you my body and blood,
but you scatter and deny and abandon me,
and you have prepared a cross for your Savior.
Holy God, have mercy upon us.

I came to you as the least of your brothers and sisters;
I was hungry and you gave me no food,
I was thirsty and you gave me no drink,
I was a stranger and you did not welcome me,
naked and you did not clothe me,
sick and in prison and you did not visit me,
and you have prepared a cross for your Savior.
Holy God, have mercy upon us.

THE LORD'S PRAYER

HYMN OR ANTHEM

DISMISSAL

I will not leave you orphans;
I will come to you.   (JOHN 14:18)

**Holy God, mighty God, ever-living God,
have mercy on us.**

*C*HE EASTER VIGIL

As early as the first century the church gathered on the Saturday night and Sunday morning to celebrate the Pasch—the passion, death, and resurrection of Christ. By the end of the fourth century the service had developed into the pattern that has remained to this day. Basically the service is intended to recall the saving acts of God in history, from Hebrew origins to God's mighty raising of Jesus Christ from the dead in triumph over death. Through bringing these events to fresh memory the participants are empowered to have a living encounter with the God who brings freedom to the enslaved, cleansing from sin, new life for the despairing, and the promise of eternal life to the dying.

The shorter passages suggested for minimal reading from Hebrew scriptures have been dramatized for choral reading. Scriptures used in this fashion are not acted out but read from the text. They should be carefully rehearsed to assure their effective reading.

The vigil is characterized by the lighting of a single large candle, the paschal candle, which is lit and brought forward to be displayed prominently on a stand of its own. Much of the strength of the service lies in experiencing Christ as the light that dispels the night of sin, destruction, and death. The whole service moves at the depths of life, centering upon life's basic elements: light, word, water, bread, and wine.

It is important, in using this service, to emphasize that it is a vigil, which means meditating long and deliberately. If the reaffirmation of baptismal vows is to be included, this should be interpreted in advance. The vigil may be adapted for varying uses:

> 1) Late Saturday evening, timed to climax after midnight.
>
> 2) Predawn Easter, beginning in darkness and concluding in the light of day.
>
> 3) Predawn Easter service of light and word; festive breakfast; service of baptism and/or reaffirmation of baptismal vows; regular Easter morning worship with the Lord's supper.

SERVICE OF LIGHT

LIGHTING A NEW FIRE

The people may assemble in silence outdoors or within the darkened church. A small fire may be started on the ground or in an urn or pan that will safely contain it. When the ceremony is held indoors, the people may face the rear of the sanctuary toward an entrance where the ceremony is held. When the fire is ready, the leader may proceed with the greeting.

GREETING

The congregation stands as a leader greets the people in these or other words.

Grace to you from Jesus Christ,
　　who was, and is, and is to come.

Sisters and brothers in Christ, on this most holy night
　　when our Savior Jesus Christ passed from death to life,
we gather with all the church throughout the world
　　in vigil and prayer.

This is the Passover of Jesus Christ:
Through light and the word,
　　through water and the bread and wine,
　　we recall Christ's death and resurrection,
　　we share Christ's triumph over sin and death,
and with invincible hope, we await Christ's coming again.

Hear the word of God:
In the beginning was the Word,
　　and the Word was with God, and the Word was God.
In the Word was life,
　　and the life was the light of all humanity.
The light shines in the darkness,
　　and the darkness has not overcome it.

BLESSING OF NEW FIRE

A leader, located near the flame, may offer the following or a similar prayer.

Let us pray.
Eternal God, giver of light and life,
　　bless this new flame,
　　that by its radiance and warmth
we may respond to your love and grace,
and be set free from all that separates us
　　from you and from each other;
　　through Jesus Christ, the Sun of Righteousness. Amen.

LIGHTING OF THE PASCHAL CANDLE

A leader, using a taper, may take a flame from the fire and light the paschal candle, saying these or similar words.

May the light of Christ, rising in glory,
　　illumine our hearts and minds.

FIRST RAISING OF THE PASCHAL CANDLE

Immediately after the words above, the bearer may raise the paschal candle, and the following words may be said or sung responsively.

Christ our light.
Thanks be to God.

If individual candles are provided for the congregation, the process of lighting them may begin after the first raising of the paschal candle. The one bearing the paschal candle, and all other leaders, may process toward the table. When the ceremony is held outdoors, the entire congregation may share in the processional into the church. When the ceremony is held indoors, the smaller procession may move from the entrance to the chancel. As the procession moves forward, all candles other than those on the table may also be lighted.

SECOND RAISING OF THE PASCHAL CANDLE

If the congregation is processing into the church from outdoors, the second raising of the candle may be held at the entrance door. If the people are already in the sanctuary, the paschal candle may be elevated midway of the aisle.

Christ our light.
Thanks be to God.

THIRD RAISING OF THE PASCHAL CANDLE

The paschal candle may be raised the third time at its stand in the center of the chancel, between the table and the congregation.

Christ our light.
Thanks be to God.

EASTER PROCLAMATION

Rejoice, heavenly powers! Sing, choirs of angels!
    Jesus Christ, our Light, is risen!
    Sound the trumpet of salvation!
Rejoice, O earth, in shining splendor,
    radiant in the brightness of your Sovereign!
Christ has conquered! Glory fills you!
    Night vanishes for ever!
Rejoice, O servant church! Exult in glory!
The risen Savior shines upon you!
    Let this place resound with joy,
    echoing the mighty song of all God's people!

God be with you!
And also with you.
Lift up your hearts.
We lift them to God.
Let us give thanks to God Most High.
It is right to give God thanks and praise.

It is truly right that with full hearts and minds and voices
    we should praise you, the unseen God, the eternal Creator,
    and your only begotten one, our Savior Jesus Christ.
For Christ has ransomed us with his blood
    and for our salvation has paid you the cost of Adam and Eve's sin!

This is our Passover feast, when Christ, the true lamb, is slain,
  whose blood consecrates the homes of all believers.
This is the night when first you saved our ancestors:
    You freed the people of Israel from their slavery
    and led them dry-shod through the sea.
This is the night when the pillar of fire
    destroyed the shadows of sin!
This is the night when Christians everywhere,
    washed clean of sin and freed from all defilement,
    are restored to grace and grow together in holiness.
This is the night when Jesus Christ broke the chains of death
    and rose triumphant from the grave.
Therefore, gracious Creator, in the joy of this night,
    receive our sacrifice of praise, your church's solemn offering.
Accept this Easter candle,
    a flame divided but undimmed,
    a pillar of fire that glows to your honor, O God.
Let it mingle with the lights of heaven and continue bravely burning
    to dispel the shadows of this night!
May the Morning Star which never sets find this flame still burning:
    Christ, the Morning Star, who came back from the dead,
    and shed your peaceful light on all creation,
    your only begotten one who lives and reigns for ever. **Amen.**

At the conclusion of the Easter proclamation, if individual candles have been provided for the congregation, ask the people to extinguish their candles and be seated. As this is done, only those electric lights necessary for reasonable vision should be turned on.

SERVICE OF THE WORD

The number of readings from Hebrew Scriptures traditionally read for the vigil varies from two to twelve. The reading of Exodus 14 is always included. Four readings with accompanying prayers are suggested here. The drama-tized readings are adapted from the New Revised Standard Version Bible. *Characters' voices may be combined, with a single reader doing several parts.*

Other readings traditionally used are:

Genesis 7:1–5, 11–18; 8:6–18; 9:8–13 (Noah and the flood)
Ezekiel 36:16–17a, 18–28 (A new heart and a new spirit)
Ezekiel 37:1–14 (The valley of the dry bones)
Jonah 3:1–10 (Our missionary calling)
Zephaniah 3:14–20 (The gathering of God's people)
Isaiah 54:5–14 (Love calls us back)
Isaiah 4:2–6 (Hope for Israel)
Daniel 3:1–29 (Song of three men)

It is customary for certain psalms or canticles to be sung following particular readings. These have been noted.

The people serving as readers may stand around the paschal candle and move after each reading so that the one reading faces the congregation and is flanked by the other readers. The readers may hold their candles during the readings.

GREETING

A leader may introduce the Service of the Word in these or similar words.

Dear brothers and sisters in Christ, we have begun our solemn vigil. As we watch and wait, let us listen to the word of God,
    recalling God's saving acts throughout history
    and how, in the fullness of time,
God's Word became flesh and dwelt among us:
    Jesus Christ, our Redeemer!

We do not live by bread alone,
    but by every word that proceeds from the mouth of God.

READINGS FROM HEBREW SCRIPTURE

First Reading: Genesis 1:1, 26–31—The Creation

NARRATOR 1: Then God said,

GOD: Let us make humankind in our image, according to our likeness; and let them have dominion over the fish of the sea, and over the birds of the air, and over the cattle, and over all the wild animals of the earth, and over every creeping thing that creeps upon the earth.

NARRATOR 2: In the beginning when God created the heavens and the earth, and created humankind in his image, in the image of God he created them.

NARRATOR 1: Male and female he created them. God blessed them, and God said to them,

GOD: Be fruitful and multiply, and fill the earth and subdue it; and have dominion over the fish of the sea and over the birds of the air and over every living thing that moves upon the earth. (*Pausing*) See, I have given you every plant yielding seed that is upon the face of all the earth, and every tree with seed in its fruit; you shall have them for food. And to every beast of the earth, and to every bird of the air, and to everything that creeps on the earth, everything that has the breath of life, I have given every green plant for food.

NARRATOR 2: And it was so.

NARRATOR 1: God saw everything that he had made, and indeed, it was very good. And there was evening and there was morning, the sixth day.

Then may be read, or sung by a cantor:

Psalm 33:1–11 *or* Psalm 46:5–10

Let us pray:

Almighty God, who wonderfully created,
    yet more wonderfully restored,
    the dignity of human nature,
grant that we may share the divine life
    of the one who came to share our humanity:
Jesus Christ, our Redeemer. Amen.

Second Reading: Genesis 22:1–18—Abraham's and Sarah's Faithfulness

NARRATOR 1: After these things God tested Abraham. He said to him,

GOD: Abraham!

NARRATOR 1: And Abraham said,

ABRAHAM: Here I am.

GOD: Take your son, your only son, Isaac, whom you love, and go to the land of Moriah, and offer him there as a burnt offering on one of the mountains that I shall show you.

NARRATOR 1: So Abraham rose early in the morning, saddled his donkey, and took two of his young men with him, and his son Isaac.

NARRATOR 2: He cut the wood for the burnt offering, and set out and went to the place in the distance that God had shown him.

NARRATOR 1: On the third day Abraham looked up and saw the place far away. Then Abraham said to his young men,

ABRAHAM: Stay here with the donkey; the boy and I will go over there; we will worship, and then we will come back to you.

NARRATOR 1: Abraham took the wood of the burnt offering and laid it on his son, Isaac, and he himself carried the fire and the knife.

NARRATOR 2: So the two of them walked on together.

NARRATOR 1: Isaac said to his father, Abraham,

ISAAC: Father!

ABRAHAM: Here I am, my son.

ISAAC: The fire and the wood are here, but where is the lamb for a burnt offering?

ABRAHAM: God himself will provide the lamb for a burnt offering, my son.

NARRATOR 1: So the two of them walked on together.

NARRATOR 2: When they came to the place that God had shown him, Abraham built an altar there and laid the wood in order. He bound his son Isaac, and laid him on the altar, on top of the wood.

NARRATOR 1: Then Abraham reached out his hand and took the knife to kill his son.

NARRATOR 2: But the angel of the LORD called to him from heaven, and said,

ANGEL: Abraham, Abraham!

ABRAHAM: Here I am.

ANGEL: Do not lay your hand on the boy or do anything to him; for now I know that you fear God, since you have not withheld your son, your only son, from me.

NARRATOR 1: And Abraham looked up and saw a ram, caught in a thicket by its horns. Abraham went and took the ram and offered it up as a burnt offering instead of his son.

NARRATOR 2: So Abraham called that place "The LORD will provide"; as it is said to this day, "On the mount of the LORD it shall be provided."

NARRATOR 1: The angel of the LORD called to Abraham a second time from heaven,

ANGEL: By myself I have sworn, says the LORD: Because you have done this, and have not withheld your son, your only son, I will indeed bless you, and I will make your offspring as numerous as the stars of heaven and as the sand that is on the seashore. And your offspring shall possess the gate of their enemies, and by your offspring shall all the nations of the earth gain blessing for themselves, because you have obeyed my voice.

Then may be read, or sung by a cantor:

Psalm 33:12–22 *or* Psalm 16

Let us pray:

Gracious God of all believers,
through Sarah's and Abraham's trustful obedience
you made known your covenant love to our ancestors and to us.
By the grace of Christ's trustful obedience, even unto death,
fulfill in your church and in all creation
your promise of a new covenant,
written not on tablets of stone,
but on the tablets of human hearts;
through Jesus Christ our Savior. Amen.

Third Reading: Exodus 14:15–15:1 or Exodus 14:21–29
    —Israel's Deliverance at the Red Sea

Dramatized Reading: Exodus 15:1–19—The Song of Moses

NARRATOR 1: Then Moses stretched out his hand over the sea. The LORD drove the sea back by a strong east wind all night, and turned the sea into dry land; and the waters were divided. The Israelites went into the sea on dry ground, the waters forming a wall for them on their right and on their left.

NARRATOR 2: The Egyptians pursued, and went into the sea after them, all of Pharaoh's horses, chariots, and chariot drivers.

NARRATOR 1: At the morning watch the LORD in the pillar of fire and cloud looked down upon the Egyptian army, and threw the Egyptian army into panic. He clogged their chariot wheels so that they turned with difficulty.

NARRATOR 2: The Egyptians said,

EGYPTIANS 1,2: Let us flee from the Israelites, for the LORD is fighting for them against Egypt.

NARRATOR 1: Then the LORD said to Moses,

GOD: Stretch out your hand over the sea, so that the water may come back upon the Egyptians, upon their chariots and chariot drivers.

NARRATOR 1: So Moses stretched out his hand over the sea, and at dawn the sea returned to its normal depth.

NARRATOR 2: As the Egyptians fled before it, the LORD tossed the Egyptians into the sea. The waters returned and covered the chariots and the chariot drivers, the entire army of Pharaoh that had followed them into the sea; not one of them remained.

NARRATOR 1: But the Israelites walked on dry ground through the sea, the waters forming a wall for them on their right and on their left.

NARRATOR 2: Moses and the Israelites sang this song to the LORD:

MOSES: I will sing to the LORD, for he has triumphed gloriously; horse and rider he has thrown into the sea.

ISRAELITE 1: The LORD is my strength and my might, and he has become my salvation; this is my God, and I will praise him, my father's God, and I will exalt him. The LORD is a warrior; the LORD is his name.

MOSES: Pharaoh's chariots and his army he cast into the sea; his picked officers were sunk in the Red Sea. The floods covered them; they went down into the depths like a stone. Your right hand, O LORD, glorious in power—your right hand, O LORD, shattered the enemy. In the greatness of your majesty you overthrew your adversaries; you sent out your fury, it consumed them like stubble. At the blast of your nostrils the waters piled up, the floods stood up in a heap; the deeps congealed in the heart of the sea.

ISRAELITE 2: The enemy said, "I will pursue, I will overtake, I will divide the spoil, my desire shall have its fill of them. I will draw my sword, my hand shall destroy them." You blew with your wind, the sea covered them; they sank like lead in the mighty waters.

MOSES: Who is like you, O LORD, among the gods? Who is like you, majestic in holiness, awesome in splendor, doing wonders? You stretched out your right hand, the earth swallowed them.

ISRAELITE 1: In your steadfast love you led the people whom you redeemed; you guided them by your strength to your holy abode.

NARRATOR 1: The peoples heard, they trembled; pangs seized the inhabitants of Philistia. Then the chiefs of Edom were dismayed; trembling seized the leaders of Moab; all the inhabitants of Canaan melted away. Terror and dread fell upon them; by the might of your arm, they became still as a stone until your people, O LORD, passed by, until the people whom you acquired passed by. You brought them in and planted them on the mountain of your own possession, the place, O LORD, that you made your abode, the sanctuary, O LORD, that your hands have established. The LORD will reign forever and ever.

NARRATOR 2: When the horses of Pharaoh with his chariots and his chariot drivers went into the sea, the LORD brought back the waters of the sea upon them; but the Israelites walked through the sea on dry ground.

Let us pray:

God our Savior,
even today we see the wonders of miracles you worked long ago.
You once saved a single nation from slavery,
and now you offer that salvation to all
through the grace of baptism.
May all the peoples of the world
become true daughters and sons of Abraham and Sarah
and be made worthy of the heritage of Israel;
through Jesus Christ, our only mediator and advocate. Amen.

Fourth Reading: Isaiah 55:1–11—Salvation Offered Freely to All
    Isaiah 12:2–6—The First Song of Isaiah

ISAIAH 1: Ho, everyone who thirsts, come to the waters; and you that have no money, come, buy and eat!

ISAIAH 2: Come, buy wine and milk without money and without price.

ISAIAH 1: Why do you spend your money for that which is not bread, and your labor for that which does not satisfy?

ISAIAH 2: Listen carefully to me, and eat what is good, and delight yourselves in rich food.

ISAIAH 1: Incline your ear, and come to me; listen, so that you may live. I will make with you an everlasting covenant, my steadfast, sure love for David. See, I made him a witness to the peoples, a leader and commander for the peoples. See, you shall call nations that you do not know, and nations that do not know you shall run to you, because of the LORD your God, the Holy One of Israel, for he has glorified you.

ISAIAH 2: Seek the LORD while he may be found, call upon him while he is near; let the wicked forsake their ways, and the unrighteous their thoughts; let them return to the LORD, that he may have mercy on them, and to our God, for he will abundantly pardon.

GOD: For my thoughts are not your thoughts, nor are your ways my ways. For as the heavens are higher than the earth, so are my ways higher than your ways and my thoughts than your thoughts. For as the rain and the snow come down from heaven, and do not return there until they have watered the earth, making it bring forth and sprout, giving seed to the sower and bread to the eater, so shall my word be that goes out from my mouth; it shall not return to me empty, but it shall accomplish that which I purpose, and succeed in the thing for which I sent it.

ISAIAH 1: Surely God is my salvation; I will trust, and will not be afraid, for the LORD GOD is my strength and my might; he has become my salvation.

ISAIAH 2: With joy you will draw water from the wells of salvation. And you will say in that day:

ISAIAH 1: Give thanks to the LORD, call on his name; make known his deeds among the nations; proclaim that his name is exalted. Sing praises to the LORD, for he has done gloriously;

ISAIAH 2: Let this be known in all the earth. Shout aloud and sing for joy, O royal Zion, for great in your midst is the Holy One of Israel.

Let us pray:

Eternal God, you created all things by the power of your Word,
and you renew the earth by your Spirit.
Give now the water of life to all who thirst for you,
and nourish with the spiritual food of bread and wine
all who hunger for you, that our lives on earth
may bear the abundant fruit of your heavenly reign;
through Jesus Christ, the firstborn from the dead,
who, with you and the Holy Spirit, lives and reigns forever. Amen.

HYMN OF PRAISE

The readers may return to their places, and all may stand to sing a hymn of praise.

During the singing of this hymn, the candles on or near the table may be lighted, additional electric lights may be turned on, and the church bell may be pealed joyfully. In some congregations, it is the custom not to use the organ until this hymn.

NEW TESTAMENT READINGS

The people may be seated. A collect may be said prior to the Epistle.

Epistle Reading: Romans 6:3–11
　　　—Our Death and Resurrection in Jesus Christ

Psalm 114, Psalm 118, *or* Another Hymn

The congregation stands for the reading of the Gospel suggested in the ecumenical lectionary. The reading may be introduced by singing or saying an alleluia (e.g., CH 49, last eight measures) and/or "Glory to you, O Christ." It may be followed by "Praise to you, O Christ" and/or an alleluia.

Gospel Reading—Christ's Resurrection
　　Year A: Matthew 28:1–10
　　Year B: Mark 16:1–8
　　Year C: Luke 24:1–12

SERMON *(May be omitted)*

HYMN

The congregation stands for a hymn introducing the baptism theme.

SERVICE RELATING TO BAPTISM

ACT OF BAPTISM

Baptism may follow, adapting the usual service of baptism.

REAFFIRMATION OF BAPTISMAL VOWS

In the event there are no candidates for baptism, the following order for the reaffirmation of baptismal vows may be used.

Sisters and brothers in Christ,
　　our baptism is the sign and seal of our cleansing from sin,
　　and of our being grafted into Christ.
Through the birth, life, death, and rising of Christ,
　　the power of sin was broken
　　and God's kingdom entered our world.
Through our baptism we were made citizens of God's kingdom,
　　and freed from the bondage of sin.

Let us celebrate that freedom and redemption
    through the renewal of the promises made at our baptism.

I ask you, therefore, once again to reject sin,
    to profess your faith in Christ Jesus,
    and to confess the faith in which we were baptized.

Do you renounce the forces of evil,
    which defy God's righteousness and love?
I renounce them.

Do you renounce the evil powers of this world
    which corrupt and destroy the creatures of God?
I renounce them.

Do you renounce the ways of sin
    that draw you away from the love of God?
I renounce them.

Do you turn to Jesus Christ
    and accept him as your Lord and Savior?
I do.

Do you intend to be Christ's faithful disciple,
    obeying his word, and showing his love, to your life's end?
I do.

With the whole church, let us confess our faith.

The congregation affirms the faith in the words of the Apostles' Creed or another affirmation of faith.

The water may be poured into basins or dipped from the baptistry.

The minister leads the people in prayer, saying:

Gracious God, we thank you that in every age
    you have made water a sign of your presence.
In the beginning your Spirit brooded over the waters
    and they became the source of all creation.
You led your people Israel through the waters of the Red Sea
    to their new land of freedom and hope.
In the waters of the Jordan, your Son was baptized by John
    and anointed with your Spirit for his ministry of reconciliation.
Glory to you forever and ever.

We thank you for the gift of baptism.
In the waters of baptism we were buried with Christ in his death;
    from the water, we are raised to share in his resurrection;
    through the water, we are reborn by the power of the Holy Spirit.
Glory to you forever and ever.

We praise you for claiming us through our baptism
    and for upholding us by your grace.
We remember your promises given to us in our baptism,
    that we may be empowered to do your will,
    and continue forever in the risen life of Christ,
to whom, with you and the Holy Spirit,
be all glory and honor, now and forever. **Amen.**

MUSIC

*As music is played or sung, water may be applied to the congregation one of
two ways:*

*1) While a hymn is sung, the minister may walk through the congregation
sprinkling water from the baptistry or basin with an evergreen bough, saying:*

Remember your baptism, and be thankful.

*2) While music is played, the minister, along with others, may take pitchers of
water to basins at various stations, inviting members to come to receive afresh
the cleansing water of Christ's spirit in a symbolic act of renewal. They are
instructed to come with hands folded in prayer to be blessed by the pouring of
water over them as they recall their baptism. As a small amount of water is
poured over the hands these words are spoken:*

Remember your baptism, and be thankful.

Each person receiving the water may respond:

Thanks be to God.

A person with a towel may assist in the drying of the hands.

PRAYER

One of the following prayers may be given.

Almighty God, we thank you that by the death and and resurrection of
your Son, Jesus Christ, you have overcome sin and brought us to yourself, and that by the sealing of your Holy Spirit you have bound us to
your service. Renew in *these* your *servants* the covenant you made with
them at *their* baptism. Send *them* forth in the power of that Spirit to
perform the service you set before *them*; through Jesus Christ, your Son,
our Lord, who lives and reigns with you and the Holy Spirit, one God,
now and forever. **Amen.**

Or:

Eternal God, you have declared in Christ
    the completion of your purpose of love.
May we live by faith, walk in hope, and be renewed in love,
    until the world reflects your glory, and you are all in all.
Even so; come, Lord Jesus. **Amen.**

SERVICE OF BREAD AND CUP

If desired, the worship may conclude with the Lord's supper. An ancient Orthodox tradition provides for the congregation to process out of the sanctuary and walk around it three times. While this takes place the stripped and barren sanctuary is adorned with its symbols and paraments to greet the worshipers upon their reentry with the joy of the risen Christ. The Lord's supper is then festively received.

Depending upon circumstances, the partaking of the Lord's supper may be postponed to be included in a later Easter service.

DISMISSAL AND BLESSING

Go in peace to love and serve the Lord
in the power of his resurrection. Alleluia!

The grace of the Lord Jesus Christ, the love of God
and the communion of the Holy Spirit be with you all.

Christ is risen!
Christ is risen!

Christ is risen!
Christ is risen!

Christ is risen!
Christ is risen indeed!
Alleluia, alleluia!

Easter is an annual Christian festival celebrating God's raising Jesus Christ from the dead following his crucifixion. It is celebrated on the first Sunday following the full moon that occurs on or next after March 21. The date corresponds closely to the Jewish Passover with which the last days of Christ's ministry are associated.

Although every Sunday worship service commemorates Christ's resurrection by taking place on the day Christ was raised from the dead, Easter has become a festival that illuminates the significance of all other services of Sunday worship.

The Easter service of worship usually adheres to a congregation's regular pattern of worship. It becomes a festival through an emphasis upon the Easter theme in words and music augmented by flowers, colors, banners, and other joyous expressions.

The materials below are intended for possible use at various points within the congregation's ordinary pattern of worship. Additional resources may be found in this book under the heading Worship Resources. *There each aspect of worship includes resources for special days of the Christian year.*

CALL TO WORSHIP

Alleluia. Christ is risen.
The Lord is risen indeed. Alleluia.

May his grace and peace be with you.
May he fill our hearts with joy.

Or:

The tomb is empty.
Sound the trumpet.

One trumpet plays measures one and two of "Christ the Lord Is Risen To-day."

The Lord is risen!
Sound the trumpets!

Two trumpets play measures five and six.

Christ leads us on the road to life!
Sound the trumpets!

Trumpets and organ play the Alleluia of the hymn as an introduction for the congregation to sing.

Alleluia! Christ is risen!
Christ is here! Alleluia!

OPENING PRAYER

Almighty and ever-living God,
we gather to marvel at the mystery of Christ's resurrection.
In boldness you exalted the humble, empowering the weak.
In strength you snatched victory from the jaws of death.
In love you declared your crucified Son the savior of the world.
We celebrate this good news in an Easter festival of life.
With you we join in this gladsome day.

Or:

Our Lord Jesus Christ, risen from death,
    we praise you for changed lives and new hopes at Easter:
You came to Mary in the garden, and turned her tears into joy.
For your love and your mercy:
We give you thanks, O Lord.

You came to the disciples by the lakeside,
    and turned their failure into faith.
For your love and your mercy:
We give you thanks, O Lord.

You came to the disciples on the Emmaus road,
    and turned their despair into hope.
For your love and your mercy:
We give you thanks, O Lord.

You come to us in our unworthiness and shame,
and turn our weakness into triumph.
For your love and your mercy:
We give you thanks, O Lord.

Lord Jesus, wherever there are tears, or fear,
or failure, or despair, or weakness:
come, reveal to us your love, your mercy, and your risen power;
for the glory of your name.
Alleluia!

PRAYER OF CONFESSION

O Jesus Christ, risen master and triumphant Lord,
we come to you in sorrow for our sins,
and confess to you our weakness and unbelief:

We have lived by our own strength,
and not by the power of your resurrection.
In your mercy, forgive us:
Lord, hear us and help us.

We have lived by the light of our own eyes,
as faithless and not believing.
In your mercy, forgive us:
Lord, hear us and help us.

We have lived for this world alone,
and doubted our home in heaven.
In your mercy, forgive us:
Lord, hear us and help us.

**Lift our minds above earthly things,
set them on things above.
Show us your glory and your power,
that we may serve you gladly all our days. Amen.**

PRAYER OF THE PEOPLE

Alleluia! What was dead shall live; what was dark shall shine;
what was forgotten shall be remembered,
for the Lord is risen and walks among us.
Let us confidently bring before God the needs of all our world,
asking God for renewal, responding, "Christ is risen indeed."
Christ is risen:
Christ is risen indeed.

God of life, in gratitude and great joy
we laud you for the gifts of Christ's resurrection.
On this day give us hope, for Christ is risen:

Christ is risen indeed.

On this feast day which brings joy to all Christian believers,
    may we commit ourselves to work toward the unity of the church,
    that Christ's body may be one, for Christ is risen:
Christ is risen indeed.

Honoring the gift of Christ's risen body may we rise to serve
    all those whose needs keep them from seeing themselves
    as the image of God; for Christ is risen:
Christ is risen indeed.

For all who have need of the gift of Easter;
    for all who journey from illness to health, from despair to hope,
    from grief to consolation, from loneliness to love;
    (for *Name*); for all our brothers and sisters,
that death may have no more power over us, for Christ is risen:
Christ is risen indeed.

For all who suffer and all who mourn,
    that today the Lord God will wipe away all tears,
    for Christ is risen:
Christ is risen indeed.

May we have the persistent faith of Mary Magdalene
    and the surprised belief of Peter and John.
May we long to be God's sign of life in our world, for Christ is risen:
Christ is risen indeed.

Here other intercessions may be offered.

May we be one in faith with all who have died in Christ,
    for our life is hid with Christ in God; for Christ is risen:
Christ is risen indeed.

God of life, we thank you for the mystery planted in us,
    the paradox of life from death
    and community from scattered disciples.
We praise you for the dying which saves us from death
    and for the rising which brings us life.
We pray, as we live, through Jesus the risen one,
    in the power of the Holy Spirit, now and forever. **Amen.**

OFFERTORY PRAYER
    We bring our gifts to you in response to good news.
    Christ is risen indeed and abides in us still.

May all that we do be in response to new life.
As you accept who we are, O God,
    receive what we offer,
    and transform all our being to conform with your will.
Extend your grace through us
    so that others hear of the salvation you bring. Amen.

COMMUNION PRAYER

    Loving Father, living God,
    it is right and appropriate and our joyful duty,
    always and everywhere to give you thanks,
    especially today, when we greet our risen Lord.

    We praise you, God, for all that you have done for us in Christ.
    We praise you for his life through which he showed your love;
        for his victory over evil
        and his obedience which took him to the cross;
        for his triumph over death
        and for his coming to be our living Lord.
    We praise you for this bread and wine,
        through which we remember;
        through which our faith and hope are renewed,
        through which we receive the power of your Spirit
        and share the fellowship of your undying love.
    Honor and glory and praise be to you, living God,
    here and everywhere, now and for ever.

DISMISSAL

    May the love of the cross,
        the power of the resurrection,
        and the presence of the Living Lord,
        be with you always.
    And the blessing of the Eternal God,
        Creator and Sustainer,
        Risen Lord and Savior,
        Giver of holiness and love,
        be upon you now and evermore.

    Or:

    Christ is risen!
    Christ is risen indeed!
    Go now as risen people.
    Alive in the spirit and way of Christ!

Pentecost is an annual festival of the Christian church occurring on the seventh Sunday after Easter, to celebrate the descent of the Holy Spirit upon the disciples. The Pentecost service of worship usually adheres to a congregation's regular pattern of worship. It becomes a festival through an emphasis upon the Pentecost theme in words and music augmented by flowers, colors, banners and other joyous expressions. The celebration of those gathered for the first Pentecost in which they understood one another despite barriers of language may be highlighted by the reading of scriptures or praying in various languages. Another possibility is to assign various persons to read the appropriate passage from Acts, beginning at intervals, so as to elicit a feeling of unity and understanding despite the confusion of many tongues.

The materials below are intended for possible use at various points within the congregation's ordinary pattern of worship. Additional resources may be found in this book under the heading Worship Resources. *There each aspect of worship includes resources for special days of the Christian year.*

CALL TO WORSHIP

The Lord said:
>   You shall receive power when the Holy Spirit has come upon you,
>   and you shall be my witnesses to the ends of the earth.

**Come, Holy Spirit, fill the hearts of your faithful
    and kindle in them the fire of your love. Alleluia!**

OPENING PRAYER

Kindling Spirit, build well the fire in our hearts this day.
Fan us to flame that all will see
    the Christ-presence of love blazing in our midst.
Burn the witness on our tongues: Christ's Spirit moves among us.
Jesus Christ, our risen Lord has set his church on fire
    with strength and boldness and power.
Kindling Spirit, build well the fire in our hearts this day.

A PRAYER OF CONFESSION

**Almighty God, we confess that we have sinned against you:
    for we have denied your saving presence in our lives,
        and we have grieved your Holy Spirit.
Come to us in the fire of your love,
    and set our minds on the things of the Spirit,
        that we may bear the Spirit's fruit in love and joy and peace;
        through Jesus Christ our Lord. Amen.**

A Pentecost Litany of Affirmation

At Pentecost the Holy Spirit was given to the church.
In pouring the Spirit on many people
>God overcomes the divisions of Babel.
Now people from every tongue, tribe, and nation
>are gathered into the unity of the body of Christ.

Jesus stays with us in the Spirit,
>**who renews our hearts, moves us to faith,**
>**leads us in the truth, stands by us in our need,**
>**and makes our obedience fresh and vibrant.**

The Spirit thrusts God's people into worldwide mission,
>impelling young and old, men and women,
>to go next door and far away
>into science and art, media and marketplace
>with the good news of God's grace.
The Spirit goes before them and with them,
>convincing the world of sin and pleading the cause of Christ.

The Spirit's gifts are here to stay in rich variety,
>**fitting responses to timely needs.**
We thankfully see each other
>**as gifted members of the fellowship**
>**that delights in the creative Spirit's work.**
More than enough the Spirit gives to each believer
>**for God's praise and our neighbor's welfare.**

Offertory Prayer

God of wind, word, and fire, we bless your name this day
>for sending the light and strength of your Holy Spirit.
We give you thanks for all the gifts, great and small,
>that you have poured out upon your children.
Accept us with our gifts to be living praise and witness
>to your love throughout all the earth;
through Jesus Christ, who lives with you
>in the unity of the Holy Spirit, one God, forever. Amen.

Or:

Lord our God, send down upon us your Holy Spirit, we pray you, to cleanse our hearts, to hallow our gifts, and to make perfect the offering of ourselves to you; through Jesus Christ, your Son, our Lord. Amen.

Dismissal

The blessing of God, whose love creates new life and whose fire burns away our impurities, be with you in your journey of life.

The blessing of God, whose love has the power to transform our living from old habits into new hope, be with you always.

The blessing of God, whose Spirit blesses our spirit with wisdom and vision, embolden you to proclaim the good news of God's love to all.

TRINITY SUNDAY

Trinity Sunday is observed on the first Sunday following Pentecost to emphasize the importance of knowing God the Father through Jesus Christ the Son by the power of the Holy Spirit.

Father Almighty, for your majesty and your mercy—
> loving us still in our waywardness, forgiving us in our unworthiness:
> we bring you our worship
and offer you thanksgiving.

Jesus, our Redeemer, for your humility and your sacrifice—
> sharing our joys and sorrows, dying and rising for our salvation:
> we bring you our worship
and offer you thanksgiving.

Holy Spirit of God, for your guidance and your encouragement—
> inspiring and empowering the church, revealing to us all truth:
> we bring you our worship
and offer you thanksgiving.

God of gods—Father, Son, and Holy Spirit,
eternal Lord, Three-in-One:
to you be glory, honor, and praise, forever and ever. Amen.

THE FESTIVAL OF CHRIST THE COSMIC RULER

This day is observed on the last Sunday of the Christian year just prior to Advent to celebrate the anticipation of Christ's completion of God's work of reconciliation of all things in heaven and on earth.

In the image of Christ we are created;
In the spirit of Christ we are knit together.

In the body of Christ we are reborn;
In the love of Christ we are reconciled.
O come, let us sing Hosanna to God—
**Whose fullness in Christ was pleased to dwell,
whose fullness in us desires to live!**

+ + +

Eternal God, you have declared in Christ
    the completion of all your purpose of love.
We pray for the sick and the departed:

    **the tempted and despairing;
    the sick and handicapped;
    the aged;
    the ministries of care and healing;
    those who mourn;
    the departed.**

We give thanks
    for the triumphs of the gospel that herald your salvation:

    the signs of renewal that declare the coming of your kingdom,
    the human lives that reveal your work of grace;

    for the unceasing praise of the company of heaven:

    **the promise to those who mourn that all tears shall be wiped away,
    the pledge of death destroyed and victory won;**

    for our foretaste of eternal life through baptism and eucharist:

    **our hope in the Spirit;
    the communion of saints.**

May we live by faith, walk in hope, and be renewed in love,
until the world reflects your glory and you are all in all.

Even so, come Lord Jesus. Amen.

IV

ON
SPECIAL
SUNDAYS

Even when the primary emphasis of Lord's Day worship is upon the themes of the Christian seasons, there are still special emphases that need to be made relating to the life of the congregation and its culture. This is often done by the use of a special prayer befitting the occasion.

The materials in this section serve as resources to be freely adapted as circumstances require.

THE NEW YEAR

The marking of the passing of time is emphasized at the beginning of a new calendar year. Usually of a meditative nature, it may be related to either the last Sunday of the old year or the first Sunday of the new year. It may also be an occasion for a special New Year's Eve service. Appropriate scripture readings include: Psalm 121:8, Deuteronomy 31:6, and Psalm 102:24–27.

God of all times and yet beyond time,
    you call us into this new year still to be named.
Help us travel light in faith and expectation.
    Guide us in this new venture of imagination.
Make us bold witnesses to the in-breaking of your future.
Let us rest our times in yours,
    confident that we do not enter this new year alone.

unison

+ + +

Come, that God may strengthen us with the gift of peace.

**Then justice will dwell in the wilderness,
    and righteousness abide in the fruitful field.**

The effect of righteousness will be peace,
    and the result of righteousness, quietness and trust.
Hear the promise of God: I will grant peace in the land,
    and you shall lie down, and no one shall make you afraid.

**Blessed are the peacemakers, for they will be called children of God.
Praise God in heaven! Peace on earth to everyone who pleases God.**

+ + +

Everlasting God of all the years, you have been our companion through all the mysteries of the past to uphold us when we knew not the way. Take our hand now and share our pilgrimage to an unknown future. Open our eyes to recognize your presence with us this day that we may give you praise and celebrate the goodness of your guidance. Renew us. Refresh us. Fill us with your Spirit; we pray in Christ's name. Amen.

+ + +

Eternal God, you have placed us in a world of space and time, and through the events of our lives you bless us with your love. Grant that in this new year we may know your presence, see your love at work, and live in the light of the event that gives us joy forever—the coming of your Son, Jesus Christ our Lord. Amen.

+ + +

Our God, your throne has been established
   from everlasting to everlasting.
We come to you as your people today in the stream of ongoing history.

Long ago you prepared the way for your faith family,
   the children of Israel,
and in your everlasting love,
   you lead us today across the seas of uncertainty
   and through the wilderness of indecision.

You demanded obedience and covenant from those
   who wanted to go to the promised land,
and you would ask of us the same wholehearted commitment.

We stand on the threshold of a new year,
   full of expectations and apprehensions;
yet we are calm with the assurance
   of your loving concern and constant presence.

We would examine our past sins of self-confidence and independence,
and open ourselves to your will
   through the wisdom of our heritage
   and the interpretation of our faith family,
as we face the concerns of living together
   in harmony, love, and humility,
of ministry to each other
   and commitment to grow in faithfulness.

We come to you for aid, for without you we are sure to fail.
   Give us great courage and fortitude.
   Save us from timidity and doubt.
   Open our eyes to the joy of simple pleasures.
   Give us noble tasks for our energies.
   Let us glow with the blessing of friendship.
   Help us to make this new year rich in growth, in vision, in service.
We look to you, O God, in the changing and flowing of days.
We trust in you alone for your mercy endures forever. Amen.

+ + +

This day wilt thou strengthen us. **Amen.**
This day wilt thou bless us. **Amen.**
This day wilt thou uplift us. **Amen.**
This day wilt thou visit us for good. **Amen.**
This day wilt thou inscribe us for happy life. **Amen.**
This day wilt thou hear our cry. **Amen.**
This day wilt thou accept our prayer in mercy and favor. **Amen.**
This day wilt thou support us with thy righteous hand. **Amen.**

+ + +

The new year is a time for taking stock of our life.
O Lord, you know us better than we know ourselves.
Help us to look at ourselves through your eyes.

Let us reflect on our use of time,
and resolve to deepen our experience of eternity.

Ca ll

Let us reflect on our investment of money,
and resolve to live our understanding of stewardship.

Let us reflect on our attitude toward work,
and resolve to strengthen our sense of vocation.

Let us reflect on our regard for leisure,
and resolve to respect our need for renewal.

Let us reflect on our perception of friendship,
and resolve to broaden our definition of family.

The new year is a time for letting go and taking hold.
O Lord, you know us better than we know ourselves.
Help us to let go of the things that pass away,
that we might take hold of the things that endure.

+ + +

Loving God, there is nothing that can separate us from your providence
  or the love of Christ Jesus, your Son.
Seasons pass, times change, your care of us remains,
  transparent now and often in the strong, supportive love of friends.
With your tender mercy, visit us, to guide our feet in the way of peace.
Guard our lives, our going and coming, now and forever. Amen.

$\mathcal{W}$EEK OF
PRAYER FOR CHRISTIAN UNITY

The Week of Prayer for Christian Unity, initiated by the Anglican Graymore com-
munity, has become an ecumenical occasion for those of many church traditions to
gather in prayer for the unity of Christ's church. It takes place during the octave of
January 18–25.

How very good and pleasant it is when kindred live together in unity!
From one person God made all nations who live on earth.

So then you are no longer strangers and aliens, but you are citizens with the saints and also members of the household of God,
In God we live and move and have our being.

For Christ is our peace; in his flesh he has made both groups into one and has broken down the dividing wall, that is, the hostility between us.
I looked, and there was a great multitude from every nation, from all tribes and peoples and languages, robed in white, with palm branches in their hands, singing,

"Blessing and glory and wisdom and thanksgiving and honor and power and might be to our God forever and ever! Amen."

+ + +

God of love and unity, we come to you now to pray for your church, the body of Christ on earth. Forgive us for the sin of disunity: forgive us for the times when we have allowed personal preferences to become more important than Christ's message of love and salvation; forgive us for the times when we have been intolerant and overcritical of one another—forgive us for our judgmental attitudes. Forgive us for wounding Christ's body again and again and causing you grief.

Lord, we ask you to cleanse us and lead us into the full light of your Holy Spirit, so that we may cast aside distrust and truly embrace all our sisters and brothers. Fill our hearts with your love so that we shall be ready to accept any difference and learn from each other with meekness and humility. Let every decision and action to be fruit of our shared love for you; let this love be paramount in every cherished hope or plan. Grant us the grace and courage to worship in unity beneath your canopy of love and peace. Father, make us one, for our dear Lord's sake. Amen.

+ + +

O God, you are the giver of life.
    We pray for the church in the whole world.
Sanctify its life, renew its worship,
    give power to its witnessing, restore its unity.
Give strength to those who are searching together
    for that kind of obedience which creates unity.
Heal the divisions separating your children one from another.
    so that they will make fast with bonds of peace,
    the unity which the Spirit gives. Amen.

+ + +

We grieve that the church
    which shares one Spirit, one faith, one hope,
    and spans all time, place, race, and language
    has become a broken communion in a broken world.

When we struggle for the purity of the church
and for the righteousness God demands,
we pray for saintly courage.
When our pride or blindness blocks the unity of God's household,
we seek forgiveness.
We marvel that the Lord gathers the broken pieces to do his work,
and that he blesses us still with joy, new members,
and surprising evidences of unity.
We commit ourselves to seeking and expressing
the oneness of all who follow Jesus.

+ + +

We pray, O God, for a deeper understanding of Christ's union with his church, and his will for it, and for the renewing action of your Holy Spirit so that your church may become one. Uniting Spirit,
Graciously, hear our prayer.

We pray for a growing awareness of the scandal of Christian divisions among the different churches. Uniting Spirit,
Graciously, hear our prayer.

We pray for the awakening of a desire of Christians in this land to meet together, to work and witness and worship together. Uniting Spirit,
Graciously, hear our prayer.

We pray for a better cooperation among all branches of Christ's church, so that the oneness of your holy, catholic, and apostolic church in which we believe and to which we belong may become manifest. Uniting Spirit,
Graciously, hear our prayer.

We pray for all who are seeking church union in this land: that they may grow into such unity, worship, and mission as will please you through Christ, the head of the church. Uniting Spirit,
Graciously, hear our prayer.

We pray for the work done by the World Council of Churches, the National Council of Churches, and all communities of churches: that they may assist Christians to unite together in mission and service in a fuller expression of what it means to be the church. Uniting Spirit,
Graciously, hear our prayer.

We pray for the ecumenical movement and for all who suffer, pray, and work in the cause of unity: that all these efforts may bear good fruits to the honor and glory of your most holy name. Uniting Spirit,
Graciously, hear our prayer.

We pray for your Spirit of truth and love to guide those who are working toward Christian unity, and for more earnest and faithful prayer for unity. Uniting Spirit,
Graciously, hear our prayer.

+ + +

Creating God, from the waters of chaos
    you brought forth order in the unity of creation.
Giving God, in every time you send messengers
    to call your people back to you.
Listening God, in the fullness of time,
    you sent us Jesus, the Christ,
        who lived out the artistry of your love
        and prayed to you that all his followers might be one.
    Forgive us for our divisive ways,
        the separate lives we lead in Christ's church,
        the judgments and suspicions we harbor
        about those whose faith expressions are different from our own.
    Forgive us for the violence we do to our sisters and brothers in Christ,
        for the lines of oppression we draw against those not like us.
Brooding God, move restlessly among us
    as you breathed on the primordial waters.
    Call us out from the depths of our chaotic differences.
    Stir in us a passion for unity.
Embracing God, gather your people from all the divisions we create.
    Help us find our common roots of faith.
    Teach us to celebrate the richness of diversity.
Loving God, hear us, heal us of our divisions.
    Make us truly one as Jesus prayed. Amen.

+ + +

The unity of the church is a gift of God in Jesus Christ,
    to be made visible before the world.
Diverse as the people of God are by reasons of race, sex,
    physical or mental condition,
    nationality, tongue, politics, vocation, or religious heritage,
we belong to one another,
    by our creation in the image of God
    and by baptism into the one body of Christ.
Just as Christ is one and undivided,
    so it is essential that the church be one. Alleluia!

OWEEK OF COMPASSION

A Week of Compassion offering is received in the congregations of the Christian Church (Disciples of Christ) on the third and fourth Sunday in February. The offering, which is part of One Great Hour of Sharing, funds the alleviation of suffering throughout the world.

Compassionate God, your Christ wept for the people
　　because of the hardness of their hearts.
Warm our hearts with your love,
　　so that we might care deeply for the people of our nation and world.
Transform our caring into bread for the hungry, healing for the sick,
　　and hope for those who hunger and thirst after justice,
　　　　to the glory of your name. Amen.

+ + +

Gracious God, you have given your Son for us all,
　　that his death might be our life and his affliction our peace.
We pray for the suffering:
　　the hungry;
　　the refugees;
　　the prisoners;
　　the persecuted;
　　agents of sin and suffering;
　　ministries of care and relief.

We give thanks for the cross of Christ at the heart of creation;
　　the presence of Christ in our weakness and strength;
　　the power of Christ to transform our suffering;

for all ministries of healing;
　　all agencies of relief;
　　all that sets humanity free from pain, fear, and distress.

for the assurance that your mercy knows no limit;
　　the privilege of sharing your work of renewal through prayer.

In darkness and in light, in trouble and in joy,
help us to trust your love,
　　to serve your purpose,
　　to praise your name;
　　through Jesus Christ our Lord. Amen.

+ + +

RESPONSE:　　**Lift every voice and sing, till earth and heaven ring.**
　　　　　　Let them resound loud as the rolling sea. (*CH* p. 755)

O God, just as the disciples heard Christ's words of promise
    and began to eat the bread and drink the wine
    in the suffering of a long remembrance and in the joy of a hope,
grant that we may hear your words,
spoken in each thing of everyday affairs:
    coffee, on our table in the morning;
    the simple gesture of opening a door to go out, free;
    the shouts of children in the parks;
    a familiar song, sung by an unfamiliar face;
    a friendly tree that has not yet been cut down.   **R**

May simple things speak to us of your mercy,
    and tell us that life can be good.
And may these sacramental gifts make us remember
those who do not receive them:
    who have their lives cut every day,
        in the bread absent from the table;
    in the door of the hospital, the prison, the welfare home
        that does not open;
    in sad children, feet without shoes, eyes without hope;
    in war hymns that glorify death;
    in deserts where once there was life.   **R**

Christ was also sacrificed; and may we learn
    that we participate in the saving sacrifice of Christ
    when we participate in the suffering of his little ones. Amen.

CELEBRATIONS HONORING SCOUTING

These are materials that may be adapted for use to give special recognition to community youth organizations.

O God, your will is that all your children
    should grow into fullness of life.
We lift to you the ministry of scouting.
We offer you thanks for camping,
    to teach us that the world is our great home;
    for study and work, to build character;
    for service, to see our responsibility to those in need;
    for encouragement in genuine patriotism and vital faith.
Bless the work of scouting, in this place and around the world,
    that, through its efforts, the young may, like our Lord,
    increase in wisdom and in stature,
    and in favor with you and all people. Amen.

STEWARDSHIP SUNDAY

Stewardship Sunday may be observed any time in the year and is often related to the making of financial commitments undergirding the work of the church.

O God, Creator of us all,
>everything we are and everything we have is really yours,
>but placed in our care for a while.
So now we make this offering,
>as a sign of our admission that we are yours,
>and that we are only in this world to fulfill your purposes.
We lay before you our bodies,
>that they may be living sacrifices,
>instruments ready for your to use in working out your plan.
We lay before you our minds,
>seeking that we may learn to think in harmony with your thoughts,
>so that we may do your will with understanding.
We lay before you our money, our homes, our possessions,
>that they may find their rightful use in your service
>and that we may be saved from soul-destroying selfishness.
We lay before you the whole life of this congregation,
>that your life-creating power may reach out through us,
>putting new life into a dying world.
We thank you that all over the world
>men and women like ourselves are offering themselves to you
>and we pray that we may all receive new power
>to teach humankind the right use of the world's resources.

+ + +

This litany can be offered as a responsive action between the choir singing and the congregation responding, or with the congregation singing as one or more worship leaders read the words of the prayer. The hymn (in bold print) is found in CH 606.

God, whose giving knows no ending,
>**from your rich and endless store,**
Giving God, we struggle to imagine even in part
>the vastness of your love.
We live in a finite world, limited by our senses,
>bound by our constant fears of "not enough,"
>and yet we are well rehearsed in the strains of your passion's song.

Nature's wonder, Jesus' wisdom,
>**costly grace, grave's shattered door:**

Your world itself calls us to mindfulness of your unstinting care.
You lavish beauty upon beauty on all your creation.

To every generation, you have offered the waters of your Life Abundant
    to slake our thirst, if we will but drink.

Gifted by you, we turn to you,
    offering up ourselves in praise;

Warmed to action by the love-light of your infinite generosity,
    we bring these our earthly gifts to you.
Bless them, multiply them, that they might fund
    miracles of hope and reconciliation in Christ's name.
Open our hearts, as we open our hands,
    so we can truly offer you the fullness of who we are
    as readily as we give away the surplus of our means.
Fill us with your gracious Spirit, that we can give
    graciously and gratefully of the resources you have entrusted to us.

Thankful song shall rise forever,
    gracious donor of our days.

Giving God, make of us willing and faithful stewards of all your gifts.
Grant us creativity, honesty, and integrity
    so we can best honor your sacred trust.
God, your giving knows no ending. Make us generous of heart,
    confident that our giving will ever find its rightful end in you.

The litany may be continued by singing the two remaining stanzas of the hymn.

 # *E*ARTH STEWARDSHIP SUNDAY

*Earth Stewardship Sunday is observed in many congregations on the Sunday fol-
lowing Earth Day, April 22. See CH 688–698 for hymns and other resources particularly relevant to this emphasis.*

"The earth is the Lord's and all that is in it."
    So we sing, and so we also acknowledge.
Yet we know, Lord, that while the earth is yours,
    you have appointed us stewards of your property.
Keep us faithful to our trust;
    and make us mindful of our responsibility
    both to conserve the earth's resources
    and to distribute its benefits justly and unselfishly,
    for the good of humankind, and for your great glory.

+ + +

Most provident God, you graciously give us all good gifts. Teach us to care for our earth: to till our soil responsibly, to keep our air pure, to free our waters from pollution, to harvest the warmth of our sun, and to respect the rights of all species. May we willingly share the gifts of your goodness with one another. We ask this of you, God of our universe. Amen.

+ + +

O God, the only source of life and energy and wealth,
    defend our planet Earth.
Teach us to conserve and not to squander the riches of nature,
    to use aright the heritage of former generations,
    and to plan for the welfare of our children's children.
Renew our wonder, awaken our concern,
    and make us better stewards and more careful tenants
    of the world you lend us as our home.
Hear us, O Lord, our Creator and Redeemer, in the name of Christ.

+ + +

Lord Jesus Christ,
through whom and for whom the whole universe was created,
    we mourn with you the death of forests,
    fruitful lands that have become deserts,
    wild animals left without grass,
    plants, insects, birds, and animals threatened with extinction,
    lands ravaged by war, people left homeless.
As the earth cries out for liberation,
    we confess our part in bringing it toward the brink of catastrophe.
Through ignorance, but often willfully,
    we thought we could serve God and mammon,
    unable to resist the temptation
    to spend and acquire more and more possessions,
    with little thought of the consequences for future generations.
Savior of the world, you call us to repentance:
    to be transformed by your love, deny ourselves,
    take up the cross and follow in your way.

+ + +

The words in bold may be sung by choir or congregation. They are from CH 58.

Many and great, O God, are thy things,
    Maker of earth and sky.

O God, we thank thee for this universe, our great home;
    for its vastness and riches, for the manifoldness of the life
    that teems upon it and of which we are a part.

Thy hands have set the heavens with stars;
    thy fingers spread the mountains and plains.

We praise thee for the arching sky and the blessed winds,
    for the driving clouds and the constellations on high.

**Lo, at thy word the waters were formed;
    deep seas obey thy voice.**

We praise thee for the salt sea and the running water,
    for the everlasting hills, for the trees,
    and for the grass under our feet.

**Grant unto us communion with thee,
    thou star-abiding one;**

We thank thee for our senses
    by which we can see the splendor of the morning,
    and hear the jubilant songs of love,
    and smell the breath of the springtime.

**Come unto us and dwell with us;
    with thee are found the gifts of life.**

Grant us, we pray thee, a heart wide open to all this joy and beauty,
    and save our souls from being so steeped in care
    or so darkened by passion that we pass heedless and unseeing
    when even the thornbush by the wayside
    is aflame with the glory of God.

**Bless us with life that has no end,
    eternal life with thee.**

Mother's Day is an annual celebration of mothers and motherhood observed the second Sunday in May.

The voicing for "Choir 1" and "Choir 2" in the following litany may be done in any manner of division that is appropriate for your worship setting.

LEADER: Let us now praise mothers,
    and all who are mothers of mothers.
In the name of Shaddai, our Mother,
    we call blessings upon your name.

ALL: **May mercy and peace accompany you
    and follow you all the way home.**

LEADER: For all mothers who bring to birth
    and contribute to God's creation:

CHOIR 1: For young mothers and old mothers,
  first-time mothers and experienced mothers,
  teenage mothers and Third World mothers,
  women who have contracted AIDS and are mothers.

CHOIR 2: For adoptive mothers and spiritual mothers,
  and all whose love is like that of mothers,
  all who give birth to ideas or music,
    artistic works or any creation
    that helps them think and feel like mothers,
    whose creativity brings to birth in others.

ALL: **May God's creativity accompany you
  and follow you all the way home.**

CHOIR 1: Impoverished mothers,
CHOIR 2: abandoned mothers,

CHOIR 1: mothers of suicides,
CHOIR 2: mothers of genocide,

CHOIR 1: mothers of anorexics,
CHOIR 2: mothers of the murdered,

CHOIR 1: mothers of victims of violent abuse,
CHOIR 2: mothers of crib death,

CHOIR 1: mothers of the dying,
CHOIR 2: mothers of the missing,

CHOIR 1: mothers of children slaughtered in war,
CHOIR 2: mothers of children slain in the streets,

CHOIR 1: mothers of kidnapped children,
CHOIR 2: mothers of children who are in prison,

CHOIR 1: mothers of children who are criminally insane,
CHOIR 2: mothers of children who ran away from home,

CHOIR 1: mothers whose children will never come home,
CHOIR 2: mothers whose home has never had children,

ALL: **May God's comfort accompany you
  and follow you all the way home.**

LEADER: For all mothers who reach out to other people,
  who nurture and feed the world.

CHOIR 1: For mothers in leadership positions:
  in public life, in business,
  in academic institutions, in the arts and communication,
  in religion, in the church;

CHOIR 2: For mothers who are behind the scenes:
at home with the family, in service jobs,
in voluntary organizations, in household industries,
in religion, in the church;

ALL: **May the Spirit of God empower you
and follow you all the way home.**

LEADER: May Shaddai, our Mother, bless all our mothers.
May their spirit inspire forever.

Unism

+ + +

O God of grace and love,
we thank you for all that you have given us
through the loving care and hard work of our mothers.— *mothers in family and spiritual mothers as well.*
We pray for your richest blessing upon all mothers:
for those with difficult homes,
whose children *feel* are more a problem than a blessing;
for those with no husband
or with husbands who find it hard to be constant and loving;
for those with loved ones far away
and those who are lonely;
for those who find it hard to make ends meet,
~~or who go short themselves for the sake of their families;~~
for those who are nearly at the end of their tether;
for those who are trying to make Christ real to their families;
for those who do not know ~~him as their Savior,~~
~~nor~~ how to cast their care on ~~him.~~ *God*
For each one according to her need, hear our prayer,
and draw all mothers closer to you today; *we pray*
through your Son, Jesus Christ, our Lord. Amen.

+ + +

call

o O God, the true Mother, as well as the Father, of all men and women,
m   from whom we come, to whose breast we turn at last,
o   we thank you this day for all good mothers
a   (and especially for our own).
For their care and patience and love in childhood's earliest days,
for the prayers they offered, the counsels they gave,
the example they set,
we bring you our praise; through Jesus Christ our Lord.

*C*HRISTIAN FAMILY WEEK

Christian Family Week is observed either the first or second Sunday in May for the purpose of strengthening family life.

O holy and loving God,
  your knowledge of each of us is infinite,
  and your love for each of us is boundless;
you place us within human families,
  and incorporate us into the beloved household of faith:
We yield ourselves to your providence and grace.
We rejoice that you have called us from our varying human backgrounds
  to be brothers and sisters together in faith and devotion.
We renew our commitments to each other,
  to mothers and fathers, to sisters and brothers,
  to neighbors and acquaintances,
through Jesus Christ, our Savior, elder brother, companion. Amen.

+ + +

God, father and mother of us all,
  we pray for families in their JOY.

Where parents are loving and children are lively;
  where home is comfortable and jobs are secure,
we pray that our joy may be hallowed by thanksgiving
  and our happiness increased by sharing it.
Amid the blessings you send, keep us mindful of you,
  the one who sends them.

Son of God, Savior of all, joy and sword for Mary's heart,
  we pray for families in their SORROW.

Where grief has come for a loved one, or where love is no more;
where jobs or home are lost or health has failed;
where neighbors or relatives make trouble and children are wayward;
where one or another is left coping with more than he or
  she bargained for, and nobody laughs or sings.
Lord Jesus, in our desert and our Gethsemane,
  give us your grace of strength and peace.

Holy Spirit of unity, wisdom, and love,
  we pray for families in their GROWING.

Reconcile us with the fact of change in one another and in ourselves.
Teach us that love need not be unaltering in order to be constant.
Strengthen our relationships by contradiction and temper,
  as well as by acquiescence and peace.

**Creator Spirit, help us grow toward mature humanity
measured by nothing less than the full stature of Christ.**

+ + +

God, our Mother,
    we call ourselves a family in Christ but we are still learning what that means. For some, our families are centers of abuse and pain. We would bring our fear, our distrust, our rage against violation to you but our ambivalence paralyzes our emotions. Some of us come from homes racked by catastrophic illnesses. We bring our exhaustion and frustration to you.

God, our Father,
    we call ourselves family but we are still learning what that means. We thank you for those who challenge policies that ignore the violence in our homes. We thank you for those who work with children, parents, and spouses who have been victimized by acts of rage. We thank you for those who become families to us by choice. Their gifts of depth, caring, and mutual respect are precious to us.

Loving God,
    hold close to your compassionate heart all those who know the loneliness of being without a family, all those who have lost loved ones to death, all those who lose their loved ones to indifference, all those who struggle daily to survive.

Help us reach deeply into ourselves to discover the unique gift we are. And help us find the way we can bring that gift as offering to our family. We pray in the name of Christ, who recognizes as sisters and brothers those who struggle to be faithful. Amen.

+ + +

Loving God, help us build our homes,
because if you are not with us our toil is useless;
help us protect our families,
because if you do not guard them we waste our efforts.
Help us in our work—our overworking, too, is useless,
because you can bless us equally when we are asleep!

The children you have given us,
they are a real blessing—our great happiness:
thank you, Lord. Amen.   (BASED ON PSALM 127)

+ + +

God of infinite love,
    help us to see each other and every human being through your eyes,
    and to reach out to one another with your tender concern.

In every aspect of our family life, let the love of Christ release us,
> lifting us above selfish fears, unworthy thoughts, unkind actions,
> so that our homes and bodies may be temples
> where we see the likeness of the appearance of your glory
> and are moved to thankfulness and praise.

# ✝ *ᏃᏋEMORIAL DAY/REMEMBRANCE*

Memorial Day is observed in the United States on or near May 30 for honoring persons who have died in the service of their country. The materials may be appropriate for any occasion of remembrance of those who have died.

We pray for all who suffer as a result of war:

For the injured and the disabled, for the mentally distressed, and for those whose faith in God and in other people has been weakened or destroyed, we lift our hearts to you:
O God of mercy, hear our prayer.

For the homeless and refugees, for those who are hungry, and for all who have lost their livelihood and security, we lift our hearts to you:
O God of mercy, hear our prayer.

For those who mourn their dead; for those who have lost husband, wife, children, or parents, and especially for those who have no hope in Christ to sustain them in their grief, we lift our hearts to you:
O God of mercy, hear our prayer.

Here follows a short silence, then:

O Lord, hear our prayer:
for the sake of our Savior, Jesus Christ. Amen.

+ + +

As we remember those who died in war for the cause of peace:
Lord, make us peacemakers.

As we look to the future of our children and grandchildren:
Lord, make us peacemakers.

As we think of the war-torn, blood-stained, sorrowful world:
Lord, make us peacemakers.

Lord, hear our prayer
and come to us in perfect love, to drive away our fear;
in the name of the Prince of Peace, Jesus Christ our Lord. Amen.

+ + +

Memories are joyful and painful, but we cannot live without them.
Let us pray that we may never forget.

For leaders who send young men and women to war,
that their judgments be sound
and their motives be pure, we pray.

For soldiers who lay down their lives for others,
that the love which inspires their sacrifice
be fulfilled in the love of Christ, we pray.

For soldiers who have been maimed or brutalized by war,
that our love for them may make their scars less hurtful
and make their brutality yield to the tenderness of returning love,
we pray.

For those who have been left behind,
that they may live on the strength of the love that they knew,
we pray.

For those who suffer most from war,
that the homeless, the orphaned, the hungry, and the innocent
may help us turn from warlike ways to pursue the potential of peace,
we pray.

God of Peace, help us never to forget that war is hell.
Help us to honor its saints, and to pray for its sinners and victims,
through the Victim for our sakes, Christ Jesus, our Lord.

*Father's Day is an annual day of commemoration of fathers and fatherhood ob-
served on the third Sunday in June.*

Silent prayers may follow each petition.

For our fathers, who have given us life and love,
    that we may show them respect and love,
we pray to the Lord...

For fathers who have lost a child through death,
    that their faith may give them hope,
    and their family and friends support and console them,
we pray to the Lord...

For men, though without children of their own,
who like fathers have nurtured and cared for us,
we pray to the Lord…

For fathers, who have been unable to be a source of strength,
who have not responded to their children
and have not sustained their families,
we pray to the Lord…

God our Father, in your wisdom and love you made all things.
Bless these men, that they may be strengthened as Christian fathers.
Let the example of their faith and love shine forth.
Grant that we, their sons and daughters,
may honor them always with a spirit of profound respect.
Grant this through Christ our Lord. Amen.

*N*ATIONAL OBSERVANCE

These materials are suitable for the observance of United States Independence Day or any occasions relating to the nation.

Let the peoples praise you, O God;
let all the peoples praise you.
Let the nations be glad and sing for joy,
for you judge the peoples with equity
and guide the nations upon earth.   (PSALM 67:3–4)

+ + +

Praise the LORD, all nations;
All peoples, glorify God,
Whose grace, like a wave, surges over us,
Whose faithfulness lasts for all time.
Praise the LORD!   (PSALM 117, CHAMBERLAIN)

+ + +

Almighty God, giver of all good things:
We thank you for the natural majesty and beauty of this land.
They restore us, though we often destroy them.
Heal us.

We thank you for the great resources of this nation. They make us rich though we often exploit them.
Forgive us.

We thank you for the men and women who have made this country strong. They are models for us, though we often fall short of them.
Inspire us.

We thank you for the torch of liberty that has been lit in this land. It has drawn people from every nation, though we have often hidden from its light.
Enlighten us.

We thank you for the faith we have inherited in all its rich variety. It sustains our life, though we have been faithless again and again.
Renew us.

Help us, O Lord, to finish the good work here begun. Strengthen our efforts to blot out ignorance and prejudice, and to abolish poverty and crime. And hasten the day when all people, with many voices in one united chorus, will glorify your holy Name.
Amen.

+ + +

O Judge of the nations, we remember before you with grateful hearts the men and women of our country who in the day of decision ventured much for the liberties we now enjoy. Grant that we may not rest until all the people of this land share the benefits of true freedom and gladly accept its disciplines. This we ask in the name of Jesus Christ our Lord. Amen.

+ + +

We have come to sing,
    rejoicing in the good that walks this land by day.
We have come to be silent,
    repenting of the evil that stalks it by night.
We have come to this place because here we are reminded
    that you are both our creator and our conscience.
Here all of our loyalties are put in their proper place,
    ordered behind our allegiance to you.
Be with us in our celebration and our confession,
    that our citizenship might become more responsible,
    our nation more humble, and our world more dependable.

+ + +

We pray for this nation in which you have set us,
    for its men and women of government,
    for the leaders of commerce and of industry,
    for those who through newspapers and television lead in thought.
Human cleverness alone cannot heal our nation's sickness,
    treaties and armaments cannot safeguard our real interests,
    more luxuries and leisure cannot meet our deepest needs.

O may your Living Word speak afresh to our people.
Raise up men and women who can speak words of insight and integrity,
    that new life may inspire us and set us right.
O Prince of Peace, despised and rejected by the wise ones of this world,
    we pray for this world,
        that the people who grope in the darkness may see a great light,
        the light of your love for every human being.

+ + +

You gather us together in faith, O God, as a loving mother and a gentle father. Help us to remember that your dwelling place is built upon love and peace, and that to bring about your reign on earth we must follow your way of peace. We pray for all governments and legislatures that they may be mindful of the rights of all peoples of this world to live in peace and dignity. Grant this in the name of Jesus. Amen.

+ + +

Come, Lord God, and rule the world:
    all the nations are yours.
Let laws be just, let justice be impartial,
    let the rights of the poor and of children be defended,
    help us to rescue the innocent from the power of those who do evil;
        let the ignorant be taught,
        let corruption be purged,
        let righteousness prevail.
Come, Lord God, and rule the world:
    all the nations are yours.   (BASED ON PSALM 82)

Labor Day is observed in the United States and Canada on or near the first Monday in September in honor of workers.

Bring yourselves before the Lord!
We offer our faithful works, our loving labors
    and our constant hopes to the glory of God.

Bring yourselves before the Lord!
We await the gospel, in word and in power,
    in the Holy Spirit and in full conviction!

+ + +

We praise you, O God, that you dwell within this sheltering home of faith we call the church. We gather around to feed on your word and to sup at your table. Nurture us in ways that strengthen us to go forth to work for the good of all. We pray in the name of Christ who to the end did the work you gave him to do. Amen.

+ + +

May the Lord give us peace in our work.

God, send us into our work with new resolves.
Help us to work out the problems that have perplexed us,
    and to serve the people we meet.
May we see our work as part of your great plan
    and find significance in what we do.
We do not know what any day will bring us,
    but we do know the hour for serving you is always present.
We dedicate our hearts, minds, and wills to your glory,
    through Jesus Christ our Lord. Amen.

+ + +

God of the rough-worn hands, as we honor workers this day,
    let us not forget all those whose work is without honor:

    those homemakers who watch over children and homes
        but are not recognized as workers because they are not paid;
    those who are forced out of jobs by corporate changes,
        those forced into early retirement,
        those who are denied employment because of their age;
    those who live far from home,
        struggling to save a bit of money to send to their loved ones;
    those who must work illegally in order to survive;
    those who lose jobs because employers use undocumented labor.

Christ of the aching back, you worked the rough wood,
    you walked the long and dusty roads,
    you know the bitter thirst of the poor.
Let our thirst become a passion for justice.
Help us to work toward transformation of economic policies
    that allow only a few nations to hoard the world's wealth,
    policies that pay women as only half a person or less,
    policies that do not recognize the worth of labor exacted without pay.

Spirit of creative power, move among us this day.
Heal the wounds we carry because of jobs we hate but must do,
    jobs we want but cannot have.
Heal all those who labor to survive.
Renew in us our sense of vocation.
Help us discern your Presence in even the lowliest tasks we face. Amen.

The Reconciliation program was established by the Disciples in 1967. The mission of Reconciliation is to address the basic causes of racism and poverty. A special offering is received by congregations on the last Sunday in September or the first Sunday in October.

Gracious God, you show us the meaning of reconciliation
   in the life of Jesus Christ.
In his touch, his words, his actions,
   Jesus reconciled people to God and to the community.
We gather to renew ourselves that we too might reconcile others
   with a touch, a word, or an act.

We sing your praise, O God,
   we proclaim your power to reconcile,
   we pray for your realm to break in on our lives!

+ + +

Our God, we are one in solidarity
   with those who live in danger and struggle.
   Whether near or far, we share their anguish and their hope.
Teach us to extend our lives beyond ourselves
   and to reach out in sympathy to the frontiers
   where people are suffering and changing the world.
Make us one in solidarity with the aliens we ignore,
   the deprived we pretend do not exist, the prisoners we avoid.
God, let solidarity be a new contemporary word for this community
   into which you are constantly summoning us.
But, God, may our solidarity be genuine,
   and not a dishonest maneuver.
May our solidarity be effective,
   and not just consist of wordy declarations.
May our solidarity be grounded in hope,
   and not in the tragedy of disaster.
May our solidarity be in humility,
   because we cannot bear all the world's troubles.
God, purify us in our solidarity with others;
   may it be genuine, fruitful, fervent, and humble.
We ask it in the name of him
   who was resolutely one in solidarity
   with abandoned, despised humankind,
   Jesus Christ, your son, our brother. Amen.

WORLD COMMUNION SUNDAY

World Communion Sunday seeks to enhance the oneness of the church through an awareness of all Christians on that day being seated about Christ's one table within their separate communities. It is observed the first Sunday in October.

We gladly join with fellow Christians everywhere to affirm both the freedom of our particular customs and the spiritual kinship that we feel with all who love the Lord Jesus Christ.

How very good and pleasant it is when kindred live together in unity!

(PSALM 133:1)

Grant us, O God, to seek your understanding, and to approach the measure of your love.

There is one body and one Spirit, just as you were called to the one hope of your calling, one Lord, one faith, one baptism, one God and Father of all, who is above all and through all and in all.   (EPHESIANS 4:4–6)

Help us to acknowledge your Lordship in all our ways, O God, and to put our trust in your steadfast love.

Now there are varieties of gifts, but the same Spirit; and there are varieties of services, but the same Lord; and there are varieties of activities, but it is the same God who activates all of them in everyone.   (1 CORINTHIANS 12:4–6)

Within the world fellowship of Christ's people, teach us to respect all forms and practices, and to put devotion to your Sovereignty above all creeds and structures.

Let us hear again the words of our Lord Jesus Christ, who spread to all his disciples the love he had received from the Father, and who commanded us that we should continue in God's love, entering with the heart into the joys and sorrows of one another.

Grant unto us—men and women of many traditions and many names, of diverse places and successive generations—to realize our unity with the one, holy, catholic, and apostolic church of Jesus Christ. As communions with cherished memories we also look beyond to the risen Christ as our common ground, that in him we may accord to each other the fullest possible recognition.

Remember that you are called to be a spiritual household in the midst of the world, that walking together in love you may be renewed in mind and heart to do God's will.

On this Sunday of World Communion, we pray for all the members of your universal church, that your people may be bound together by spiritual ties, and labor together for the coming of your reign.

With all lowliness and humility, with long-suffering and mutual forbearance, let us endeavor to build up the body of Christ,

Until all of us come to the unity of the faith and of the knowledge of the Son of God, to maturity, to the measure of the full stature of Christ.

(EPHESIANS 4:13)

+ + +

Sung response: CH 387

We praise you, Nurturing God, for feeding us at Christ's table here and all the world around. Patiently you plant the seeds of faith, waiting to harvest the fruits of our lives. Busily you grind the grains of our experience, mixing the dough. Quietly, restlessly you yeast Christ's church to life.

Bread of the world, in mercy broken,

We thank you, Nourishing God, for the strength we draw from the shared witness of our sisters and brothers who partake of this holy meal today. Make us bold to seek justice, and quick to act in compassion. Shape us well that we might become the Bread of Life to those who need us.

wine of the soul, in mercy shed,

We rejoice in you, Surprising God, for your abiding presence. Spark our imaginations that we might share your dream of unity. Open our hearts so Christ's healing love may flow from your gathered church into a parched, thirsty world.

and be thy feast to us the token,

We pray to you, Healing God, that your people find sustenance at Christ's table this day. Feed our spirits that we might work together as the body of Christ around the world: preaching good news to captives, restoring health to those in pain, proclaiming God's year of Jubilee!

that by thy grace our souls are fed.

ALL SAINTS DAY

All Saints Day is a church festival in honor of all saintly persons observed on November 1 or the preceding Sunday.

Love the LORD, all God's saints.
Be strong, and let your heart take courage,
   all you who wait for the LORD.   (PSALM 31:23–24, ALT.)

+ + +

Rejoice in the Lord, you righteous.
Sing for joy, all upright hearts.
Heaven, blaze in gladness;
All saints, apostles, prophets.

+ + +

Since we are surrounded by so great a cloud of witnesses,
   let us also lay aside every weight and the sin that clings so closely,
   and let us run with perseverance the race that is set before us,
   looking to Jesus the pioneer and perfecter of our faith.
God calls us to be saints, together with all those
   who in every place call on the name of our Lord Jesus Christ.

In the company of all the saints we cry:
Praise God! Salvation, glory, and power belong to our God!

+ + +

We give thanks to you, O Lord our God,
for all your servants and witnesses of time past:
   for Abraham, the father of believers, and for Sarah, his wife;
   for Moses, the lawgiver, and Aaron, the priest;
   for Miriam and Joshua, Deborah and Gideon;
   for Samuel and Hannah, his mother;
   for Isaiah and all the prophets;
   for Mary, the mother of our Lord;
   for Peter and Paul and all the apostles,
   for Mary, Martha, and Mary Magdalene;
   for Stephen, the first martyr,
   and all the saints and martyrs in every time and in every land.
In your mercy, give us, as you gave them,
   the hope of salvation and the promise of eternal life;
   through the firstborn from the dead, Jesus Christ our Lord.

+ + +

Sung response: CH 67

The souls of the righteous are in the hand of God
    and no torment will ever touch them.
In the eyes of the foolish they seem to have died,
    and their departure was thought to be a disaster,
and their going from us to be their destruction;
    but they are at peace.
For though in the sight of others they were punished,
    their hope is full of immortality.

O God, our help in ages past, our hope for years to come,
our shelter from the stormy blast, and our eternal home!

Having been disciplined a little, they will receive great good,
    because God tested them and found them worthy;
like gold in the furnace God tried them,
    and like a sacrificial burnt offering God accepted them.
In the time of their visitation they will shine forth,
    and will run like sparks through the stubble.
They will govern nations and rule over peoples,
    and the Lord will reign over them for ever.
Those who trust in God will understand truth,
    and the faithful will abide in love,
because grace and mercy are upon the elect,
    and God watches over the holy ones.

O God, our help in ages past, our hope for years to come,
our shelter from the stormy blast, and our eternal home!

(WISDOM OF SOLOMON 3:1–9, ALT.)

+ + +

Eternal God, make us this day to remember
the unseen cloud of witnesses who compass us about:
    those who in every age and generation
        witnessed to their faith in life and in death;
    those who by their courage and their sacrifice
        won for us the freedom and the liberty we enjoy.
    those who served their sisters and brothers
        at the cost of pain, of persecution and of death;
    those for whom all the trumpets sounded
        as they passed over to the other side;
    those whom we have loved and who have gone to be with you,
        and whose names are written on our hearts.

Help us to walk worthily of those
in whose unseen presence life is lived.
Help us to have in our lives
their courage in danger;
their steadfastness in trial;
their perseverance in difficulty;
their loyalty when loyalty is costly;
the love which nothing can change;
their joy which nothing can take away.

So grant to us in your good time to share with them the blessedness
of your nearer presence, that we also may come to that life,
where all the questions are answered;
where all the tears are wiped away;
where all shall meet again, never to be separated from them,
those whom we have loved and lost awhile;
where we shall be forever with our Lord.

So grant to us in this life never to forget those who have gone before,
so that in the life to come we may share their blessedness;
through Jesus Christ our Lord. Amen.

+ + +

May God, who has given us, in the lives of saints, patterns of holy living
and victorious dying, strengthen your faith and devotion, and enable you
to bear witness to the truth against all adversity. Amen.

*Thanksgiving Day is a national holiday set apart for giving thanks to God. It is
celebrated in the United States on the fourth Thursday of November and in Canada
on the second Monday of October.*

O give thanks to God, for God is good;
God's steadfast love endures forever.
Let them give thanks for God's steadfast love,
for God's wonderful works to humankind.
For God satisfies the thirsty,
and fills the hungry with good things.
Let the peoples praise you, O God;
let all the peoples praise you.

The earth has yielded its produce;
    God, our God, has blessed us.
God provides food for all living creatures,
    for God's faithful love endures forever.
Give thanks to the God of heaven,
    for God's faithful love endures forever.

+ + +

Let us gather together in thanksgiving to God.
For God has made us and this earth which gives us nurture.
Let us gather together in gratitude to one another.
For we are the bearers of God's blessing and love
    for the earth and to all people.
Let us praise God; let us join hands;
    let us reach out in care and courage
    so that the goodness of life may be for all God's children. Amen.

+ + +

O God, as our Father you have lavished on us gifts of life abundant.
But we must confess that we have often used your gifts carelessly,
    and acted as though we were not grateful.
When we enjoy the fruits of the harvest, but forget they come from you,
    then in your fatherly mercy,
Forgive us and help us.

When we are full and satisfied,
    but ignore the cry of the hungry and those in need,
when we are thoughtless, and do not treat with respect or care
    the wonderful world you have made,
    God as our Mother have mercy on us,
Forgive us and help us.

When we store up goods for ourselves alone,
    as if there were no God and no heaven, God in your mercy,
Forgive us and help us.

Grant us thankful hearts and a loving concern for all people;
through Jesus Christ our Lord. Amen.

+ + +

Let us give thanks for all God's gifts so freely bestowed upon us:

For the beauty and wonder of your creation, in earth and sky and sea;
For all that is gracious in the lives of men and women,
    revealing the image of Christ;

For our daily food and drink, our homes and families, and our friends;
For minds to think, and hearts to love, and hands to serve;

For health and strength to work, and leisure to rest and play;
For the brave and courageous,
>   **who are patient in suffering and faithful in adversity;**

For all valiant seekers after truth, liberty, and justice;
For the communion of saints, in all times and places.

Above all, we give you thanks for the great mercies and promises
>   given to us in Christ Jesus our Lord.
To him be praise and glory, with you, O Father, and the Holy Spirit,
now and forever. Amen.

+ + +

Sung response: CH 716

O God, we give you thanks for all that you have done for us:
>   that you have created us, and have given us the gift of life
>> and set us to live in this fair earth;
>   that you have given us work to do, and the strength to do it;
>   that you have kept us all our days,
>> and have brought us in safety to this present hour:
Now thank we all our God with heart and hands and voices.

We give you thanks for all that others have done for us.
>   for those who taught us when we were children;
>   for those who in the days of youth gave us the guidance which
>> kept us from going astray;
>   for those who to this day love us and surround us with their care;
>   for those who pray for us, and who bear us to the throne of grace:
Now thank we all our God with heart and hands and voices.

We give you thanks for the gift of your Holy Spirit:
>   for your Spirit to remind us of the words of Jesus,
>> when we are in danger of forgetting them;
>   for your Spirit to lead us into new knowledge and new truth;
>   for your Spirit to tell us what we must do and what we must say;
>   for your Spirit to inspire us with strength and courage
>> for life and for living:
Now thank we all our God with heart and hands and voices.

We give you thanks for all that your church has done for us:
>   for all the teaching we have receive within the church;
>   for strength and guidance each week for life's way;
>   for the friendship and the fellowship which we here enjoy;
>   for the sacraments of your grace, and the prayers of your people:
Now thank we all our God with heart and hands and voices.

We give you thanks for all that you have done for us in Jesus Christ.
　　that in him you have shown us the length and breadth
　　　　and depth and height of your great love for us;
　　that in him you have opened to us
　　　　a new and living way into your presence;
　　that in him you have given us forgiveness of sins and peace with you:
Now thank we all our God with heart and hands and voices.

We give you thanks for everything which has given us
　　strength for earth and hope for heaven.
Accept this our sacrifice of praise for your love's sake.
Now thank we all our God with heart and hands and voices.

National Bible Week is observed the fourth week in November to recognize the importance of the Bible within the Christian community. Sometimes this emphasis is related to the observance of the second Sunday in Advent.

Almighty and most merciful God, you have given the Bible to be the revelation of your great love to us, and of your power and will to save us: grant that our study of it may not be made in vain by the callousness or carelessness of our hearts, but that by it we may be confirmed in penitence, lifted to hope, made strong for service, and above all, filled with the true knowledge of yourself and of your Son Jesus Christ.

+ + +

Lord, grant us this blessedness of your own promise.
Give us ears to hear, eyes to see, and a heart to understand,
　　by diligent reading of the Scriptures,
　　in the holy offices of your church,
　　in private prayer,
　　to hear, mark, learn, inwardly digest, and thoroughly obey:
Blessed are they who hear the Word of God and keep it.

To hear your Word, by the kindling of the Holy Spirit,
　　in the seeking, reasoning mind,
　　in the hungering, thirsting heart,
　　in the womb of the soul:
Blessed are they who hear the Word of God and keep it.

To hear, O Lord, your Word;
 not the new, but the true;
 not the partial, but the full;
 the final and the eternal:
Blessed are they who hear the Word of God and keep it.

To hear it, O Lord,
 and with all your saints and servants
 not only hear, but keep;
 and bring forth fruit—
 thirty, sixty, a hundredfold.
Blessed are they who hear the Word of God and keep it.

+ + +

Thank you, Lord, for the Bible: for its ability to give us each day new vision and new power; for its capacity to reach to the roots of our inner life and to refresh them; for its power to enter into the innermost structures of mind and spirit and fashion them anew. For the Bible, and its power to beget faith and to sustain it, we give you thanks and praise; through Jesus Christ our Savior. Amen.

$\mathcal{A}$IDS SUNDAY

This day may be observed on a Sunday close to December 1, which is recognized as International AIDS Day.

Gracious God, you are merciful and loving,
 Hear our prayers on behalf of all who suffer with AIDS:

For all who live in fear of the disease,
 grant them peace in their hearts,
 wisdom in the choices they make,
 and courage to face the days ahead.

The congregation may offer petitions for persons for whom prayers are desired.

For all who live with the disease of AIDS,
 grant them the gift of your love,
 hope for their future,
 friends to comfort and sustain them,
 the will to live,

**and faith that resurrection is a promise for now
as well as for eternal life.**

The congregation may offer petitions for persons for whom prayers are desired.

For all who minister to the needs of persons with AIDS,
**grant them compassionate hearts,
tenderness and patience in their daily tasks,
and dedication in their ministry to all who suffer.**

The congregation may offer petitions for persons for whom prayers are desired.

For all whose loved ones are affected by AIDS.
**grant them hope each day,
an awareness that love is forever binding,
the knowledge that Christ shares their suffering.**

The congregation may offer petitions for persons for whom prayers are desired.

For all who have died of AIDS,
**grant them rest eternal;
may light perpetual shine upon them,
may we always remember them in our hearts.**

The congregation may offer petitions for persons for whom prayers are desired.

O God of love, whose mercy has always included
those whom we have forgotten,
those whom we have isolated, and those who suffer:
bless, we beseech you, all who are afflicted with AIDS.
Comfort them in their pain,
sustain them by your Holy Spirit in their days of hopelessness
that they may engage in living.
Receive them into the arms of your mercy in their dying.
Open our hearts to provide for their needs,
to take away their isolation,
to share their journey of suffering and sorrow as well as hope and joy,
and to be present with them in their dying,
that no one need suffer or die alone.
Strengthen all who care for those who are ill,
that their service may be filled with
the tenderness of your compassion and the fullness of your love,
that their words and deeds may make your presence
a living reality for those whom they serve.
Bless those who mourn the death of their friends and lovers,
that they may not be overwhelmed by death
but may receive comfort and strength to meet the days ahead
with trust and hope in your goodness and mercy.
In Jesus' name we pray. **Amen.**

PEACE/SHALOM SUNDAY

This day is observed in the Christian Church (Disciples of Christ) on the first or second Sunday in December, during Advent.

We remember all who are held hostage
 by people bearing arms or by history;
 by politics based on a balance of terror,
 by their own fears and prejudices.
We remember families who are separated
 and people who are exiled from the land of their birth
 by frontiers, by barbed wire,
 by division in the minds of men and women.
We remember places long held as holy by people of different faiths
 which have become territory to be fought over,
 their names meaning suffering—modern Golgothas.
We pray for redemption—
 for prisoners, for victims of injustice,
 for our common humanity.

+ + +

Come, behold the works of God,
 who has wrought desolations in the earth,
making wars cease to the end of the earth,
 breaking the bow, shattering the spear,
 and burning the chariots with fire!
"Be still, and know that I am God.
 I am exalted among the nations,
 I am exalted in the earth!"
The God of hosts is with us;
 the God of Jacob is our refuge.

(Psalm 46:8–11, I–L)

+ + +

Lord Jesus, in a dark hour you spoke of the gift of peace;
 we beg that gift for ourselves, that we may have
 the inner serenity that cannot be taken from us,
then we may be messengers of your peace to a strife-torn world.

Give peace in our time, Lord.
Help us to live in peace.

We pray for those who are fighting,
 injury, disfigurement, and death their constant companions,
 nerves and bodies strained beyond endurance,
 the streams of compassion drying up within them,
 their only goal the destruction of the 'enemy.'

Whatever the color of their skin—we pray for them.
Whatever the sound of their tongue—we pray for them.
Whatever the insignia they wear—we pray for them.

Give peace in our time, Lord.
Help us to live in peace.

We pray for all who have been broken in battle;
    for those who weep and those who cannot longer weep;
    for those who feel the anguish
        and for those who have lost the capacity to feel;
    for all prisoners—and all jailers;
    for those who exist in war-torn lands
        and for those who no longer have a homeland.

Give peace in our time, Lord.
Help us to live in peace.

We pray for all who stir up strife;
    for all who make a profit out of the misery of others;
    for all who are led into vice as they seek a momentary forgetfulness;
    for all who believe that war is inevitable.

Give peace in our time, Lord.
Help us to live in peace.

The desire to press self-interest is deeply rooted in us.
We defend our attitudes when we should be ashamed of them.
We compare the noblest aspects of our own cause
    with the basest of that of our opponents.
We are reluctant to admit that our own selfish desires
    could contribute to the miseries of others.

Give peace in our time, Lord.
Help us to live in peace.

We bring to you particular needs...
and we remember those who have died...

O Lord, support us all the day long of this troubled life,
    until the shadows lengthen, and the evening comes, and
    the busy world is hushed, the fever of life over, and our work done.
Then, Lord, in thy mercy grant us safe lodging, a holy rest,
    and peace at the last; through Jesus Christ our Lord.

Give peace in our time, Lord.
Help us to live in peace.

+ + +

Remember, O God, the peoples of the world divided into many nations
and tongues; deliver us from every evil that obstructs your saving purpose; and fulfill your promises of old to establish your realm of peace.

From the curse of war and all that begets it,
>   O **Lord, deliver us.**
From believing and speaking lies against other nations,
>   O **Lord, deliver us.**
From narrow loyalties and selfish isolation,
>   O **Lord, deliver us.**
From fear and distrust of other nations,
from all false pride, vainglory, and self-conceit,
>   O **Lord, deliver us.**
From the lust of the mighty for riches,
that drives peaceful peoples to slaughter,
>   O **Lord, deliver us.**
From putting our trust in the weapons of war,
and from want of faith in the power of justice and goodwill,
>   O **Lord, deliver us.**
From every thought, word, and deed that divides the human family
and separates us from the perfect realization of your love,
>   O **Lord, deliver us.**

+ + +

Let us pray for the world that is immeasurable,
>   a society of millions of people and newspapers full of news.

Let us pray for the smaller world around us:
>   for the people who belong to us, for the members of our families,
>   our friends and those who share our worries.

Let us pray for the leaders of governments
>   and those whose words and actions
>   will influence the situation in the world—
>>   that they may not tolerate injustice, seek refuge in violence,
>>   or make rash and ill-considered decisions
>>   about the future of other people.

Let us also pray for all who live in the shadow of world events,
>   for those who are seldom noticed:
>   the hungry, the poor, the broken, and unloved.

We beseech you, O God, send your Holy Spirit
>   to help us give a new face to this earth that is dear to us.
May we help create peace wherever people live.
Give us the wisdom to see where we can make a difference
>   in the great nuclear debate that goes on around us,
>   and grant us the courage to form our conscience in the image of Christ.
Let your Spirit have power over us
>   and put us on the path that leads to peace. Amen.

+ + +

Show forth your power, O Lord of the nations,
    and do a new thing among your people
    and establish justice, peace and true community.
Our hearts are heavy, our wounds are deep;
    do not wait, O Lord, but bring your healing
    before we can no longer forgive;
    before, consumed with hatred, we lose the ability to love.
When death had done its worst, you brought your Son to new life.
You revealed the power of your love and your victory over evil.
Break our bonds and set us all free
    that we may know that you are the Lord.

+ + +

God of power and of the poor:
We rejoice at the growing role of women in society;
    we confess that they are still oppressed,
    that with children they are still hardest hit by poverty.
We rejoice that in some communities human dignity is affirmed;
    but we confess that in many places people are persecuted
    in their search for basic rights; food, shelter, employment.
We rejoice that the churches are speaking out together
        against oppression;
    but we confess the role of our leaders
    in supporting oppressive governments.
We rejoice in the generous response of people of all faiths
        to the crises of hunger around the world;
    we are concerned that many people,
    throughout the world, are still hungry.

The date of this emphasis on the global mission of the church varies among those congregations that hold such an observance.

Give thanks to the Lord, call on God's name;
make God's deeds known in the world around.
Sing to the Lord, sing praise to God;
tell of the wonderful things God has done.
Glory in God's holy name;
let those who seek the Lord rejoice! Amen.

+ + +

We are one worldwide family in Christ. We give thanks for people in every generation who have shared this vision and responded to God's call to serve overseas, remembering especially pioneers who willingly faced dangers of travel, climate, disease, and persecution to fulfill their calling.
We thank you, O God, that we are one family in Christ.

Let us thank God for those who were missionaries in their own lands: for their courage in answering Christ's call and facing persecution by their own people.
We thank you, O God, that we are one family in Christ.

Let us praise God for the work of the world church today; for the development and growth of national church leadership.
We thank you, O God, that we are one family in Christ.

Let us thank God for our partnership in mission throughout the world; for those who go overseas and for those who come as missionaries to our land to enrich our faith.
We thank you, O God, that we are one family in Christ.

Heritage Sunday is a local observance to celebrate a congregation's connection with its past.

God, whom we gather to worship,
    is aware of the gifts of sacrifice and love
        that went into the building of this place of worship;
    recalls the hosts of persons
        who have ushered worshipers to their places,
        who have sung the gospel and lifted prayers in harmony,
        who have served as prophets in the pulpit,
        who have presided over baptisms, and
        who have served the sacred meal.
The Lord affirms that other persons have labored,
    and that we have entered into their labors.
Come, let us worship God, and to God let us pray.

+ + +

Lord God, we thank you for our heritage of faith:

For the vision of apostles and evangelists who brought it to us,
     gracious Lord,
we give you thanks and praise.

For the courage of martyrs and teachers who secured it for us,
     gracious Lord,
we give you thanks and praise.

For the devotion of preachers and pastors who proclaimed it to us,
     gracious Lord,
we give you thanks and praise.

For the love of families and friends who nourished it within us,
     gracious Lord,
we give you thanks and praise.

For the freedom to speak of it in the world about us,
and to share it with our neighbors,
     gracious Lord,
we give you thanks and praise.

For the resources & commitment to live it out in deeds of compassion & justice, Gracious Lord

Lord God, we thank you for our heritage of faith:
give us the will and the strength to pass it on to others
for the glory of your name; through Jesus Christ our Lord. Amen.

+ + +

We pray to you, our good and gracious God,
     as a people who cherish the memories that are ours,
     and who claim a common history as a sacred gift.
We ask you to renew your grace in us,
     that we might recognize your presence in our midst
     and hear the call of the gospel
     in the human needs that surround us.
Through the power of your compelling Spirit
     may we grow in courage,
     that our actions might reflect the love we profess.
We ask this in the name of your child, Jesus. Amen.

+ + +

Living God, we give you thanks
     for our fathers and mothers in the faith;
     those who have revealed to us your grace in Christ
     through their lives, preaching and in hymns.
Strengthen the fellowship of the church,
     and our sense of belonging to a worldwide family.

For a Church Anniversary

Lord, thank you for this building
    where we come for cleansing,
    where we gather round your table,
    where we sing aloud your praise,
    where we proclaim all you have done for us;
Lord, we love the house where you meet us,
    the place where your glory dwells:
    in the assembly of your people
    we stand and praise the Lord! Amen.

V

SPECIAL

Worship

OCCASIONS
IN THE LIFE OF
THE CHURCH

RECOGNITION OF THE GIFTS OF THE PEOPLE OF GOD

INSTALLATION OF A MINISTER

This service has been designed to be a complete service in itself. It may be adapted to a regular Lord's Day service by using only the Covenant of Installation.

INSTRUMENTAL VOLUNTARY

HYMN

CALL TO WORSHIP

Thank the LORD with all your heart,
    in the gathered assembly of God's people.
Mighty are the deeds of the LORD,
Great are the works of the LORD,
    studied by all who have pleasure in them.

Holy and awesome is God's name!
To worship the LORD is the highest wisdom;
    Those who do so know all that is good—
God's praises will last forever.   (PSALM 111:1–2, 9B–10, CHAMBERLAIN)

OPENING PRAYER

The following, or another suitable prayer, may be used.

Eternal God, help us to worship you in spirit and in truth;
        that our consciences may be quickened by your holiness,
        our minds nourished by your truth,
        our imaginations purified by your beauty,
        our hearts opened to your love,
        our wills surrendered to your purpose;
and may all this be gathered up in adoration
as we ascribe glory, praise, and honor to you alone,
through Jesus Christ our Lord. Amen.

GLORIA PATRI OR OTHER DOXOLOGICAL RESPONSE

STATEMENT OF PURPOSE

READING FROM THE HEBREW SCRIPTURE

VOCAL MUSIC

READING FROM THE EPISTLES

READING FROM THE GOSPEL

SERMON

HYMN

COVENANT OF INSTALLATION
There are different gifts,
But it is the same Spirit who gives them.
There are different ways of serving God,
But it is the same God who is served.
Each one is given a gift by the one Spirit,
To use for the common good.
Together we are the body of Christ,
And individually members with one another.

Within our common ministry some members are chosen for particular work as ministers of the Word. They are ordained to a representative ministry and charged:

to lead in transmitting the Christian tradition
    from one generation to another;
to interpret the scriptures and proclaim the gospel of Christ;
to administer the sacraments,
    serving to maintain a company of Christians
    in continuity with the life and faith of the apostles;
to serve God's people with pastoral care and to share in
    the strengthening of the church in its life and mission;
and to act as pioneers and leaders
    in the church's reconciling work in the world.

We now come to this moment in which one of the church's ordained ministers, having been called with due seriousness to minister within this congregation, is to be officially received and installed to this office.

The new minister will stand.

Name, as the minister called to provide spiritual leadership and pastoral care for this congregation, do you reaffirm your profession of faith in Jesus Christ?

I reaffirm my baptism and confession of faith that Jesus is the Christ, and give myself in full commitment to be Christ's disciple.

Do you reaffirm your ordination vows?

I reaffirm my ordination vows and promise faithfully to fulfill my ministry among this people through preaching and teaching the word of God; administering the sacraments of the church; ministering to those who are sick and troubled; sharing in leadership to strengthen

the church's life; representing in a worthy manner what it means to live in faithful response to God's abiding grace.

The congregation will stand.

Having called *Name* to be your minister, do you renew your baptismal vow and commit yourself to support *her/him* with your prayers and shared responsibilities?

We reaffirm our baptism and our commitment to Jesus the Christ and our loyalty to Christ's church. We covenant to uphold our pastor with our prayers; to share *her/his* joys and sorrows; to attend to *her/his* preaching and teaching of God's word; to welcome *her/his* pastoral care; and honor *her/his* leadership.

NEW MINISTER: **Standing with you, I promise to be your pastor; and in the strength and grace of Jesus Christ I covenant to serve this congregation in all faithfulness for the glory of God.**

Let us unite in affirming our common faith.

The Preamble to the Design of the Christian Church, or another affirmation, may be said responsively or in unison.

INSTALLATION PRAYER

Almighty God, give us the grace to do the work to which you have called us in Jesus Christ. Fill this community of faith by your Spirit, that it may work together as one people to be the body of Christ in his reconciling ministry. Blend together the variety of gifts manifested within this congregation to strengthen its fellowship for service to the world. In solidarity with all your people of every time and place we pray that your will may be done here on earth through our worship, witness, and work. We ask this in the spirit of Jesus Christ, who gave his life that others may live. Amen.

DECLARATION

In the name of Jesus Christ, the head of the church, we declare you properly installed as minister of this congregation; and we commend you to the grace of God in the discharge of all your duties as a minister of the gospel. May God count you worthy of your calling, and bring to fulfillment in you every good purpose and every act inspired by faith.

HYMN

BENEDICTION

INSTRUMENTAL VOLUNTARY

INSTALLATION OF A MINISTER
ON A MULTIPLE STAFF:
A CELEBRATION OF PARTNERSHIP

VOLUNTARY

HYMN

PRAYER

Open our hearts to your presence, Holy God, that we may give ourselves fully to the covenant of partnership we make this day. Strengthen
our resolve to live in community with our sisters and brothers in Christ.
Amen.

WELCOME AND STATEMENT OF PURPOSE

GREETINGS FROM CHURCH REPRESENTATIVES

READING FROM THE HEBREW SCRIPTURE

VOCAL MUSIC OR INSTRUMENTAL VOLUNTARY

READING FROM THE EPISTLES

READING FROM THE GOSPEL

SERMON

HYMN

COVENANTING TOGETHER IN MINISTRY

Inasmuch as the installation of a minister involves mutual obligations
among all parties involved, members of the ministerial staff, this
congregation, and the regional church will all covenant together in
ministry.

A charge is given to the new staff member:

Do you accept the responsibilities of the office to which you have been
called by this congregation? Do you reaffirm your ordination vows,
and do you promise to give yourself wholly to your ministry, and to
conduct yourself in such a manner as to reflect credit to Christ and
Christ's church?

**Willingly I reaffirm my ordination vows, believing with all my heart
that Jesus is the Christ. It is my desire to devote myself to the ministry of Christ's church and to bring credit to the gospel of Christ that
I preach and teach. I promise to fulfill to my utmost ability the office
of a good minister of Jesus Christ. I will diligently and faithfully**

perform all my duties on behalf of this congregation and the church at large.

A charge is given to the present ministerial staff:

Because of the relationship that must exist between the ministers of the church, I call upon you to reaffirm your ordination vows and your calling as minister(s) of this congregation. Will you affirm the ministry of *Name*, seeing *her/him* as a peer of equal standing within the Christian Church (Disciples of Christ)? Will you help *her/him* fulfill the ministerial responsibilities to which *she/he* is called, affirming *her/his* special gifts and talents, being both counselor and friend, guide and listener?

Willingly I affirm my ordination vows, believing with all my heart that Jesus is the Christ. I gladly covenant with you to continue in service as a minister of the Word in the congregation. I promise to affirm *Name's* gifts of ministry, and to help *her/him* fulfill the responsibilities to which *she/he* has been called. I welcome *her/him* to a ministry of partnership in Christ's church in this place.

The congregation is invited to stand.

You, too, are called to become part of this covenant. Will you affirm your calling into the ministry of Jesus Christ that you received at your baptism, understanding with celebration that the Holy Spirit has given to you the gifts needed for service?

We believe that Jesus is the Christ, the Son of the living God, our Lord and Savior, in whose name we were baptized and in whose body we live. Understanding that we have received the gifts of service, we recommit ourselves to our own unique ministries in this congregation and in this community.

Will you affirm your covenant with our region and the general manifestation of the Christian Church (Disciples of Christ) in the United States and Canada, praying for our ministers and leaders, and supporting them through your financial support?

We pledge our continuing support of our Region and the Christian Church (Disciples of Christ) in the United States and Canada. We shall pray for its leaders and ask God to bless the world with the gospel of Christ.

A regional representative is called upon to offer the following response of the region to the congregation:

The Christian Church (Disciples of Christ) manifests itself organizationally in geographical units called regions. The mission of regions includes in part: (1) to extend the ministry of Christ in mission, witness and service among the people and social structures of the region, and

(2) to establish, receive, and nurture congregations in the region, providing help, counsel, and pastoral care to members, ministers, and congregations in their mutual relationships and relating them to the worldwide mission and witness of the whole church. As a representative of the *name of region*, I affirm on behalf of our region, our covenant with *congregational name*.

PLEDGE OF LOYALTY

The moderator of the board or chair of elders will address the congregation, which then responds.

Having committed ourselves to a ministry of partnership, let us join in completing this covenant.

We, the members of *congregational name*,
    affirm our call to ministry in the name of Jesus, the Christ.
As God's servant people we accept these charges:
    to gather in common worship,
    to minister to all who seek spiritual nurture,
    to extend the hand of charity,
    to loose the bonds of bigotry, malice, hatred and ill will,
    to share the good news of God's love in deed and word,
    to seek knowledge, that each generation may gain in wisdom.
Committed to these principles,
    we gladly receive *Name* as one of our ministers,
    affirming *her/his* gifts of ministry.
We pledge to *her/him* our support for *her/his* ministry among us.
We promise this day the best that is in us
    to *her/him* and to one another.
We promise to work with our ministers,
    along with our regional church,
    understanding that ours is a shared ministry.

PRAYER OF INSTALLATION

Eternal God, hear the vows we have made to one another this day. Strengthen us to carry out the work laid before us. Gather the varied fibers of our being and fashion us into a living tapestry of loving service—a community in the world witnessing to your Son our Lord, Jesus Christ. Amen.

HYMN

BENEDICTION

INSTRUMENTAL VOLUNTARY

☙ RECOGNITION, COMMISSIONING, OR ORDINATION OF ELDERS

According to the Design of the Christian Church: The offices of the eldership and the diaconate are ordered by the congregations, through election and recognition with appropriate ceremony, for the performance of certain functions of ministry appropriate to the offices. (a) A person elected to the eldership is authorized to exercise within the congregation which elects him or her the ministerial functions which it assigns for periods of time which it specifies, such as: sharing in the ministration of baptism and the Lord's supper and the conduct of worship, and sharing in the pastoral care and spiritual leadership of the congregation. Eldership is a voluntary ministry, each congregation having a plurality of elders.

(P<small>ARAGRAPH</small> 97 <small>OF</small> S<small>ECTION</small> VI, "M<small>INISTRY</small>")

The following service allows for such recognition to include the laying on of hands with prayer if that is a congregation's policy. If this is done, the intentions, including such matters as length of service and locale and limits of authority, should be clearly stated.

S<small>TATEMENT OF</small> P<small>URPOSE</small>

We come to this glad and solemn moment in which this congregation recognizes God's gift of elders to serve the church in Christ's ministry. All ministry is a gift from Jesus Christ who is the chief minister, the great high priest, of the entire people of God. Through the action of the Holy Spirit, Christ's ministry of reconciling, healing, teaching, and serving is the basis of all ministries. While the whole people of God through baptism is commissioned to share in this servant ministry, the church from earliest times has set some persons apart with prayer to serve in designated ministries.

An eldership has been established through which those named as elders serve together in a shared responsibility of congregational leadership. Together they serve as colleagues of the minister(s) who represent the reconciling work of Christ and the whole church in the present day. The responsibility of the eldership is:

> to teach and express the nature of the church
> > and the spirit of Christian living in word and deed;
> to give wise counsel to individual members
> > and to the congregation as a whole
> > in the face of the perplexities of its life together;
> to represent with disciplined clarity
> > the church's understanding of the significance of
> > communion at the Lord's table through its prayers;
> to set forth to the people of God
> > an engaging vision of the congregation's mission and ministry;

to share in positions of church leadership
in accordance with this congregation's practices.
to guard in all things the purity, unity,
and peace of Christ's holy church.

PRESENTATION OF CANDIDATES

Those who are to be recognized are called forth.

The church has with prayer and deliberation affirmed your call to the eldership of this congregation. Each of you have accepted this call as God's intention for your life. We therefore now proceed to *install/commission/ordain* you to the office of elder.

In the light of your calling to this new responsibility, do you reaffirm your faith that Jesus is the Christ, the Son of God; and do you promise to follow him and to seek to do and to bear his will all the days of your life?
I do.

Do you believe that the word of God in the Old and New Testaments, discerned under the guidance of the Holy Spirit, is the supreme authority for the faith and conduct of all God's people?
I do.

Do you commit yourself to the well-being of the church and through God's grace fulfill a servant ministry of care and concern for all the church's members?
I do, God being my helper.

May the Lord bless you and give you grace to keep these vows.

PRAYER

If the elders are to be set apart by prayer and the laying on of hands, the minister and those elders appointed to do so attend to each elder one at a time. The candidates kneel for the laying on of hands with prayer.

If this is not done, the following prayer may be adapted for general use.

Gracious God, the giver of every good and perfect gift, we thank you for raising up these elders in our midst to serve you and the church in strengthening the church. By your grace assist them in the building up of the church into the fullness of the stature of Jesus Christ. *(Repeat for each elder being recognized):* We thank you for *Name* and ask that you fill *her/him* with all the good graces of your Spirit that *she/he* may faithfully fulfill the ministry of Christ.

INDUCTION

I now ask the congregation to join with its elders in a covenant affirmation:

Reaffirming our faith that Jesus is the Christ, the Son of God, we gladly receive these elders as leaders in our life together. We covenant to support them with our prayers, encouragement, and respect. We celebrate with thanksgiving the shared responsibilities for Christ's ministry which is ours as the church. Praise be to God.

DECLARATION

In the name of Jesus Christ, the head of the church, and in accordance with the actions of this congregation, I declare that you are now members of the eldership in this church.

BLESSING

May grace and peace be yours in abundance in the knowledge of God and of Jesus our Lord.   (2 PETER 1:2)

☙ RECOGNITION OF THE DIACONATE

According to the Design of the Christian Church: The offices of the eldership and the diaconate are ordered by the congregations, through election and recognition with appropriate ceremony, for the performance of certain functions of ministry appropriate to the offices. (b) A person elected to the diaconate is authorized to serve in the congregation which elects him or her for periods of time which it specifies, by assisting in the ministration of baptism and the Lord's Supper, in the conduct of worship, and in the pastoral care and spiritual leadership of the congregation. The diaconate is also a voluntary ministry.

(PARAGRAPH 97 OF SECTION VI, "MINISTRY")

The following service assumes that other church officers are recognized separately.

STATEMENT OF PURPOSE

Through the gifts of the Spirit, God calls men and women within Christ's church to serve as deacons in ministry. All ministry derives from the life, death, and resurrection of Jesus Christ, who embodies God's ministry to all the world. Within the church all ministry is a rich interweaving of word and worship, work and witness. In different ways, members of the body of Christ share responsibility for the church's government, administration, discipline, instruction, worship, and pastoral care.

A diaconate has been established through which those designated as deacons serve together in shared responsibility of church leadership. Together they represent to the people of God servant ministry within a congregation. Together they are those:

who assist generally in worship and particularly in
the ministration of baptism and the Lord's supper;
who assist in pastoral care, looking after
the needs of the sick and those in distress;
who take shared responsibility for the disciplined spiritual life
of the congregation and its collective expressions of the gospel;
who fulfill designated administrative responsibility in
the ordered life and mission of the church.

In all things the diaconate is called to exemplify the interdependence of worship and mission in the life of the church.

PRESENTATION OF CANDIDATES

Those who are to be recognized are called forth.

The church has prayerfully considered your gifts of ministry for service in its diaconate and has duly called you to be a deacon. Each of you has accepted this call as God's intention for your life. In the light of your calling to this responsibility,
do you reaffirm your faith that Jesus is the Christ, the Son of God;
do you seek the peace, unity and purity of the church;
and do you, in accepting the office of deacon in this congregation,
promise faithfully to perform all the duties
pertaining to your calling?

I do, God being my helper.

Do you, the members of this church, receive these persons as deacons within the shared ministry of Christ's mission, and do you covenant to encourage and support them in the fulfillment of their responsibilities?

We do, God being our helper.

Let us pray: Gracious God, we thank you for these your servants who have been called into the church's diaconate. As we set them apart for this special ministry we ask you to fill them with all the graces needed to fulfill their responsibilities. Grant them the spirit of compassion for human needs, and devotion to the well-being of your church, that together we may grow ever more fully into the likeness of Christ. Amen.

INDUCTION

I now ask the congregation to join with its deacons in a covenant affirmation:

Reaffirming our faith that Jesus is the Christ, the Son of God, we gladly receive these deacons as servant leaders in our life together. We covenant to support them with our prayers, encouragement, and

respect. **We celebrate with thanksgiving the shared responsibilities for Christ's ministry which is ours as the church. Praise be to God.**

DECLARATION

In the name of Jesus Christ, the head of the church, and in accordance with the actions of this congregation, I declare that you are now members of the diaconate of this church.

BLESSING

May grace and peace be yours in abundance in the knowledge of God and of Jesus our Lord.   (2 PETER 1:2)

🍷 *A GENERAL INSTALLATION*

This service of installation expresses the responsibilities of leadership through an adaptation of the Preamble to the Design of the Christian Church (Disciples of Christ). It may be preceded by announcing the names of those to be installed and giving a brief description of their respective responsibilities. The responses, in bold, are to be spoken by those being installed.

Let us remember the model of leadership provided by our Lord, who came not to be served, but to serve, and who said to his disciples, "Whoever would be great among you must be your servant, and whoever would be first among you must be slave of all."

In Christ's name and by his grace we accept our mission of witness and service to all people.

Let us remember the unity that God has given us: one body, one spirit, one hope of our calling; one Lord, one faith, one baptism; one God and Creator of all, over all, through all, and in all.

We rejoice in God, maker of heaven and earth, and in the covenant of love which binds us to God and to one another.

Let us remember the church we are chosen to serve using the gifts with which we are equipped "for the work of ministry, for building up the body of Christ."

We are joined together in discipleship and in obedience to Christ.

Let us remember the commission the head of the church gave his followers to go into all the world witnessing, making disciples, baptizing, teaching, and serving, and realize that charge is intended for those who would lead the church.

In the bonds of Christian faith we yield ourselves to God that we may serve the One whose kingdom has no end.

Do you now gladly accept the particular office to which you have been elected, and do you promise to fulfill its duties?

I do, the Lord being my helper. *trusting in God*

Let us pray. We thank you, God, for these who have accepted special servant roles in a particular part of the church. We see gifts in them that can be put to good use in building up the body of Christ and in the ministry of reconciliation. Preserve the resolve each of these servants has at this moment. We pray in the name of our Lord Jesus Christ, the head of the body of which we are members. Amen.

I declare that you now are installed to your respective offices in the church. May the Lord provide grace for the service you have resolved to perform. *God*

service to the world,

Guide each of them in your way.

☿ INSTALLATION OF OFFICERS

STATEMENT OF PURPOSE

Within the whole family of God on earth, the church appears wherever believers in Jesus Christ are gathered in his name. This congregation manifests itself as Christ's church as a community of disciples bound together for worship, for fellowship and for service. To this end we are structured for mission, witness and mutual discipline, and for the nurture and renewal of our members.

God graces the church with leaders equipped for its work by gifts of the Holy Spirit. Today we rejoice in the rich blessings of God as represented in the leaders who have been called to Christ's service and who now acknowledge this calling by the dedication of their lives to Christ's servant ministry.

PRESENTATION OF THOSE BEING INSTALLED

Those having been called to service may be named along with the titles of their respective offices. They may stand as named, and/or come forward to the front of the sanctuary.

READING OF SCRIPTURE

The apostle Paul, in writing to the church at Corinth, reminds us of the way various members of the church function in mutual responsibility toward one another in the life of a congregation:

Now there are varieties of gifts, but the same Spirit; and there are varieties of services, but the same Lord; and there are varieties of activities, but it is the same God who activates all of them in everyone. To each is given the manifestation of the Spirit for the common good.

(1 Corinthians 12:4–7)

For just as the body is one and has many members, and all the members of the body, though many, are one body, so it is with Christ. For in the one Spirit we were all baptized into one body—Jews or Greeks, slaves or free—and we were all made to drink of one Spirit. Indeed, the body does not consist of one member but of many. If the foot would say, "Because I am not a hand, I do not belong to the body," that would not make it any less a part of the body. And if the ear would say, "Because I am not an eye, I do not belong to the body," that would not make it any less a part of the body. If the whole body were an eye, where would the hearing be? If the whole body were hearing, where would the sense of smell be? But as it is, God arranged the members in the body, each one of them, as God chose. If all were a single member, where would the body be? As it is, there are many members, yet one body.

(1 Corinthians 12:12–20, alt.)

Now you are the body of Christ and individually members of it.

(1 Corinthians 12:27)

Charge to Officers and Congregation

There follow brief descriptions of the responsibilities of those to be recognized. These may be adapted to the specific circumstances of the occasion.

Some among us are elders. They are gifted with a grasp of the gospel exemplified in word and deed. They give disciplined expression of the faith in teaching and in praying at the Lord's table. They have a vision of the church and its mission and are dedicated to expressing it in wise counsel.

Some among us are deacons. They are gifted with the ability to assist in the ministration of baptism and the Lord's supper. They assist in pastoral care and in spiritual discipline. They fulfill administrative responsibilities in the conduct of the church's work.

Some among us are trustees. They serve faithfully to represent the will of the church in all its legal actions.

Some of us are board officers. They serve in leadership capacities as the church seeks to fulfill its ministry under the headship of Christ. They seek to build up the church in every way.

Some of us are teachers. They serve to nurture the spiritual growth of all who are entrusted to their care. They embody God's good news in Jesus Christ and seek to communicate it to others in life transforming ways.

Those to be installed are now addressed:

Do you each accept the office to which you have been called, and do you promise, the Lord being your helper, to fulfill its duties faithfully? **I do.**

The congregation is now addressed:

Will you pledge your eager support to the work of God in this congregation under the leadership of these with whom you share ministry in this body of Christ; and pray God's blessing upon as together we seek to support one another in selfless service? **We do.**

PRAYER OF INSTALLATION

Let us pray: Almighty God, we rejoice that you have called us to be your people in this time and place. Help us to fulfill the mission to which you call us as we seek to know what faithfulness requires of us. Strengthen the resolves that have here been made and uphold your leaders with hope and encouragement that they may endure every frustrating difficulty. Fill this congregation with your loving Spirit that each may work together harmoniously so that all members may work together for the common good and to your glory. We pray in Christ's name. Amen.

DECLARATION

In the name of Jesus Christ, the head of the church, and by the authority of this congregation, I declare you properly installed to your respective offices for the terms to which you have been called.

BLESSING

May grace and peace be yours in abundance in the knowledge of God and of Jesus our Lord.   (2 PETER 1:2)

ADDITIONAL RESOURCE

A PRAYER OF BLESSING FOR CHURCH OFFICERS

Loving God, source of all blessings, give these your servants grace and power to fulfill their ministry. Make them faithful to serve, ready to teach, constant in advancing your gospel; and grant that, always having full assurance of faith, abounding in hope, and being rooted and grounded in love, they may continue strong and steadfast in your Son, Jesus Christ our Lord; to whom, with you and your Holy Spirit, belong glory and honor, worship and praise, now and forever. Amen.

☥ *INSTALLATION OF CHURCH SCHOOL TEACHERS*

Through baptism into the body of Christ, God calls every member into the service of the church. The Holy Spirit pours out gifts uniquely upon each one of us that we may build up the body of Christ. Today our congregation recognizes the gift of teaching. We celebrate with thanksgiving those who have responded to God's call to nurture others in the faith and knowledge of Christ.

Those to be installed may be named, identifying their respective responsibilities.

We thank God for the gifts that each of you holds. We are grateful for your responding to this high calling of the church. We charge you:

> In the name of Christ, the great teacher from God, to lead a life worthy of the calling to which you have been called, with all humility and gentleness, with patience, bearing with one another in love, making every effort to maintain the unity of the Spirit in the bond of peace. Equip those whom you teach for the work of ministry, for building up the body of Christ, until all of us come to the unity of the faith and of the knowledge of the Son of God, to maturity, to the measure of the full stature of Christ.   (EPHESIANS 4:2–3,12–13, ADAPT.)

Let us pray:

Gracious God, in every generation you have raised up prophets and teachers to make yourself known and to shape a servant people. We rejoice that you have called these persons to be your teachers among us. Pour out your Spirit upon them that they may be faithful to those they serve. Give them strength and courage to teach wisely. Fill them with a love that communicates by their very lives the good news of your abiding friendship. Let them know they are not alone. You are with them. We as a church stand with them. Together we share responsibility to nurture one another in the faith and every good work. May we as your people become full-grown, reflecting fully the mind of Christ. Amen.

Or:

Holy Wisdom, Giver of Life, we thank you for the gifts of insight and communication you have bestowed on these teachers. Help them discover the gifts you have hidden deeply within them. Give them the courage to be curious, the tenacity always to ask "why?" even when answers are not forthcoming. Strengthen them and give them courage when your Holy Spirit leads them to teach what is dangerous, when your holy passion for justice conflicts with popular opinion. Guide them as they continue to journey in faith. Cultivate the soil of our spirits so we can sink our roots deeply in your love and grow to bear good fruit in Christ's name. Amen.

INSTALLATION OR RECOGNITION OF PERSONS IN MUSIC MINISTRIES

This service is intended to take place within a regular Sunday service of worship. It may be used for the installation or recognition of persons engaged in a variety of roles in music leadership in the congregation—choirs, directors, song leaders, and instrumentalists.

STATEMENT OF PURPOSE

The author of Ephesians encourages us to "sing psalms and hymns and spiritual songs among yourselves, singing and making melody to the Lord in your hearts, giving thanks to God the Father at all times and for everything in the name of our Lord Jesus Christ." (5:19–20)

Through the gifts of the Spirit, God calls men and women *(and children and youth)* within Christ's church to serve in ministries of music. To direct, to sing, and to play instruments are ministries of Christ among us. We celebrate with thanksgiving those who share their gifts with us through music.

PRESENTATION OF MUSIC LEADERS

Those having been called to serve in positions of music leadership may be named. They may stand as named, and/or come forward to the front of the sanctuary.

CHARGE TO MUSICIANS AND CONGREGATION

The persons being recognized or installed are now addressed:

Making music to the praise of God in the congregation is a ministry that requires devotion and discipline. Do you accept responsibility for this ministry?

I do.

Will you be faithful to the disciplines of music?

We will.

The congregation is now addressed:

To these persons has been given the ministry of music in the church. Will you sustain them with your encouragement and your prayers, as together we seek to offer praise to God?

We will.

PRAYER OF BLESSING

Holy God, Master Musician,
bless these, your servants.
Grant them creativity, and stir their imaginations.

Tune their ears ever to hear your song of life,
  echoing through the music of the spheres
  and pulsing through their veins.
When discord comes upon them, help them and us
  to look on it as a prelude to new ideas,
  new harmonies, new possibilities for resolution.
Composer of the grand symphony of creation,
  help us all to remember you have written a part
  unique to each one of us in your sacred song.
Let the music of these, your servants
  be the constant reminder of, and challenge to,
  our own ministries of grace.
Grant that our music will ever glorify you. Amen.

HYMN   When in Our Music God Is Glorified (*CH 7*)

 COMMISSIONING TO MISSION

This service is intended to take place within a regular Sunday service of worship.

The commissioning ceremony begins with remarks about the person(s) being commissioned and the task to which he/she/they are being commissioned. This may be done by a staff representative of the mission agency.

QUESTIONS OF COMMITMENT
  Do you believe in your heart
    that God has called you to serve in location?
  I/We **do.**

  Are you willing to take these new responsibilities
    in service for Christ?
  I am/We are **willing.**

  Will you seek to share with those around you the good news that
    in Jesus Christ there is reconciliation with God, forgiveness of sins,
    and power for righteous and holy living as children of God?
  God being *my/our* **helper,** *I/we* **will.**

CHARGE TO CONGREGATION
  You have heard the nature of the work to which *Name (and Name) have/ has* been called and *their/his/her* readiness to respond to this call. *They/ He/She are/is* part of you and as *they/he/she go(es)*, you will be going with *them/him/her. They/He/She* will keep in contact with you, and you will want to keep in contact with *them/him/her.* As *they/he/she assume(s)* this

responsible position, *they/he/she need(s)* the assurance of your participation by support and prayer so *they/he/she* can go forth with a real
sense of joy and encouragement.

CONGREGATIONAL RESPONSE

**We have heard your commitment and we thank God for your obedi-
ence to this call to service. Through the calling of God's Spirit and
the commissioning of the church, the servants of Christ are scattered
throughout the world.**

**We accept your service in location as an extension of the ministry of
this congregation, and pledge our support and prayers that your
ministry may be effective. May the Lord watch over us and the Holy
Spirit guide us while we are absent one from another.**

ACT OF COMMISSIONING

In the name of the Lord Jesus Christ and his church, and on behalf of
the mission agency, we commission you to this service in *location*. May
God bless you, and make you a blessing. Amen.

RESPONSES

From the candidate(s)

From the congregation

PRAYER OF CONSECRATION

CONGREGATIONAL RECOGNITIONS

WELCOME TO NEW MEMBERS

The following congregational response is also available as CH 341.

**Reaffirming our own faith in Jesus the Christ,
we gladly welcome you into this community of faith,
    enfolding you with our love
    and committing ourselves to your care.
In the power of God's Spirit
    let us mutually encourage each other to trust God
    and strengthen one another to serve others,
that Christ's church may in all things stand faithful.**

+ + +

Let us, the members of this congregation,
express our welcome and affirm our mutual ministry in Christ.

We welcome you with joy in the common life of this church.
We promise you our friendship and prayers
  as we share the hopes and labors of the church of Jesus Christ.
By the power of the Holy Spirit
  may we continue to grow together in God's knowledge and love
  and be witnesses of our risen Savior.

PRESENTATION OF BIBLE TO YOUNG READERS

This service is intended to be a part of a regular Sunday service of worship in which those who have completed the third grade are presented Bibles.

INTRODUCTION

Name and Name have been asked to come forward today to receive a special gift and blessing from the congregation. This marks a significant point in their personal religious development.

Having learned to read, you are now ready to receive your own Bible for study and inspiration. Therefore your community of faith presents to each of you a copy of the Bible as a token of its love and joy in your growth and development.

The Bibles are presented individually to each person.

CHARGE TO THE RECIPIENTS

In ancient times the Lord commanded his holy community of faith to keep God's words in their hearts; to recite them to their children and talk about them when at home and away, upon lying down and upon rising up. (DEUTERONOMY 6:4–7, ALT.)

In this spirit we as a part of God's faith community seek to fulfill our responsibility to develop an atmosphere in which God is known and loved and trusted. We do this by living out our faith before one another as a caring community. Faith is caught as much as it is taught.

At the same time we are always undergirded by God's holy story told in the Bible. It serves as a means through which God still speaks to us in every circumstance of life. As the Bible itself says, "All scripture is inspired by God and is useful for teaching, for reproof, for correction, and for training in righteousness, so that everyone who belongs to God may be proficient, equipped for every good work." (2 TIMOTHY 3:16–17)

Firmly convinced of the central place of the Bible in a Christian's life, your church presents you with your own copy to read and study as you grow to Christian maturity. Treasure it as among your greatest possessions. Use it in church school and at home that you may grow up into the full humanity to which God calls you. May you hear God speak to you through these sacred pages and bless you deeply.

☙ COMMISSIONING YOUTH FOR CAMP AND CONFERENCE

We of the congregation want those of you going to camp this summer to grow in your faith as Jesus grew in his faith.

"And Jesus increased in wisdom and stature and in favor with God and people."

We hope that you will grow in the spirit of God and bear fruit that reflects the kingdom of heaven.

"The fruit of the spirit is love, joy, peace, patience, kindness, goodness, faithfulness, gentleness, self-control."

We want you to learn the lessons of nature that Jesus taught.

"Look at the birds of the air, consider the lilies of the field, do not be anxious about your life, but seek first the kingdom of heaven and all will be yours."

We remember the contributions of individuals who make the camp and conference program possible; the time, the imagination, and the money that comes from people in this congregation and other congregations around us.

"I have received full payment from the gifts you sent, a fragrant offering, a sacrifice acceptable and pleasing to God."

We hope your experience at camp will go well. Hold us in your prayers as we will hold you in our prayers.

"I thank my God in all my remembrance of you, in every prayer of mine for your partnership in the gospel from the first day until now."

 BEGINNING OF A NEW SCHOOL YEAR

CH 518, *This Is a Day of New Beginnings, may be sung.*

At the beginning of a new school year, O God of wisdom,
  we offer thanks and praise for the gift of new beginnings
  and for the opportunity to learn and to wonder.
We pray for teachers, students, and staff
  that this year might be rewarding for all.
Be with us as we face the challenge of new tasks,
  the fear of failure, the expectations of parents, friends, and self.
In our learning and our teaching,
  may we grow in service to others and in love for your world,
    through Jesus Christ our Savior. Amen.

HONORING GRADUATES

For life, O Lord,

We give you thanks!

We give you thanks this day especially for the lives of *Names of graduates.*
Give them strength. Give them courage. Give them a vision of the persons
you have redeemed them to be.

**Endow them with the grace of kindness and compassion; enrich them
with Christian endurance when generous service wearies them.**

Awaken their minds to the wholeness of your creation; grant that they may
remain curious about the nature of things and that their daily inquiries
may reveal to them your presence.

**Grant us the grace to unite with them in the body of Christ, heeding
together Christ's call to lives of service and praise.**

Bind our hearts in Christian love.

**Unite us by your Spirit wherever the enterprise of life takes us, in the
name of the Father, and of the Son and of the Holy Spirit. Amen!**

🍷 *FOR AN ENGAGED COUPLE*

We praise you, loving God, for your gentle plan that draws together your children, *Name* and *Name*, in their love for each other. Strengthen their hearts, so that they will keep faith with each other, please you in all things, and so come to the happiness of celebrating their marriage. We ask this through Christ our Lord. Amen.

🍷 *FOR THOSE WHO INTEND TO ENTER CHRISTIAN SERVICE*

God, you showed yourself most fully in one who took basin and towel to wash his friends' feet. In all times you call leaders to serve your people. We pray that you strengthen *Name* in *her/his* resolve to follow Christ in ministry and service. Give *her/him* discernment to hear your call. Quicken *her/his* imagination to find ways of communicating the wonders of your abiding presence to us all. Fill our hearts with love for *her/him*. Let our caring actions be a source of strength and assurance for *her/him*. Amen.

🍷 *ON THE SABBATICAL OF A MINISTER*

The congregation is invited to pray, in unison:

As a family of Christians,
    we proclaim our love for God, Jesus, and one another.
As a family of Christians,
    we send our love with our pastor on *his/her* journey of faith.
As a family of Christians,
    we share, over time and space, our God, our Savior, the Holy Spirit.
As a family of Christians,
    we know that time and distances do not separate us
    from love for one another in Christ.
As a family of Christians,
    we pray, dear God, that you will bless *Name* and this congregation
    during this sabbatical, so that we all may grow in faith.
We ask this in the name of Christ,
    who connects us all in the Holy Spirit. Amen.

☉ *UPON RETIREMENT*

CH *518, "This Is a Day of New Beginnings," may be sung.*

Eternal God, you hold the times and seasons,
    endings and beginnings, in your hands.
Bless *Name*, who now enters a new time of life.
We give you thanks for tasks accomplished,
    for the joys and pains woven into the fabric of *his/her* years.
Give *Name* the guidance of your Holy Spirit.
May days no longer filled with old obligations
    be free for new activities and associations.
May fears and uncertainties about the future
    be transformed into quiet confidence.
May each new day be received as a sacred trust and lived to your glory,
    through Jesus Christ our Savior. Amen.

☉ *FAREWELL TO A MEMBER OR MINISTER*

Lord, you have called *Name* to another place,
    another community, another task.
We are sad to see *her/him* go,
    but we recognize that, just as *she/he* has been your gift to us,
    so now *she/he* goes as a gift to another group of your people.

We pray for each other now
    as our once-parallel roads of pilgrimage diverge.
We thank you for all that we have done or learned or shared together

We pray for *Name* as *she/he* explores and clarifies and puts into action
    the call that takes *her/him* onward from here.
May *she/he* grow in your grace and in the knowledge of your love,
    so that *she/he* may be a blessing to many.

We pray for the community to which *she/he* goes,
    that they will value *her/him*, support *her/him*,
    learn from *her/him*, and encourage *her/him*.
We pray for ourselves as we stay,
    that you will keep us faithful to the vision we have shared,
    and that you will show us what we should do,
    how we should be, now that *Name* is no longer with us.

As we part, we reaffirm that it has been your Spirit
    who brought us together in the first place,
    your Spirit who has enlivened our fellowship;

your Spirit who goes with *Name*
and your Spirit who stays with us;

your Spirit who keeps us all together
in the worldwide family of your church.
Thanks be to God. Amen.

+ + +

Go in peace,
with our love, our forgiveness, our prayers supporting you.
Go in strength,
with the gifts we have shared in our time together.
Go in joy,
with the assurance that the bonds of our love in Christ
cannot be broken.
You are a part of our family,
Here you will always be at home.
Go in peace. Amen.

☙ *A DIALOGUE OF CONFESSION AND FORGIVENESS*

This may be shared by minister and congregation on the occasion when a ministry comes to a close.

One of the hardest parts of saying good-bye is sorting through our memories and feelings.

Memories of good times and bad times come flooding into our conscious minds, each one evoking deep feelings within us.

We are reminded of our accomplishments.

And we are filled with pride.

We are reminded of our failures.

And we are filled with disappointment.

We are reminded of times when we stopped to minister to the needs of a brother or sister, reaching out in love.

And we lift our heads to hear the acclamation of our Lord saying, "Well done, good and faithful servant."

We are reminded of times when we found our brother or sister lying hurt on the side of life's road, in need of our help, and yet we crossed the road and walked by on the other side.

And we hang our heads and cover our ears lest we hear the condemnation of our Lord. But even with our ears covered, we feel Christ's pain in our hearts.

O God, you promise to forgive us, and call us to forgive one another.

Hear our litany of confession and forgiveness.

My friends, for the times when I have said the wrong thing or left things unsaid, when I have done the wrong thing or left something undone, or when I have been there at the wrong time or failed to be there at all, I ask your forgiveness.

We hear your confession and offer the gift of our forgiveness. And we give thanks to God for those times when you have offered God's word of hope, demonstrated God's grace, and made flesh God's love in our lives.

Thanks be to God.

Our friend, for the times when we have said the wrong thing or left things unsaid, when we have done the wrong thing or left something undone, or when we have been there at the wrong time or failed to be there at all, we ask your forgiveness.

I hear your confession and offer the gift of my forgiveness. And I give thanks to God for those times when you have offered God's word of hope, demonstrated God's grace, and made flesh God's love in my life and in the lives of my family.

Thanks be to God.

My friends, let us hold fast to the promises of God. In Christ Jesus, each death is an opportunity for new life.

In Christ Jesus, there is grace sufficient enough for each one of us.

(ALL:) Thanks be to God. Amen.

Occasional
PRAYERS WITHIN THE CHURCH

⚱ *BEFORE A COMMITTEE MEETING*

We thank you, God, for the gift of leadership you have gathered here. Give us wisdom and courage to make decisions that are in harmony with the in-breaking of your reign in our midst. Help us to be discerning and willing servants on Christ's behalf in the world. Amen.

+ + +

Lord, guide us as we meet together
    that we may think calmly and carefully, decide wisely and well,
    in order that everything may be done in accordance with your will.
Help us to make your concerns our concerns,
    so that through us you may be able to carry on
    your work here on earth, for Jesus Christ's sake. Amen.

⚱ *OPENING A CHURCH GATHERING*

Gathered together in Christ's name, we seek God's guidance and counsel, that what we undertake may be established in God's wisdom and infused by the power of God's Spirit.

Read Ephesians 4:11–16

We are the body of Christ and gifted members who seek to build up and strengthen the church into the fullness of Christ. Therefore let us pray:

Grant, O God, that we may have the mind of Christ
    who bore witness to the truth as it was given him;
    who empties himself, taking on the form of a servant;
    who exalted others that he may be abased;
    who, having loved his own, loved them to the end.
Help us in all that we do
    to put aside cunning and craftiness;
    to regard others better than ourselves;
    to speak the truth in love
    to contribute to the well-being of the whole body.
Join and knit us together by your grace
    that our endeavor, being grounded in love,
    may flourish through the gifted contribution of each member. Amen.

☙ *AT A CONVENTION/CONFERENCE*

We give you thanks, our God, for these days of *name of convention/confer-ence*: for the mingling of minds and personality, for the clash of provoca-tive thought and expression, for the great variety of skills, talents and gifts represented here. Let your Holy Spirit flow into our lives, that all these abilities may be used to fulfill your purposes and extend the kingdom of our Lord Jesus Christ. Amen.

☙ *WHEN THERE IS DIVISION IN THE CHURCH*

Holy God, giver of peace, author of truth:
    we confess that we are divided and at odds with one another,
    that a bad spirit has risen among us,
    and set us against your Holy Spirit of peace and love.
Take from this congregation mistrust, party spirit, contention,
    and all evil that now divides us.
Work in us a desire for reconciliation, so that,
    putting aside personal grievances,
    we may go about your business with a single mind,
    devoted to our Lord and Savior, Jesus Christ. Amen.

*O*CCASIONS OF PASTORAL CARE

☙ *FOR GOD'S BLESSING ON A HOME*

Good Lord, just as you were pleased to relax
    in the home of Martha and Mary,
    abide also, we pray, in *our homes/this home*.
Bestow upon *them/these* an atmosphere of Christian love
    where your presence can be found, your word made known,
    your will accepted, and your purpose worked out.

+ + +

O God, make the door of this house
    wide enough to receive all who need human love and fellowship;
    narrow enough to shut out all envy, pride, and strife.

Make its threshold smooth enough to be no stumbling block to children
    or to straying feet,
    but rugged and strong enough to turn back the tempter's power.
God, make the door of this house
    the gateway to thy eternal kingdom.

☸ AFTER CHILDBIRTH

Holy Creator of Life,
    we celebrate the glorious mystery of birth.
You love your children into existence
    and place them in human arms for tender nurture.
We are grateful for a safe deliverance
    and ask that you bless this mother
    with physical strength and spiritual fortitude
    to fulfill her responsibilities in the days ahead.
Surround this child with fatherly care
    and the supporting love of friends and family.
We bless you for this great gift of life,
    and ask that your peace be with us all our days. Amen.

+ + +

We rejoice before you, Creator God, in all your marvelous works.
We bless you for the miracle of new life,
    and that you have called men and women to share in this wonder.
Today we especially thank you for the safe delivery of this child;
    praying that *she/he* may grow physically to healthy adulthood,
    and spiritually to know and love you,
        whom to know is eternal life, in Jesus Christ our Lord. Amen.

☸ AFTER A DIFFICULT BIRTH

God of all mercy, we pray for your healing touch upon this mother. Give
her rest. And strengthen her that she will be able soon to care for her child
as she so desperately desires. Calm her fears and hold her close to your
heart just as we, her family and friends, hold her close to ours. Holy God,
your mystery of life astounds us. Your abundant mercy overflows our hearts
with thanks. Amen.

☿ FOR PARENTS OF A STILLBORN CHILD OR AT THE DEATH OF A NEWLY BORN CHILD

Merciful God, you strengthen us by your power and wisdom.
Be gracious to *Name* and *Name* in their grief,
    and surround them with your unfailing love;
    that they may not be overwhelmed by their loss,
    but have confidence in your goodness,
    and courage to meet the days to come;
        through Jesus Christ our Lord. Amen.

☿ PRAYER FOR ONE WHO HAS BEEN MOLESTED

Most loving God,
    she/he has been severely wounded,
    hurt beyond words with the betrayal of trust,
    physical violence and abuse,
    and the absence of love.
Bless *her/him* with the abundance of your love
    and with the support of loving people
    who will help to heal the wounds,
    restore confidence and trust,
    and teach *her/him* to love again;
in the name of Jesus Christ we pray. Amen.

+ + +

God of light, grant that your love will overcome the darkness,
    the terror of this moment.
Wash this one's heart with your tears
    and comfort *her/him* with your presence.
Let *her/him* know you are one who can always be trusted.
Help *her/him* discover the holiness of rage.
    Bless *her/his* anger.
Shape it into the power to tell the truth in all things
    and to fight back the shadows of secrets.
Surround *her/him* with people who care, who listen well,
    who can help bring love once again to light. Amen.

FOR THOSE IN A COMA OR UNABLE TO COMMUNICATE

Eternal God, you have known us before we were here
and will continue to know us after we are gone.
Touch *Name* with your grace and presence.
As you give your abiding care,
assure *him/her* of our love and presence.
Though we are unable to respond to each other,
assure *him/her* that our communion together remains secure
and your love for *him/her* is unfailing.
In Christ, who came through to us, we pray. Amen.

WHEN A LIFE-SUPPORT SYSTEM IS WITHDRAWN

God of compassion and love,
you have breathed into us the breath of life
and have given us the exercise of our minds and wills.
In our frailty we surrender all life to you from whom it came,
trusting in your gracious promises;
through Jesus Christ our Lord. Amen.

BLESSINGS FOR CONGREGATIONS AND BUILDINGS

DEDICATION OF A CHURCH BUILDING

Almighty God, to whose glory we celebrate
the *dedication/consecration* of this house of prayer:
We praise you for the many blessings
you have given to those who worship here;
and we pray that all who seek you in this place may find you,
and being filled with the Holy Spirit
may become a living temple acceptable to you;
through Jesus Christ our Lord. Amen.

REDEDICATION OF A CHURCH SANCTUARY

For use when a sanctuary has been renovated. A choice is given between two styles of dedication. The moment of dedication may either be a responsive Prayer of Rededication *or a responsive* Act of Rededication. *One identifies the people with God's activity in its midst; the other focuses on the congregation's action to fulfill God's purposes.*

If this takes the place of a regular Sunday morning worship service, or if the congregation so desires, the Lord's supper may be celebrated at an appropriate time within the service.

INSTRUMENTAL VOLUNTARY

CALL TO WORSHIP

Lift up your heads, O gates!
and be lifted up, O ancient doors!
that the Holy One of Glory may come in.
Who is this glorious Holy One?
Our God, strong and mighty,
our God, mighty over every foe.

Lift up your heads, O gates!
and be lifted up, O ancient doors!
that the Holy One of Glory may come in.
Who is this glorious Holy One?
The God of hosts,
whose name we come to glorify. (PSALM 24:7–10, ADAPT.)

Or: Spoken individually or in unison

Make a joyful noise to God, all the lands!
Serve God with gladness!
Come into God's presence with singing!
Know that the Sovereign is God!
It is God who made us, and to God we belong;
we are God's people, and the sheep of God's pasture.
Enter God's gates with thanksgiving,
and God's courts with praise!
Give thanks to God, bless God's name!
For God is good;
God's steadfast love endures forever,
and God's faithfulness to all generations. (PSALM 100, I-L)

HYMN

If there is a procession, the hymn may precede the call to worship.

DECLARATION OF PURPOSE

We have gathered as a family of God to celebrate with thanksgiving the renovation of this sanctuary and to rededicate it to the glory of

God. Aware of our rich heritage, we celebrate the lives of those who in times past have devoted themselves to the upbuilding of this congregation and who now surround us as a great host of witnesses to the power of God at work in the church. Holding this heritage in sacred trust, we come now to consecrate afresh this house of God and this body of Christ—the church—to the worship of God and the service of the world. Let us, then, celebrate with joy this festive occasion with praise and prayer to God.

Prayer

God of all glory, whose habitation is the whole of creation, we rejoice that you make yourself known particularly in the midst of those who gather as your people in Christ's name. May this place be a holy meeting ground between you and your people. Make yourself known afresh to us today as we dedicate anew this building and ourselves to your service. May this sanctuary ever resound to praises of your glorious name; through Christ our Lord. Amen.

Or:

O God, you are our God. We seek you,
    our souls thirst for you;
our flesh faints for you,
    as in a dry and weary land where there is no water.
**So we have looked upon you in the sanctuary,
    beholding your power and glory.**

Because your steadfast love is better than life,
    our lips will praise you.
**So we will bless you as long as we live;
    we will lift up our hands and call on your name.**

(PSALM 63:1–4, ALT.)

Gloria Patri or Doxology

Greetings

This may be an occasion to welcome visitors, to introduce special guests, to receive brief greetings. If deemed appropriate, the architect and contractor may present their work for acceptance. If specific items are to be memorialized, they may be dedicated at this point. All of this should be brief.

Recalling This Church's Story

A congregation needs occasions to tell and retell its own personal story, particularly as a means to incorporate new members into its life. This is one such worthy occasion to accomplish this purpose.

AFFIRMATION OF FAITH

The congregation, either responsively or in unison, affirms its Disciples heritage by reading aloud the Preamble to The Design of the Christian Church (Disciples of Christ), CH 355.

HYMN OR ANTHEM

SCRIPTURE(S)

Suitable readings include:

1 Kings 8:22–30	Matthew 16:13–20
Psalm 42	Matthew 21:10–14
Psalm 48	1 Corinthians 3:9–13, 16–17
Psalm 84	1 Peter 2:1–9
	Revelation 21:2–7

MESSAGE

An appropriate choral presentation or instrumental concert may substitute for the Message.

PRAYER OF REDEDICATION

Wondrous God, the skies and the highest heavens cannot contain you, much less temples made by human hands. Yet you dwell on this earth among us and make yourself known in sacred space and time. Receive this house afresh for your glory as we rededicate it and ourselves to your service.

Fill this sanctuary with your Holy Spirit. May its walls, its furnishings, its holy emblems, declare your praise.

Consecrate afresh this building to your service and this church to Christ's ministry. May we show forth your loving-kindness as a light upon a stand that leads others to see our good works and give you praise.

Accept the praise of our lips, the songs of our hearts, the adoration of our spirits, that in all things we may glorify you and enjoy you for ever.

Attend to every prayer uttered aloud or in secret, touching each heart with the certainty that no prayer goes unanswered.

Proclaim your word by the reading of the scripture and the preaching of the gospel. May all take heart and believe to their salvation and to renewal of the world.

Reveal yourself to your people gathered around the Lord's table in the breaking of bread and in communion with one another.

Greet with outstretched arms newborn children entrusted to your care, embracing them with a love that draws them ever nearer to you.

Enfold in your loving care those who are baptized. Grant that they may know themselves to be members of the body of Christ through God's everlasting covenant.

Bless by your presence those who pledge themselves to one another in a holy marriage, adding your strength to their vows.

Reconcile by the power of your Spirit those who feel themselves estranged from you and one another. Within this body grant them your peace, putting an end to all hostility.

Comfort all who gather in mourning for the loss of a loved one, giving them courage to celebrate the gift of life and to know your eternal love.

Sanctify all that we are, all that we have, all that we shall become, and make us wholly yours.

Blessing and glory and wisdom and thanksgiving and honor and power and might be to you, our God, forever and ever! Amen.

Or:

ACT OF REDEDICATION

This may be used in place of the Prayer of Rededication.

We rejoice in having completed the renovation of our place of worship. With heartfelt gratitude we now reconsecrate this chancel and church to the glory of God.
In the name of the Lord Jesus Christ we do this.

We rededicate this house to the glory of God,
    who has called us by sheer grace:
        to the glory of Jesus Christ, who loves us and gave himself for us:
        and to the glory of the Holy Spirit, who illumines and sanctifies us.

We rededicate this house
    for the worship of God in praise and prayer;
    for the preaching of the gospel of Jesus Christ,
        crucified, risen, and exalted;
    and for the celebration of the holy sacraments of God's grace.

We rededicate this house
    for the giving of comfort to all who mourn;
    of strength to all who are tempted;
    of light to all who seek the way.

We rededicate this house
    for the hallowing of family life;
    for the teaching and guiding of the young;
    for the upbuilding of all who believe,
    and the perfecting of the saints;

We rededicate this house
    for the increase of righteousness;
    for the spread of the spirit of love;
    and for the extension of the reign of God.

And now, as a people within the household of God
    in the unity of faith;
    in the communion of the saints;
    in love and goodwill to all;
    in gratitude for the gift of this house
        to be a dwelling place of God through the Spirit;
we dedicate ourselves to the worship of God
    and the service of God's mighty realm;
    in the name of the Father, and of the Son,
    and of the Holy Spirit. Amen.

HYMN

BLESSING

If there is a recessional, the blessing may precede the singing of the hymn.

Peace be to this house, and all who worship here.
Peace be to those who enter, and to those who go out.
Peace be to those who love this house,
    and who love the name of Jesus Christ our Lord.

INSTRUMENTAL VOLUNTARY

☙ *DEDICATION PRAYER FOR EDUCATIONAL SPACES*

God of grace and wisdom, we offer this building to you as a learning and teaching place. Grant that we will join you as co-adventurers, learning and teaching your Holy Word. Help us to be bold explorers, seeking the truth about our responsibilities as stewards of creation. Awaken our compassion, our conviction to bring change to our world. Embrace us all as children of your Word as we embrace learners of all ages. Fill us with your Spirit. Bathe us all in the light of your love. Amen.

☙ *DEDICATION PRAYER FOR A FELLOWSHIP HALL*

Laughing God,
  Hallow our laughter in this place.
Reaching God,
  Your yearning love brings us to life. Let that yearning grow within us together with all who seek your presence in our community.
Surprising God,
  Your gifts to us are new every morning. We take joy in anticipating the surprises we will encounter in this space.
Blessing God,
  Be with us as we gather here. Grant that the meals and celebrations we share here will be food not only for our bodies but for our spirits. Let your Spirit of caring bind us together as one people—not to the exclusion of those who are outside these walls—but as a witness to Jesus, the Christ, who gathered his friends to celebrate your rich blessings to us all. Make this a place of witness to your abiding love. Amen.

☙ *DEDICATION OF AN ORGAN OR OTHER MUSICAL INSTRUMENTS*

This service is intended to be used within a service of worship. If the instrument is given in memory of a person who has died or in honor of someone living, the phrase in parentheses may be included.

The donor, or someone designated to present the instrument, stands before the congregation and says:

We present this *instrument* to be consecrated to the glory of almighty God and for service in this congregation (in *loving memory/honor* of *Name*).

Pastor and people respond:

It is good to give thanks to the Lord,
to sing praises to your name, O Most High,

to declare your steadfast love in the morning,
and your faithfulness at night,

to the music of the lute and the harp,
to the melody of the lyre.

For you, O Lord, have made me glad by your work;
at the works of your hands I sing for joy.

A Gloria Patri (CH 35–37) or Doxology (CH 46–50) may be sung.

Dedicatory music may be played on the instrument(s) being consecrated.

Eternal God, whom the generations have worshiped through the gift of music, accept our praise to you in the sound of this instrument, which we consecrate in your name and to your glory. Grant that its music may be a blessing to all who worship here, and that they may be consecrated to you, whose sound has gone out through all the earth and whose words to the end of the world. Let our music be so joined to your holy Word that your glory may surround us and empower us for the service to which you call us in the world; through Jesus Christ our Lord. Amen.

☻ CONSECRATION OF SPECIAL GIFTS TO THE CHURCH

It is appropriate within a service of worship to receive and set apart with thanksgiving gifts that facilitate the worship of God. This may appropriately take place within the context of the congregation's joys and concerns.

This congregation is the grateful recipient of the gift of (   ) for the purpose of (   ). It is given *in appreciation of/in memory of Name* by *Name*. The psalmist declares:

Sing and bless the name of the Lord;
    Proclaim God's salvation, day after day.
Majestic and grand is God's presence;
    Strength and splendor are in God's temple.
Give to the Lord glory and strength.
    Bring a gift and come to God's court.
Bow to the Lord in holy splendor;
    Tremble before God, all the world.   (Psalm 96: 2, 6–9, Chamberlain)

Let us enter into a litany of thanksgiving and consecration.

We praise you, O God, for this church which calls us together in the name of Christ to worship and serve you.

We celebrate the good news that through Christ you have reconciled the world to yourself. May we be faithful in our ministry of reconciliation.

We rejoice in those who have through the years gladly given of themselves in the service of your church. Particularly do we remember to you with thanksgiving the *life/lives* of *Name(s)*, recalling all the goodness and influence of such lives that have been passed on to us.

We are grateful for the thoughtfulness of *Name(s)* who *has/have* glorified your name and facilitated the work of the church through this gift. May we show our thankfulness by using it according to your will.

With praise to you, O God, for all your goodness, we consecrate this gift to your worship and service.

Blessing and glory and wisdom and thanksgiving and honor and power and might be to you, our God, forever and ever! Amen.

VI

RESOURCES

$\mathscr{I}$NVITATION TO WORSHIP

The invitation to worship calls upon the community of faith to center its worship upon God. This may be done simply by the quoting of appropriate scriptural sentences. Another form consists of a greeting that is followed by a congregational response. The call to worship, always addressed to the people, has the sole purpose of calling the congregation to its stated purpose: to worship God. The importance of clarifying for those assembled the purpose of its gathering cannot be underestimated. If a congregational response is made, it should be to affirm the purpose of the people's gathering.

SCRIPTURAL CALLS TO WORSHIP

It is appropriate to open worship with this simple invitation:

Let us worship God.

Then may follow a variety of scriptural sentences that express the theme of the service. The sentences may either be read responsively, as occasionally indicated, or spoken entirely by the worship leader.

1
Sing to the LORD, all the earth.
    Tell of God's salvation from day to day.
Declare God's glory among the nations,
    the Creator's marvelous works among all the peoples.
For great is the LORD, and greatly to be praised.   (1 CHRONICLES 16:23–25, ALT.)

2
Wait for the LORD;
    be strong, and let your heart take courage;
    wait for the LORD.
We wait for the LORD.   (BASED ON PSALM 27:14)

3
Ascribe to the LORD, O heavenly beings,
    ascribe to the LORD glory and strength.
Ascribe glory to the LORD's name;
    worship the LORD in holy splendor.   (PSALM 29:1–2, ALT.)

4

Rejoice in the Lord, O you righteous;
    praise befits the upright.
Our souls are waiting for you, O Lord;
    you are our help and our shield.
In you do our hearts find joy;
    we trust in your holy name.
Let your love be upon us, O God,
    as we place our hope in you.   (Psalm 33:1, 20–22, alt.)

5

I will bless the Lord at all times;
    God's praise shall continually be in my mouth.
My soul makes its boast in the Lord;
    let the humble hear and be glad.
O magnify the Lord with me,
    and let us exalt God's name together.   (Psalm 34:1–3, alt.)

6

"Be still, and know that I am God!
    I am exalted among the nations,
    I am exalted in the earth."
The Lord of hosts is with us;
    the God of Jacob and Leah is our refuge.   (Psalm 46:10–11, alt.)

7

O Lord, open our lips;
    and our mouths shall sing forth your praise.
Praise the Lord.
    The Lord's name be praised.   (based on Psalm 51:15)

8

Make a joyful noise to God, all the earth;
    sing the glory of God's name;
    give to God glorious praise.   (Psalm 66:1–2, alt.)

9

I will sing of your steadfast love, O God, forever.
    With my mouth I will proclaim your faithfulness
        to all generations.
I declare that your steadfast love is established forever;
    your faithfulness is as firm as the heavens.
Let the heavens praise your wonders, O Lord,
    your faithfulness in the assembly of the holy ones.   (Psalm 89:1–2, 5)

10

It is good to give thanks to the Lord,
    to sing praises to your name, O Most High;

to declare your steadfast love in the morning,
and your faithfulness by night,
to the music of the lute and the harp,
to the melody of the lyre.
For you, O Lord, have made me glad by your work;
at the works of your hands I sing for joy.
How great are your works, O Lord!
Your thoughts are very deep!   (Psalm 92:1–5)

11

O come, let us sing to the Lord;
let us make a joyful noise to the rock of our salvation!
Let us come into God's presence with thanksgiving;
let us make a joyful noise to God with songs of praise!

(Psalm 95:1–2, alt.)

12

O worship the Lord in the beauty of holiness.   (Psalm 96:9, KJV)
Honor and majesty are rightfully God's;
strength and joy are where God abides.   (1 Chronicles 16:27, alt.)
For our sovereign God is a sun and shield
who bestows favor and honor.
No good thing does God withhold
from those who walk uprightly.   (Psalm 84:11, alt.)

13

Make a joyful noise to the Lord, all the earth;
break forth into joyous song and sing praises.
Sing praises to the Lord with the lyre,
with the lyre and the sound of melody.
With trumpets and the sound of the horn
make a joyful noise before the King, the Lord.   (Psalm 98:4–6)

14

Make a joyful noise to the Lord, all the earth.
Worship the Lord with gladness;
come into God's presence with singing.
Know that the Lord is God.
It is God that made us, and we are God's;
we are God's people, and the sheep of God's pasture.

(Psalm 100:1–3, alt.)

15

The sung responses are the first stanza of "Joyful, Joyful, We Adore Thee" (CH 2).

Make a joyful noise to the Lord, all the earth.
Joyful, joyful we adore thee, God of glory, Lord of Love.
Worship the Lord with gladness; come into God's presence with singing.

Hearts unfold like flowers before you, opening to the sun above.
Know that the LORD is God.
Melt the clouds of sin and sadness, drive our fear and doubt away.
It is God that made us, and we are God's;
We are God's people, and the sheep of God's pasture.
Giver of immortal gladness, fill us with the light of day!
Come, let us worship God!   (PSALM 100:1–3, ADAPT.)

16

ᵊ Enter God's gates with thanksgiving,
      and God's courts with praise.
   ᴺ Give thanks to God, bless God's name.
 ᵒ **You are truly good, O God.**
      ᵐ **Your steadfast love endures forever,**
      ᴀ **and your faithfulness extends to all generations.**   (PSALM 100:4–5, ALT.)

17

 ᵒ I will bless you, God!
      You fill the world with awe:
 ᴺ You dress yourself in light,
      rich, majestic light.
 ᵒ You pitched the sky like a tent,
      built your house beyond the rain.
 ᵐ You ride upon the clouds,
      the wind your wings,
 ᵒ the wind your words,
      ᴀ the fire your willing tongues.   (PSALM 104:1–4, ICEL)

18

O give thanks to the LORD, call on God's name,
      make known God's deeds among the peoples.
Sing to the Holy One, sing praises to our Sovereign;
      tell of all God's wonderful works.
Glory in God's holy name;
      let the hearts of those who seek the Lord rejoice.   (PSALM 105:1–3, ALT.)

19

O give thanks to God who is good;
      whose steadfast love endures forever.
We thank you, God, for your steadfast love,
      for your wonderful works to humankind;
For you satisfy the thirsty,
      and fill the hungry with good things.
Fill our hearts with wisdom
      that we may ponder the majesty of your loving deeds.
                                              (PSALM 107:1, 8–9, 43, ADAPT.)

20

Praise the LORD, who is faithful,
  who works such wonders for mortals.
Let the congregation exalt the LORD,
  and the council of elders, sing praise to God. (PSALM 107:31–32, CHAMBERLAIN)

21

Praise the LORD!
Praise, O servants of the LORD;
  praise the name of the LORD.
Blessed be the name of the LORD
  from this time on and forevermore.   (PSALM 113:1–2)

22

What shall we return to the LORD
  for all the LORD's bounty to us?
**We will lift up the cup of salvation
  and call on the name of the LORD.**   (PSALM 116:12–13, ALT.)

23

This is the day the LORD has made;
  let us rejoice and be glad in it.   (PSALM 118:24)

24

This is the day the LORD made,
let us rejoice and be glad.   (PSALM 118:24, ALT.)
Come, bow down and worship,
kneel to the LORD our Maker!   (PSALM 95:6, ALT.)

25

Praise the LORD!
    Praise the name of the LORD;
    give praise, O servants of the LORD,
you that stand in the house of the LORD,
    in the courts of the house of our God.
Praise the LORD, for the LORD is good;
    sing to God's name, for God is gracious.   (PSALM 135:1–3, ALT.)

26

Praise the LORD!
How good it is to sing praises to our God;
  for God is gracious, and a song of praise is fitting.   (PSALM 147:1, ALT.)

27

Sing to the LORD with thanksgiving;
    make melody to our God on the lyre.
God covers the heavens with clouds,
    prepares rain for the earth,
    makes grass grow on the hills.   (PSALM 147:7–8, ALT.)

28

Praise the LORD!
Praise the LORD from the heavens;
    praise God in the heights!
Praise God, all the angels;
    praise God, all the heavenly host!   (PSALM 148:1–2, ALT.)

29

Praise the LORD!
Sing to the LORD a new song,
    God's praise in the assembly of the faithful.   (PSALM 149:1, ALT.)

30

Praise the LORD!
Praise God in the sanctuary;
    praise God in the mighty firmament!
Praise God's mighty deeds;
    praise God's surpassing greatness!
Let everything that breathes praise the LORD!
    Praise the LORD!   (PSALM 150:1–2, 6, ALT.)

31

Those who wait for the LORD shall renew their strength,
    they shall mount up with wings like eagles,
they shall run and not be weary,
    they shall walk and not faint.   (ISAIAH 40:31)

32

For thus says the high and lofty one
    who inhabits eternity, whose name is Holy:
I dwell in the high and holy place,
    and also with those who are contrite and humble in spirit,
to revive the spirit of the humble,
    and to revive the heart of the contrite.   (ISAIAH 57:15)

33

Thus says the LORD:
>Do not let the wise boast in their wisdom,
>do not let the mighty boast in their might,
>do not let the wealthy boast in their wealth;

but let those who boast boast in this,
>that they understand and know me,
>that I am the LORD;
>I act with steadfast love, justice, and righteousness in the earth,

for in these things I delight, says the LORD.   (JEREMIAH 9:23–24)

34

The steadfast love of God never ceases.
>**Your mercies never come to an end.**

They are new every morning.
>**Great is your faithfulness.**   (LAMENTATIONS 3:22–23, ALT.)

35

But the hour is coming, and is now here,
when the true worshipers will worship the Father in spirit and truth,
>for the Father seeks such as these to worship him.

God is spirit, and those who worship him
>must worship in spirit and truth.   (JOHN 4:23–24)

36

Grace to you and peace from God our Father and the Lord Jesus Christ.
Blessed be the God and Father of our Lord Jesus Christ,
>**who has blessed us in Christ with every spiritual blessing**
>**in the heavenly places.**

Let us praise the God of glorious grace,
>for the free gift bestowed on us in the Beloved.   (EPHESIANS 1:2–3, 6, ADAPT.)

37

Let us give thanks to the God of our Lord Jesus Christ.
>**God has blessed us in Christ with every spiritual blessing.**

Before the world was made, God chose us in Christ,
>**that we might be holy and blameless before God.**

(EPHESIANS 1:3–4, ADAPT.)

38

By grace you have been saved through faith,
>and this is not your own doing; it is the gift of God—
>not the result of works, so that no one may boast.

We are God's workmanship,
>**created in Christ Jesus for good works,**
>**which God prepared in advance for us to do.**   (EPHESIANS 2:8–10, ALT.)

39
Sing psalms, hymns, and sacred songs;
    let us sing to God with thanksgiving in our hearts.
Let everything you do or say be done in the name of the Lord Jesus,
    giving thanks to God through Jesus Christ.

                                  (COLOSSIANS 3:16–17, ADAPT.)

40
Since we are receiving a kingdom that cannot be shaken,
    let us give thanks,
by which we offer to God an acceptable worship
    with reverence and awe.

                                  (HEBREWS 12:28)

41
Draw near to God,
    and God will draw near to you.
Humble yourselves before the Lord,
    and the Lord will exalt you.

                                  (JAMES 4:8A, 10, ALT.)

42
Grace and peace be yours in abundance
    in the knowledge of God
    and of Jesus our Lord.

                                  (2 PETER 1:2)

43
Hear Christ's call:
"Listen! I am standing at the door, knocking;
    if you hear my voice and open the door,
I will come in to you and eat with you,
    and you with me."

                                  (REVELATION 3:20)

ADVENT

44
Then the glory of the LORD shall be revealed,
    and all people shall see it together,
    for the mouth of the LORD has spoken.

                                  (ISAIAH 40:5)

45
Blessed be the Lord God of Israel,
    who has visited and redeemed God's people,
and has raised up a mighty savior for us
    in the house of David.
By the tender mercy of our God,
    the dawn from on high will break upon us,
to give light to those who sit in darkness and in the shadow of death,
    to guide our feet into the way of peace.

                                (LUKE 1:68–69, 78–79, ALT.)

46

Now is the moment for you to wake from sleep.
For salvation is nearer to us now than when we became believers;
    the night is far gone, the day is near.
Let us then lay aside the works of darkness
    and put on the armor of light.   (ROMANS 13:11–12, ALT.)

CHRISTMAS

47

The people who walked in darkness
    have seen a great light.
The light shines in the darkness,
    and the darkness has not overcome it.
Those who lived in a land of deep darkness—
    on them light has shined.
We have beheld Christ's glory,
    glory as of the only Son of the Father.
For a child is born for us,
    a Son given to us.
In him was life,
    and the life was the light of all people.   (ISAIAH 9:2, 6; JOHN 1:4–5, 14, ALT.)

48

How beautiful upon the mountains
    are the feet of the messenger who announces peace,
who brings good news,
    who announces salvation,
    who says to Zion, "Your God reigns."   (ISAIAH 52:7)

49

God is love.
That love was revealed to us in this way:
    God sent the Son into the world
    so that we may live through him.   (1 JOHN 4:8–9, ADAPT.)

50

God's love was revealed among us in this way:
    God's only begotten Son was sent into the world
    so that in him we might have life.   (1 JOHN 4:9, ADAPT.)

51

I heard a loud voice from the throne saying,
    "See, the home of God is among mortals.
    The Holy One will dwell with them as their God;
    they will be God's peoples,
    and God in person will be with them."   (REVELATION 21:3, ALT.)

Epiphany

52

O God was making friends of all people through Christ.

M God did not keep an account of their sins against them,

All   and God has given us the message how to make them friends.

(2 Corinthians 5:19, TEV, alt.)

Lent

53

Christ humbled himself
  and became obedient to the point of death—
  even death on a cross.   (Philippians 2:8)

54

Christ himself bore our sins in his body on the cross,
  so that, free from sins, we might live for righteousness;
  by his wounds we have been healed.   (1 Peter 2:24, alt.)

Palm Sunday

55

Hosanna!
  Blessed is the one who comes in the name of the Lord!
  Hosanna in the highest!   (Mark 11:9–10, adapt.)

56

Blessed is the one who comes in the name of the Lord.
  Hosanna in the highest!
Praise the Lord.
  The Lord's name be praised.   (based on Matthew 21:9)

Good Friday

57

Is it nothing to you, all you who pass by?
Look and see if there is any sorrow like my sorrow.   (Lamentations 1:12)
But God proves eternal love for us in that while we still were sinners
  Christ died for us.   (Romans 5:8, alt.)
"Here is the Lamb of God
  who takes away the sin of the world!"   (John 1:29)

EASTER

58

Christ is risen. He is risen indeed. Alleluia.
Thanks be to God, who gives us the victory
    through our Lord Jesus Christ.   (1 CORINTHIANS 15:57, ADAPT.)

59

Grace and peace to you in fullest measure.
Praise be to the God and Father of our Lord Jesus Christ,
    who in great mercy gave us new birth into a living hope
    by the resurrection of Jesus Christ from the dead!   (1 PETER 1:2b–4, NEB)

ASCENSION

60

Lift up your heads, O gates!
    and be lifted up, O ancient doors!
    that the King of glory may come in.   (PSALM 24:7)

61

Jesus lifted up his hand.
While blessing his disciples, he parted from them. Alleluia!
Christ went up, above and beyond the heavens,
to fill the whole universe with his presence. Alleluia!
        (BASED ON LUKE 24:50–51; EPHESIANS 4:10)

62

Since, then, we have a great high priest
    who has passed through the heavens,
    Jesus, the Son of God,
let us approach the throne of grace with boldness,
    so that we may receive mercy
    and find grace to help in time of need.   (HEBREWS 4:14, 16, ALT.)

PENTECOST

63

The Lord said:
You shall receive power when the Holy Spirit has come upon you,
    and you shall be my witnesses to the ends of the earth.
Come, Holy Spirit, fill the hearts of your faithful
    and kindle in them the fire of your love. Alleluia!
        (BASED ON ACTS 1:8)

64

God's love has been poured into our hearts
    through the Holy Spirit that has been given to us.   (ROMANS 5:5)

☧ LEADER'S CALLS TO WORSHIP

65

Friends in Christ,
    we are gathered to give thanks
        for all we have received from God's good hands:
    to praise God's holy name;
    to acknowledge and confess our sins;
    to hear God's holy word;
    and to ask those things needful for life.
Let us draw near to God in all humility
    and celebrate God's infinite goodness and mercy.

66

Let us praise our God,
    Holy Mystery, Source of all being, Word and Spirit.
Let us praise and exalt God above all forever.

67

All praise to you, Eternal Spirit,
    Source of life and Savior of the world.
With faithful people of every generation, we praise you;
    through Jesus Christ, with you and the Holy Spirit,
    one God forever and ever. Amen.

68

Sing a new song to our God!
    Songs of celebration, songs of joy!
Gather all the melodies together into one great harmony of praise.
Let the music of our hearts become part of God's great song,
    pulsing through all creation.
Sing a new song to our God!

69

Let us gather within the covenant of love
    which binds us to God and one another.
Let us gather at the table of the Lord
    to celebrate with thanksgiving
    the saving acts and presence of Christ.

Let us gather to remember our baptism into Christ
>by which we enter into newness of life
>and are made one with the whole people of God.
Let us gather to worship the maker of heaven and earth
>to whom be blessing and glory and honor forever!

70

Within the whole family of God on earth,
>we gather as God's church in the name of Jesus Christ
>>for worship, for fellowship, and for service;
>>for mission, witness, and mutual discipline;
>>and for our nurture and renewal as disciples of Christ.
Transcending all barriers within the human family
>we receive the gift of ministry and reconciliation.
All dominion in the church belongs to Jesus Christ,
>its Lord and head, upon whom the whole body depends.

71

O People of God, look about and see the faces of those we know and love—
>*M* (neighbors and friends, sisters and brothers—
>a community of kindred hearts.
D People of God, look about and see the faces of those we hardly know—
>*M* (strangers, sojourners, forgotten friends,
>the ones who need an outstretched hand.
O People of God, look about and see all the images of God assembled here.
>*M* (In me, in you, in each of us,
>God's spirit shines for all to see.
O People of God, come. Let us worship together.

72

Come together as God's people with signs all about us of God's presence:
>a baptistry reminding us of God's redeeming grace;
>a Bible breaking to us the bread of life;
>a cross declaring God's sacrificial love;
>a table where the living Christ bids us welcome.
Come, draw near to God, for God is with us.

73

Come to Christ, the living bread,
>who satisfies those who hunger and thirst for what is right.
Come to Christ, who gives living water,
>that you may never thirst again.
Come to Christ, that being filled yourself,
>you may minister to the hunger and thirst of others.
Come to God, in worship and praise,
>through Jesus Christ, who gives us life.

74

O   Come apart from the chaos awhile
    M   and dwell in the presence of God who is our source of being.
O   God calls us to renew ourselves and our life's purpose
    M   and we gather with others who are searching.
    Let us be at prayer together.
    All Come, let us open our hearts & minds to God

75

God calls us out of our isolation to join hands
    with our sisters and brothers in this community of faith.
God calls us out of our confusion to speak to us from the Word
    and to inspire us by the Spirit.
God calls us out of our sin to cleanse us through the Son
    and to enhance our lives with beauty and usefulness.

76

In the beginning God created the heavens and the earth.
    The earth was without form and void,
    and darkness was upon the face of the deep,
    and the Spirit of God moved across the face of the waters.
Come celebrate the beginning!
Come celebrate the time before all time
    and the people before our people
    and the fishes and birds before all people.
Come celebrate the beginning
    and the mystery hiding there—
        beneath civilization,
        beyond civilization,
        before civilization—
The mystery in the womb of living water,
    giving birth to earth and sea and people and culture.
Come celebrate!

77

O   We have come together because of God:
M   We are created and sustained by the power of God's love.
O   We have come together because of Jesus:
M   We accept his revolutionary example that shows us what life means.
O   We come together because of the Spirit:
M   We experience that presence that inspires and blesses our fellowship.
A   Let us worship God through Jesus in the Spirit.

78

Rejoice, for God is among us.
Give thanks, for in Christ we are a new people.
Sing praise, for we come to worship God.

79

God knows us and our hungers.
God loves us like a father and nurtures us like a mother.
God draws us to each other and claims us as the people of God.
Knowing this, let us worship God.

80

We gather to worship with many needs,
    and in many morning moods:
Some are ready to shout:
    "Make a joyful noise unto the Lord...."
Some echo the psalmist's anguish:
    "Out of the depths I cry to you, O Lord. Lord, hear my voice...."
Some are looking for guidance and direction from the Word of God:
    "more to be desired are they than gold...
    sweeter also than honey and the honeycomb...."
Some long passionately to be close to God:
    "As a deer longs for flowing streams,
    so my soul longs for you, O God...."
God stands ready and able to respond to our needs.
In that assurance, let us worship God.

81

O Let us sing to the Lord our God,
  M majestic in holiness,
   O awesome in glory,
  M working wonders:
O for God is highly exalted
  A and God will reign forever and ever.

82

This is the place and this the time; *– 2 x one 1st many 2nd*
  o here and now God waits to break into our experience:
    m to change our minds,
    o to change our lives,
    m to change our ways;
  o to make us see the world and the whole of life in a new light;
  m to fill us with hope, joy, and ~~certainty~~ *confidence* for the future.
o This is the place, as are all places;
  m this is the time, as are all times.
All Here and now, let us praise God.

GOOD FRIDAY

83

Holy God, we dare not raise our eyes
    for the cross is too horrible a sight before us.
Yet we see a love that refuses to let go—
    the love for Christ the women expressed at the foot of the cross,
    standing in lonely vigil after the men had scattered.
Fill our hearts with that same stubborn love—
    a love that lasts even as our frail hope dies.
We do not presume to understand the depth of your love for us—
    the love that would go to the cross for our sakes.
For such gifts of love we thank you.
    Abide with us as we enter the struggles of this day.
    Keep us close to your heart of love.

EASTER

84

Christ is risen! He is risen, indeed! Hallelujah!

☷ RESPONSIVE CALLS TO WORSHIP

85

We gather on this Lord's Day, about the Lord's table
    to celebrate with thanksgiving
    the saving acts and presence of Christ:
        who touches us with healing and makes us whole;
        who teaches us God's love and brings us to life;
        who washes us in baptism's waters and frees us from sin;
        who reconciles us to God and unites us with others;
        who feeds us with bread and wine and comes to us;
        who shapes us as servants and equips us for ministry.
Blessing, glory, and honor be to God forever. Amen.
Let us worship God who is holy goodness.
Let us bring our praises to the God of deepest reality.
We come offering ourselves to God in awesome wonder:
Holy, holy, holy, God of hosts; all earth is full of your glory.

86

Come now to worship God with justice and truth.
Let us speak the truth to one another,
    rendering true judgments that make for peace.

Let justice roll down like waters,
　　and righteousness like an everflowing stream.
Teach us to do good, seek justice,
　　rescue the oppressed, defend the helpless.
Hear God's demand and promise:
　　Maintain justice, and do what is right,
　　for soon my salvation will come, and my deliverance be revealed.

87

Out of the fullness of the lives God has given us
　　we have come to worship and to praise.
With thanks we offer to God the creativity of our minds,
　　the warmth of our hearts, and the joy of our spirits.
We love because God has first loved us,
　　freeing us from the power of sin and death.
With glad hearts let us join together in singing praise to God:
　　Creator, Word, and Holy Spirit. Amen.

88

Come, Holy Spirit, come.
Come to comfort us in our suffering;
Come to cheer us in our sorrow;
Come to encourage us in our failings;
Come to persuade us in our doubting;
Come to exhort us in our waning zeal;
Come to urge us forward in following Christ.
Renew our strength, O God, as we wait upon you;
Fill us with abounding hope through the power of the Holy Spirit.

89

In worship of God, let us
　　quicken our conscience by God's holiness;
　　nourish our minds by God's truth;
　　purify our imagination by God's beauty;
　　open our hearts to God's love.
Let us surrender our wills to God's purpose,
　　and gather ourselves selflessly before God in adoration.

90

We come to worship God, not to boast in ourselves.
Our wisdom, our might, our wealth—all these are gifts from God.
If we must boast, then let us boast in this:
We come, to understand and know God,
　　to honor God's sovereign majesty.
God acts with steadfast love, justice, and righteousness in the earth.
In these things God takes delight.
Come, let us worship God.

91

God is our constant companion.
There is no need that God cannot fulfill.
> When our pain is severe,
> when our burden is heavy,
> when our depression darkens the soul,
> when we feel empty and alone,

God fills the aching vacuum.
We trust in God's promises. God will not let us go.

92

God anointed Jesus to console the afflicted.
Come, let us worship Christ our Comforter!
God anointed Jesus to emancipate the enslaved.
Come, let us worship Christ our Liberator!
God anointed Jesus to bind up the wounded.
Come, let us worship Christ our Healer!
God anointed Jesus to deliver the troubled.
Come, let us worship Christ our Savior.

93

Come, let us celebrate the supper of the Lord.
Let us make a huge loaf of bread
> **and let us bring abundant wine, as at the wedding in Cana.**

Let the women not forget the salt.
Let the men bring along the yeast.
Let many guests come, the lame, the blind, the poor.
Come quickly. Let us follow the recipe of the Lord.
All of us, let us knead the dough together with our hands.
> **Let us see with joy how the bread grows.**

Because today we celebrate the meeting with the Lord.
Today we renew our commitment to the Kingdom.
Nobody will stay hungry.

94

Come, thank God for the whole of creation,
> for all the works of God's hands,
> for all God has done in our midst,
> through Jesus Christ, our Lord.

We praise your majesty, Almighty God, with all the living;
We bow before you and adore you, exclaiming,
> **Holy, holy, holy Lord, God of all living things;**
> **earth and heaven are filled with your glory,**
> **we bless your name.**

95

Come along with me as a sojourner in faith.
Bring along a sense of expectancy
 a vision of high hopes
 a glimpse of future possibility
 a vivid imagination.
For God's creation is not done.
We are called to pioneer a future yet unnamed.
As we venture forward, we leave behind our desires for
 a no-risk life,
 worldly accumulations,
 certainty.
Let us travel light in the spirit of faith and expectation,
 toward the God of our hopes and dreams.
May we be witnesses to God's future breaking in.
Come along with me as sojourners in faith
 secure in the knowledge that we never travel alone.

96

Gathered together in this community of faith,
 we are a focusing point in time
 for the worship of all God's children in earth and heaven.
Wherever we are gathered,
 In whatever numbers, small or great,
 we show forth life of the great church invisible.
As the redeemed of God,
 let us enter into the communion of the saints.
We offer our lives to God,
 forgetting ourselves in the great company of those who trust in God.

97

Be still before the mystery of Life,
 before your Creator who made it,
 before Jesus who said that he was Life,
 before the Spirit who breathes life into us all,
 before life as we see it in God's good world.
Gracious God, let us revere you in your gift of Life,
 and grant to our reverence, insight into your holy purpose.
With praise and thanksgiving we open our lives to you.

98

Sisters and Brothers, we are called:
Called to follow Jesus.
 What a challenge!
 What an opportunity!

[handwritten:] All: Called to follow Jesus.

[handwritten margin notes:] O M O A

Called to move, as he did, among the people;
    to feel with them;
    to care for them;
    to touch them and be touched by them.
Called to name, as he did, the oppressions that destroy our world:
    those of which we are already aware,
    and those injustices we have not yet learned to recognize or to name.
Called to discern those gifts of life
    God has hidden deep within each one of us.
Called to discover and to share
    those gifts of our hearts, our hands, our whole selves.
Called to place our gifts in God's hands:
    the holy hands from which they came.
Called to follow Jesus
    and yes, we can answer;
    we can follow, because we have been called first to love.
Called to be God's children.
Called by name.

99

Grateful hearts need no special season to offer thanks to God.
Life abundant is itself reason for praise.
In the face of Love's mysteries given such bountiful expression
    what gifts of praise have we?
We have gifts enough for praise:
    Our hands, our strength, our singing hearts.
Let us worship God.

100

The world belongs to God,
    the earth and all its people.
How good and how lovely it is
    to live together in unity.
Love and faith come together,
    justice and peace join hands.
If the Lord's disciples keep silent
    these stones would shout aloud.
Lord, open our lips,
    and our mouths shall proclaim your praise.

101

Rejoice, people of God!
Celebrate the life within you,
    and Christ's presence in your midst!
Our eyes shall be opened!

The present will have new meaning,
    and the future will be bright with hope.
Rejoice, people of God!
Bow your heads before the One
    who is our wisdom and our strength.
We place ourselves before our God,
    that we may be touched and cleansed
    by the power of God's spirit.

102

Sisters and brothers, we have come together to worship God
    who offers us freedom through our Lord Jesus Christ.
For the spirit of life in Christ Jesus
    has set us free from the law of sin and death.
For we did not receive the spirit of slavery to fall back into fear
    but we have received the spirit of the children of God.

103

In the name of our God who shares divinity with us,
in the name of our God who shares humanity with us,
in the name of our God who unsettles and inspires us,
    let us give praise and thanks!
Amen!

104

Rejoice in our God always!
Again, I say, rejoice!
For God has gathered us together
    from all the corners of the earth
    to be present now,
    and to know the joyful unity
    of being one with Christ.
Rejoice in our God always!
Again, I say, rejoice.

105

Life is a journey with others;
We travel as a people, on a winding road.
We share our lives, our experiences, our hopes, our fears.
With joy and hope we welcome other travelers to share our lives.
We learn from each other.
We laugh and cry with each other.
We are at home with each other.
Life is a series of hellos and good-byes.

There are those who arrive to be with us.
There are those who move ahead of us beyond death.
Both in laying hold and letting go we celebrate God's goodness.
We affirm the Spirit's presence in the journey,
      in being Home.

106

O God, of the whirlwind and fire,
      sweeps into our presence in this hour.
M **Glory be to God,**
      who strengthens us and blesses all people with peace.
O God, who called all worlds into being,
      calls forth new life in us today.
M **Glory be to God,**
      in whose creative purpose we are claimed and empowered.
O God, whose Spirit unites all people in a common language of love,
      confirms God's gifts in us as we gather here.
A **Glory to be God,**
      who created light in which we can walk in confident expectation.

107

Let us praise the God who formed the mountains and created the wind.
Let us sing to the One who made the stars,
      who turns deep darkness into morning and day into night.
Let us turn to God, ~~hating~~ what is evil and loving what is just. *turning from*
So may justice roll down like waters,
      and righteousness like an ever-flowing stream. Amen.

108

Sing praises to God, O you saints, and give thanks to God's holy name!
We exalt you, O God, for you have restored us to life!
We may cry through the night, but your joy comes with the morning.
You hear us, O God, and you are gracious in our distress.
You turn our mourning into dancing!
Our souls cannot be silent!
O God, our Savior, we give thanks to you forever!

109

Listen for the voice of God—
God will speak peace to God's people.
But do not be surprised if God's peace comes in the form of judgment.
Do not expect God to whitewash the truth.
We will listen and take heart in God's presence.
Surely God's salvation is at hand for those who fear God,
      that glory may dwell in our land.
God's glory is not that of wealth or power.

God's glory is found in compassion and works of justice.
We will listen and give ourselves anew to God's reign.
Listen for the voice of God—
God will speak peace to God's people.

110

As a shepherd seeks a lost sheep,
  so God seeks and saves the lost.
Like a woman who searches for a lost coin until it is found,
  so God rejoices over one soul restored to wholeness.
As a father receives a returning wayward son,
  so God welcomes us, and lets the past be the past.
Therefore, let us praise God in thanksgiving that we are received.
**Let us receive and welcome and rejoice over one another
  in the name of Jesus Christ.**

111

The Spirit of God calls to us,
  with sighs too deep for words.
The Spirit of God calls to us,
  claiming us,
  summoning us to become more than we now are;
  calling us by name: God's children.

112

Let us sing a hymn in unison,
  for we are not many, but one!
Let us praise our God in harmony,
  for we are not one, but many.
Members are we, one of another:
  the body of Christ, the people of God.
**Let our melody rise as if from one voice,
  while the chorus swells from each mouth of creation.**

113

I will sing of your steadfast love, O God, forever.
With my mouth I will proclaim your faithfulness to all generations.
Let people of all ages bring praise to God:
  **the laughter of children,
  the questioning of youth,
  the determination of young adults,
  the experience of middle years,
  the wisdom of elders.**
We will sing of your steadfast love, O God, forever.
With our mouths we will proclaim your faithfulness to all generations.

114

The sung response for this introit is found in CH 44.

All works of God: bless the living God;
    praise and magnify God forever.
Bless the Lord, O my soul, blessed art thou, O God.
Servants of God: bless the living God;
    praise and magnify God forever.
Bless the Lord, O my soul,
    and all that is within me bless God's holy name.
Holy and humble of heart: bless the living God;
    praise and magnify God forever.
Bless the Lord, O my soul,
    and all that is within me bless God's holy name.

115

The sung response for this introit is found in CH 282.

I will bless you, God! You fill the world with awe!
    You dress yourself in light—rich, majestic light.
Light of light eternal, all things penetrating.
    For your rays our souls are waiting.
To you, O God, we lift up our souls.
As the tender flowers, willingly unfolding
    to the sun their faces holding.
My soul, bless God!
    All my being, bless God's holy name!
Ever so would we do, light from you obtaining,
    strength to serve you gaining.

ADVENT

116

The Spirit and the church cry out:
    Come, Lord Jesus.
All those who await his appearance pray:
    Come, Lord Jesus.
The whole creation pleads:
    Come, Lord Jesus.

117

Mary was a virtuous woman, a woman of strength,
    a woman who lived according to the rules of her time.
On a certain day she heard the voice of an angel sent by God.

And the angel said:
"Hail, O favored one, the Lord is with you."
This greeting was odd and unfamiliar. Mary was troubled,
>VOICE 1: frightened,
>VOICE 2: anxious,
>VOICE 3: startled,
>VOICE 4: disturbed.

And she thoughtfully pondered what it could mean.
And the angel said: "Do not be afraid, Mary,
for you have found favor with God.
>VOICE 1: You will conceive in your womb,
>VOICE 2: you will bear a son,
>VOICE 3: you will call his name Jesus."

And the angel sang on about the greatness of her child.
But Mary was a woman who knew herself, and asked,
>VOICE 4: "How shall this be? I have no husband."

And the angel said:
"The Holy Spirit will come upon you,
the power of the most high will overshadow you,
the child to be born will be called holy."
Out of the shadows,
>out of the darkening experience of the overshadowing of God,
>will emerge what is holy.

118

Let us sing praise to the God of all creation.
Let us sing praise to the Spirit who gives life to all.
Let us sing praise to Jesus Christ,
>in whom the fullness of God was pleased to dwell,
>>**that everything and everyone in all creation**
>>**might be reunited with God ~~through Christ.~~** *in love.*

We sing with the faithful of all ages, tongues, and races!

CHRISTMAS

119

Come to Bethlehem to behold God and humanity made one.
>Here kneel before a humble child who brings God close.

O Christ, we come, just as we are, to receive you.
>**We come that you may bless us with your reconciling peace.**

120

Blessed be God, who has come among us to dwell.
Blessed be God Immanuel.

121

Come, holy people, redeemed of God,
    to follow the way prepared for you.
Glory to God in the highest,
    and peace on earth among those who please God.
Once again the earth is surprised at a manger,
    as the glory of God transforms the commonplace.
Let us go to Bethlehem to see
    what God has made known to us.
Experience anew the wonder of God's ways.
    Kneel in awe before life that is fresh and new.
Let us glorify and praise God
    for all that we have seen and heard!

122

Come, all who await God's coming; there is good news of great joy!
God has come among us in a baby of humble birth.
Our salvation has come; let heaven and earth rejoice!
Give thanks to God's holy name, for God's light has dawned among us.
Join the multitudes who sing, "Glory to God in the highest."
God has redeemed us and calmed our fears;
we are God's own, sought out and not forsaken.

123

Let us rejoice in God, our Sovereign,
    whose salvation comes in everyday events.
In the face of a child God is revealed.
In the babe of Bethlehem we are healed.
Let us give thanks with our whole hearts,
    for God is gracious and merciful.
In the food we eat God's love is shown.
As the bread is broken our worth is known.
Let us worship the God of wondrous works,
    who offers to enter into covenant with us.
In the gift of Christ we receive a new name.
Salvation comes and nothing is the same.

124

Lift up your hearts in prayer. Lift up your voices in praise.
Let your eyes rise in expectation, and your hands in exultation,
For the Lord has drawn near, and dwells among us.
We lift them up. Amen.

125

We come to celebrate a God of love.
We come to celebrate that God is Love.
We come to celebrate that Love revealed:
**Jesus, God's only son, has come into the world
    so that in him we might have life!**
Let our celebration begin!

126

Such a large star for such a tiny babe,
Such a fuss over a poor child in a manger,
Such a loud song for such a quiet gift,
Such celebration for a little stranger,
Such a Love to enter our lives so softly,
Such a Life to fill our hearts with Love!

127

CHOIR: *(a cappella)*
O come, let us adore him, O come, let us adore him,
O come, let us adore him, Christ, the Lord!

The people stand, singing with organ accompaniment (CH 148):

**O come, all ye faithful, joyful and triumphant,
O come ye, O come ye to Bethlehem;
Come and behold him, born the King of angels;
O come, let us adore him, O come, let us adore him,
O come, let us adore him, Christ, the Lord!**

The people who walked in darkness
    have seen a great light;
those who dwelt in the land of deep darkness—
    on them has light shined.   (ISAIAH 9:2, ALT.)

**For to us a child is born, to us a son is given;
    and the government will be upon his shoulder,
    and his name will be called "Wonderful Counselor,
    Mighty God, Everlasting Father, Prince of Peace!"**   (ISAIAH 9:6, KJV ALT.)

**Sing, choirs of angels, sing in exultation,
Sing, all ye citizens of heaven above!
Glory to God, all glory in the highest;
O come, let us adore him, O come, let us adore him,
O come, let us adore him, Christ, the Lord!**

And the Word became flesh and lived among us,
    and we have seen his glory,
the glory as of a father's only son,
    full of grace and truth.   (JOHN 1:14)

Yea, Lord, we greet thee, born this happy morning,
Jesus, to thee be all glory given;
Word of the Father, now in flesh appearing;
O come, let us adore him, O come, let us adore him,
O come, let us adore him, Christ, the Lord!

EPIPHANY

128

Blessings to God, who gives hope in the darkness of our lives.
Blessings to Jesus Christ, who reveals God's love unto the world.
Blessings to the Holy Spirit, who empowers us to be a light for others.
Blessings, honor, and glory to God, today and forever. Amen.

129

Have you seen the star of Bethlehem?
    Arise, people of God; let it shine in your lives.
We have seen Christ's star and have come to worship.
    We are ready to let God lead and direct us.
Come from the shadows of earth
    to the light of God's eternal purposes.
We see the glory of God in our midst
    and our hearts rejoice in expectation.
The promises of the gospel are for us,
    and for all people everywhere.
We are here to be equipped by God
    to carry good news into the world. Amen.

130

God's ways are not our ways. God's thoughts are not our own.
    God watches over us far beyond the powers of human reasoning.
God searches for us.
    Yet we will find God hidden deep in our hearts.
Let us turn away from evil
    and God will have mercy on us.

ASH WEDNESDAY

131

The day of the Lord is coming! The day of the Lord is near!
The time is fulfilled! The reign of God is at hand!
O people, repent! Believe in the gospel!
Come, let us turn and follow the Lord!

PASSION/PALM SUNDAY

132

Jesus set his face resolutely toward Jerusalem.
We gather this day to be strengthened.
Should there come a day
    when we must stand fast against the forces of evil,
        or say "No" to a terrible injustice,
    help us not be broken by the consequences of our decision or action,
    even though a dream we followed lies in fragments at our feet.
Let us worship God
    and celebrate the arrival of the Servant-King.

133

Cry out, people of faith!
    Rejoice and praise God!
If we did not sing praise, the very stones would cry out!
Cry out, people of faith,
    for your Savior draws near to Jerusalem.
Hosanna! God saves!
    Blessed is the One who comes in God's name!
Blessed is Jesus Christ, who did not turn back for fear of the cross.
Let us praise the God who loves us,
    sharing Christ's sufferings,
    and facing with courage our path of faith.
Hosanna! God saves!
    Blessed is the One who comes in God's name!

134

This is the day to remember Jesus' journey from Jerusalem to Calvary:
    the day to remember the deeds of those who inflicted the pain;
the day to remember the acts of those who partook of the burdens;
    the day to remember that we, like the chief priests,
    betray the Lord by stealth;
the day to remember that we, like the woman with the ointment,
owe the Lord our best;
    the day to remember that we, like Judas,
    sell the Lord for silver;
the day to remember that we, like Pilate,
reject conscience for the crowd;
    the day to remember that we, like Simon of Cyrene,
    can bear the Savior's cross;
the day to remember that we, like Jesus,
must die to self to live for God.

HOLY THURSDAY

135

This is a day to remember.
We remember the Passover Jesus shared with his disciples.
We remember his new covenant of broken bread and cup.
We remember his night alone in the garden in prayer.
We remember his arrest, his trial, his suffering,
    the denial of his friend.
We remember this day
    and thank God for Jesus' presence with us then and with us now.

136

On the night before he died, Jesus, knowing what lay in store for him,
    drew his disciples to his side.
He had loved them throughout the years
    and now loved them in ways that words alone could not convey.
Jesus took up a basin of water and a towel and began to wash their feet.
And the disciples recognized Jesus in the act of service.

EASTER

137

Christ is risen!
Let the gospel trumpets speak, and the news as of holy fire,
    burning and flaming and inextinguishable,
    run to the ends of the earth.
Christ is risen!
Let all creation greet the good tidings with jubilant shout;
    for its redemption has come,
    the long night is past, the Savior lives!
    and rides and reigns in triumph
    now and unto the ages of ages.

138

Alleluia. Christ is risen.
Christ is risen indeed. Alleluia.
Alleluia. Christ is risen and the Lord is here.
Christ is risen and the Spirit is with us. Alleluia.
Alleluia. Christ is risen for God has worked wonders.
Christ is risen in glory and power forever. Alleluia.

139

Jesus Christ is risen from the dead.
Alleluia, Alleluia, Alleluia!
We are illumined by the brightness of his rising.
Alleluia, Alleluia, Alleluia!

Death has no more dominion over us.
Alleluia, Alleluia, Alleluia!

140
We are risen with Christ—
the Lord is risen!
Eternal life is ours—
the Lord is risen!
Death has met its master—
the Lord is risen!
The way to heaven is open—
the Lord is risen!
He is risen indeed—
Alleluia! Amen.

EASTERTIDE

141
The risen Christ says: Peace be with you.
We are filled with joy because he lives! Alleluia!
The risen Christ says: Reach out, touch, and believe!
Our Lord and our God! Alleluia!   (BASED ON JOHN 20:26–28)

142
Let us praise God for the mighty deeds wrought through Jesus Christ.
Praise God for loosing the chains of sin!
Let us praise God for the mighty deeds wrought through Jesus Christ.
Praise God for breaking the bonds of death!
Let us praise God for the mighty deeds wrought through Jesus Christ.
Praise God for releasing the forces of love!
Let us join with God's people everywhere
    and praise Jesus Christ the Lord!

PENTECOST *call*

143
Kindling Spirit, build well the fire in our hearts this day.
Fan us to flame that all will see
    the Christ-presence of love blazing in our midst.
Burn the witness on our tongues: Christ's Spirit lives among us.
Jesus Christ, our risen Lord, has set his church on fire
    with strength and boldness and power.
Kindling Spirit, build well the fire in our hearts this day.

RAYER

 CALLS TO PRAYER

The purpose of a call to prayer is to clarify the significance of the praying that is to take place. It is a reminder to the congregation of the importance of what they are called upon to do. Pastoral guidance is helpful when it is expressed as an invitation rather than as an instruction.

See CH 301–306 for choral calls to prayer.

144

Let us remember that God is with us now.
    There is no place where God is not.
    Wherever we go, there God is.
Now and always God encompasses us,
    looks upon us with mercy,
    and is ready to hear us when we call.
Therefore let us pray.

145

Let our prayer arise before you.
And may your grace descend upon the world.
Accept our prayers with all who are praising you this very moment.
And send your spirit to renew the face of the earth.
Give to us, God, eyes for seeing.
And ears to hear your word.

146

Come to our aid, Compassionate One.
We have need of your mercy.
Listen to us now as we pray.
Open our eyes to your works,
and our hearts to your words of life.

147

As a deer longs for flowing streams, so my soul longs for you, O God.
    My soul thirsts for God, for the living God.
    When shall I come and behold the face of God?   (Psalm 42:1–2)
"Blessed are those who hunger and thirst for righteousness,
    for they will be filled."   (Matthew 5:6)

Ho, everyone who thirsts, come to the waters;
    and you that have no money, come, buy and eat!
    Come, buy wine and milk without money
        and without price.   (Isaiah 55:1)

"They will hunger no more, and thirst no more;
    and God will wipe away every tear from their eyes."
                                                            (Revelation 7:16a,17b)

148

On God rests my deliverance and my honor;
    my mighty rock, my refuge is in God.
Trust in God at all times, O people;
    pour out your heart before the Holy One;
    God is a refuge for us.   (Psalm 62:7–8, alt.)

149

O come, let us worship and bow down,
    let us kneel before the Lord, our Maker!
For this is our God, and we are the people of God's pasture,
    and the sheep of God's hand.   (Psalm 95:6–7a, alt.)

150

From the rising of the sun to its setting
    the name of the Lord is to be praised.   (Psalm 113:3)
Let our prayers be counted as incense before you,
    and the lifting up of our hands as an evening sacrifice.   (Psalm 141:2, alt.)

151

While God may be found, we will seek God;
    while God is near, we will call;
let the wicked forsake their way,
    and the unrighteous their thoughts;
let them return to the Lord;
    for they will find mercy and abundant pardon from God.
                                                              (Isaiah 55:6–7, alt.)

152

If we say that we have no sin,
    we deceive ourselves, and the truth is not in us.
If we confess our sins,
        God who is faithful and just will forgive us our sins
        and cleanse us from all unrighteousness.   (1 John 1:8–9, alt.)

Ⓨ *OPENNESS TO GOD*

Although God is always present to every human being, humanity is not always present to God. One aspect of public prayer is to facilitate a people's openness to God. It is assuming a discipline of attending to God. By paying attention to God, we know God better and learn what faithfulness requires. There is much in life that shuts us away from God. A prayer of openness centers attention upon breaking down these barriers.

153
Almighty God, to you all hearts are open,
    all desires known,
    and from you no secrets are hidden:
Cleanse the thoughts of our hearts
    by the inspiration of your Holy Spirit,
that we may perfectly love you,
    and worthily magnify your holy name;
through Jesus Christ our Lord. Amen.

154
Bless us, O God, with a reverent sense of your presence,
that we may be at peace and may worship you
with all our mind and spirit; through Jesus Christ our Lord. Amen.

155
Almighty God, your Son has opened for us
a new and living way into your presence.
Give us pure hearts and steadfast wills
to worship you in spirit and in truth;
through the same Jesus Christ our Lord. Amen.

156
Eternally present God,
    you journey with us through wilderness and through desert.
No matter the circumstance
    the signs of your presence are always with us:
        sometimes in fire and cloud;
        sometimes in bread from heaven and water from a rock.
As we your people gather in praise and prayer,
    reveal yourself to us in cross and candle, Bible and pulpit.
Above all, make yourself known to us through Christ
    in the breaking of bread.
We wait for you in glad reverence and expectant awe.

157

As on a first day you began the work of creating us;
as on a first day you raised your Son from the dead;
so on this first day, good Lord, freshen and remake us:
and as the week is new, let our lives begin again
because of Jesus who shows us your loving power. Amen.

158

God of the faithful in every time,
    today you have called us into your church
    to be one body in Jesus Christ.
You have bestowed upon us the gifts we need for your service.
Grant that we may willingly take our part;
    that we may support one another;
    and that we may seek the greatest gift, which is love.
Knead us together into one loaf
    with all your people throughout the world,
    through your Spirit of unity. Amen.

159

Most holy God, your majesty is exceeded only by your love;
grant us, in this our worship of you,
penitence in the presence of your holiness,
reverence at the thought of your majesty,
and confidence in the knowledge of your love;
through Jesus Christ our Lord. Amen.

160

O God, you are the unsearchable abyss of peace,
    the ineffable sea of love, the fountain of blessings,
    and the bestower of affection,
    who sends peace to those that receive it.
Open to us this day the sea of your love
    and water us with plenteous streams
    from the riches of your grace
    and from the most sweet springs of your kindness.
Make us children of quietness and heirs of peace;
    enkindle in us the fire of your love;
    strengthen our weakness by your power;
    bind us closely to you and to each other
    in our firm and indissoluble bond of unity.

161

Spirit God, in the beginning you gave life and movement,
    color and harmony to the universe.
Everything moves by your power and is one through you.
But most of all you move in the minds and spirits of men and women.
You give vision and insight, speaking spirit to spirit.
You stir the sleeping conscience, rouse the dormant mind,
    to seek justice, express beauty, declare truth.
Most of all you come in the power of Jesus,
    bringing love and joy and peace,
    patience, kindness, goodness,
    faithfulness, gentleness, self-control.
So move us now in mind and conscience;
    stir and quicken us with beauty and truth;
    and give us all your harvest, now and always. Amen.

162

Living God, we seek your presence now.
Our minds cannot understand you,
    yet our hearts cry out for a living relationship with you.
Our eyes cannot see you,
    yet without you there would be nothing to see.
Our faith cannot grasp you,
    yet in you we live and move and have our being.
Our way ahead into this week is hidden from us,
    but we trust that you have prepared a way through for us.
Renew our vision of the eternal truths
    in the light of which our day-to-day lives must be lived.
Open our eyes to see your presence
    in the simple glories of everyday things.
Light up our relationships with other people
    by the living word of love in Jesus.
Help us so to see where we went wrong in the past,
    that we shall be able to take our bearings afresh for the way ahead.
In Christ's name we pray. Amen.

163

Eternal God, we thank you for this house of prayer
    in which you bless your family on its pilgrimage.
Help us to worship you in spirit and in truth;
    that our consciences may be quickened by your holiness,
    our minds nourished by your truth,
    our imaginations purified by your beauty,
    our hearts opened to your love,
    our wills surrendered to your purpose;
and may all this be gathered up in adoration

as we ascribe glory, praise, and honor to you alone,
through Jesus Christ our Lord. Amen.

164

God of love,
   take hold of us in this act of worship,
   and do not let us go until we have been blessed by a vision of love,
      infinitely generous, gentle and forgiving;
      simple, wholesome, mysterious, profound;
   in which all are accepted and no one rejected;
   love that never ends.
Living God, Love itself,
live in our hearts now and forever.

165

Living God, we praise you for Christ's coming to the temple
   to restore true worship.
We praise you that he still comes,
      thrusting aside all that hinders our approach to you,
      all that deprives us of your light,
      and all that prevents our hearing your demands.
We welcome his coming, even when he comes as Judge,
      because we know he always comes in mercy.
Let his coming transform us again,
      so that all our worship and all our lives may honor you forever.

166

Most merciful God,   revealed our freedom
      through Jesus Christ you have set us free from slavery to sin,
      that we might become your children;
help us in this our service of praise,
      to sing of our freedom with joy,
      to long for it in our prayers,
      and to be assured of it in the proclamation of your word;
through the same Jesus Christ our Lord. Amen.

167

O Lord our God! You know who we are:
      people with good consciences and with bad,
      persons who are content and those who are discontent,
      the certain and the uncertain,
      Christians by conviction and Christians by convention,
      those who believe, those who half-believe, those who disbelieve.
And you know where we have come from:
      from the circle of relatives, acquaintances, and friends
         or from the greatest loneliness,

     from a life of quiet prosperity
          or from manifold confusion and distress,
     from family relationships that are well ordered
          or from those disordered or under stress,
     from the inner circle of the Christian community
          or from its outer edge.
But now we all stand before you, in all our differences, yet alike
     in that we are all in the wrong with you and with one another,
     that we must all one day die,
     that we would all be lost without your grace,
     but also in that your grace is promised and made available to us all
          in your dear Son, Jesus Christ.
We are here together in order to praise you
     through letting you speak to us.
We beseech you to grant that this may take place in this hour,
     in the name of your Son, our Lord. Amen.

168

God, confront us in this time of worship.
Confront us with the fears we hold so tightly,
     the favorite sins to which we cling.
Confront us with our closedness.
Knock at all the locked doors of our hearts.
Do not let us rest until you gain entrance.
Tell us the painful truth about ourselves
     that we might receive the truth of Christ—
     the very truth that will set us free. Amen.

169

God of abundant grace:
Grant to each of us a singing heart—
     a heart open and ready to join in your love song.
Grant to each of us a dancing heart—
     willing to embrace all our many partners
     in your great dance of creation.
Grant to each of us a laughing heart,
     that we might come into your holy presence
     with praise, thanksgiving, and joy. Amen.

170

Gathered in your name, O God, we ask you to bless our worship.
May this be an occasion in which kindness and truth shall meet;
     justice and peace shall kiss.
Through the communion of the Holy Spirit
     give us new life that we may rejoice in your goodness.

Embolden us to make real in daily living
    what we experience within this fellowship of your love. Amen.

171

Loving God, we gather in the name of Christ who has called us friends.
    In friendship we come to share life with the one we love.
Within this fellowship make Christ so known to us
    that we shall eagerly seek to please him in all that we say and do.
May the glow of this friendship last into the coming days
    and be known to others as we share life with them. Amen.

172

Revealing God, we would see Jesus.
Open our eyes now to Christ's living presence
    as we attend to your word in holy scriptures
    and listen for the voice of Christ speaking to us.
Through prayer and praise, through bread and wine, *and song,*
    let us know that Christ is in our midst and communes with us. Amen.
    speaking to and through

173

Your steadfast love to us is our joy, righteous God.
We gather to rejoice in your salvation,
    to sing praises to you for all your healing gifts to us.
You have called us to faith
    and have given us strength to live out that faith.
You have joined us together in the life of Christ.
Hear our prayers and our praise in Christ's name. Amen.

174

God of the quiet places, God of the stormy seas,
    we gather in your calming presence.
Silence the crashing waves of trouble in our hearts.
Let us hear your promise to us in Christ's whispered, "Be still."
And in our stillness, let us know within our whole selves
    that you and you alone are our God. Amen.

175

Holy God, ages ago you announced your presence to your people
    through fire and cloud, earthquake and trumpet blast.
We are no longer a people of signs
    but we still long for the reassurance of your touch.
Move among us this day.
Gather us into one people, worthy of your presence.
Anoint this gathering with your grace
    that we might offer you our fullest praise. Amen.

176
Giving God, your generosity to us knows no bounds.
    You have lavished the gifts of life and health upon us.
You freed your people from their bonds in Egypt
    and raised them up to your glory.
Free us from our stubbornness,
    our refusal to know you as our only God.
Raise us up to your honor and praise
    as we gather in your presence this day.
Hear us as we make festival before you.
    Hear our songs and shouts of praise.
Giving God, we return to you our thanks.
    Let all that we do and say bring honor to your name. Amen.

177
Gather us close to your mothering heart, loving God.
Lift us up from where we have fallen.
Help us respond to your persistent call in this time of worship.
Tell us once more that your love is constant in spite of our waywardness.
For such constancy we give you our thanks and praise.

178
God of all seasons,
    your light breaks across our consciousness like the first morning.
We gather with anticipation in your presence
    as spring struggles free of winter's heavy coat.
We have heard the first bird songs and we come to sing you our joy.
    Praise for the singing!
    Praise for the morning!
    Praise to you for your re-creation of our new days!

179
O Faithful God, your mercies to us are new every morning.
M In your presence we gather to give you our thanks and praise.
O You know our hearts in their depths.
    Your knowledge is not limited by human perspective.
M Your creation unfolds its gifts for us daily—
    a great tapestry of love you have spread for our care.
O What can we offer you but our worship and love?
All Great is your faithfulness unto us!

180
Loving God, too often we play hide and seek with you.
We know you are always ready to receive us
    but we are not as ready to open ourselves to your abiding presence.
Ready or not, God, here we come.

bounding into your presence enlivened by your own spirit
rushing energy through all our veins.
Ready or not, here we come,
knowing all too well that we are the ones
who hide ourselves from you.
You are the seeking one,
you are the God who finds our lost hearts.
Ready or not, here we come,
some of us struggling to quiet ourselves,
some of us trying hard to get excited.
Stir in us all a spirit of expectation and a love of surprises.
Gather us together: your children, one and all—
ready to laugh
ready to cry
ready to sing
ready to love and be loved.
Ready or not, God, here we come!

181
Bounteous God, increase our faith as we gather as your people.
Pour forth your love upon us and shower us with gifts of the Spirit.
In our turning to you, *show us your*
grace us this hour, with your abounding love, joy, peace, and patience, *always.*
Fill us with kindness, faithfulness, gentleness, and self-control.
Strengthened in faith,
may we share your generosity with all the world.

182
Creator of the universe, we gather as a portion of your world centered in
Christ. As your community of faith strengthen us this hour, not to be conformed to the world, but transformed by the renewal of our minds. Equip
us to express the kind of world you intended when you spoke it into existence. Join us together with all your people to do your good and perfect
will. Grant that your great day may come when all creation fully pleases
you.

183
O Lord, our God, around us are the symbols of our faith;
symbols of Christ, of your presence, of your love.
Let them speak to us as we worship.
May their beauty, their color, their perfection
cause us to probe our hearts, to recognize our imperfections,
and with contrition, to lay them aside. In Jesus' name. Amen.

184

Lord of life, we gather as your people to give you glory
    and to receive your goodness into our lives.
Lend flavor to our lives
    that we may be the salt of the earth.
Light us with the fire of your Spirit
    that we may shine as lights of prophetic truth.
Fit us this hour for usefulness in your world
    that our words and deeds may add to your praise.

185

Just as a woman caresses her child, O God,
    you wrap us in gentle care.
Make yourself known to us now to still our anxious hearts.
Within this household of faith
    comfort us with the gospel of your abiding love.
Nurture us with the Bread of Life that satisfies.
Free us from all earthly securities
    that we may rely solely upon your strength.

So we may be free at last.

186

We shall fill this sanctuary, O God, with words as we worship.
Let them not substitute for honest acts of faith lived out in daily living.
Make us doers of *the* Word and not speakers only.
Take ~~what we~~ *speak* and turn them into deeds of love and mercy.
Transform ~~our words~~ *what we say* into a living testimony to your Word,
which became flesh in service to humanity.

187

O Bread of Life,
    we come with minds that are hungry for truth;
O Water of Life,
    we come with souls that are thirsty for forgiveness;
O Way of Life,
    we come with wills that are searching for direction;
O Spirit of Life,
    we come with spirits that are yearning for power.
In this holy place, O Lord,
    feed us, refresh us, forgive us, empower us,
    and send us on our way rejoicing.

188

The paint on the canvas, O Lord;
   the chisel against the stone; the speed of the shutter;
none has captured completely the joy, the sorrow;
   the laughter, the tears; the freedom, the burden,
   that we have found in Jesus, our Master and Friend.
May he live in us, as we live for you;
   that we may become his canvas, his stone, his likeness. Amen.

189

Bountiful God, who gathers your church and feeds it through word and
sacrament, fill us, we pray, with the joy of your presence. Turn us from
lessons of war to lessons of peace. Turn us from a craving for the things of
this world to a hunger for that which satisfies forever. We pray, dearest
God, that as you have ushered in this Lord's Day so you will usher in that
day of your holy realm of peace. Help us to live so that our lives are signs,
however small, of its coming. In the name of Christ we pray. Amen.

190

O God, distant yet near,
   we gather as witnesses to your promise
   that if we seek you with all our hearts,
   we will find you.
Be among us this day.
Hear the confessions of our mouths
   and the yearnings of our hearts.
Help us change the narrowness of our vision
   and the pettiness of our living.
Make us new again with your holy grace.
Grant us the maturity to accept your many gifts in humility
   and to use them with faithfulness.
Grant to us your spirit
   that our worship may have integrity and energy,
   ever witnessing to your holy presence in our lives.
We praise and give thanks to you, Eternal Presence;
   through Jesus Christ we pray. Amen.

191

Like the sun that is far away and yet close at hand to warm us,
so God's Spirit is ever present and around us.
Come, Creator, into our lives.
We live and move and have our very being in you.
Open now the windows of our souls. Amen.

192

O God, in mystery and silence you are present in our lives,
    bringing new life out of destruction,
    hope out of despair, growth out of difficulty.
We thank you that you do not leave us alone
    but labor to make us whole.
Help us to perceive your unseen hand in the unfolding of our lives,
    and to attend to the gentle guidance of your Spirit,
    that we may know the joy you give your people. Amen.

193

O God, we do not pretend to come to you with more faith than we really
have. We do not come to make promises that are beyond our grasp. We do
not come seeming to be more than we are. We come to offer these words,
these actions, and ourselves, trusting that you hold in your hands our faith,
our promises, our lives.

194

Living God, we come to worship you,
    praising you for the past
    and trusting you for the future!
We come to join our will to your will,
    make your purpose our purpose,
    and your love our love.
We come in the name of Jesus Christ our Lord.
Amen.

195

Grant, Holy One,
    that thinking, we may think your thoughts;
    that speaking, we may speak your word;
    that singing, we may sing your praise;
    that hearing, we may hear your truth;
    and that willing, we may make your will our own,
so that going out at the end of our worship,
    we may walk in your love and your peace,
    and departing from one another, not depart from you.
Through Jesus Christ our Lord. Amen.

196

Loving God,
open our eyes to see what is beautiful,
our minds to know what is true,
and our hearts to love what is good;
for Jesus' sake. Amen.

197
O God, we expect to meet you here and now
    in bread and drink,
      by word, written and spoken,
      through your people present with us,
      and as the Holy Spirit among us:
Receive our adoration for your power and wisdom,
    our gratitude for your glorious creation,
      our response of trust and obedience to your mercy and love.
Bind us together anew
      as a loving, forgiving, rejoicing company of disciples of Jesus,
and commission us each afresh to be channels of your mercy
      to all other persons; for your name's sake. Amen.

198
Come to our aid, Compassionate One.
We have need of your mercy.
Listen to us now as we pray.
And teach us your words of life.

199
God of life, we rejoice in your love
    which has filled creation from the beginning
    and which calls all life into being.
We praise you for Jesus Christ
    who reveals most fully your loving purpose for all people.
We bless you for your Spirit
    who draws all humanity into the circle of your tender love.
Gracious God, bless us with your presence
    so that our worship and our lives
    may be a true celebration of your love in Jesus Christ,
    in whose name we pray. Amen.

200
Eternal God, into the peace of your presence
    we bring our restless lives.
Down through the ages men and women have sought you
    and found that your faithfulness has no end.
Your people long ago journeyed by your guidance
    and rested on your love.
So guide us as a pillar of cloud by day and fire by night,
    that our imaginations may be filled with your beauty,
    our minds fired by your truth,
    and our hearts overflowing with your love;
    for without you life has no source, or purpose, or destiny.
Refresh our faith, restore our confidence,
    and lay your guiding hand on our lives.
We ask this through Jesus Christ our Lord. Amen.

201

Eternal Light, shine into our hearts,
Eternal Goodness, deliver us from evil,
Eternal Power, be our support,
Eternal Wisdom, scatter the darkness of our ignorance,
Eternal Pity, have mercy upon us;
      that with all our heart and mind and soul and strength
          we may seek your face
      and be brought by your infinite mercy to your holy presence;
          through Jesus Christ our Lord. Amen.

202

God, we are seeking you:
Let yourself be found.
God, we are calling you:
Listen to our prayers.
    We enter your courts with singing.
    We walk through your gates with thanksgiving.
    Receive your people with gladness!
    Welcome us with blessings!

ADVENT

203

God of Israel, with expectant hearts
    we your people await Christ's coming.
As once he came in humility,
    so now may he come in glory,
that he may make all things perfect
    in your everlasting kingdom.
For he is Lord forever and ever. Amen.

204   *Mother*

Father, in heaven, our hearts desire the warmth of your love
    and our minds are searching for the light of your Word.
Increase our longing for Christ our Savior *Jesus' coming*
    and give us the strength to grow in love,
that the dawn of his coming may find us rejoicing in his presence,
    and welcoming the light of his truth, *following his way of*
We ask this in the name of Jesus the Lord. *justice & peace, born*
amen in compassion

205

Father of our Lord Jesus Christ,
    ever faithful to your promises
    and ever close to your church:

The Earth rejoices in hope of the Savior's coming
and looks forward with longing to his return at the end of time.
Prepare our hearts and remove the sadness that hinders us
from feeling the joy and hope that his presence will bestow,
for he is Lord forever and ever. Amen.

206

Lord, oil the hinges of our hearts' doors
that they may swing gently and easily to welcome your coming.

207

Expectant God, teach us in this time of worship the lessons of waiting.
Calm our restless hands
so we may learn deeply the ways of quiet preparation.
Help us know the wisdom of being faithful in your presence.
Waiting God, grant that we learn to live with our questions
rather than demanding instant answers.
Guide us to live in peace with what we cannot understand.
Help us rest in the confidence of your abiding presence
and your abundant promises, soon to be fulfilled.
Indwelling God, fill our hearts with your love
that we may offer praise befitting your holiness.
Strengthen us that all we do and say, all we think and feel,
will be avenues of your praise—
one great magnificat of love lifted to you.
All this we pray in the name of the coming Christ. Amen.

208

God, You wait for us until we are open to you.
We wait for your word to make us receptive.
Attune us to your voice, to your silence;
speak and bring your Son to us—Jesus, the word of your peace.
Your word is near, O Lord our God, your grace is near.
Come to us, then, with mildness and power.
Do not let us fail to hear you,
but make us receptive and open to Jesus Christ your Son,
who will come to look for us and save us
today and every day, forever and ever.
You, God, arouse faith in our hearts, whoever we are.
You know and accept all your people,
whatever their thoughts are of you.
Speak to the world, then, your word,
come with your heaven among us,
give to the good and to the bad your Son,
forever and ever. Amen.

209

God of all wisdom, our hearts yearn for the warmth of your love,
    and our minds search for the light of your Word.
Increase our longing for ~~Christ our Savior,~~ *you*
    and strengthen us to grow in love,
that at the dawn of ~~his~~ coming   *Jesus'*
    we may rejoice in his presence
    and welcome the light of his truth.
~~This we ask in the name of Jesus Christ.~~ Amen.

CHRISTMAS

210

Almighty God, Creator and Ruler of all worlds,
    who in the beginning created light to dispel darkness:
We bless you for the light of your love
    seen in the face of Jesus Christ.
We worship and adore you with heartfelt thanks
    for the fulfillment in him of the promise of the ages.
Blessed are you, Lord God most holy,
    for you have visited and redeemed your people;
    and holy is your name. Amen.

211

For all the light and loveliness that shines upon our lives at Christmastime
we bless you; but above all, for the Babe of Bethlehem. With humble footsteps and reverent hearts we come to the manger of the Child. Lead us
away from our pride and conceit to the humility of childlikeness today.
May the kingdom of heaven belong to us because we have become teach-
able as children. Amen.

212

Inhabit our hearts, God of history,
    as you once inhabited human flesh.
Be here among us with all of your wisdom,
        all of your power,
        all of your mercy,
        all of your love,
    that we might learn to be like God   *one of*
    from our God who came to be like us.
Holy are you.
Holy are we
    who are one with you forever. Amen.

213

Lord our God, with the birth of your Son,
    your glory breaks on the world.

Through the night hours of the darkened earth
    we your people watch for the coming of your promised Son.
As we wait, give us a foretaste of the joy that you will grant us
    when the fullness of his glory has filled the earth,
    who lives and reigns with you forever and ever.

214

Immanuel, God with us, show us where you may be found today:
    in each human birth, in family joy, in relentless tragedy,
    in treasured babes, and homeless families.
Immanuel, we rejoice that you are with us—
    in everything, through everything.
Lord Christ, be born in us today.
Word of God, become flesh in us that we might live your gospel.
Light of the world, shine in us and through us for the sake of your world.
Loving God, help us to see your grace,
    hear your voice, and follow in your way;
        through Jesus Christ our Savior. Amen.

LENT

215

Light of light, in you is found no shadow of change
    but only the fullness of life and limitless truth.
Open our hearts to the voice of your Word
    and free us from the original darkness that shadows our vision.
Restore our sight that we may look upon your Son
    who calls us to repentance and a change of heart,
        for he lives and reigns with you forever and ever.

216

The colors of our lives have become muddied and dull, O God.
We long desperately to hear the message of the Easter angels;
    but our weekday morning lives reflect only a shadow
    of the promise of resurrection.
The world brands us fools.
We pray that our foolishness is not in vain.
Some call you a fool as well,
    but we know you as Creator,
    Giver of all good gifts.
Yet reality's harsh glare blinds us at times
    to the dawn of your quiet triumphant presence.
So help us rehearse our lines once more
    with the fresh colors of new life refashioning our faces.
Send us forth yet again as messengers of your redeeming folly.
Lead us with joy once more into the great carnival of life.
Help us to live as your April fools. Amen.

EASTER

217

Dressed in our finest we gather as a community of faith, O God,
(its) *(around The world)*

to sing to you Easter alleluias and to offer you our Sunday best.
Christ is risen, bringing a deadening world to new life.
As we celebrate this good news with joy and gladness,

reclothe us inwardly with the splendor of your compassion,
kindness, humility, meekness, and patience, *and*
Above all, make us fashion statements of love, *your*

which binds everything together in perfect harmony.
We pray in the name of the one who is creating all things new.

PENTECOST

218 *unison*

Holy Spirit, come like a mighty rushing wind

and awaken us out of our complacency, our apathy, our indifference.
Disturb us, for we are too content to let things go on as they are

and to let people go on not knowing your *love.*
Penetrate the closed gates of our hearts and make us live again.
O Holy Spirit, create among us a mighty Christian revolution *transformation*

and cast the fear of the unknown out of our lives.

219

Living God, your powerful Spirit

made the apostles bold on the day of Pentecost,
and set them free from self-consciousness and fear
to proclaim the good news of Christ.
As we are together here for praise and prayer,

fill us with the same Spirit,
so that we may be bold to proclaim the good news again,
to the ends of the earth; to the honor of your great name.
                a blessing to all creation.

☻ GLORY AND ADORATION

One way of praying is to give God glory. The Protestant reformer John Calvin asserted humanity's chief end is to live joyfully to the glory of God always. Another way of expressing this is to center in admiration upon the very nature of God. It is to revel in the presence of God who is with us. It is saying how good it is to share communion with our God known to us in the Spirit through Jesus Christ.

220
Who is like you, Lord our God—majestic in holiness,
    awesome in glory, working wonders?
In your unfailing love you will lead your redeemed:
    in your strength you will guide us.
To you we sing, for you are highly exalted:
    you will reign forever and ever. Amen.

221
The response may be sung to the first line of "What Wondrous Love Is This," CH
200.

In this the love of God was made manifest among us, that God sent his
only Son into the world, so that we might live through him. For God so
loved the world that he gave his only Son, that whoever believes in him
should not perish but have eternal life. For God sent the Son into the world,
not to condemn the world, but that the world might be saved through him.

                                        (1 JOHN 4:9; JOHN 3:16–17, ALT.)

What wondrous love is this, O my soul, O my soul,
what wondrous love is this, O my soul!

In this the love of God was made manifest among us, that God sent his
only Son into the world, so that we might live through him. In this is love,
not that we loved God but that he loved us and sent his Son to be the ex-
piation for our sins. He destined us in love to be his children through Jesus
Christ, according to the purpose of his will, to the praise of his glorious
grace which he freely bestowed on us in the Beloved. In him we have redemption through his blood, the forgiveness of our trespasses, according
to the riches of his grace which he lavished upon us.

                                (1 JOHN 4:9–10; EPHESIANS 1:5–8, ALT.)

What wondrous love is this, O my soul, O my soul,
what wondrous love is this, O my soul!

Who shall separate us from the love of Christ? Shall tribulation, or distress, or persecution, or famine, or nakedness, or peril, or sword? No, in all
these things we are more than conquerors through him who loved us. For
I am sure that neither death, nor life, nor angels, nor principalities, nor
things present, nor things to come, nor powers, nor height, nor depth, nor
anything else in all creation, will be able to separate us from the love of
God in Christ Jesus our Lord.   (ROMANS 8:35; 37–39, ALT.)

What wondrous love is this, O my soul, O my soul,
what wondrous love is this, O my soul!

Let us have this mind among ourselves, which is ours in Christ Jesus, who,
though he was in the form of God, did not count equality with God a thing
to be grasped, but emptied himself, taking the form of a servant, being

born in human likeness. And being found in human form he humbled himself and became obedient unto death, even death on a cross. Therefore God has highly exalted him and bestowed on him the name which is above every name, that at the name of Jesus every knee should bow, in heaven and on earth and under the earth, and every tongue confess that Jesus Christ is Lord, to the glory of God the Father. (PHILIPPIANS 2:5–11, ALT.)

**What wondrous love is this, O my soul, O my soul,
what wondrous love is this, O my soul!**

So we have known and believe the love that God has for us. God is love, and those who abide in love abide in God, and God abides in them. Hope does not disappoint us, because God's loves has been poured into our hearts through the Holy Spirit that has been given to us. (1 JOHN 4:16; ROMANS 5:5)

222

You are holy, God the Creator, giving us richly all things to enjoy.
You are holy, Christ the Savior of the world, made flesh to set us free.
You are holy, Spirit of truth and love, willing to dwell in us.
You are holy and blessed, O God, eternal Trinity, and we worship you.

223

Lord God, we come to adore you. You are the ground of all that is.
     You hold us in being, and without you we could not be.
Before we were born, before time began,
     before the universe came into being, you were.
When time is finished, when the universe is no more, you will still be.
     Nothing can take your power from you.
And in your presence we can only be silent
     before the mystery of your being,
     for no words of ours can do justice to your grandeur.
(*Silence*)
Yet you have spoken to us.
Out of universal silence your living word has sprung.
     You have spoken, and given form and beauty to the world.
     You have spoken, and given purpose to human life.
     You have spoken, and declared the forgiveness of our sin.
     You have spoken, and freed us from the fear of death.
Lord Jesus Christ, divine Word, speak to us now.
Show us the beauty of life; unite us to the eternal purpose;
     remove our guilt; conquer the fear of death in our hearts.
Speak and let us hear, for your name's sake.

224

O Lord, we adore you, the Word, the Truth, the living God.
With worshiping hearts and listening ears, we bow before you,
    whose voice has sounded over all the earth
        in the thunder of the commandments,
        in the preaching of prophets and apostles,
        and in the teaching of Jesus Christ.
Speak to us now, O God,
    and may we not forget what we hear but act upon it always;
through Jesus Christ, your Son, our Savior. Amen.

225

Holy Lord, God of power and might,
    heaven and earth are full of your glory.
You chose to become one of us in Jesus Christ,
    sharing our joy and sorrow,
    manifesting your greatness in the child of the manger,
    revealing your Lordship in the master's
    washing his disciples' feet,
    showing forth your glory in the shame of the cross, _surprising us_
And so we praise you for your love   _Easter morning._
    which is great enough to embrace the universe,
    yet close enough to enter our hearts.
~~During our worship,~~ Surprise us with your grace
    that we, with the rest of the church
    and the whole creation, may praise and adore you,
    O God, our Creator and Redeemer. Amen.

226

God of the insistent Spirit,
    we feel you within us,
    rearranging our loves and desires,
    refurbishing our hearts as your home.
God of the intimate Spirit,
    you not only treasure all that once happened—
    you are the promise of all that is yet to come;
    you do not hold yourself far away from us;
    you know our deepest needs as your own.
God of the dancing Spirit,
    how can it be that we matter to you?
    You have choreographed the electrons and the galaxies,
        the infinitesimal and the infinite;
    yet you hold us in high esteem; you care for us.
From this assurance we draw our hope,
    our confidence, our strength.

227

I worship you, Lord; I bless you, God the Good;
   I beg you, Most Holy; I fall down before you, Lover of humankind.
I give you glory, O Christ, because you, the Only Begotten,
    the Lord of all things, who alone are without sin,
     gave yourself to die for me, a sinner unworthy of such a blessing:
    you died the death of the cross
      to free my sinful soul from the bonds of sin.
What shall I give you, Lord, in return for all this kindness?
   Glory to you for your love.
   Glory to you for your mercy.
   Glory to you for your patience.
   Glory to you for forgiving us all our sins.
   Glory to you for coming to save our souls.
   Glory to you for your incarnation in the virgin's womb.
   Glory to you for your bonds.
   Glory to you for receiving the cut of the lash.
   Glory to you for accepting mockery.
   Glory to you for your crucifixion.
   Glory to you for your burial.
   Glory to you for your resurrection.
   Glory to you that were preached to men and women.
   Glory to you in whom they believed.
   Glory to you that were taken up into heaven.
   Glory to you who sit in great glory at the Father's right hand.
   Glory to you whose will it is that the sinner should be saved
     through your great mercy and compassion.

ADVENT

228

Holy God, we adore you because you have come to us in the past.
   You have spoken to us in the Law of Israel.
   You have challenged us in the words of the prophets.
   You have shown us in Jesus what you are really like.
Holy God, we adore you because you still come to us now.
   You come to us through other people and their love and concern for us.
   You come to us through men, and women who need your help. *and children*
   You come to us as we worship you with your people.
Holy God, we adore you because you will come to us at the end.
   You will be with us at the hour of death.
   You will still reign supreme when all human institutions fail.
   You will still be God when our history has run its course.
We welcome you, the God who comes,
   Come to us now in the power of Jesus Christ our Lord. *your Spirit.*

229

This is one variation of the "Advent Antiphons." See CH 120 for a different ren-
dering. The praying of the Antiphons can be interspersed with the singing of "O
Come, O Come, Emmanuel," CH 119.

O Wisdom, coming forth from the mouth of the Most High,
    pervading and permeating all creation,
    you order all things with strength and gentleness:
    come now and teach us the way to salvation.
        Come, Lord Jesus.
O Adonai, Ruler of the house of Israel,
    you appeared in the burning bush to Moses
    and gave him the Law on Sinai:
    come with outstretched arms to save us.
        Come, Lord Jesus.
O Key of David, Scepter over the house of Israel,
    you open and no one can close,
    you close and no one can open:
    come to set free the prisoners
    who live in darkness and the shadow of death.
        Come, Lord Jesus.
O Radiant Dawn, splendor of eternal light, Sun of Justice:
    come, shine on those who live in darkness
    and in the shadow of death.
        Come, Lord Jesus.
O Ruler of the nations, Monarch for whom the people long,
    you are the Cornerstone uniting all humanity:
    come, save us all, whom you formed out of clay.
        Come, Lord Jesus.
O Emmanuel, our Sovereign and Lawgiver,
    Desire of the nations and Savior of all:
    come and save us, O Lord our God.
        Come, Lord Jesus.

CHRISTMAS

230

The sung RESPONSE *is the refrain from "Angels We Have Heard on High," CH*
155.

In the beginning of the world's creation,
from chaos, God brought all things into being.
In the beginning was the Word with God.
Without the Word nothing was made that was made.
The Word was God.   **R**

The Word is Christ, eternal,
uncreated, untarnished mirror of God's active power.
For the Word the earth was made, and all the living,
the boundless universe, the things we see, and things unseen.   R

God said: Let there be light, and there was light.
The Word is life, true light of every human heart.
The Word came down to earth and was made flesh,
to dwell with all humanity.   R

The Word, our Christ, is the shoot sprung up from Jesse's root,
the child of God and Mary's virgin womb.
Redeemed by Christ, we too are children of God,
whose glory Christ has destined us to share in endless life.   R

PASSION/PALM SUNDAY

231

We pray that the Lord of Palm Sunday will bless us today:
    Come into our city, Lord; bring hope and a cause for joy.
        Hosanna to the King
        who comes in the name of the Lord!
    Come into our fellowship, Lord;
    cleanse it of all that is not in accordance with your will.
        Hosanna to the King
        who comes in the name of the Lord!
    Come into our hearts, Lord; teach us your love and your truth.
        Hosanna to the King
        who comes in the name of the Lord!
Lord Jesus, as you entered into Jerusalem and its temple,
    so come to us, that we may be a holy people,
        worthy of your presence, bringing glory to your name. Amen.

232

God our Maker, today in remembrance and awe
        we tread the holy ground of Calvary:
    this place of abandonment
            that has become the scene of our adoration;
    this place of suffering
            that has become the source of our peace;
    this place of violence
            that has become the battlefield on which love is victorious.
Loving God, as we relive the events of this day
    it is with awe that we count again the cost of our salvation.
Words cannot be found to utter our thanksgiving.
Accept our silent adoration; in Jesus' name. Amen.

EASTER

233

Christ is risen!

Mighty God, we have no words that can express
your power and our awe.

Christ is risen! You raised him from the dead.

Blessing and honor and glory and power be yours, almighty God,
forever and ever.

Christ is risen! You raised him from the dead.

All creation sings the glory of the risen and victorious Son.

Christ is risen! You raised him from the dead.

We are free from the power of sin and death.

Christ is risen! You raised him from the dead.

Mighty God, we have no words that can express
your power and our awe. But with adoring hearts we now affirm:

Christ is risen! You raised him from the dead. Alleluia! Amen.

 *DOXOLOGIES*

The doxology is a sung liturgical praise to God. It has often begun with the traditional words beginning "Praise God from whom all blessings flow." Dissatisfaction of some with this traditional formulation has led to the development of fresh expressions intended to more inclusive.

See CH 46–50 for appropriate doxology tunes.

234

Praise God, from whom all blessings flow;
Praise Christ, all creatures here below;
Praise Holy Spirit evermore;
One God, triune, whom we adore. Amen.   (CH 48)

235

Praise God, from whom all blessings flow;
Praise God, all creatures here below;
Alleluia! Alleluia!
Praise God, the source of all our gifts!
Praise Jesus Christ, whose power uplifts!
Praise the Spirit, Holy Spirit!
Alleluia! Alleluia! Alleluia!   (CH 50)

236

Praise God, from whom all blessings flow.
Let songs rise up from earth below.
Let stars and galaxies enthrone.
Creator, Christ, and Spirit, One. Amen.

237
Praise God, from whom all blessings flow,
in heaven above and earth below;
one God, three persons, we adore—
to you be praise for evermore! Amen.

238
Praise God, the Source of life and birth.
Praise God, the Word, who came to earth.
Praise God, the Spirit, holy flame.
All glory, honor to God's name! Amen.

(🍷) *PRAISE AND THANKSGIVING*

Prayers of praise and thanksgiving contemplate with gratitude what God has done and continues to do in the life of the world. They recall and recite what God has done in creation and redemption with severe mercy toward a wayward people. They are a means of grateful response to the good news of the God who judges with mercy and whose loving-kindness is everlasting.

239
Compassionate God, in your holy presence we gather.
We bless you for your steadfast love, for your abundant mercy.
Your life-giving gifts to us never end:
    our strength is renewed like the eagle's.
We thank you for your forgiveness,
    for removing the burden of our sins from us.
With your angels, and all your people, we sing to you our praise.

240
Eternal God, you are the power that created the universe,
    the energy that fires everything,
    the strength that sustains our world.
Eternal Father, you are the love that encircles us,
    the grace that enables us,
    the truth that enlightens us.
Eternal Savior, you are the glory of the cross of Christ,
    the hope of the resurrection,
    the life of the Holy Spirit.
God of love, power, and glory: we praise you. Amen.

241

Great and merciful God,
>   your life is the source of the whole world's life;
>   your mercy is our only hope;
>   your eyes watch over all your creatures;
>   you know the secrets of our hearts.

By your life-giving Spirit, draw us into your presence,
>   that we may worship in the true life of your Spirit,
>   with lives moved by your love,
>   through him who has led us to your heart of love,
>   even Jesus Christ our Lord.

242

God of the galaxies, yet accessible to every human heart;
Mind behind the universe, yet one whom we can call our Father; *our Mother;*
Infinite, yet within our reach;
Awesome and majestic, yet compassionate and tender;
Above and beyond us, yet here beside us:
We praise your name, through Jesus Christ our Lord.

243

Lord, you are our shepherd;
>   you give us all we need.
You make us lie down in green pastures;
>   you lead us beside still waters;
>   you restore our soul.
You guide us in the paths of righteousness.
Even though we walk through the valley of the shadow of death
>   you are with us, and you comfort us.
Let your goodness and your love follow us all the days of our life,
>   until we live in your presence for ever. Amen.

244

Almighty God, we give you thanks
>   for this life and all its blessings,
>   for joys great and simple,
>   for gifts and powers more than we deserve,
>   for love at the heart of your purpose
>   and a surpassing wisdom in all your works,
>   for light in the world brought once in Christ
>   and shining ever through his Spirit.
We pray, through Jesus Christ our Lord,
>   for that light to dawn upon us daily,
>   that we may always have a grateful heart,
>   and a will to love and to serve to the end of our days.
Lord, hear our prayer and our praises:
Alleluia, we bless you, O God.

245

Our gracious God, out of chaos and darkness in the beginning you brought
into being the splendor of the universe and the world in all its beauty.
God, we praise you: **We give you thanks.**
At the right time you sent your Son to be the Light of the world, to lead us
out of spiritual darkness into the marvelous brightness of your truth. In
him has dawned the day of resurrection life.
God, we praise you: **We give you thanks.**
Above all the noise and movement of this world today, we look for the
coming of the new heaven and earth, "the holy city of God." Lord Jesus,
you are coming again in great power and glory.
God, we praise you: **We give you thanks.**
We thank you that you are in this world, by your Spirit preparing a people
for this next great cosmic event.
God, we praise you: **We give you thanks.**
We thank you that you are healing lives that have been torn and broken by
sin, and that you are filling us with joy and hope.
God, we praise you: **We give you thanks.**
Lord God, we await the dawning of the new day when the earth shall be
filled with the glory of God as the waters cover the sea.
To God be praise and thanks forevermore. Amen.

246

We give you thanks, most gracious God,
    for the beauty of earth and sky and sea;
    for the richness of mountains, plains, and rivers;
    for the songs of birds and the loveliness of flowers.
We praise you for these good gifts,
    and pray that we may safeguard them for posterity.
Grant that we may continue to grow
    in our grateful enjoyment of your abundant creation,
    to the honor and glory of your name, now and forever. Amen.

247

Lord God, maker of all worlds, we praise and adore you:
    thank you for our beautiful planet moving in space;
    thank you for light, and warmth, and food,
        and life in all its forms;
    thank you for magnificent rainbows
        and night skies patterned with stars;
    thank you for a glimpse of your majestic universe;
    thank you for humankind,
        and for creating each one of us in your image;
    thank you for Jesus whose name is over all. Amen.

248

Thank God for life, for living
Thank God for love, for giving
Thank God for death:
an ending, a beginning.

Thank God for lips, for speaking
Thank God for hearts, for seeking
Thank God for weakness:
a stumbling and upsurging.

Thank God for eyes, for seeing
Thank God for soul, for being
Thank God for absence:
a longing and unfolding.

Thank God for life, for loving
Thank God for death, for longing
Thank God with singing.

249

We praise you, O God, and thank you,
        for your merciful kindness is great toward us
        and your faithfulness endures forever.
Save us from being so steeped in care,
        so darkened by passion or so thoughtless of your presence,
        that we pass unseeing and unheeding,
                even when the bush by the wayside is aflame with your glory.
Open the eyes of our minds
        to the tokens of your power and goodness around and within us.
And fill our hearts, O God, with your love,
        our mouths with your praise, and our lives with your obedience,
                to the glory of your name. Amen.

250

O God, Creator, Redeemer, and Sanctifier,
        we thank you that we may be together
        to hear your word of life and hope.
We are all equal before you.
You know our life in its deepest recesses.
You have not forgotten us.
You love us, and again and again you fill the empty hands
        that we stretch out toward you.
Through the suffering and death of your Son Jesus Christ,
        you took our darkness and fear upon yourself
        in order that we might know light and joy.

251

The following response may be read or sung. The tune is found in Canticles and
Gathering Prayers *by John P. Mossi and Suzanne Toolan (Winona, Minnesota:
Saint Mary's Press, 1989), p. 35.*

**You are the One who gathers us,
loving, compassionate God.**

Blessed are you, Loving God.
　　You are our wellspring and omega point.
Your Spirit binds us together in respect, dignity, and service.
　　Gather our community together now and in the future. Amen.　　**R**

Blessed are you, Creator of All that Is!
　　In your image we are made;
　　in your likeness you fashion and form us.
Your breath gives us life,
　　that we may know you, O Creator.
Day by day you pour out your love to us,
　　that we might see the beauty of all you have done.　　**R**

Blessed are you, Steadfast Lover!
　　You are ever faithful;
　　your promises endure through all generations.
Though we wander far from you,
　　your ardent desire to be our God ever calls us back.
With a love spilling over its bounds you draw us to yourself.　　**R**

Blessed are you, Gracious Giver of Salvation!
　　Your great power wells up within us to be our strength,
　　to be our hope, to be our glory.
With your mighty arms you shelter us in times of distress.
You go before us,
　　that with your grace we may win victory over death.　　**R**

Blessed are you, Source of All Compassion!
　　You tremble as a mother giving birth.
For when we, your people, suffer in darkness,
　　you bring forth light and life.
The warmth of your love for us melts away fear and sadness.
　　You bring to new birth the dawning child of mercy.　　**R**

Gather us now into one holy union.
　　Give us the grace to look beyond all divisions.
Show us the oneness that we are called to be.
　　Guide us to the source of all community.
Infuse our hearts with one desire,
　　and bring us to the fullness of your one love!　　**R**

In communion with our Savior, Jesus Christ,
    and with the Holy Spirit, who remains our guide,
    we, your gathered people, give you all praise,
    all honor, and all glory,
for by your gracious love,
    we are a holy people for all generations,
    world without end. Amen.

252

Let us give thanks for all God's goodness to us:
For creating the world and for preserving it until now:
    we give you thanks, O Lord,
    and praise your holy name.
For the regular return of day and night, and of the seasons:
    we give you thanks, O Lord,
    and praise your holy name.
For the wonder of nature and the beauty of the earth:
    we give you thanks, O Lord,
    and praise your holy name.
For our memory, which enables us to build on the experience of the past:
    we give you thanks, O Lord,
    and praise your holy name.
For our imagination which admits us to a wider world
        than we could otherwise know:
    we give you thanks, O Lord,
    and praise your holy name.
For the grace by which you have revealed yourself to us:
    we give you thanks, O Lord,
    and praise your holy name.
For your patience with our waywardness
        and your forgiveness for our sinfulness:
    we give you thanks, O Lord,
    and praise your holy name.
Above all we thank you for the promise of all things made new,
    and for our re-creation in your dear Son, Jesus Christ our Lord. **Amen.**

253

Creator God, we thank you for the beauties of nature, for shape and color;
for times and seasons; for our dependence upon the earth and our responsibility as its stewards; for our care of animals and plants and for all signs
of new life at this time of year.
    Creator of the Universe,
    We thank you.

Creator God, we thank you for giving birth to the human family; for our variety of race and culture. We praise you that you did not create us to live in isolation but to share with others in loving relationships.

Creator of us all,
We thank you.

Creator God, we thank you for your supreme gift in Jesus Christ; for his life on earth and oneness with the poor and outcast; for his dying and rising again to open new relationships; for gifts of choice and decision; for the ability to respond and be changed.

Creator of Life,
We thank you.

Creator God, we thank you for family relationships here and now; for bonds of love that endure stress and strain; for mutual respect and the opportunity to develop our full potential, for the cooperation that makes us free to be ourselves and uphold our Christian values.

Creator of feelings and sustainer of life,
We thank you.

Creator God, we thank you for continent and climate; for transport and travel; for the bonds of friendship and groups; for our fellowship with the family of the world church; for the challenge and friendship of people of other faiths.

Creator of all that is and shall be,
We thank you.

254

Mother of the world,
   to you we sing praise and adoration for life's abundance and grace.
You provide for our needs with the bounty of your womb.
You bless us with the touch of your breath upon our souls.
You caress us with your love in our hearts.
Praise and thanksgiving to you we raise,
   with grateful lives and joyful hearts. Amen.

255

Almighty and eternal God:
We thank you that you created the universe
   and that you have revealed yourself to us in human form
   in Jesus Christ your Son, our Lord.
We thank you that he chose to identify himself
   with us and all humanity, and accepted baptism in water
   as the means by which we might declare your will and purpose
   and be filled with the Holy Spirit.

We thank you for the mission of love
    that Christ's baptism inaugurated;
    for his offering of himself upon the cross;
    for his mighty resurrection and his glorious ascension.
We thank you that our baptism has united us with Christ,
    incorporated us into his mission,
    and made us part of his body, the church.
We thank you that, as by baptism we share in Christ's death,
    so by your grace we share in his victory over death.
We thank you that you still dwell within us,
    refreshing us by your Spirit,
    and making us able to serve you in the world Christ came to save.
Almighty and eternal God,
    you have made us yours by baptism and the Holy Spirit;
    we offer ourselves again to you,
    and pray that we may be your faithful soldiers and servants
    to our life's end, in the name of Jesus Christ our Lord. Amen.

256

O   We give you thanks, God of abundant life,
    M   for bread and friendship and hope.
O   With these gifts of your grace we are nourished.
    M   With these signs of your presence we are able to be faithful.
O   Continue to nourish us, inspire us, and call us,
    All   that we might help make your reign more of a reality in our day.

257

We give you thanks, God our Creator,
because you have given us life.
You have made us in your image and breathed your Spirit into us.
We are alive with divinity and your glory is made manifest in us;
we have been touched by God!

258

God of all glory:
On this first day of the week you began creation,
    bringing light out of darkness.
On this first day you began your new creation,
    raising Jesus Christ out of the darkness of death.
On this Lord's Day, grant that we,
    the people you create by water and the Spirit,
    may be joined with all your works
    in praising you for your great glory.
Through Jesus Christ in union with the Holy Spirit,
    we praise you now and forever. Amen.

259
Thank you, Lord.
>You are the light that never goes out.
>You are the eye that never closes.
>You are the ear that is never shut.
>You are the mind that never gives up.
>You are the heart that never grows cold.
>You are the hand that never stops reaching.

Thank you, Lord. And let us be receptive to you.

260
We thank you, God, that you are here with us and in us. We discover you through those who listen to our loneliness and celebrate our happiness. We meet you when we share the anxious hours and triumphant moments of others. We offer ourselves as grateful agents of your spirit and joyful channels of your love. In Jesus' name. Amen.

ADVENT

261
Almighty God, we thank you for the holy scriptures, in which you have revealed to us your Son Jesus Christ as the fulfillment of the law and the prophets, the promised Messiah of Israel, and the Redeemer of humankind. Grant that we, who gratefully celebrate his advent and acknowledge him as your living Word, may walk in the light of his truth and make known the good news of his kingdom in all the world, to the glory of your name.

CHRISTMAS

262
A child is born in Bethlehem. Alleluia.
Come, let us rejoice. Alleluia. Alleluia.
This is the day we have long awaited,
>the reality foretold by all the prophets.

We thank you. We praise you. We rejoice in you.
You are our God who shares divinity with us.
We thank you. We praise you. We rejoice in you.
You are our God, Emmanuel, ever in our hearts and lives each day.
We thank you. We praise you. We rejoice in you.

263
The Word was made flesh,
Alleluia. Alleluia!
and dwelt among us,
Alleluia. Alleluia!

Jesus, Son of the living God, Splendor of the Father, Light eternal:
Glory to you, O Lord!
Jesus, King of glory, Sun of righteousness, born of the Virgin Mary:
Glory to you, O Lord!
Jesus, Wonderful Counselor, Mighty God, Everlasting Lord:
Glory to you, O Lord!
Jesus, Prince of Peace, Source of life, perfect in holiness:
Glory to you, O Lord!
Jesus, Friend of all, Protector of the poor, Treasure of the faithful:
Glory to you, O Lord!
Jesus, Good Shepherd, inexhaustible Wisdom,
    our Way, our Truth, and our Life:
Glory to you, O Lord!
Jesus, Joy of the angels, and Crown of all the saints:
Glory to you, O Lord!

264
Surprising God,
    We thank you for the openness of Mary,
        for her stubborn strength to bear the Christ Child,
        as a woman not yet married.
    We thank you for her indomitable spirit that allowed her
        to brave the fearful consequences
        of bearing a child outside wedlock.
    We thank you for the sacred passion
        that helped her protect the life growing within her.
    We thank you for Mary's gift of life, offering her own body
        as a temple for your Spirit taking human flesh.
Dreaming God,
    We thank you for Joseph of Nazareth.
    We thank you for his sensitivity, his understanding
        of his inner voice, his ability to act upon his dreams.
    We thank you for his largeness of heart,
        for his abundant love for Mary and the child she carried.
    We thank you for Joseph's care,
        for his imagination in getting Mary and the child to safety
        when their lives were threatened.
Imagining God,
    We thank you for your gifts of Mary and Joseph to us—
        the care they gave to Jesus, your Son,
        the human qualities they model for us,
        the parts they played in your drama of salvation.
Surprising God,
    Thank you for your gifts of love to us.
    Let the Christ child be born anew in our hearts, we pray. Amen.

PASSION/PALM SUNDAY

265

God of infinite love,
     on this day above all days
     we sing the praise of him who died,
     of him who died upon the cross.
We bless you for the words he uttered,
     for the anguish he endured,
     for the sacrifice he offered,
     for the triumph he won over sin and death.
Accept our gratitude, our worship, our adoration,
     and make us more worthy of all that he has done for us,
     our Lord and Savior Jesus Christ.

EASTER

266

The Lord is risen! and we are risen with him.
The Lord is risen! and life eternal is ours.
The Lord is risen! and death has met its master.
The Lord is risen! and the way to heaven is open.
The Lord is risen! He is risen indeed!
Alleluia!

267

Lord, we are your people.
You have gathered us together to share in your purpose
     and advance your ~~kingdom~~ of love, justice, and peace.   reign
In our worship and devotion open our minds to know your will.
We come like people at the first Easter,
     raised by Christ to be his presence in the world.
We come joyfully and gladly to offer
     praise and adoration to the living God.
In the name of Jesus, accept our praise.
We come to worship.
     God is with us,
     Christ our Savior is raised from death to redeem us.
     God's Holy Spirit is present to guide and encourage us.
In the name of Jesus, accept our praise.

268

Living God, we worship you today
          with joy in our hearts and thanksgiving on our lips.

When the powers of evil had done their worst,
  crucifying your Son, and burying him in death,
you raised him to life again:
  an act of power giving hope to the world.
Lord Jesus, we rejoice that death could not keep you in its grip;
  that you were raised to life, alive for evermore.
You greeted your friends and now you stand among us
  in your risen power.
Spirit of God, you are always giving life to the people of God,
  giving birth to children of God.
Remodel us in the image of Jesus,
  fill us with his love and enable us with his risen power,
  that we might be faithful to his way,
  used by you in the redeeming of your world.

PENTECOST

269

O God, whose Spirit did brood upon the waters when darkness was upon
the face of the deep, and by your power brought forth light out of darkness
and created the world out of chaos,
  Glory and praise be yours, O God.
O Most Loving, who in the name of Jesus sent forth the Holy Spirit to be
our Comforter and Guide, the Spirit of wisdom and understanding, the
Spirit of counsel and might, the Spirit of truth and holiness, the Spirit of
God, Spirit of Christ,
  Glory and praise be yours, O God.
For the inspiration of your Spirit to the prophets of old, for the overshad-
owing of Mary by the power of the Most High, for the descent of the Spirit
like a dove upon Christ at his baptism, for the outpouring at Pentecost like
a rushing mighty wind and cloven tongues of fire,
  Glory and praise be yours, O God.
That the gifts of the Spirit may be poured out upon the whole church in
our time; that the world may be convinced of sin, of righteousness, and of
judgment,
  Send forth your Spirit, O God.
That we may be led out of the bondage of fear into the glorious liberty of
the children of God, and by the witness of your Spirit know ourselves to be
children of God and joint heirs with Jesus Christ,
  Send forth your Spirit, O God.
That the Spirit may help our infirmities and teach us how to pray; that our
bodies may be the dwelling place of the Spirit, walking no more after the
flesh but after the Spirit, bringing forth its fruits abundantly,
  Send forth your Spirit, O God.
Receive now the Holy Spirit!
  Amen.

☿ *CONFESSION*

Although communion and fellowship with God and our neighbors in loving devotion is our aim, we mar these relationships through sin. We fail in our loving and trusting. A prayer of reconciliation seeks healing and wholeness in broken relationships with God and those about us. Traditionally this takes the form of a confession of sin, repentance, the receiving of forgiveness, and the renewal of life in the knowledge of God's grace. Since before God all have sinned and fall short of the glory of God, both leader and the people share in the act of reconciliation.

Some of these prayers of confession conclude with words of pardon or assurance. Where that is not the case, the prayer should be completed by using one of the words of assurance at the end of this section.

270

(A call to confession:)
If we say that we have no sin,
    we deceive ourselves, and the truth is not in us.
If we confess our sins,
    God who is faithful and just will forgive our sins
    and cleanse us from all unrighteousness.   (1 JOHN 1:8–9, ALT.)
In humility and faith, let us confess our sin to God.

271

Most merciful God, we confess that we have sinned against you
    in thought, word, and deed,
    by what we have done, and by what we have left undone.
We have not loved you with our whole heart;
    we have not loved our neighbors as ourselves.
We are truly sorry and we humbly repent.
For the sake of your Son Jesus Christ, have mercy on us and forgive us;
    that we may delight in your will, and walk in your ways,
    to the glory of your name. Amen.

272

For our failure to appreciate and enjoy
    the good things you provide for our lives, in your mercy:
        Lord, forgive us.
For our insensitivity to the needs of others,
    and for our oversensitivity when we are hurt by them, in your mercy:
        Lord, forgive us.
For becoming consumed in the business of life,
    and for losing faith in your sovereignty and power, in your mercy:
        Lord, forgive us.

For moods of disobedience
and for outright rejection of your will, in your mercy:
Lord, forgive us.
For consenting to wrong practices by our cool silence,
and for listening to scandal, in your mercy:
Lord, forgive us.

**Reform our will, reinforce our courage:
create in us a new heart, O God,
and put your righteousness in us;
through Jesus Christ our Lord. Amen.**

273

O God, you gave us a garden of Eden
and we chose to wander in deserts of our own making.
You gave us the Light of the world
and we chose to do our night-crawling.
Forgive us our squandering,
our wandering,
our lack of commitment.
Forget not your covenant with us, O God,
and choose us still to tell your good news
to give all that we have that we might be one in your shalom.
In Jesus' name we pray. Amen.

274

Almighty and everlasting God,
you are always more ready to hear than we to pray,
and to give more than we either desire or deserve.
Pour upon us the abundance of your mercy,
forgiving us those things of which our conscience is afraid,
and giving us those good things for which we are not worthy to ask,
except through the merits and mediation of Jesus Christ our Savior;
who lives and reigns with you and the Holy Spirit,
one God, forever and ever. Amen.

275

God, your Son Jesus Christ has taught us that power belongs to you.
You have shared your power with us.
Yet, we confess we have not accepted the power you have given us.
We have allowed others to use power to dominate people and nations,
exploiting them, creating wars, and accumulating wealth.
Today you offer us your power,
so that we can help change the world, announce your kingdom,
and acknowledge you, the source of all power.
For yours is the kingdom, and the power,
and the glory, forever and ever. Amen.

276

Lord, you come to us but we do not recognize you;
    you call but we do not follow;
    you command but we do not obey,
    you bless us but we do not thank you.
Please forgive and help us.
Lord, you accept us but we do not accept others;
    you forgive us but we do not forgive those who wrong us;
    you love us but we do not love our neighbors.
Please forgive and help us.
Lord, you showed us how to carry out your mission,
        but we still insist on our own;
    you identified yourself with outcasts, the needy and the poor,
        but we do not bother to find out what is happening to them;
    you suffered and died for the sake of all,
        but we do not give up our comfortable lives.
Please forgive and help us.

277

"Be kind and compassionate to one another, forgiving each other,
    just as in Christ God forgave you."   (EPHESIANS 4:32, ALT.)
Let us confess our lack of love, and our need of grace:

When we lose patience, when we are unkind,
when we are envious, when we are rude or proud,
when we are selfish or irritable, and when we will not forgive:
    have mercy on us, O God.
Help us not to delight in evil, but to rejoice in the truth;
help us always to protect, to trust, to hope and to persevere:
then shall we see you face to face, and learn to love as you love us
    in Jesus Christ our Lord. Amen.

278

We confess, Lord,
    that we have not loved you or our neighbor as we should.
We have often neglected opportunities of good;
    sometimes we have done actual harm.
Our consciences accuse us over trifles,
    but let us blithely ignore your weightier demands.
We know that a mere apology will not do.
We resolve to turn from the sins we know.
We ask you to show us the sins we do not recognize.
We resolve to forgive any who have wronged us;
    and to seek reconciliation with any from whom we are estranged.
And now we beg your pardon and ask your help.

279

Merciful God, we admit the mistakes of our life which we cannot undo.
Help us to accept their consequences without bitterness,
    and within their limits to see our immediate obedience,
    and to act upon it with joy.
Through Jesus Christ, our Lord. Amen.

280

Most gracious and most merciful God,
    we confess to you and to one another that time after time
    we have entered your presence with countless prayers
    but with hearts that have been closed to your grace.
We have lifted our hands to you in praise
    but our feet have still walked in the ways of evil.
We have rehearsed your commandments
    but have refused to see your face in the needs of our neighbor.
We pray you, Lord, to forgive our lack of faith
    and to pardon our acts of injustice.
Grant us the healing that comes from your presence
    and the cleansing of your all-powerful word;
        through Jesus Christ our Lord. Amen.

281

Our Maker God, we sinners confess to you what we are.
    We like the path of life to be easy, comfortable, untroubled.
    We like problems to melt away, hardships to be smoothed over,
        stones to turn into bread for us.
    We do not want the hard way that Jesus takes.
    We like every step to be free from fears.
    We like to see mighty power helping us at every turn.
    We like miracles to be happening for our benefit.
    We do not want the faithful way that Jesus takes.
Merciful God, by all the grace of those forty desert days,
    arm us against those temptations,
    alert us to their corruption,
    forgive us our sins.
Teach us to tread the way that Jesus takes; for his sake. Amen.

282

Creator God, you have given us the power of imagination,
    through which the future grasps our lives today.
We confess that we do not give our lives over
    to the transforming power of your spirit.
We choose not to hear you calling to us. We deny the gifts you grant us.

We fail to live in ways that build up the life of your whole creation.
Forgive us, and give us courage, that we may open ourselves
    to the new creation you seek to bring within and among us.
Draw us into the future toward the new world you are creating
    through the grace of Jesus the Christ. Amen.

283

God of justice, you have shown us what is right:
    to act justly, to love mercy,
    and to walk humbly with you.
Forgive all in the life of our nation
    that falls short of what you require.
Forgive the poverty of body, mind, and spirit
    that still exists among us;
Forgive all the broken lives and all the broken hearts
    that are not tended;
Forgive us for the lives of young children
    that are being perverted and degraded,
    and all the social casualties that are not lifted up.
Forgive us, as individuals and as a nation,
    for not being big enough, broad-minded enough,
    hopeful enough, or loving enough
        to create a just society.
Forgive us and help us, so that our life as a nation,
    and the contribution we make to the life of the world,
    may honor you and do justice to your demands:
        through Jesus Christ our Lord. Amen.

284

We have life, and the power to live it, from God.
Let us acknowledge it and admit our faults.

We fail to live the lives God wants.
We are ungrateful to God and to other people;
    arrogant and self-confident when things go well;
    frightened and despairing when things go wrong.
We forget the goodness of God and the needs of other people.
We are short of love.

285

Living God, from the beginning
    you have been teaching us what goodness is
    and how human beings should live together:
    with integrity and justice, each one a refuge for the others.
Forgive our hard-heartedness, our lack of imagination,
    our inability to read the value of each person
    and to bring out the best in everyone we meet.

God, forgive us: we have made such a chaos of the earth.
Forgive our babel sounds, our lust for power and religious strife,
    separating us from one another and sapping all life's joys.
Teach us humility, keep our hope alive,
        sustain our love for all humanity,
        until conflict is stifled and we stand together in your silence
        which is filled with eternal praise: with Jesus Christ our Lord.

286

Living God, you have made us in your image
    and we, both willfully and helplessly,
        have marred that image in us.
You have charged us to be the evidence of your presence with humanity,
        and we have made you seem far away,
        uncaring, unnecessary.
You have made us for each other
        so that no human being should be left alone,
        and we have neglected, hurt, and abused our fellow men and women.
Though we have marred your image,
        hidden you from other people's faith
        and failed to unite the human family,
        continue to have mercy on us and to give us hope
            through our crucified and risen Lord. Amen.

287

Righteous God, we live in a world where human life is exploited and
abused. Violence is taken lightly, and people are often viewed as objects.
Images of hunger and war and murder flash before us until we become
nearly hardened. If we have taken on these values of the world, forgive us.
Give us tender hearts, help us to reflect your righteousness, and give us
courage to challenge the wrongs we see; through the power of the Holy
Spirit. Amen.

288

Forgive us, O God, for everything that has spoiled our home life:
        for the moodiness and irritability that made us difficult to live with;
        for the insensitivity that made us careless of the feelings of others;
        for the selfishness that made life harder for others.
Forgive us, O God, for everything that has spoiled our witness for you;
        that so often people would never have known
            that we had been with Jesus and pledged ourselves to him;
        that we have so often denied with our lives
            that which we said with our lips;
        for the difference between our creed and our conduct,
            our profession and our practice;
        for any example that made it easier
            for people to criticize your church or for another to sin.

When we think of ourselves
>   and of the meanness and ugliness and weakness of our lives,
>   we thank you for Jesus Christ our Savior.
Grant unto us a true penitence for our sins.
Grant that at the foot of the cross,
>   we may find our burdens rolled away.
And so strengthen us by your Spirit that in the days to come,
>   we may live more nearly as we ought.
Through Jesus Christ our Lord. Amen.

289

Source of goodness, who remembers not our sins, open our lips this day to speak your praise! We give thanks that you are the hope of all the earth, the one for whom we yearn and yet from whom we so often turn away. We confess that we live possessive lives as if all we have were not a gift from you. We confess that we live prideful lives as if we were the center of creation. We confess that we live diminished lives, jealous and resentful, as if we were not enriched by another's joy. Forgive us, Lord. Ground our lives in your perfect love that never ends. We pray it in the name of him by whom we know love, Christ our Lord. Amen.

290

Most merciful God,
>   we have done little to forward your kingdom in this world,
>   to foster the unity of your family,
>   and to establish love as the law of life.
We have allowed self to make us callous, pain to embitter us.
We have forgotten that
>   whatever is done to one of the least of your children is done to you.
Pardon our shortcomings. Forgive our neglect.
Give us pure hearts intent on pleasing you.
Help us in all our seeking
>   to seek first your kingdom and your righteousness.
And make us to come, as came your Son Jesus Christ,
>   not to be ministered unto but to minister.
All this we ask through Jesus Christ our Savior. Amen.

291

We confess to you, all-knowing God, what we are.
We are not the people we like others to think we are.
We are afraid to admit, even to ourselves,
>   what lies in the depths of our souls.
But we cannot hide our true selves from you.
You know us as we are, and yet you love us.
Help us not to shrink from self-knowledge.
Teach us to respect ourselves for your sake.

Give us the courage to put our trust in your guiding power.
Raise us out of the paralysis of guilt
    into the freedom and energy of forgiven people.
And for those who through long habit find forgiveness hard to accept,
    we ask you to break their bondage and set them free;
through Jesus Christ our Redeemer. Amen.

292

We are reluctant, O Author of Love,
    to set aside our hurt, our anger, our disappointment.
Heal us with your tender touch,
    that we might be cleansed of all unclean thoughts,
    all schemes of revenge, all hope of vindictive retribution.
Open our eyes to the power of love,
    shown to us in the unselfish sacrifice
    of your Son, our Savior, Jesus Christ. Amen.

293

Have mercy on us, O God, in your goodness;
    in your great tenderness wipe away our faults.
Wash us clean of our guilt;
    purify us from our sin.
God, create a clean heart in us;
    put into us a new and constant spirit.
Be our savior again, renew our joy,
    keep our spirit steady and willing.

The Declaration of Forgiveness:
The almighty and merciful God grant us
    pardon and remission of all our sins,
    time for amendment of life,
    and the grace and comfort of the Holy Spirit. Amen.

294

I confess to Almighty God,
in the communion of the saints of heaven and earth,
and to you, my brothers and sisters,
that I have sinned through my own fault,
in my thoughts and in my words,
in what I have done,
and in what I have failed to do.
So I ask you, my brothers and sisters,
to pray for me to the Lord our God.

May the almighty and merciful God
grant unto us pardon and remission of all our sins,
true repentance, amendment of life,
and the grace and comfort of the Holy Spirit. Amen.

295

Jesus was careless about himself;
   we are careful.
He was courageous;
   we are cautious.
He trusted the unworthy;
   we trust those who have good collateral.
He forgave the unforgivable;
   we forgive those who do not really hurt us.
He was righteous and laughed at respectability;
   we are respectable and smile at righteousness.
He was meek;
   we are ambitious.
He saved others;
   we save ourselves as much as we can.
He had no place to lay his head and did not worry about it;
   **we fret when we cannot have the last convenience
      manufactured by clever science.**
He did what he believed to be right regardless of consequences;
   we determine what is right by how it will affect us.
He feared God but not the world;
   we fear public opinion more than we fear the judgment of God.
He risked everything for his Father, God;
   we make religion a refuge from every risk.
He took up the cross;
   we neither take it up nor lay it down but merely let it stand.
Merciful God, forgive, and in the freedom of your forgiveness,
   **may we climb to the threshold of our belief in you,
      take up our cross and follow your Son. Amen.**

296

Most merciful God, we humbly admit that we need your help.
We confess that we have wandered from your way.
We have done wrong, and we have failed to do what is right.
   You alone can save us.
Have mercy on us:
Wipe out our sins and teach us to forgive others.
Bring forth in us the fruit of the Spirit
   that we may live as disciples of Christ.
This we ask in the name of Jesus our Savior. Amen.

297

Let us confess our sins before God and one another.

**Almighty and merciful God,
   you created and are creating still.**

In your presence our limits lie stark before us.
We confess our unclean lips, our cold hearts,
  our turning away from neighbors,
  our broken promises, and our unrepentant hours.
Forgive us, O Holy One.

We confess that we have squandered the gifts you have given.
  We have neglected the land.
  We have grasped for goods.
  We have used each other.
  We have loved power more than people.
Forgive us, O Holy One.

Cleanse from us the illusion of innocence.
Come into our hearts, and make us new again.
We pray in the name of Jesus. Amen.

In Jesus Christ, God knows and receives us as we are.
Listen, give thanks, and live.

298

We confess that often we have failed
  to be an obedient church.
We have not done your will,
We have broken your law,
We have rebelled against your love,
We have not loved our neighbors,
  and we have not heard the cry of the needy.
Forgive us, we pray.
Free us for joyful obedience,
  through Jesus Christ our Lord. Amen.

Anyone in Christ becomes a new person altogether;
  the past is finished and gone,
  everything has become fresh and new.
Friends, believe the good news of the gospel:
In Jesus Christ, we are forgiven.

299

Creator God, breathing your own life into our being,
  you gave us the gift of life:
You placed us on this earth, with its minerals and waters,
  flowers and fruits, living creatures of grace and beauty!
You gave us the care of the earth.
Today you call us: "Where are you; what have you done?"
O God of love, you gave us the gift of peoples—
  of cultures, races and colors, to share our lives with.

Today you ask: "Where is your brother, your sister?"
The refugees, the oppressed and voiceless cry out to you.

Forgive us, Creator God, and reconcile us to your creation.
Teach us, O God of Love, that the earth and all its fullness is yours,
    the world and those who dwell in it.
Call us yet again to safeguard the gift of life.

300

The proof of God's amazing love is this:
    while we were sinners Christ died for us.   (ROMANS 5:8, ALT.)
In humility and faith, let us confess our sin to God.

Merciful God, in your gracious presence
    we confess our sin and the sin of this world.
Although Christ is among us as our peace,
    we are a people divided against ourselves
    as we cling to the values of a broken world.
The profit and pleasures we pursue
    lay waste the land and pollute the seas.
The fears and jealousies that we harbor
    set neighbor against neighbor and nation against nation.
We abuse your good gifts
    of imagination and freedom, intellect and reason,
    and have turned them into bonds of oppression.
Lord, have mercy upon us.
Help us, forgive us, and set us free to serve you in the world
as agents of your reconciling love in Jesus Christ.

(Silence)
The people stand for the Assurance of Pardon and the Peace as the minister says:

Hear the good news!
Who is in a position to condemn?
Only Christ, and Christ died for us,
    Christ rose for us,
    Christ reigns in power for us,
    Christ prays for us.
Anyone who is in Christ is a new creation.
    The old life has gone; a new life has begun.
Friends, believe the gospel.
    In Jesus Christ, you are forgiven.
Since we are reconciled to God in Christ,
    let us share the sign of peace with one another.
May the peace of our Lord Jesus Christ be with you all.
And also with you.

Let us offer each other a sign of peace.
The peace of Christ be with you.
The people will reach out to one another with an appropriate sign of peace.

301

We know that nothing is able to separate us
    from the love of God in Jesus Christ.
Let us, therefore, be free to confess the wrong we have done.

God of mercy; as we gather to celebrate your gift of love
    we recall with sorrow the times when we forget you
    and are divided one from the other.
How often our thoughts, our words, and our actions
    have betrayed the goodness you have shown to us.
Forgive us, merciful God.
Mend what is broken.
Heal the wounded relationships
    that separate us from you and one another;
through Jesus Christ our Lord.

While it is true that we have sinned,
    it is a greater truth that we are forgiven
    through God's love in Jesus Christ.
To all who humbly seek the mercy of God I say,
    in Jesus Christ your sin is forgiven.
Thanks be to God.

May the peace of our Lord Jesus Christ be with you all.
And also with you.
Let us offer each other a sign of peace.
The peace of Christ be with you.

302

Let us confess our sin against God and each other.
Merciful God, we know that you love us
    and that you call us to fullness of life,
but around us and within us
    we see the brokenness of the world and of our ways.
Our successes leave us empty; our progress does not satisfy.
    Our prosperous land is not the promised land of our longing.
Forgive our willful neglect of your word,
    our insensitivity to the needs of others,
and our failure to feed the spirit that is within us; *All this we are bold*
    through Jesus Christ our Redeemer. Amen. *who has shown us the way.*

to confess + to ask

303

If we say we have no sin,
    we deceive ourselves, and the truth is not in us.
If we confess our sins, God is faithful and just
    and will forgive our sins and cleanse us from all unrighteousness.
Sisters and brothers, in the words of the psalmist,
    let us ask for the forgiveness we need.
Have mercy on us, O God,
    according to your steadfast love.
According to your abundant mercy
    blot out our transgressions.
Wash us thoroughly from our iniquity,
    and cleanse us from our sin.
Create in us a clean heart, O God,
    and put a new and right spirit within us.
Restore to us the joy of your salvation,
    and sustain in us a willing spirit. Amen.

(1 JOHN 1:8–9, PSALM 51:1–2, 10, 12, ALT.)

304

God of life, forgive our denial of life,
    our destruction of its hopes,
    our denial of its needs,
    our distorting of its possibilities.
Fill us with your Spirit of life, that we might be
    people of life, servants of life, encouragers of life,
    signs of Christ, the life of the world.
In his name we pray. Amen.

305

Most loving and gracious God, forgive us our sins:
    those we commit knowingly,
    and those we do without perception of how we have hurt others.
Open our hearts to hear your truth,
    to understand our failure,
    and to reach a new level of wisdom,
that in all we do and say,
    we may bring glory to your name
    and love and compassion unto our neighbor.
In Christ's name we pray. Amen.

WORDS OF ASSURANCE

306

Jesus looked up and said to a sinner:
Where are your accusers? Has no one condemned you?
Neither do I condemn you; go, and do not sin again.
Thanks be to God.

(BASED ON JOHN 8:10–11)

307

Since we are justified by faith,
we have peace with God through our Lord Jesus Christ.
Through Jesus Christ
we have obtained access to this grace in which we stand,
and we rejoice in our hope of sharing the glory of God.

(ROMANS 5:1–2, ALT.)

308

God proves his love for us in that while we still were sinners,
Christ died for us. (ROMANS 5:8)
Anyone in Christ is a new creation; the old has passed away;
behold, the new has come. (2 CORINTHIANS 5:17, ALT.)

309

Anyone in Christ becomes a new person altogether;
the past is finished and gone,
everything has become fresh and new. (2 CORINTHIANS 5:17, ALT.)
Friends, believe the good news of the gospel:
In Jesus Christ, we are forgiven.

310

Here are words you may trust, words that merit full acceptance:
Christ Jesus came into the world to save sinners.
To all who confess their sins and resolve to lead a new life
he says: "Your sins are forgiven,"
and he also says: "Follow me."
Now to the one who rules all worlds,
immortal, invisible, the only wise God,
be honor and glory forever and ever. Amen." (BASED ON 1 TIMOTHY 1:15, 17)

311

Hear these comforting words:
If you repent and believe in God's redeeming mercy,
your sins are forgiven.
Trust in God's promises and begin anew your life
with God and all people.
In the name of Jesus Christ. Amen.

312

God hears the confession of our hearts and lips.
Through Jesus Christ we are forgiven all our sins,
and by the Holy Spirit we are empowered for new life.
We believe the good news of Jesus Christ. Amen.

313

In Jesus Christ, God knows and receives us as we are.
Listen, give thanks, and live.

314

God's pardon flows like a river in a continuing stream.
We come to God and wash and we are clean.
As the blood of Christ was poured from his body on the cross,
    so the grace of God is poured into our hearts,
        to bring us back from death to life.

315

Rejoice that in the eyes of God we are forgiven through Jesus Christ. Leave
your past. Close the door. And turn with hope to the future. Let Christ
have rule of your life. I declare, in the name of Christ, that we are a forgiven people.

316

When we walk out of the light of God, we stumble. God accepts and forgives our stumbling and is always there to help us back into the light. Yes,
we are accepted, forgiven, and made new by God. Thanks be to God.

317

Listen—here is good news:
Christ Jesus came into the world to save sinners,
    to forgive you in your failure;
    to accept you as you are;
    to set you free from evil's power
        and make you what you were meant to be.
Listen to him, for through him his Father says
    to all who have come to him as you have come to him:
        "You are accepted.
        You are forgiven.
        I will set you free."
O depth of wealth, wisdom, and knowledge in God!
    How unsearchable his judgments, how untraceable his ways!
Source, Guide, and Goal of all that is—
    to him be glory for ever! Amen.

ADVENT

318

Almighty God, Light of the World, you caused light
    to shine out of darkness in the advent of Jesus our Christ;
    you continually open to us the ways we are to prepare.

We confess our unwillingness to see the light and to walk in your ways.
We have not always opened our eyes to the needs of others,
   and our feet have wandered from the paths of justice and peace.
We ask that the Spirit of Christ be born anew within us,
   that our hearts may be stirred to glorify the nativity
   with acts of compassion and service. Amen.

CHRISTMAS

319

Merciful God, if we have spent so much time shopping
   that we have had little time to spend
   with those for whom we are shopping,
Forgive us and give us sensitivity.
If we become so busy practicing for the Christmas programs
   that we forget to think about what they mean,
Forgive us, and give us understanding.
If we decorate our houses
   but neglect the inner beauty of our homes,
Forgive us, and grant us love.
If we are worried about how much Christmas is going to cost us,
   but have given little thought to how much Christmas cost God,
Forgive us, and give us perspective.
If we are so consumed with thinking about Christmas
   that we have little consideration
   of the meaning of the first Christmas,
Forgive us and give us insight. Amen.

EPIPHANY

320

Lord Jesus Christ,
   wise visitors from the East worshiped and adored you;
   they brought you gifts—gold, frankincense, and myrrh.
We too have seen your glory, but we have often turned away.
      Lord, in your mercy,
      forgive us and help us.
We too have gifts,
but we have not fully used them or offered them to you.
      Lord, in your mercy,
      forgive us and help us.
We too have acclaimed you as King,
but we have not served you with all our strength.
      Lord, in your mercy,
      forgive us and help us.

We too have acknowledged you as God,
but we have not desired holiness.

>Lord, in your mercy,
>**forgive us and help us.**

We too have welcomed you as Savior,
but we have failed to tell others of your grace.

>Lord, in your mercy,
>**forgive us and help us.**

**Make our trust more certain, make our love more real,
make our worship more acceptable; for your glory's sake. Amen.**

deeply joyful.

ASH WEDNESDAY

321

In fear, but also in hope, we come together with ashes on our heads. The planet is dying in our hands; people turn to each other for food and strength only to be shoved away. Each day we deal in death, yet pretend that we are good. Let us take forty days to look hard at our so-called goodness and see what it covers up. Then, we will join together in taking up the cross of living in the world as it is, for there is only one earth, and, as far as we know, only one human race.

Each of the following petitions may be offered by a different speaker. Each should be followed by a time of silence.

That as Christians we might start using our hands, feet, money, time, and energy for the good of the poor, let us pray to the Lord.

That citizens everywhere will realize that care for their neighbor consists in more than the mere giving of money, let us pray to the Lord.

For those in need, that they will not have to remain despondent and alone, let us pray to the Lord.

For all of us here that we will be honest enough to admit what we are selfish about, and what we can do to remedy our lack of love, let us pray to the Lord.

For those who share Christ's charity toward sinners, let us pray to the Lord.

The celebrant concludes:

Lord, the ashes are our pledge to take up the cross of life. We came from the earth and we will go back to it. In the meantime, beginning with these forty days, we will try to live here and make it a better home for everyone. Through Christ our Lord. Amen.

322

As disciples of Jesus Christ,
>we are called to struggle against everything
>that leads us away from the love of God and neighbor.

Repentance, fasting, prayer study, and works of love
   help us return to that love.
I invite you, therefore,
   to commit yourselves to love God and neighbor
   by confessing your sin
   and by asking God for strength to persevere in your Lenten discipline.

Silence may be observed for reflection and prayer.

Let us pray.
Most holy and merciful God, we confess to you and to one another,
   and to the whole communion of saints in heaven and on earth,
   that we have sinned by our own fault in thought, word, and deed,
   by what we have done, and by what we have left undone.
We have not loved you with all our heart, and mind, and strength.
We have not loved our neighbors as ourselves.
We have not forgiven others as we have been forgiven.
Have mercy on us, O God.
We have been dead to your call to serve as Christ served us.
We have not been true to the mind of Christ.
We have grieved your Holy Spirit.
Have mercy on us, O God.
We confess to you, O God, all our past unfaithfulness.
The pride, hypocrisy, and impatience in our lives,
We confess to you, O God.
Our anger at our own frustration
   and our envy of those more fortunate than ourselves,
We confess to you, O God.
Our intemperate love of worldly goods and comforts
   and our dishonesty in our daily life and work,
We confess to you, O God.
Our negligence in prayer and worship
   and our failure to commend the faith that is in us,
We confess to you, O God.
Accept our repentance, O God, for the wrongs we have done.
For our neglect of human need and suffering
   and our indifference to injustice and cruelty,
Accept our repentance, O God.
For all false judgments, for uncharitable thoughts toward our neighbors,
   and for our prejudice and contempt toward those who differ from us,
Accept our repentance, O God.
For our waste and pollution of your creation
   and our lack of concern for those who come after us,
Accept our repentance, O God.
Restore us, O God,
   and let your anger depart from us.
Favorably hear us, O God, for your mercy is great. Amen.

Lent

323

Great and giving God, we enter into the wilderness of this Lenten season with mixed feelings. We appreciate the disciplines of Lent and the opportunities for growth. We sense a stark, bare beauty to the days ahead, and we acknowledge your promise of provisions to carry us through.

Yet we balk at our Lenten journey's beginning. We are often entirely comfortable in our customary places and spaces. We are content with relying upon sources of sustenance other than your presence. We are inclined to trust our own sense of direction and are reluctant to follow the leadings of your Spirit.

Forgive us. Give us the will to journey far. May the season of lengthening days be a season for strengthening spirits. In the name of Jesus Christ we pray. Amen.

Passion/Palm Sunday

324

On Palm Sunday the crowds worshiped Jesus; on Good Friday they shouted for him to die. Let us who also worship him confess that we sometimes reject him, and ask his forgiveness:

Lord Jesus Christ, you come to us in peace,
>but we shut the door of our mind against you. In your mercy:
>**forgive us and help us.**
You come to us in humility,
>but we prefer our own proud ways. In your mercy:
>**forgive us and help us.**
You come to us in judgment,
>but we cling to our familiar sins. In your mercy:
>**forgive us and help us.**
You come to us in majesty,
>but we will not have you to reign over us. In your mercy:
>**forgive us and help us.**
Lord, forgive our empty praise; fill our loveless hearts;
come to us and make our lives your home forever. Amen.

Easter

325

God of endless possibility, we confess that
>we do not always perceive the opportunities you place before us.
Caught up in our own hopes, plans, and fantasies,
>and crushed when they disappoint us,
>we are slow to see the open pathways you set before us.

Open our eyes, that we may accept the new life that you offer us,
and thus show forth the resurrection of Jesus Christ. Amen.

ASCENSION

326

Lord Jesus Christ, crucified, risen and ascended for us:
we have not loved you as our Redeemer,
or obeyed you as our Lord;
we have not brought our prayers to you,
or heeded your tears shed over the world.
Forgive us, we pray;
breathe into us a new spirit of service,
and make us joyfully obedient to your will:
for your glory's sake. Amen.

PENTECOST

327

Almighty God, we confess that we have sinned against you:
for we have denied your saving presence in our lives,
and we have grieved your Holy Spirit.
Come to us in the fire of your love,
and set our minds on the things of the Spirit,
that we may bear the Spirit's fruit in love and joy and peace;
through Jesus Christ our Lord. Amen.

328

Loving God, we confess that we have stifled your Spirit within us.
You have sent us the Spirit of love,
but we have preferred to hate those who oppose us.
You have sent us the Spirit of joy,
but we have taken your gifts for granted and been ungrateful.
You have sent us the Spirit of peace,
but we have allowed our selfishness
to cause division and disharmony.
You have sent us the Spirit of patience,
but we have been worried and anxious when we have not seen
immediate results from our efforts, or evidence of your love.
You have sent us the Spirit of kindness,
but we have been indifferent to other people's needs.
You have sent us the Spirit of goodness,
but through thoughtlessness, as well as our deliberate wrongdoing,
we have sinned.
You have sent us the Spirit of faithfulness,
but we have been fickle in our resolve, unreliable disciples of Jesus.
You have sent us the Spirit of gentleness,
but we have been insensitive to the feelings of others.

You have sent us the Spirit of self-control,
but we have lived recklessly, without disciplining ourselves.
Forgive us, merciful God.
Teach us how much we need the power of your Spirit in our lives;
and breathe new life into us; for Jesus Christ's sake. Amen.

☉ SEEKING PERSONAL HELP

The most primitive cry of prayer is for help. We know we are not self-sufficient but depend upon a power greater than ourselves to bring our lives to full fruition in God. Although God sustains all of life in every living moment, there is a need to share our deepest concerns with God as friend to Holy Friend. In seeking personal help we dare to claim this friendship, recognizing the power that inheres in this loving relation. At the same time we understand that our Holy Friend has the freedom in love to respond as is deemed appropriate.

329   *For the Graces of Christian Character*
Caring God, by whom we are supported day and night,
    assist us during our waking hours
    to resist the temptations that beset us,
    so that, with your help, the graces of Christian character
    may more and more take shape in our lives.
Give us, O God, a warm heart,
    that no coldness may chill our love of people,
    or restrict our charitable deeds.
Give us, O God, a wide vision,
    that no prejudice may limit our understanding of others,
    or make us intolerant and unjust.
Give us, O God, a pure mind,
    that no evil thoughts may corrupt us,
    or turn the light that is in us to darkness.
Give us, O God, a strong will,
    that no weakness may cripple our good intentions,
    or disable us from doing and saying what is right.
Give us, O God, a great desire
    to put our feet into the print of Christ's shoes,
    and to follow him faithfully to the end of our days.

330   *Recognizing Christ in the World*
Lord Jesus Christ, you are alive in the world:
    among the poor and oppressed,
    the pavement dwellers and refugees
    of Africa, Asia, and Latin America.

Amid the garbage and ruins, in depths of despair and suffering,
    there you are.
The friendly face of a homeless child stares up at us;
    an old man smiles and blesses us;
    a beggar woman shares a handful of rice
    between her hungry children and the orphan who joins them.
        Of such is the kingdom.
Lord Jesus Christ, we cannot see you as Thomas did,
    or touch you with our hands,
but you come in unexpected ways and speak through people
    whose backgrounds and outlooks are different from our own.
Help us to listen with respect to their experiences
    and reflect upon their insights.
Free us from pride to find your dignity and presence
    wherever you are. Amen.

331   *To Turn Words into Deeds*

Save us, O Lord, from being idle bystanders—looking on and attempting to interpret the dilemmas of a broken world, yet rarely willing to act. Give us compassion for the lost and confused, the weary and the oppressed. Save us from slick and simplistic answers to human problems, which offer words but no real help. Unsettle us, and move us on from viewing the plight of sin-scarred people, to actions that promote spiritual and inward healing and liberating forgiveness. Cleanse our lives, that they may be instruments worthy of conveying your truth of abundant and everlasting life through Jesus Christ the Lord. We ask in his name. Amen.

332   *When We Are Desperate*

Lord, we love you
    because you listen to our prayers
    and give us a hearing.
But sometimes in deep distress
    we feel we will be swept away.
Help us when we feel desperate,
    when life is too much,
    when relationships are too trying
    and our own difficulties and weaknesses too hard to cope with.
Help us when we wish the ground would swallow us,
    when we find the thought of death attractive,
    even tempting.
Rescue us from death and trouble:
    keep us from stumbling,
    till we walk in your presence full of life, hope, and joy,
    praising you, with all your people, everywhere, forever. Amen.

333   *To Forgive Others*
O God, Creator of all,
    help us to forgive others as we would wish them to forgive us.
May we try to understand them
    as we in turn would like to be understood,
    in the hope that forgiveness will not be in order.
May we see with their eyes, think with their minds,
    feel with their hearts.
Then let us ask ourselves
    whether we should judge them or judge ourselves
    and accept them as children, like us, of one heavenly Father.

334   *For Help to Know God Truly*
O God, you are the light of the minds that know you,
    the life of the souls that love you,
    and the strength of the wills that serve you;
help us so to know you that we may truly love you,
    so to love you that we may fully serve you,
    whom to serve is perfect freedom; through Jesus Christ our Lord.

335   *For Overcoming Indifference to the Good News*
O Lord, we've heard the old, old story
    and we confess our sin of indifference.
God, jolt our lives to turn and look at you once more.
Give us the ears to hear your amazing story:
    that God would become one of us,
        living among us, teaching us,
        sitting down at table with us,
        breaking bread and drinking wine with us,
        and then dying among us, for us.
Amazing grace!
O Lord, we ask for your presence this day;
    brush against us when we least expect it;
    touch us with your Spirit;
    take us by the shoulders and shake us awake
        to your incredible truth.
We are your people and you are our God.
Forgive our faithlessness, Faithful God!
And see beyond our apathy, our thoughtlessness,
    our self-centeredness, our wrong choices.
See into our hearts, for you are our Treasure.
We pledge once more to give to those who need us,
    that this world might be more human.
We pledge to do away with indifference.
We pledge to tell the old, old story in new life-changing ways!
    For Jesus' sake. Amen.

336   *For a Steadfast Heart*
Grant me, O Lord, a steadfast heart,
        which no unworthy affection may drag downward;
    an unconquered heart, which no tribulation can wear out;
    an upright heart, which no unworthy purpose may tempt aside.
Bestow upon me also, O Lord my God,
    understanding to know you,
    diligence to seek you,
    wisdom to find you,
    and a faithfulness that may finally embrace you. Amen.

337   *An Affirmation of Hope*
We see ourselves, O God, people of faith and faithlessness—
    dancing in the sun one day
        and overwhelmed by our realities on the next,
    joyfully announcing the gospel sometimes
        and then trembling in our uncertainty.
We see the hope that lies among us—
    and hope that we could care *may*
    and live in community with each other and the world.

338   *For the Gift of Humility*
Merciful God, keep our hearts from pride,
    keep our eyes from haughty looks,
    keep our minds from arrogance,
    keep our spirits calm—
in childlike dependence upon you
for you are our hope now and always. Amen.

339   *For Integrity*
Deliver us, O God, from any hesitation to make a stand for justice.
May we never run from our responsibility to you.
In you, O God, we find the strength to confront the forces of evil,
    the courage to stand firm
    and to speak your truth no matter what the cost.
You are our way, our truth, our life, our integrity forever.
Holy are you, O Blessed Indwelling, now and forever. Amen.

340   *For the Growth of God's Kingdom*
Your kingdom, O God, is among us as a seed growing secretly.
    Let it burst into flower in our generation.
Where the poor are raised up,
    there is your kingdom.
Where justice flows down like the mountain streams,
    there is your kingdom;

Where men and women yield their lives to Christ
    and to the doing of his will,
        there is the hidden treasure of your kingdom.
Help us, O God, to read the signs of the times,
    to discern the kingdom's presence,
        and to make it known in prophetic words and committed lives;
through Jesus Christ our Lord. Amen.

341   *To Be God's New Creation*
Spirit of Light: let your wisdom shine on us.
Spirit of Silence: make us aware of God's presence.
Spirit of Courage: dispel the fear in our hearts.
Spirit of Fire: inflame us with Christ's love.
Spirit of Peace: help us be still and listen to God's word.
Spirit of Joy: inspire us to proclaim the good news.
Spirit of Love: help us to open ourselves to the needs of others.
Spirit of Power: give us all your help and strength.
Spirit of Truth: guide us all in the way of Christ.
Come into our hearts; make us your new creation.
    (The response could be spoken after each individual petition.)

342   *For Openness*
Blessed God, we give thanks for our many gifts: for the gifts of our race, gender, and sexual orientation, and for the sacraments of relationship and community that grow from these gifts.
Holy God, we rejoice for the healing power of salvation.
Sanctify our hearts that our lives may glorify and show forth your power.
We thank you for healing our ears to hear how racism attempts to silence a people by consensus. Open our ears to hear the silence and the language of our own racism.
God, we give you thanks because you give us the wisdom to discern injustice and the courage to stand for peace.
Give us the strength of a mountain to stand against the ignorance of sexism, the promotion of racism, and the condemnation and defamation of gay and lesbian people.
Blessed God, thank you for delivering us out of the mire of injustice that pollutes, disrespects, and dismisses the needs and concerns of women throughout the world.
Holy God, we rejoice because you are healing the blindness of sexism. Open our eyes to see how we can support women in their struggles.
Holy Spirit, our teacher, teach us to be aware of when our own freedoms infringe on the freedoms of others.
Blessed God, forgive us for participating in attitudes and behaviors that cause repression and grief for others. Make us aware and give us the power to change.

Holy Spirit of life, thank you for the gift of those who give their hearts of empathy, who reach out with support and understanding to gay and lesbian people, to those healing the injuries of racism, and to those who nurture the rights of women.
Be with us all in our struggles. Amen.

343   *For Facing into Ourselves*
Lord, we put ourselves in your hands.
Help us to face what it is in us
     that deadens our souls, and cuts us off from you.
Help us to face what it is in us
     that causes ill-feeling in our homes and strife at our work.
Help us to face what it is in us
     that deadens the work of the church and wounds the body of Christ.
Save us from wasting time blaming ourselves for things that went wrong
     when you have forgiven us and are giving us a clean start.
Save us from passing on the blame to other people,
     when we should be seeking to redeem the situation from ill-feeling.
Save us from holding on to our sense of grievance against others,
     when we should be forgiving them even as we have been forgiven.

We pray now for all those who have wronged us,
     those who have gone out of their way to hurt us,
     those who have hurt us without meaning to,
     those whose ideas are very different from our own.
As you have borne our sin, and have risen above it,
     so teach us to forgive them, and to rise above past differences.
When situations arise that tempt us at our points of weakness,
     may your Holy Spirit of love be our strength.
When we are challenged with problems too big for us to tackle,
     may your Holy Spirit of power uphold us and equip us to face them.
When we are faced by suffering or death,
     may your Holy Spirit of life fill us through and through.

Enable us, as individuals, and as a congregation
          to bear witness to your gospel of forgiveness and new life
               to all in this community.
Join us with your church throughout the world
          to preach the goodness of your forgiveness to all people. Amen.

344   *To Be Strong and Resolute*
Lord, stand with us in the fight for life.
When truth is undermined, and hope is overwhelmed—
Keep us strong and resolute.
When we are tempted to take the easy, rather than the right, way;
     and to do the selfish, rather than the loving, thing—

Keep us strong and resolute, obedient to you.
When pain and sorrow are too much for us,
    and anxiety and fear defeat us—
Keep us strong and resolute;
    give us confidence and set us free
    by the power of your joyful Holy Spirit. Amen.

345   *For Surprise in New Understanding*
God, you are no idol of our making, but the living God, coming, going,
revealed or hidden—as you decide. Give us the capacity to be surprised
into new understanding. Break through our traditions and set phrases, and
show yourself alive—the strength of our present and the promise of our
future. Give us the capacity to be surprised by each other: to recognize
truth in words spoken, movements made and glances given; seeing new
dimensions in each other.

Help us to be startled by grace where we could see no virtue, by kindness
where we could see only coldness, by the need of love where we could see
only arrogance and ingratitude, by the need of generous aid where we could
see only dirt, squalor, and laziness. Meet us, Lord, in unexpected places;
speak to us through unexpected voices; and do not let us refuse to see or
hear you anywhere.

Help us of our own free will to love and cherish one another and all people,
everywhere, until every man, woman, and child becomes aware of being
loved, cherished, forgiven, and accepted by you, and the universe rings
with loud and joyful praise to the glory of your name. Amen.

346   *To Be Taught of God*
By the prayers of Jesus,
Lord, teach us how to pray.
By the grace of Jesus,
Lord, teach us how to give.
By the labors of Jesus,
Lord, teach us how to work.
By the love of Jesus,
Lord, teach us how to love.
By the cross of Jesus,
Lord, teach us how to live. Amen.

347   *To Be Woven into God's Purpose*
O God, you are like a weaver-woman in our lives. Out of the energy of the
universe you have spun each one of us into a unique, colorful strand with
our own special hue and texture, and have woven us together into your
human family that blankets the globe. We admit that our own choices have
severed us from your loom of life and torn our human fabric.

We have allowed ourselves to be bound by the narrow contexts into which we were born and now live our daily lives. To insulate ourselves from fatigue and isolation and to ensure our own survival, we have often refused to ask the hard questions that need to be asked for the sake of the well being of all people.

O weaver-woman God, open our eyes to the mystery and power of your Spirit. Refresh us with the light of your vision so that we may once again recognize the beauty and wonder of the specially spun threads that we are and the splendor of the one colorful cloth of humanity. Reattach us to your loom so that your vision may be made plain through us.

In the name of the Christ, the one who was at one with all of life. Amen.

348   *For an Answer When We Call (a Litany)*
Eternal God, be our Help;
Eternal God, sustain us;
   Eternal God, be our Answer
   when we call upon you.
God of all being, be our Help;
Searcher of hearts, sustain us;
   Mighty Redeemer, be our Answer
   when we call upon you.
Proclaimer of justice, be our Help;
God surrounded by glory, sustain us;
   Steadfast and loving One, be our Answer
   when we call upon you.
Pure and upright One, be our Help;
Friend of the poor, sustain us;
   Inspiration to goodness, be our Answer
   when we call upon you.
Mind of the universe, be our Help;
God of power and splendor, sustain us;
   Lord arrayed in justice, be our Answer
   when we call upon you.
Eternal Ruler, be our Help;
Radiant and glorious God, sustain us;
   Upholder of the falling, be our Answer
   when we call upon you.
Helper of the weak, be our Help;
Redeemer and Deliverer, sustain us;
   Eternal Rock, be our Answer
   when we call upon you.
Holy and awesome One, be our Help;
Merciful and gracious God, sustain us;
   Keeper of the Covenant, be our Answer
   when we call upon you.

Support of the innocent, be our Help;
Mighty forever, sustain us;
Pure in your ways, be our Answer
when we call upon you. Amen.

349   *For Wisdom in Rearing Children (a Litany)*
When children live with criticism and impatience,
    they learn that they are not part of Christ's body.
May God grant us wisdom.
When children live with intolerance and are ignored,
    they wonder why they should be part of Christ's body.
May God grant us wisdom.
When children live with praise and approval,
    they, too, reflect God's love.
May God grant us wisdom.
When children live with friendliness and understanding,
    they give their energy and enthusiasm.
May God grant us wisdom. Amen.

350   *For the Church as a Household of Faith (a Litany)*
O Lord our God, we pray that your blessing
    may continually abide with this household of faith:
In our worship, our fellowship of praise and sacrament and prayer;
    in the preaching of the gospel of our Lord Jesus Christ;
    in all our activities and organizations;
O God, make manifest your power and glory.
By the giving of comfort to those who mourn;
    of strength to those who are tempted;
    of light to those who seek the way;
O God, make manifest your power and glory.
In the hallowing of family life;
    in the teaching and guiding of the young;
    in the building up of all who believe and the perfecting of the saints;
O God, make manifest your power and glory.
For the increase of righteousness;
    for the spread of the spirit of love;
    for the setting forth of your kingdom;
O God, use this church here and now.

351   *To Be Disciples (a Litany)*
Jesus said: "Whoever among you wants to be great must become the servant of all. For the Son of Man himself has not come to be served but to
serve, and to give his life to set many others free."
    Master, we hear your call;
    Lord Jesus, help us to follow.
Jesus said: "Unless you change your whole outlook and become like little
children, you will never enter the kingdom of heaven."

Master, we hear your call;
Lord Jesus, help us to follow.
Jesus said: "Blessed are the poor in spirit, for theirs is the kingdom of heaven. Blessed are the meek, for they shall inherit the earth."

Master, we hear your call;
Lord Jesus, help us to follow.
Jesus said: "You must love your enemies, and do good without expecting any return and without giving up hope on anyone: so will you be children of the Most High, because God indeed is kind to the ungrateful and wicked. Be compassionate, as your Father is compassionate."

Master, we hear your call;
Lord Jesus, help us to follow.
O God of grace and mercy, bless your church. Help us always to remember that the church is your family. And so help us within the church never to do anything to grieve your loving heart, and never to do anything to turn to bitterness the mutual love, which ought to be the very air and atmosphere of your church.

Grant us wisdom, grant us courage, for the facing of this hour.
Give your church grace to live in all godliness. In this generation give your church grace to be adventurous in thought and resolute in action; courageous in witness and generous in service. In this generation give your church grace to have wisdom in its mind, certainty in its message, love in its fellowship, and a passionate desire to win those who are still outside.

Grant us wisdom, grant us courage, for the facing of this hour.
Keep your church free from persecution from outside and from dissension inside. Strengthen your church within the world that it may stand like a steadfast rock amid the shifting sand of doubt and unbelief; like a clear light of goodness amid the falling of standards and the lowering of ideals; like a warm fire of love amid the coldness of selfishness and the callousness of self-seeking.

Grant us wisdom, grant us courage, for the facing of this hour.
So help your church, to accept nothing but your guidance; to serve nothing but your will; to seek nothing but your glory; through Jesus Christ our Lord. Amen.

352   *For the Gift of the Holy Spirit (a Litany)*
Holy Spirit, Creator,
   at the beginning you hovered over the waters;
   you breathed life into all creatures;
   without you every living creature dies and returns to nothingness,
Come into us, Holy Spirit.
Holy Spirit, Comforter,
   by you we are born again as children of God;
   you make us living temples of your presence,
   you pray within us with prayers too deep for words,
Come into us, Holy Spirit.

Holy Spirit, Lord and Giver of life,
>   you are light, you bring us light;
>   you are goodness and the source of all goodness,

Come into us, Holy Spirit.

Holy Spirit, Breath of life,
>   you sanctify and breathe life into the whole body of the church;
>   you dwell in each one of its members,
>   and will one day give new life to our mortal bodies,

Come into us, Holy Spirit.

353   *To Strengthen the Ministry of All Christians (a Litany)*

O God, who sent Jesus into the world
>   not to be ministered unto, but to minister,
>   and to give his life to set others free,
>>   shape us for your ministry.

Claim us, O God, for your service and direct us toward your will.

All members of Christ's body, one by one,
>   are graced with gifts of the Spirit to fulfill their vocation:
>>   to lead lives worthy of God's calling;
>>   to be workers who have no reason to be ashamed;
>>   to shine as lights to the glory of God.

Claim us, O God, for your service and direct us toward your will.

There are varieties of gifts, but the same Spirit;
>   and there are varieties of services, but the same Lord;
>   different forms of activities,
>>   but it is the same God who activates all of them in everyone.

You, our Creator, have granted each of us
>   **the manifestation of the Spirit for the common good.**

Given grace according to the measure of Christ's gift,
>   some are called to be apostles,
>   some prophets, some evangelists,
>   some pastors and teachers,
>>   to equip the saints for the work of ministry,
>>   for building up the body of Christ.

Grant that together we may all come to the unity of the faith
>   **and of the knowledge of the Son of God,**
>   **to maturity, to the measure of the full stature of Christ.**

Let us lead, then, a life
>   worthy of the vocation to which we were called.

Claim us, O God, for your service and direct us toward your will.

☒ INTERCESSION FOR CHURCH AND WORLD

To intercede is to plead on another's behalf. It is going beyond seeking personal help to pray for those to whom we are connected in the bundle of life. We join with the God of creation in concern for the whole world. Intercessions for church and world include supplications not only for the church and the world, but for all people and their needs.

This is a prayer of the people for all God's people. It requires the involvement of the worshipers in expressing their deepest concerns. If the intercessions take the form of pastoral prayer, it is well to incorporate vocal or written concerns expressed earlier by those assembled. If the intercessions take the form of a litany, provision may be made for the concerns of the people to be expressed either in advance or at a specific point as the litany unfolds. Another form of intercession is the bidding prayer, in which topics are suggested for either silent or public expression by the people.

354
Let us ask God for the coming of the kingdom.
O God, into the pain of the tortured:
    breathe stillness.
Into the hunger of the very poor:
    breathe fullness.
Into the deaths of your creatures:
    breathe life.
Into those who long for you:
    breathe yourself.
Your kingdom come, your will be done.
    The kingdom, the power, and the glory
    are yours now and forever.
Our God is with us.
We celebrate the miracle of living and being!
We celebrate the miracle of creation!
    Our God loves us.
    Our lives are the blessing of God.
    Let us give thanks with joy! Amen.

355
O God, be present among us, for the sake of all human beings on earth.
Open our eyes that we may see the salvation that is in you,
    and reveal yourself to a blind humanity.
Make your face shine upon those stricken with disease;
    give them your strength and your peace.
All the poor ones, the weak, all those weighed down by want,
    may they have the knowledge of you,
    so to lean on you and be filled to overflowing in you.

To the mighty and the wealthy, grant the power they are lacking;
   give them a discerning spirit,
      that they may be free by your freedom, and free to love others.
To one and all of us, may you grant your life and your peace. Amen.

356
A General Bidding Prayer
Let us pray for all people, for all nations, and for the church, offering silent prayer as we are bidden.

I ask your prayers for God's church, for *Name* and *Name*, all who serve it, for this assembly, and for all God's people everywhere. Pray for the church.
Pray silently.

I ask your prayers for the good earth, that all people may respect its resources, preserve its future, and enjoy its fruits in their season. Pray for the soil and the sea.
Pray silently.

I ask your prayers for the leaders of the nations, that they may act deliberately and dispassionately, and for the good of all. Pray for those who govern.
Pray silently.

I ask your prayers for peace, that the peoples of the world may live in safety and without fear. Pray for peace.
Pray silently.

I ask your prayers for the wealthy, the free, and the healthy, that they may use their possessions to aid those in need. Pray for compassion among people.
Pray silently.

I ask your prayers for the sick, the sorrowing, and those who are alone, *especially Name(s)* Pray for those in any need or trouble.
Here other intercessions may be offered.

I ask your prayers for the faithful departed, *especially Name(s)*, that God give *him/her/them* eternal rest. Pray for those who have died.
Pray silently.

God of all living, hear the prayers of your faithful people, and grant our requests. Strengthen us for the tasks you give us, and bring us at last to praise you forever with your saints, through Christ our Lord. Amen.

357
A General Bidding Prayer
Aware of God's gracious love for all creation, let us pray for Christ's church, the world, and all who stand in need. I bid you to pray in silent meditation your deepest concerns to God as directed.

Let us pray for the church around the world: that its communities of faith may proclaim your good news and bring reconciliation and healing to this earth. Pray for the church.

Pray silently.

Let us pray for all Christians: that each may know the power of the living Christ and serve in faithful discipleship filled with grace and love and peace. Pray for one another.

Pray silently.

Let us pray for our country: that its leaders may govern wisely and with compassion; that its citizens may act responsibly toward one another with fairness and for the common good. Pray for this country.

Pray silently.

Let us pray for all nations: that all peoples shall know peace with justice; that together they recognize their common interdependence in sharing earth's resources. Pray for the nations.

Pray silently.

Let us pray for the ties that bind us to one another: that husbands and wives love and respect one another with tender care; that children are reared with a sense of basic trust in the goodness of life; that relations between friend and friend be open in loving honesty. Pray for the strengthening of our human relationships.

Pray silently.

Let us pray for those who are in trouble or danger: that regardless of circumstance they may find hope and release; that they may know they are not alone but abide in you. Pray for those weighed down by life's burdens.

Pray silently.

Let us pray for the spread of God's good news to all the world: that people shall increasingly seek to know God and find their rest in the one who has befriended them in Christ. Pray for all who witness to God's love in word and deed.

Pray silently.

O God, you know the deepest yearnings of our hearts. Take them and use them to work your perfect will in the life of the world. Shape our lives according to our prayers. In Christ's name we pray. Amen.

358

(A Bidding Prayer allowing for the addition of specific petitions relating to the congregation's immediate concerns)

Let us with one heart and one mind offer our prayers for the whole church of Christ, and for all people according to their need. When I pray the words, "God of all mercy," respond by praying, "Hear our prayer." Let us pray.

For the peace of the world, that a spirit of respect and understanding may grow among the nations and peoples; for the governments of the nations, that there may be peace and justice among all who inhabit the earth; for all people in their daily life and work, that they may have joy in doing God's will; for...

God of all mercy,
Hear our prayer.

For all who minister to the suffering, the friendless and the needy, that God's purposes may be fulfilled; for our enemies and all who wrong us, that we may bear a Christian witness; for the suffering, the sorrowful, the aged and the dying, that they may be strengthened and comforted; for...

God of all mercy,
Hear our prayer.

For the whole church of Christ, that, professing one Lord, one faith and one baptism, all whom Christ calls may live in the unity of the one Spirit; for all who spread the gospel, that they may draw all people to you in Christ Jesus; for all who receive God's Word, that they may reveal Christ's glory; for...

God of all mercy,
Hear our prayer.

We give thanks and praise for all your saints. Help us, strengthened by their fellowship, to follow their examples, and bring us with them into the fullness of your eternal joy.

Lord God, holy and faithful, you have called us to your service; help us to know and to do your will, that we may be worthy of our calling; through Jesus Christ our Lord. Amen.

359

Loving God, in Jesus Christ you teach us to pray
    and to present our petitions to you in his name.
Guide us by your Holy Spirit,
    that our prayers for others may serve your will
    and show your steadfast love for all.
Gracious God,
    you have called together a people to be the church of Jesus Christ.
May your people be one in faith and discipleship,
    breaking bread together, and telling good news
    so that the world may believe you are love,
    turn to your ways, and live in the light of your truth.

In your abundant mercy,
Hear our prayer.

Creator God, you made all things and called them good.
May your planet Earth be held in reverence by all people.
May its resources be used wisely
    and its fragile balance between life and death respected.

In your abundant mercy,
Hear our prayer.

Eternal Ruler, in your mighty realm the nations rise and fall.
Hear our prayers for those who rule the nations,
    that they may learn wisdom and truth,
    establish justice and mercy,
    and seek the ways of peace.

In your abundant mercy,
Hear our prayer.

Prayers spoken by the people or offered silently may be included here, followed by:

In your abundant mercy,
Hear our prayer.

Concluding petition:
Eternal God, ruler of all things in heaven and earth,
    accept the prayers of your people, and strengthen us to do your will;
    through Jesus Christ. **Amen.**

360
The sung response is CH 306.
Let us pray for others and ask that the love of God may uphold and protect
them.

Creator God, from whom the whole family in heaven and earth is named,
we commend all your people in great need to your tender care and safekeeping.

Hear our prayer, O Lord.

Protect all who toil in mines, tend machinery, or travel by land, sea, or air.
And defend those who are in mortal danger because of evil surroundings.
Fill with your spirit of love and healing every hospital and nursing home,
that those whom accident has injured or disease attacked may be treated
with skill and compassion and be restored to health and strength.

Hear our prayer, O Lord.

Govern our nation and its leaders, that here religion may be upheld, laws
justly administered, and human rights maintained. Abolish all that mars
our social life and causes misery, that everyone may have work and food,
health and happiness.

Incline thine ear to us.

O God of peace, break down the suspicion and fear that keep the nations
apart. Rebuke those who foster racial and color prejudice. And teach us all,
through obedience to Christ, to live together in peace.

And grant us thy peace.

Fill with your Holy Spirit, O God, every member of your church. Grant us the faith that removes mountains of difficulty, the hope that makes all things new, and the love that works miracles of healing and deliverance. Thus may we more effectively serve you, whose will it is that all should be saved and come to the knowledge of your truth.

Hear our prayer, O Lord,
hear our prayer, O Lord,
incline thine ear to us,
and grant us thy peace.

361

Spirit of power, we find it hard to come together in the church
    even within a single congregation.
How shall we learn to be one family
    loving and serving the whole of humankind?
Lead us into such unity of purpose that we may receive power:
    not the power to threaten or destroy
    but the power to restore waste places.
Use us to declare your glory
    that all eyes may see, all ears, hear,
    and the cynical be brought to faith.
Spirit of the Living God,
Hear our prayer.

Spirit of truth, we live in a modern Babel
    where words are used to conceal meaning
    rather than make it plain.
Lead the peoples of the world into such a love of truth
    that nation may speak with nation,
    not seeking to confuse but to understand and to be understood,
    whereby trust is created, out of which
    a truly international community may be born.
Spirit of the Living God,
Hear our prayer.

Creator Spirit, you give people the capacity
    to dream dreams and to see visions,
    but because we exalt ourselves and our desires
    to the place that is yours alone,
    our visions are visions of horror and our dreams nightmares.
Raise up artists and prophets among us
    with the will and the ability to inspire and cleanse our society,
    to set our hearts aflame and turn our spirits to the heights.

Spirit of the Living God,
Hear our prayer.

Source of all comfort, we pray for the lonely, the sick, the sad,
　　the bereaved and all who suffer or are ill at ease…
We claim for them the gift of your peace,
　　that their troubled hearts may be set at rest
　　and their fears banished.

Spirit of the Living God,
Hear our prayer.

Giver of life, we remember those who have died…
May they enter into the kingdom
　　where your presence is all in all.

Spirit of the Living God,
Hear our prayer.

362

Be merciful, gracious God, to all those in trouble:
　　those who are exhausted,
　　those who are deep in sorrow,
　　those whose lives are ebbing away,
　　those who are without friends,
　　those who are forgotten by the world.
Ever loving God, we entrust them to your care.
In Jesus' name. Amen.

363

O God, source of love and compassion
　　in the sufferings of all your children,
　　we offer our compassion also for the hungry,
　　and the sick in body, mind, or heart,
　　the depressed and the lonely,
　　all living in fear and under stress,
　　all stricken in grief,
　　the unemployed and the rejected,
　　and those burning with hatred.
Strengthen us to work for their healing
　　and inspire us to build with you the kingdom of love
　　where none shall cause suffering to others
　　and all be caring, loving children of yours.
Our compassionate, all-embracing God,
　　ever present, ever loving, never failing.

364

Gracious God, the story of your love makes us realize
    that there are many others as well as ourselves
    who need your help and your grace;
    so we bring our prayers to you:
for those who suffer pain,
    and for those whose loneliness is soul-destroying;
for those whose minds are disturbed,
    and for those who live lives of quiet despair;
for those who have not had the opportunities
    to realize their potentialities;
for those who are satisfied with something less
    than the life for which they were made;
for those who know their guilt, their shallowness,
    their need, but who do not know of Jesus;
for those who know that they must shortly die;
    for those who cannot wait to die.
Gracious God, your Son has taken all our sufferings
    upon himself and has transformed them.
Help us, who offer these prayers,
    to take the sufferings of others upon ourselves, and so,
    by your grace, become the agents of your transforming love:
Through Jesus Christ our Lord. Amen.

365

Lord, we pray for this modern world
    in which faith comes hard,
    where people find it difficult to raise their eyes
    above the material things that are so necessary to life.
We pray for those who find it hard to believe
    because they have too many things,
    and for those who find it hard
    because they haven't enough.
We pray for those who have more to eat than they need,
    and those who are dying from lack of food.
We pray for parents who, because of their poverty
    and a lack of concern on the part of others,
    must watch their children die.
We pray for those who suffer from disease,
    from confusion and guilt, from depression and fear.
We pray for those who face each day with dread
    because their lives are so dominated by the power of others.
We pray for those who are so lonely
    that life is robbed of all loveliness and hope.
Lord, we pray because our love for you is a love for One
    whose compassion embraces all human suffering.

366
We pray, O God, for the nations;
    for their right dealing one with another;
    for the breaking down of barriers of race and color;
    for political freedom;
    for educational development;
    and for a more just economic structure.
In the faith that your love is a healing love,
        your power a healing power,
        your peace a healing peace,
    we bring to you the needs of all those
        who suffer from disease, hunger, unemployment, loneliness,
        confusion and fear, sorrow, depression and guilt.
Enable them to turn to you in faith so that they can receive
    the healing that each one needs.
Grant to your church throughout the world
    that people may respond joyously to your love,
        by committing themselves in obedience and service,
    with a faith that is strengthened
        by a living experience of Christ's presence,
    with hearts warmed to love and with freedom and courage to follow
        where Christ leads; for his name's sake. Amen.

367
We pray for the household of the faith, the church,
    charged with the task of proclaiming the word.
May we all, members and ministers,
    be faithful to our baptismal dignity and responsibilities.
We pray for our nation and the family of nations,
    facing serious ethical and moral, social and economic judgments.
Guide those who lead us in their concern for justice, charity, and peace.
We pray for all married couples,
    who have pledged to be faithful to each other.
May the fervor of their love show to the world
    your regard and care for the church.
We pray for all parents, parents without partners,
    the married and single, widowed, separated, and divorced.
Help them to share their faith and show their trust
    as they listen to, affirm, and support their children.
We pray for infants and children,
    especially the abused and those without parents.
Let them know your love
    through the tenderness of all who care for them.
We pray for all young men and women
    as they approach life's decisions.

Give them a full and happy youth,
   and open their hearts to your world's goodness and beauty.
We pray for all who are single by choice or circumstance,
   living in the workaday world.
**May their lives of generous service to others
   bring them the reward of deep friendships.**
We pray for all who are celibate for the sake of your reign.
**Support them in the joy of their vocations,
   that their lives may manifest the reign of God.**
We pray for all who have no family or home.
**Show the gentleness of your presence
   to those who are alone and have no hope but you.**
We pray for all in the autumn of life
   with its prospects of loneliness and diminished health.
**Grant them a secure and serene old age,
   and guide their steps on the road of peace.**
We pray for all who have lost a spouse or child.
Let your compassion heal their hearts.
We pray for all our beloved dead, *especially Name(s).*
**Grant eternal rest to them, O Lord,
   and let perpetual light shine upon them.**
Gracious God, give us all a share of joy and happiness,
   that we may constantly discover your love and praise
   and glorify you in our daily lives.
May we arrive at the perfect joy, which is to live with you,
   your Son, and the Holy Spirit, forever and ever. **Amen.**

368
Caring God, as we think of other people, hear our prayer.
For all who are ill, *especially Name(s)*, we ask your healing.
   In your mercy:
   hear our prayer.
For those who are lonely, frightened, and unhappy, we ask your help.
   In your mercy:
   hear our prayer.
For those who are suffering from war, and for refugees, we ask your care.
   In your mercy:
   hear our prayer.
For children who are handicapped, we ask your protection.
   In your mercy:
   hear our prayer.
For those who are in trouble because of foolish behavior,
we ask your correction and restoration.
   In your mercy:
   hear our prayer.

For those who are hungry or homeless or in inadequate housing,
we ask your compassion.
>In your mercy:
>**hear our prayer.**
For your church in every part of the world, we ask your compassion.
>In your mercy:
>**hear our prayer.**
For all who labor for the peace of the world
and the freedom of all peoples, we ask your guidance and strength.
>In your mercy:
>**hear our prayer.**

Caring God, you promise to hear
>**those who are gathered to pray in your name:**
receive our prayer for all in need,
>**and grant your salvation to them and to us;**
through our Savior, Jesus Christ. Amen.

369

God, every family in heaven and earth takes its name from you. We pray for all Christian parents, that they may always be aware of their responsibility to give to the lives of their children that extra dimension of faith in Christ, and that they may be helped and supported in this by the church.

We pray for the children of Christian families, that with Christ central to their lives they may grow up confident, full of hope, merciful, gentle, and creative in all their dealings with other people.

We pray, too, for parents who have seen their children destroyed by violence or hunger: that there may be some comfort for their deep grief and forgiveness for this world in which such grief is possible.

We pray for all children orphaned by war.

We pray for the families in our own country who are homeless and separated, or who live in unhealthy, degrading, brutalizing conditions: that justice may be done and mercy shown before the children of such families find themselves against the law. Where moral breakdown has already occurred, let mercy, deep wisdom, and right understanding restore hope.

We pray that social workers and national and local government and the earnest will of society as a whole may strengthen and sustain family life, so that children may more and more grow up able to enjoy life to the fullest, creatively, for the good of the whole community.

Almighty God, what is impossible with us, will you accomplish in us, so that we may do justice to your holiness and your love, which are stronger and surer than all our evil.

Be merciful: give all we need to live well and die graciously, with Jesus Christ our Lord. Amen.

370

We pray an end to all corruption in politics or commerce;
    to all greedy exploitation of people's emotions, desires or pain,
    and to all cynical or mindless violence.
We look for total honesty and a spirit of service
        in politicians, business men and women, trade unionists;
    for purity of mind and purpose in journalists,
        writers, filmmakers, publishers;
    and for a mind to imagine other people's fear and pain,
        with a heart that is merciful, in all who turn to violence now.
Deliver us from evil!
Let your will be done: through Jesus Christ our Lord. Amen.

371

O Spirit, help us so to serve you, that all the world might hear
    and rejoice in the greatness of your name:
WOMEN: **Lord of hosts, God of gods, Ruler of glory,**
    Judge of earth, Lover of justice, Avenger of wrong;
MEN: **Upholder of life, Lifter of heads,**
    Parent to the orphan, Protector of the weak;
ALL: **Maker, Savior, Redeemer, Deliverer, Helper,**
    Shepherd, Keeper, Midwife, sheltering Wings, forgiving God!

O Spirit, help us so to serve you, that all the world might hear
    and rejoice in the greatness of your hand:
WOMEN: **the Hand that opens, stretches forth, anoints,**
    lifts up, rescues, saves;
MEN: **the Hand that leads, abides, receives our spirits,**
    helps, holds our times;
ALL: **the Hand that holds the cup—a strong hand,**
    exalted, high, but forgotten!

O Spirit, help us so to serve you, that all the world might hear
    and rejoice in the greatness of your arm:
WOMEN: **the Arm that creates the heavens and earth**
    and all who dwell therein, that performs great signs and wonders;
MEN: **the Arm that rules, that triumphs,**
    that scatters the wicked and makes them still;
ALL: **the Arm that brings slaves out of bondage,**
    that gathers the lambs and all who are scattered—
    the Arm that is bared before all the nations!

372

Jesus says: I am the bread of life.
I am the bread that came down from heaven.
Those who eat this bread will live forever.   (JOHN 6:35, 41, 51, ALT.)

Lord, give us this bread always.   (JOHN 6:34, ALT.)

Jesus says: I am the vine, and you are the branches.
Whoever remains in me will bear much fruit,
for you can do nothing without me.   (JOHN 15:5, ALT.)

Lord, we believe you are the Holy One who has come from God.

                                                      (JOHN 6:69, ALT.)

Jesus says: I am the gate.
Whoever comes in by me will be saved.   (JOHN 10:9, ALT.)

Lord, Lord! Let us in!   (MATTHEW 25:11, ALT.)

Jesus says: I am the light of the world.
Whoever follows me will have the light of life
and will never walk in darkness.   (JOHN 8:12, ALT.)

Send us your light and your truth.   (PSALM 43:3, ALT.)

Jesus says: I am the good shepherd.
I know my sheep and they know me,
and I am willing to die for them.   (JOHN 10:14–15, ALT.)

Lord, make us one flock with one shepherd.   (JOHN 10:16, ALT.)

Jesus says: I am the resurrection and the life.
Whoever lives and believes in me will never die.   (JOHN 11:25, ALT.)

Lord, I do believe that you are the Messiah, the Son of God.   (JOHN 11:27)

Jesus says: I am the way, the truth and the life;
no one goes to the Father except by me.   (JOHN 14:6, ALT.)

Teach me your ways, O Lord.   (PSALM 25:4, ALT.)

Jesus says: I am the one who knows everyone's thoughts and wishes.
I will repay each one of you according to what you have done.

                                                      (REVELATION 2:23, ALT.)

Examine me, O God, and know my heart.   (PSALM 139:23, ALT.)

Jesus says: I am descended from the family of David;
I am the bright morning star.   (REVELATION 22:16, ALT.)

Son of David, have mercy on me!   (MATTHEW 15:22, ALT.)

Jesus says: I am the Alpha and the Omega,
the beginning and the end, the first and the last.   (REVELATION 22:13, ALT.)

Lord, you know us that the first shall be last and the last first.

                                                      (MATTHEW 19:30, ALT.)

373
Jesus, Son of God,
        you loved us and sacrificed yourself for us;
        God forbid that we should boast in anything except your cross.
May we be crucified with you,
        be set free from the narrow and selfish standards of the world,
        and experience the liberty of children of God.

**May we cease to live for ourselves, and live for you
    who for our sake died and rose again.**
Jesus, Shepherd and Guardian of our souls,
        by your sufferings you set us an example;
        it is for us to follow in your steps.
**May we follow you in your patience and your forgiveness,
        not shrink from sharing your baptism and your cup,
        and give ourselves in sacrificial service to humankind.**
Jesus, Head of the church,
        you gave yourself up for the church,
        so that it might be holy and without blemish.
**Cleanse and renew by your word the whole body of the church,
        so that it may enjoy the peace and unity you want it to have,
        and not be slack in carrying out its mission to the world.**
Jesus, Good Shepherd,
        you laid down your life to gather the scattered children of God
        and to draw all people to yourself.
**Bring home to the hearts and consciences of all people
        the reality of your love and the meaning of your sacrifice,
        so that they may gladly give themselves to you
        and receive the benefits of your passion.**
Jesus, by your death
        you broke down the barriers between Jew and Gentile,
        Greek and barbarian, male and female, slave and free.
**Heal the tragic divisions of our world,
        between East and West, black and white, Arab and Jew,
        so that each may respect the other as someone for whom you died.**
Jesus, by God's gracious will
        you have gone through death for every human being
        and destroyed its power.
**May all who profess themselves Christians have such faith in you,
        that they may not fear the hour of their death,
        but with reverent hope look upon it as the entrance to fuller life.**
Jesus, you proved your Father's love to us
        by dying for us while we were still sinners.
**Arouse in us an answering love, ready to work, to speak,
        to think or to suffer in obedience to your perfect will. Amen.**

374
Eternal God, you have raised Jesus Christ from the dead
        and exalted him to your right hand in glory,
        and through him called your church into being,
        that your people might know you,
        and that we might make your name known.
We pray for the church:
        the church, universal and local;

the unity of the church;
the ministries of the church;
the mission of the church;
the renewal of the church;
all Christians in this place.
We give thanks:
for the apostolic gospel committed to your church:
for the continuing presence and power of your Spirit,
the ministry of word, sacrament, and prayer.
for the divine mission in which we are called to share;
for the will to unity and its fruit in common action,
the faithful witness of those who are true to Christ;
for all works of Christian compassion;
for every service that proclaims your love.
In peace and unity
may your people offer the unfailing sacrifice of praise,
and make your glory known;
through Jesus Christ our Lord. Amen.

375
O living God, come and make our souls temples of your Spirit.
Sanctify us, O Lord!
Baptize your whole church with fire,
that the divisions soon may cease, and that it may stand
before the world as a pillar and buttress of your truth.
Sanctify us, O Lord!
Grant us all the fruits of your Holy Spirit:
love, joy, peace, patience, goodwill and faithfulness.
Sanctify us, O Lord!
May your Holy Spirit speak by the voice of your servants,
here and everywhere, as they preach your word.
Sanctify us, O Lord!
Send your Holy Spirit, the Comforter, to all who face adversity,
or who are the victims of human wickedness.
Sanctify us, O Lord!
Preserve all nations and their leaders from hatred and war,
and build up a true community among nations,
through the power of your Spirit.
Sanctify us, O Lord!
Holy Spirit, Lord and source of life, giver of the seven gifts,
sanctify us, O Comforter.
Sanctify us, O Lord!
Spirit of wisdom and understanding, Spirit of counsel and strength,
Sanctify us, O Lord!
Spirit of knowledge and devotion, Spirit of obedience to the Lord,
Sanctify us, O Lord!

376

God has so adjusted the body, that there may be no discord in the body, but that the members may have the same care for one another. If one member suffers, all suffer together; if one member is honored, all rejoice together. Now we are the body of Christ and individually members of it. Therefore, let us pray:

For the whole church of Christ, scattered abroad on six continents, and bearing many names, that it may no longer be torn asunder, divided in itself, or weak, but may become a glorious church, without spot or blemish, fulfilling your perfect will:

Your will be done in your church, we pray.

For the churches that are passing through times of suffering and persecution, that their faith and courage may not fail or their love grow cold:

Save them and us, we pray.

For the churches that are strong in faith, that they may abound in grace and in knowledge and love of you:

Use them and us, we pray.

For all weak and struggling churches, that they may persevere and be strong, overcoming those forces that hinder their growth or threaten their existence:

Sustain them and us, we pray.

For newer churches of Asia, Africa, and the islands of the sea, that they may grow into the full stature of the completeness of Christ, bringing new treasures into the church of the ages:

Direct their steps and ours, we pray.

For our fellowship as Christians, that we may hold fast to the truth, be delivered from all error, and walk with one another in the way of love and unity:

Teach us and guide us, we pray.

For the ecumenical councils of churches, that through them Christians may more quickly overcome their reluctance to cooperate with one another, transcend their differences, and be knit together in a fellowship of understanding and love:

Draw all churches near to one another, we pray.
O Sovereign and almighty God,
    bless all people and all your flock.
Give your peace and your love to us your servants
        that we may be united in the bond of peace,
        in one body and one spirit,
        in one hope of our calling,

**in your divine and boundless love,
for the sake of Jesus Christ,
the great Shepherd of the sheep. Amen.**

377

God of Abraham and Isaac, of apostles and prophets: in every age you have picked out people to work for you, by showing justice and doing mercy. Let the church share Christ's own work as prophet, priest, and king, reconciling the world to your law and your love, and telling your mighty power.

Give thanks to God for the church of Jesus Christ.

We are a chosen people.

You have called us out of the world, O God, and chosen us to be a witness to nations. Give us your Spirit to show the way, the truth, and the life of our Savior Jesus Christ.

Forgive our silence and stubbornness. Help us to be your chosen people.

Give thanks to God for the church of Jesus Christ.

We are a royal priesthood.

You have appointed us priests, O God, to pray for people everywhere and to declare your mercy. Give us your Spirit; that, sacrificing ourselves for neighbors in love, they may be drawn to you, and to each other.

Forgive our hypocrisy and lazy prayers. Help us to be your royal priesthood.

Give thanks to God for the church of Jesus Christ.

We are the household of God.

You have baptized us into one family of faith, and named us your children, the sisters and brothers of Christ. Give us your Spirit to live in peace and serve each other gladly.

Forgive our pride and unloving divisions. Help us to be your household.

Silence

Give thanks to God for the church of Jesus Christ.

We are a temple for your Spirit.

You have built us up, O God, into a temple for worship. Give us your Spirit to know there is no other foundation for us than Jesus Christ, rock and redeemer.

Forgive our weakness and lack of reverence. Help us to be a temple for your Spirit.

Give thanks to God for the church of Jesus Christ.

We are a colony of heaven.

You have welcomed us as your citizens, O God, to represent our homeland here on earth. Give us your Spirit to do your will, speak your language, and to show by our style of life your kingdom's courtesy and love.

Forgive our injustice and going along with the world. Help us to be a colony of heaven.

Give thanks to God for the church of Jesus Christ.

We are the body of Christ.

You have joined us in one body, O God, to live for our Lord in the world. Give us your Spirit that, working together without envy or pride, we may serve our Lord and Head.

Forgive our slack faith and separate ways. Help us to be the body of Christ.

O God, we are your church, called, adopted, built up, blessed and joined to Jesus Christ. Help us to know who we are, and in all we do to be your useful servants.

We are a chosen people, a royal priesthood, a household of God, a temple for the Spirit, a colony of heaven , the body of Christ.

Give thanks to God,

for the church of Jesus Christ.

Give thanks to God,

and trust the Holy Spirit. Amen.

378

Lord, grant us this blessedness of your own promise.
Give us ears to hear, eyes to see, and a heart to understand,
    by diligent reading of your scriptures,
    in the holy offices of your church,
    in private prayer,
    to hear, mark, learn, inwardly digest, and thoroughly obey:
To hear your Word, by the kindling of the Holy Spirit,
    in the seeking, reasoning mind,
    in the hungering, thirsting heart,
    in the womb of the soul:
To hear, O Lord, your Word;
    not the new, but the true;
    not the partial, but the full;
    the final and the eternal:
To hear it, O Lord,
    and with all your saints and servants
    not only hear, but keep;
    and bring forth fruit thirty, sixty, a hundredfold.

379

Hate what is evil, hold fast to what is good.
   Let our love be genuine!
Love one another with real affection.
   Let our love be genuine!
Never lack zeal, be on fire with the Spirit, serve the Lord.
   Let our love be genuine!
Rejoice in hope, be patient in tribulation, be constant in prayer.
   Let our love be genuine!
Serve the community, practice hospitality.
   Let our love be genuine!
Bless those who persecute you; bless and do not curse.
   Let our love be genuine!
Rejoice with those who rejoice, weep with those who weep.
   Let our love be genuine!
Live in harmony with one another.
   Let our love be genuine!
Make real friends with the poor. Do not become self-satisfied.
   Let our love be genuine!
Seek only the highest ideals.
Do all you can to live at peace with everyone.
   Let our love be genuine!
Do not be overcome by evil, but overcome evil with good.
   Let our love be genuine!   (BASED ON ROMANS 12:9–21)

380

Creator, Redeemer, Sanctifier, Sacred Mystery, One God:
Help us to be a constructive part of the world in which we live.
That we may urge our hearts and minds to love of excellence
      in every routine task we must perform,
Lord, grant us dedication.
That we may understand and know,
      as we know breath and bone, and pain and joy,
      a duty half performed is time with you forever lost,
Lord, grant us dedication.
That we may portion gladness to each day,
      accepting, not seeking, giving, not asking,
      embracing, not rejecting, waiting, not running,
      surrendering, not commanding, until lost in your companionship
      we find a loving friendship with each other—
      that all of this may be,
Lord, grant us dedication.

381

In the midst of hunger and war
> **we celebrate the promise of plenty and peace.**

In the midst of oppression and tyranny
> **we celebrate the promise of service and freedom.**

In the midst of doubt and despair
> **we celebrate the promise of faith and hope.**

In the midst of fear and betrayal
> **we celebrate the promise of joy and loyalty.**

In the midst of hatred and death
> **we celebrate the promise of love and life.**

In the midst of sin and decay
> **we celebrate the promise of salvation and renewal.**

In the midst of death on every side
> **we celebrate the promise of the living Christ.**

382   *A Litany of Healing*

Let us name before God those for whom we offer our prayers.

The people audibly name those for whom they are interceding.

God the Father, your will for all people is health and salvation;
We praise you and thank you, O Lord.
God the Son, you came that we might have life,
> and might have it more abundantly;

We praise you and thank you, O Lord.
God the Holy Spirit, you make our bodies the temple of your presence;
We praise you and thank you, O Lord.
Holy Trinity, one God, in you we live and move and have our being;
We praise you and thank you, O Lord.
Lord, grant your healing grace to all who are sick, injured, or disabled,
> that they may be made whole;

Hear us, O Lord of life.
Grant to all who seek your guidance,
> and to all who are lonely, anxious, or despondent,
> a knowledge of your will and an awareness of your presence;

Hear us, O Lord of life.
Mend broken relationships, and restore those in emotional distress
> to soundness of mind and serenity of spirit;

Hear us, O Lord of life.
Bless physicians, nurses, and all others who minister to the suffering,
> granting them wisdom and skill, sympathy and patience;

Hear us, O Lord of life.

Grant to the dying peace and a holy death,
>   and uphold by the grace and consolation of your Holy Spirit
>   those who are bereaved;
Hear us, O Lord of life.
Restore to wholeness whatever is broken by human sin, in our lives,
>   in our nation, and in the world;
Hear us, O Lord of life.
You are the Lord who does wonders:
You have declared your power among the peoples.
With you, O Lord, is the well of life;
And in your light we see light.
Hear us, O Lord of life:
Heal us, and make us whole.
Let us pray.

A period of silence follows.

Almighty God, giver of life and health: Send your blessing on all who are sick, and upon those who minister to them, that all weakness may be vanquished by the triumph of the risen Christ; who lives and reigns for ever and ever. Amen.

383   *God's Church in Mission (a Litany)*
God calls the church to fulfill its mission to the world, telling us, "You are a chosen race, a royal priesthood, a holy nation, God's own people, in order that you may proclaim the mighty acts of the one who called you out of darkness into his marvelous light."   (1 PETER 2:9, ALT.)
Help us, O God, to proclaim your mighty acts in word and deed.
God in Jesus Christ reminds the church of its mission, saying, "You are the salt of the earth; but if salt has lost its taste, how can its saltiness be restored? You are the light of the world. A city built on a hill cannot be hid."
(MATTHEW 5:13A, 14)
Help us, O God, to proclaim your mighty acts in word and deed.
God has inspired Jesus Christ to undertake God's mission by declaring: "God has anointed me to bring good news to the poor. God has sent me to proclaim liberty to the captives and recovery of sight to the blind, to let the oppressed go free, to proclaim the year when the Lord will save his people."
(LUKE 4:18–19, ALT.)
Help us, O God, to proclaim your mighty acts in word and deed.
God has commissioned the church to make manifest the word of God's redeeming action, that "Christ died for all, so that those who live might live no longer for themselves, but for the one who died and was raised for them. So if anyone is in Christ, there is a new creation: everything old has passed away; see, everything has become new!"   (2 CORINTHIANS 5:15, 17, ALT.)
Help us, O God, to proclaim your mighty acts in word and deed.

"God has reconciled the church to himself through Christ, and has given us the ministry of reconciliation. That is, in Christ, God was reconciling the world to himself, not counting their trespasses against them, and entrusting the message of reconciliation to us. So we are ambassadors for Christ, since God is making his appeal through us."   (2 CORINTHIANS 5:18–20A, ALT.)

Help us, O God, to proclaim your mighty acts in word and deed.

God joins us in discipleship with Christ who blesses and commissions us, saying: "Peace be with you. As the Father has sent me, so I send you."

(JOHN 20:21)

Help us, O God, to proclaim your mighty acts in word and deed.

ADVENT

384

At the beginning of this Advent season, let us offer our prayers to God, saying: Gentle God, have mercy.

That our gracious Savior may rouse us from sleep and make us attentive to the nearness of his presence, let us pray to the Lord:

Gentle God, have mercy.

That we may discover God's word in every sound of this world, God's touch in every human embrace, and God's love in every gesture of self-sacrifice among us, let us pray to the Lord:

Gentle God, have mercy.

That divine energy and holy grace may bring our hearts to vigilance and make us see with uncovered eyes the Christ who suffers in his people's agonies, let us pray to the Lord:

Gentle God, have mercy.

That we may come to recognize in our holy assembly gathered for prayer that Jesus the Christ is with us here to make our songs of praise and pleading his own, let us pray to the Lord:

Gentle God, have mercy.

That God's coming into the days and years of our human history may be always new, always brimming with light to drive all darkness away, let us pray to the Lord:

Here other intercessions may be offered.

Make ready our hearts for your coming, O Lord, and receive our prayers in the name of the one who comes, our gracious Savior, Jesus, the Christ.

385

God, the host of every sacred meal,
   you have gathered us around this table.
Let your Word shake us out of our easy ways
   that we may repent and take positive steps in our witness to you.
That Lent may bring a return to the covenant
   in which we love God and our neighbor as Jesus teaches,
   we earnestly pray:
Lord, renew the face of the earth.
That Lent may be a time for truth, justice, and peace
   in the decisions of state, national and world governments,
   we earnestly pray:
Lord, renew the face of the earth.
That Lent may be a time for positive efforts
   toward renewal of our covenant promises to love,
   we earnestly pray:
Lord, renew the face of the earth.
That Lent may provide each family with time
   to strengthen bonds of love and communication,
   we earnestly pray:
Lord, renew the face of the earth.
That Lent's prayers and sacrifices may bring relief
   to those suffering from any need,
   we earnestly pray:
Lord, renew the face of the earth.

Other personal intentions may be added.

These are our prayers.
We join to them our promise to live Jesus' way of love.
We seal this prayer and promise with this bread and cup.

PASSION/PALM SUNDAY

386

O God, your son Jesus Christ entered Jerusalem on Palm Sunday as a king of peace. Reconcile all people to you and to one another, that there may be an end to wars and fighting among us.

As Christ fulfilled your will with no thought for self, fill the church with that same spirit. Inspire it to work for your reign and not for its own glory, to struggle for the salvation of the world and not for its own safety. Guide the councils and assemblies of the church in all perplexities of belief and conduct, that we may hold fast that which is true, and firmly maintain the Christian virtues.

We pray for all engaged in public life or in the professions, who have to make difficult decisions that affect the lives of others. Let not the shouts of the crowd, or the prejudice of the mob, influence their judgment. Encourage them to seek your will and, having found it, to act fearlessly upon it.

Merciful God, so willing and able to comfort us in trouble, we pray for all in distress at this time. Cheer the sick, and help doctors and nurses to relieve their pain. Protect and provide for widows and orphaned children. Guide and guard those who are exposed to danger. Befriend the aged who have outlived their former companions. Smooth the pillows of the dying, and wipe away the tears of the bereaved. And in the silence we bring to you the names of our friends who particularly need your help.

The people silently name those for whom they are interceding.

Be pleased, O God, to answer these prayers, for the sake of the one who bore our griefs and carried our sorrows, even Jesus Christ our Lord. Amen.

EASTER

387

O risen Lord, who in your first appearance to Mary
    was mistaken for the gardener:
Be present, be present, O Jesus, good High Priest,
    as you were in the midst of your disciples,
    and show yourself to us in all our mistakes and uncertainties.
O risen Lord, who appeared to your dejected disciples
    on the road to Emmaus, and opened to them the scriptures
    so that their hearts burned within them:
Be present, be present, O Jesus, good High Priest,
    as you were in the midst of your disciples,
    and set our hearts on fire with love for you.
O risen Lord, who gave to your distraught and distracted followers
    the assurance of healing and forgiveness:
Be present, be present, O Jesus, good High Priest,
    as you were in the midst of your disciples,
    and bring together all Christians in peace and harmony.
O risen Lord, who mindful of the needs of your disciples
    prepared a meal by the shores of the Sea of Galilee:
Be present, be present, O Jesus, good High Priest,
    as you were in the midst of your disciples,
    and make yourself known to us in all acts of hospitality and sharing.
O risen Lord, who in your final appearance on the Mount of Olives
    lifted up hands of blessing on all humankind:

Be present, be present, O Jesus, good High Priest,
  as you were in the midst of your disciples,
  and grant that our prayers and praises today
  may be taken up into yours on behalf of the whole world.

ASCENSION DAY

388

On this day of the ascension of Christ, let us pray with amazement, wonder, awe, astonishment. Joining Christ who intercedes for all the world before God, let us offer our prayers to God, saying: O God of wonder, "hear our prayer."

O God, we stand amazed; for Christ ascended from the earth in order to be everywhere at once. We are in awe; for in leaving, Jesus has not left us alone. We thank you, O God, for the life of your Son. Turn our eyes continually to see, to gaze with wonder at your miraculous ways.
  O God of wonder,
  hear our prayer.
Turn the eyes of ordinary people, young and old, poor and rich, to see signs of Jesus. Show us everywhere the signs of Jesus, who is raised up and giving freedom and working power and justice.
  O God of wonder,
  hear our prayer.
Turn the eyes of your church to see the poor places in which Christ now dwells. Help us to see the body of Christ, wounded and yet bright with the light of the Spirit.
  O God of wonder,
  hear our prayer.
Turn the eyes of the leaders of nations to envision a new world in which peace and harmony reign. Turn the eyes of all in power to see the oppressed and the needy. For all who live by your inner sight, we give thanks. For more such people to lead the peoples, we pray.
  O God of wonder,
  hear our prayer.
Turn the eyes of all gathered here beyond this place. Help us to look toward our glorified Lord, and then to look back anew.
  O God of wonder,
  hear our prayer.

Here other intercessions may be offered.

O God, keep us in the spirit of amazement. Keep us believing when we cannot see; keep us hoping while we wait; keep us looking for your presence. Fix our eyes on the glorious one who ascended to intercede, who will come in greatest glory, Jesus Christ our Lord.

(Y) *PRAYERS BY THEME*

There are occasions in public worship when attention needs to be focused upon a specific subject. These are prayers by theme. Some of them may serve to introduce the particular theme of the day. These are traditionally called "collects." They collect the thoughts of the people around a common theme. Although contemporary expression has broken through the collect's traditional formulation, the purpose remains the same.

Other prayers by theme focus upon a specific concern that needs to be included in the congregation's praying because of concerns that have arisen among the people. Circumstances require their praying. These may stand alone in the service or be incorporated into various other times of praying.

389   *For All Who Are Abused*
You chose, O loving God,
    to enter this world quietly, humbly, and as an outcast.
Hear our prayers on behalf of all who are abused:
    for children, who suffer at the hands of parents
        whom they trust and love;
    for spouses, beaten and destroyed by the very one
        who promised to love and to cherish them forever;
    for all people ignored, hated, and cheated by the very neighbor
        who could be the closest one to offer your love.
Hear the cry of the oppressed.
Let the fire of your Spirit fill their hearts
    with the power of vision and hope.
Grant to them empowerment to act,
    that they may not be passive victims of violence and hatred.
Fulfill for them the promises you have made,
    that their lives may be transformed and their oppression ended.
Turn the hearts of oppressors unto you,
    that their living may be changed by your forgiving love
    and their abusive actions and oppressive ways may be brought to an
        end.
In the name of Jesus Christ, who came to liberate the world, we pray.
Through Christ and in us may your holy name be praised,
    this day and forever. So be it. Amen.

390   *For Agricultural Workers*
Thank you, Holy Friend, for our companions who, through work in field and farm, earn their livelihood by providing us with ours. Give them good working conditions, happy relations with the rest of the community, a fair reward for their labors, and the satisfaction that can come from seeing the words of the Lord in the labor of their hands; through Jesus Christ our Lord. Amen.

391   *For Persons with AIDS*
Hear our prayer, O God of mercy and love,
    for all who suffer with AIDS.
Grant unto them tender and loving companions
    who will support them in the midst of fear.
Give them hope for each day to come,
    that every day may be lived with courage and faith.
Bless them with an abundance of your love,
    that they may live with concern for others
    and not be obsessed with their own illness.
Pour upon them the peace and wholeness that you alone can give.
Through Jesus Christ, our Savior, who came to give us abundant life,
    we pray. Amen.

392   *For Animals*
Hear our humble prayer, O God, for our friends the animals. We entreat
for them all your mercy and pity, and for those who deal with them we ask
a heart of compassion, gentle hands, and kindly words. Make us ourselves
to be true friends to animals and so to share the blessing of the merciful.
For the sake of your Son, the tenderhearted Jesus Christ our Lord. Amen.

393   *For Those in the Armed Forces*
Almighty God, we commend to your gracious care and keeping all the
men and women of our armed forces at home and abroad. Defend them
day by day with your heavenly grace; strengthen them in their trials and
temptations; give them courage to face the perils that beset them; and grant
them a sense of your abiding presence wherever they may be; through Jesus
Christ our Lord. Amen.

394   *For Benefactors*
We remember, O God, with gratitude those who use the gifts
with which you have enriched their lives to benefit others:
    those who promote and encourage art and music;
    those through whose endowments knowledge is increased
        and made freely available;
    those who enable charitable organizations
        to continue their works of mercy;
    those who ensure that the churches maintain their witness
        and that the gospel is offered without price;
    those who make it possible for people to explore the secrets
        of the universe and share with others the healing mysteries.
From those to whom much is given, much will be expected.
May they be wise in the use of their gifts, offering them humbly
    without hope of gain, or self-seeking, or desire for recognition. Amen.

395   *For the Bible*

O God, we thank you for the sacred scriptures; for the comfort the Bible has brought to the sorrowful, for guidance offered to the bewildered, for its gracious promises to the uncertain, for its strength given to the weak, and for its progressive revelation of yourself.

We thank you for the people of God who speak to us still from its pages, and for the messengers of God whose learning has made those pages live. We thank you most of all that it reveals to us your Son, the Word made flesh.

Help us to ponder this record of your ways with humanity, that your Word may be indeed a lamp to our feet and a light to our path; through Jesus Christ our Lord.

396   *For the Brokenhearted*

O God, whose love restores the brokenhearted of this world:
Pour out your love, we beseech you,
    upon those who feel lonely, abandoned, or unloved.
Strengthen their hope to meet the days ahead.
Give them the courage to form new life-giving relationships,
    and bless them with the joy of your eternal presence.
This we ask in the name of Jesus Christ. Amen.

397   *For Holy Calm*

So teach us to number our days that we may apply our hearts to wisdom.
Lighten, if it be your will, the pressure of this world's care,
    and, above all, reconcile us to your will,
    and give us a peace that the world cannot take away,
through Jesus Christ our Lord. Amen.

398   *Candor Before God*

All-seeing God, teach us to be open with you about our needs,
to seek your support in our trials, to admit before you our sins,
and to thank you for all your goodness; for Jesus' sake. Amen.

399   *For Cancer Sufferers*

O God, mighty giver of life, you are able to sustain what you have created: we ask you to heal the ills of those who suffer from the threat of cancer. We ask you to restore the physical body and also to cleanse the minds of the ill of worry, fear and despair, that both health of body and joy of soul may unite to undergird and uplift those who suffer, and so place them within the range of your healing power; through Jesus Christ, our Lord. Amen.

400   *For Inspiration to Care*
Save us, Lord, from hurrying away,
    because we do not wish to help,
    because we know not how to help,
    because we dare not.
Inspire us to use our lives serving others;
    through Jesus Christ our Lord. Amen.

401   *To See Christ in Every Face*
Loving Father,
    as you made your love known in a single human life,
        lived for others and laid down,
    help us to meet Christ and greet him in every human face,
    to worship and serve him in every human need,
    until with him and every man and woman born into the world
        we share with you the kingdom,
        the power, and the glory forever. Amen.

402   *To Be Crafted by Christ*
O Christ, the Master Carpenter,
    who, at the last, through wood and nails
    purchased our whole salvation:
Wield well your tools in the workshop of your world,
    so that we, who come rough-hewn to your bench,
        may here be fashioned to a truer beauty of your hand.
We ask it for your name's sake. Amen.

403   *Worldwide Church*
Heavenly Father, we thank you for making us in our baptism
    members of your worldwide family, the church,
    and for our brothers and sisters in every land who love the Lord Jesus.
Keep us loyal to one another, faithful to our promises
    and active in your service, for Jesus Christ's sake. Amen.

404   *For Cities*
God of our daily lives:
We pray for the people of the cities of this world,
    working and without work;
    homeless and well housed;
    fulfilled or frustrated;
    confused and cluttered with material goods,
        or scraping a living from others' leavings;
    angrily scrawling on walls, or reading the writing on the wall;
    lonely or living in community;
    finding their own space and respecting the space of others.
We pray for our sisters and brothers, mourning and celebrating.
May we share their suffering and hope.

405   *For Inner Cities*
Hear our prayer, compassionate God, for all whose lives
    are impoverished and beset by the problems of our inner cities.
Guide those in local and central government,
        the planners, the administrators, the decision makers;
        may they see the welfare of its citizens as the city's highest good.
Raise up in such areas men and women of integrity and energy
        as leaders, ministers, and teachers;
        in industry and commerce, in health and social services, in the police
        and in all the work of community and industrial relations.
And this we ask for Jesus Christ's sake. Amen.

406   *For the Comfortless*
Enfold, O God, within your loving-kindness
        all those who feel rejected, unwanted, or alone.
Hear our prayer for prisoners
        and all who are caught up in processes of law;
        for those enclosed within a private world of desolation
            by incapacity of mind or body,
            by age or grief or sickness,
            or because society has passed them by.
Draw near and comfort them wherever they may be;
        and move the hearts of us and all your people
        to care more deeply for the pains of others;
in the name of Jesus, the Man of Sorrows. Amen.

407   *For Those Who Serve the Community*
We thank you, creative God, for those whose work sustains our nation and this community in which we live; for all who create the wealth by which we trade, for those who grow and provide our food, or who in industry, commerce, and transport bring it to our homes.

We thank you for those who, day and night, maintain the public services; for the police, for those who respond to emergencies, and for all whose work is in health or healing or social care.

Teach us to remember that all our lives depend upon the work of many minds and hands; and we pray that we may live thankfully and in unity as members of one human family; through Jesus Christ our Lord.

408   *In Times of Conflict*
O God, you have bound us together in a common life.
Help us, in the midst of our struggles for justice and truth,
        to confront one another without hatred or bitterness,
        and to work together with mutual forbearance and respect;
            through Jesus Christ our Lord. Amen.

409   *For Those Who Suffer for the Sake of Conscience*
God of love and strength, your Son forgave his enemies
    even while he was suffering shame and death.
Strengthen those who suffer for the sake of conscience;
    when they are accused, save them from speaking in hate;
    when they are rejected, save them from bitterness;
    when they are imprisoned, save them from despair.
Give us grace to discern the truth,
    that our society may be cleansed and strengthened.
This we ask for the sake of our merciful and righteous judge,
    Jesus Christ our Lord. Amen.

410   *For Being Stewards of God's Creation*
Lord of the universe, we praise you for your creation;
    for the wonder of space, the beauty of the world,
    and the value of Earth's resources.
Keep us from spoiling these your gifts by our selfishness
    and help us to use them for the good of all people
    and the glory of your name. Amen.

411   *For the Cross*
The cross is the hope of Christians
The cross is the resurrection of the dead
The cross is the way of the lost
The cross is the savior of the lost
The cross is the staff of the lame
The cross is the guide of the blind
The cross is the strength of the weak
The cross is the doctor of the sick
The cross is the aim of the priests
The cross is the hope of the hopeless
The cross is the freedom of the slaves
The cross is the power of the kings
The cross is the water of the seeds
The cross is the consolation of the bondsmen
The cross is the source of those who seek water
The cross is the cloth of the naked
We thank you, Father, for the cross.

412   *At the Close of the Day*
O Lord our God, thank you for bringing this day to a close;
Thank you for giving us rest in body and soul.
Your hand has been over us and has guarded and preserved us.
Forgive our lack of faith and any wrong that we have done today,
    and help us to forgive all who have wronged us.

Let us sleep in peace under your protection,
    and keep us from all the temptations of darkness.
Into your hands we commend our loved ones
    and all who dwell in this place;
We commend to you all that we are—body and soul.
O God, your holy name be praised.

413   *A Prayer of Dedication*
Teach us, O gracious Lord, to begin our works with reverence,
    to go on in obedience, and finish them with love;
and then to wait patiently in hope,
    and with cheerful countenance to look up to you,
whose promises are faithful and rewards infinite;
    through Jesus Christ our Lord. Amen.

414   *For the Diaconate*
O God, through the ages you have called *women/men* to the diaconate in
your church. Let your blessing rest now on all who answer that call. Grant
them understanding of the gospel, sincerity of purpose, diligence in ministry, and the beauty of life in Christ, that many people will be served and
your name be glorified; through your Son, Jesus Christ our Lord.

415   *For Dialogue*
Give us a willingness to listen to one another,
    and even to those with whom we have sharp disagreements,
    lest in blind obedience to what we call the truth
    we do not hear your word as you elect to speak it
        through the words of others. Amen.

416   *After a Disaster*
Lord of compassion and power,
    be with those who have survived this disaster;
    minister to their needs of mind and spirit, body and circumstance;
    help those who are hurt;
    give peace to the dying;
    comfort and support the bereaved;
    and to all who are working to bring relief and restore order,
        give strength and resilience to do their work well;
    for the sake of Jesus Christ our Lord. Amen.

417   *After a Natural Disaster*
God of earthquake, wind, and fire: tame natural forces that defy control or
shock us by their fury. Keep us from calling a disaster your justice; and
help us, in good times or in calamity, to trust your mercy, which never
ends, and your power, which in Jesus Christ stilled storms, raised the dead,
and put down demonic powers. Amen.

418   *For Self-Discipline*
Almighty God,
     whose Son Jesus Christ fasted forty days in the wilderness
     and was tempted as we are, yet without sin:
give us grace to discipline ourselves in obedience to your Spirit;
     and, as you know our weakness, so may we know your power to save;
through Jesus Christ our Lord. Amen.

419   *The Diversity of Races and Cultures*
O God, you created all people in your image. We thank you for the aston-
ishing variety of races and cultures in this world. Enrich our lives by ever-
widening circles of fellowship, and show us your presence in those who
differ most from us, until our knowledge of your love is made perfect in
our love for all your children; through your Son, Jesus Christ our Lord.

420   *For the Divorced*
O Lord, we pray for all those who, full of confidence and love,
     once chose a partner for life,
     and are now alone after final separation.
May they all receive the gift of time,
     so that hurt and bitterness may be redeemed by healing and love,
     personal weakness by your strength,
     inner despair by the joy of knowing you and serving others;
through Jesus Christ our Lord. Amen.

421   *For a Public Election*
All-knowing God, we gather to hear your word
     and to pray for your guidance as we approach the time
     to elect those who will next serve the nation in public office.
Enlighten our minds with understanding and perception
     that we may continue to discover your truth.
Endow our wills with the strength to strive for justice.
Fill our hearts with love for the peace you alone give,
     that we may be at peace with one another.
May our individual lives serve the good
     of all the people of our land and beyond its shores.
We ask this through Christ our Lord. Amen.

422   *For Enlightenment*
Eternal God, all-powerful and merciful,
     your word is a torch for our path and a light for our way.
Open our eyes and enlighten our spirit that we may
     understand your revelation in all its purity and holiness.
May it transform our lives and make us worthy to bear your image;
     through Jesus Christ our Lord. Amen.

423   *For Evangelistic Visiting*

We remember, O God, that the apostle Paul proclaimed the gospel not only
    in public places but also from house to house.
Give grace to us your servants as we seek to spread the good news of Jesus
    by visiting the home of this community.
Keep us humble and make us wise;
        show us how to use our opportunities;
        help us to speak a word in season;
and in all we say and do may we commend our Master and further his
    kingdom, to the glory of your name. Amen.

424   *Evangelistic Witness*

Lord Jesus Christ, you stretched out your arms of love on the hard wood of
the cross that everyone might come within the reach of your saving embrace. So clothe us in your Spirit that we, reaching forth our hands in love,
may bring those who do not know you to the knowledge and love of you;
for the honor of your name. Amen.

425   *Faithfulness*

Holy and eternal God, give us such trust in your sure purpose,
        that we measure our lives not by what we have done or failed to do,
        but by our faithfulness to you; in Jesus our Redeemer. Amen.

426   *For Troubled Families*

O God, there are families where love is bought and sold
            and treated like a commodity,
            a thing, a power to be wielded to gain control in another's life;
        where forgiveness is given lip service
            while the offense is held ever after over the offender's head
            like a dangling sword.
How can trustworthiness grow where no trust is given?
How can love be rekindled where it has been killed?
You are the source and giver of life, O God.
Bless the children in homes without love.
Sustain them, give them hope, and people who will love them
            and teach them to love;
        in the name of Christ who loves. Amen.

427   *For Global Enlightenment*

God, our Father and our Mother, Creator and Sustainer of the universe, we
thank you for the wondrous ways in which you have revealed your love to
us through the teachings of the sages of India, the wise of the East; through
the enlightened words of the Buddha and the disciplined words of the
prophet Mohammed, and through the light of the gospel of Jesus Christ.
We pray that you will pour your love into our hearts, that with open minds
we may accept all peoples of the world as brothers and sisters, and serve
them in true humility, so that all humankind may find the joy of true freedom in you.

428   *For Those Who Govern*
Eternal God, Fount of wisdom,
    we ask you to bless the representatives we have elected.
Grant that through their discussions and decisions
    we may solve our problems effectively,
    enhance the well-being of our nation,
    and achieve together a fairer and more united society. Amen.

429   *For the Healing of Minds*
O Lord, you know our deepest thoughts, our human griefs and anxieties.
We bring to you those whose minds are troubled, whose bodies are in pain,
and who are disappointed in spirit.

We pray for little children whose minds and emotions have been molested
and tormented by the undiscipline of adults: give them confidence to share
their problems and to recover hope and strength.

We pray for those overwhelmed and consumed by habits they are power-
less to break: bring them to admit their weakness, and to seek counselors
who have sympathy and understanding and can give them help.

We pray for the callous and careless in the world who cause pain to others
and create within their own lives a bitter spirit and an unpleasant atmosphere: reveal to them the tender love of our Savior, and when we are the
victims of unhelpful comment and unjust criticism, keep us from all re-
sentment and all bitterness.

Channel our energies into your service, secure us by our almighty strength,
and help us to find our healing in you, for Jesus' sake. Amen.

430   *Thanksgiving for Those Restored to Health*
We join today in thanking you, God,
    for all who have been restored again to better health;
    for faith and patience granted to us;
    for healing in body, mind, and spirit;
    for the skill and friendship and generosity of others;
    for the possibility of prayer and the comfort of the Bible;
    for sins forgiven and pardon assured;
and through it all, for your unfailing presence
    we give you thanks and praise, through Jesus Christ our Lord. Amen.

431   *For a Sense of History*
Give us, O Lord, a sense of history. Forgive our preoccupation with the
present moment. Teach us to recognize your hand in the stories of peoples
and nations. Help us to be thankful for evidence of your loving eye upon
our own lives. Encourage us for the coming days in the knowledge that
your touch has still its ancient power; through Jesus Christ our Lord. Amen.

432   *For the Holy Spirit's Blessing*

Holy Spirit, we meet you in countless ways and find you in many forms:
  breath, wind, fire, water, dove.
Often you comfort us, often you inspire us,
  sometimes you surprise us, always you bless us.
Holy Spirit, enfold us, so that we are an echo of God's love,
  a reflection of Christ's light, and a pathway for your peace. Amen.

433   *For a Ray of Hope*

O Dawn of the new creation,
  spill a ray of hope to lift the hearts of your sons and daughters,
  for we are bound by a vision that is not always clear to see.
As we live into your promises,
  help us to help each other, for we truly need each other,
  as you need us and we need you every day of our lives. Amen.

434   *For the Hospitalized*

O God, Creator of us all, to whom alone is known the mystery of suffering,
hear our prayers on behalf of those in hospitals who are bearing the burden of illness or pain or have to undergo an operation: in their weakness
and anxiety draw near to them with your comfort and strength, and give
them the assurance that, sharing their suffering, you will also share with
them your peace, in Jesus Christ our Lord. Amen.

435   *For This House of Prayer*

O God, make the doorway of this house
  wide enough to receive all who need human love and fellowship;
  narrow enough to shut out all envy, pride, and strife.
Make its threshold smooth enough to be no stumbling block to children,
  or barrier to the elderly and disabled.
Let its door be rugged and strong to turn back the tempter's power,
  but open and inviting to those who are your guests.
God, make this house the doorway to your eternal kingdom;
  through Jesus Christ our Lord. Amen.

436   *For a Sense of Humor*

Give us a sense of humor, Lord, and also things to laugh about.
Give us the grace to take a joke against ourselves,
  and to see the funny side of the things we do.
Save us from annoyance, bad temper, resentfulness against our friends.
Help us to laugh even in the face of trouble.
Fill our minds with the love of Jesus; for his name's sake. Amen.

437   *For the Imprisoned*
Many of your children are imprisoned, and often they are so denied human dignity that their confinement is only a punishment and not a means of rehabilitation. Prevent that from happening, and enlighten correction officers and others who are involved in this work, that those imprisoned may be returned to useful and responsible lives within society.

438   *For Industry*
Almighty and everlasting God, we pray for all who work in industry.
Bless all meetings between employers and employees.
Remove all bitterness, distrust, and prejudice from their deliberations.
Give to all a spirit of tolerance, and an earnest desire
        to seek justice and truth;
    that all may work together for the common good,
        through Jesus Christ our Lord. Amen.

439   *For the Judiciary and the Police*
God of truth and justice, we ask you to help the men and women
    who administer and police our laws.
Grant them insight, courage, and compassion;
    protect them from corruption and arrogance;
    and grant that we, whom they seek to serve,
    may give them the support and affection they need.
So may our people be strengthened more and more
    in respect and concern for one another. Amen.

440   *About Justice and Trust*
God of nations, help us to reflect and share the goodness that surrounds us. Help us to win justice for poor and rich alike, and bring trust and friendship to all our different races. Amen.

441   *For Our Labor*
O God, we thank you for the gifts you have given to each of us, and for the satisfaction of a task well done—whether for ourselves, for our family, for our church, for our employer, or for a friend. Help us to do all that we do, as Jesus did, to bring honor and glory to your name. Amen.

442   *For Those We Love*
Everloving God, we bring to you in our prayers all whom we love,
    knowing that your love for them is so much greater than ours,
    and that your will for them is all that is for their good.
So, guard them in your keeping, O Lord,
    and give them now and always your richest blessing;
    for Jesus Christ's sake. Amen.

443   *For the Marginalized*

Loving God, we pray for millions of silent people today: the homeless, the refugees—forced to live in tents or shacks, often in camps, herded together. We pray for people whose harvest has failed for years, who must listen to the sobs of children with daily hunger pains. Strengthen every missionary, every church organization, every national fund seeking to help the forgotten millions, and show us how we can best love these our neighbors in need. Hear our prayer and enliven our response, for Jesus' sake. Amen.

444   *For Marriages Under Stress*

O Lord God, we thank you for the gift of marriage—
    that gift which leads to the heights of shared joy
    or to the depths of shared bitterness.
We pray for those who are suffering hurt in marriage;
    for those who inflict it,
    and for those whose greatest unhappiness
        stems from the closeness of their partner.
O Lord, who in love created the complexities of the human mind,
    and in power conquered the evil that invades it:
Bring unity to those who are divided,
    and wholeness to those who long for it,
    that we may all finally be united with you and with one another;
        through Jesus our Redeemer. Amen.

445   *For Ministers of the Church*

We thank you, O God, for those whom you have called through the centuries to serve in the ministry of the church. Pour your blessing on those whom you have called today *and especially on your servant(s) whom we now remember;* that by word and deed they may bear witness to your saving love and power, and enable your people to grow up into him who is the Head, our Lord and Savior Jesus Christ, to whom be praise and honor forever.

446   *Mission*

May the Spirit of the Lord be upon us
    that we may announce good news to the poor,
    proclaim release for the prisoners,
    and recovery of sight for the blind;
    that we may let the broken victim go free,
    and proclaim the year of the Lord's favor;
according to the example of Christ and by his grace. Amen.

447   *For the Use and Understanding of Money*

Help us and all people, dear Lord, to understand the purpose and place of money in our life. Keep before us the peril of loving it. Help us to make it our servant, and never our master. And let neither the lack of it, nor the possession of it, in any degree loosen our grasp upon reality, which is ours through the love of Jesus Christ our Lord. Amen.

448 *For Mothers-to-Be*

Lord Jesus, whose holy mother was told by the message of an angel
    that the fruit of her womb would be blessed:
    we pray for all mothers who are awaiting the birth of a child.
Keep them in your peace, guard them from harm,
    and grant them the fulfillment of their joy, for your name's sake.

449 *For Music and Musicians*

Eternal God, source of all beauty and harmony, we praise you for the gift of music; for the inspiration given to those who compose it, for the skill and devotion of those who perform it, for the faculties and powers that enable us to enjoy it; and we pray that as by this gift our lives are enriched and renewed, so we may glorify you in a fuller dedication of ourselves, giving thanks always for all things in the name of our Lord Jesus Christ. Amen.

450 *Thanksgiving for Music*

Creator God, we thank you for the many ways we can express ourselves, but above all for the gift of music. We thank you for the way it can describe every emotion: joy and delight; melancholy and sadness; wonder and worship; love and devotion. We thank you that music can soothe the soul and bring solace to those who mourn. And we thank you, too, that like the Israelites of old, we can make merry before you and show our joy in music and song, singing and making melody in our heart, through Jesus Christ our Lord. Amen.

451 *For One's Nation/Community in Time of Trial*

Lord almighty, heaven is your throne and earth your footstool.
    Our *country/city/town/village* is in pain.
Extend to us your peace like a river, and restore to us prosperity.
As a mother comforts her children, so comfort us—
    that our hearts may rejoice,
    and that we may flourish like a garden tended by your hand;
Lord, in your mercy hear us. Amen.

452 *For Our Neighbors*

Jesus Christ, you have taught us
    that what we do to each other, we do to you.
Make us quick to help and slow to hurt,
    knowing that in our neighbor
    it is you who receive our love or our neglect. Amen.

453   *For the Outcast*
God of compassion,
    do not forsake the ones cast out from the center of the circle.
Move closer to the core of them as others move away.
Cast your circle wider than our small circumference,
        so that all who are out are in
        and blessed in your own loving way. Amen.

454   *For Peace*
O God of many names,
    Lover of all nations,
we pray for peace:
    in our hearts,
    in our homes,
    in our nation,
    in our world;
the peace of your will,
the peace of our need.

455   *For an Awareness of the Poor*
They sleep in doorways;
    they sleep at home.
They wear ragged clothes and carry shopping bags;
    they look like us.
They use poor grammar and smell;
    they have good educations and are well groomed.
All-knowing God, show us the poor—
    not just the ones who have been pushed aside
        in the wake of competition,
    but the ones who are losing self-confidence,
    the ones who are victims of the system they helped to build,
    the ones whose jobs no longer exist.
Show us there is also is a poverty of the heart
    when saving is more important than sharing.
Help us to find security in sharing all our resources
    so that through our total effort
    we will have answered your call to be a friend in need. Amen.

456   *That Prayer Be Answered*
Almighty God, you have given us grace at this time to make our prayers to
you with one accord and you have promised that when two or three are
gathered together in your name you will grant their requests. Fulfill now
the desires of your servants, if it is fitting; and give us knowledge of your
truth in this world and eternal life in the world to come, through Jesus
Christ our Lord. Amen.

457   *For Prisons*
Grant your grace, O God, to those who have the care of prisoners, the police and wardens, the prison governors, chaplains and doctors, the prison
visitors, and those working for discharged prisoners; grant to them your
gifts of wisdom, courage, and patience in all their difficulties. When their
work is dangerous and unrewarding, grant your special grace, that they
may be saved from attitudes of cruelty and indifference. Let your love be
always present with them and let your mercy guide them, through Jesus
Christ our Lord. Amen.

458   *For the Fulfillment of God's Purpose*
God of all times and places,
    may we live by faith, walk in hope, and be renewed in love,
    until the world reflects your glory and you are all in all.
Even so, come Lord Jesus. Amen.

459   *For Racial Inclusivity*
Almighty God, as your Son our Savior was born of a Hebrew mother,
    but rejoiced in the faith of a Syrian woman and of a Roman soldier,
    welcomed the Greeks who sought him,
    and suffered a man from Africa to carry his cross,
so teach us to regard the members of all races
    as fellow heirs of the kingdom of Jesus Christ our Lord. Amen.

460   *To Be Ready*
Rouse our spirits, Lord Jesus,
    that whenever you come to the door and knock
    you may find us awake, ready to admit and serve you. Amen.

461   *For Reconciliation*
God, who formed all humankind as a family to live in harmony and peace:
we acknowledge before you our divisions, quarrels, hatreds, injustices, and
greed. Let your church demonstrate before the world the power of the gospel to destroy divisions, so that in Christ Jesus there may be no barriers of
wealth or class, age or intellect, race or color, but all may be equally your
children, members one of another and heirs together of your everlasting
kingdom. To your name be glory forever and ever. Amen.

462   *For Reconciling of Divisions*
O God the Father of all, you ask every one of us to spread
    love where the poor are humiliated,
    joy where the church is brought low,
    and reconciliation where people are divided:
        father against son
        mother against daughter

husband against wife
believers against those who cannot believe
Christians against their unloved fellow Christians.
You open this way for us,
so that the wounded body of Jesus Christ, your church,
may be leaven of communion for the poor of the earth
and in the whole human family.

463   *A Psalm on Separation*
O One to whom we are connected by unbreakable bonds of love,
you tell us that nothing can separate us
from your providential mercy and your covenant of care.
Our grateful beings praise you.
You are the substance of our hope that life can and will go on.
Pour out on all our relationships the possibility of forever,
and when we must sever an inseparable bond,
strengthen us and support us so that life may continue
around us and in us, forever and ever. Amen.

464   *Make Us Servants*
Lord Christ, you remain, unseen, at our side,
present like a poor man who washes the feet of his friends.
And we, to follow in your footsteps,
we are here, waiting for you to suggest signs of sharing
to make us into servants of your gospel.

465   *For Healing from Sin*
We need your healing, merciful God:
give us true repentance.
Some sins are plain to us;
some escape us, some we cannot face.
Forgive us; set us free to hear your word to us;
set us free to serve you. Amen.

466   *For Victims of a Tragedy*
God of compassion, you watch our ways
and weave out of terrible happenings wonders of goodness and grace.
Surround those who have been shaken by tragedy
with a sense of your present love, and hold them in faith.
Though they are lost in grief, may they find you and be comforted;
through Jesus Christ, who was dead, but lives,
and rules this world with you. Amen.

467   *For Travelers*

We pray for those soaring into the skies,
    sailing across the seas, and driving on the roads.
Give strength and wisdom to all who use the machines of travel,
    and those who have responsibility for other people's lives.
Save us all from selfishness and from taking undue risks;
    give us patience and the ability to move in this world in peace.
We ask this for our health's sake, and for the glory of the Lord of life,
    our Savior Jesus Christ. Amen.

468   *For Unity in the Church*

Help each one of us, gracious God,
    to live in such magnanimity and restraint
    that the head of the church
    may never have cause to say of us:
This is my body, broken by you.

469   *For Wider Vision*

God of all cultures, God of all people,
    help us not to label anyone inferior or second-class.
Help us overcome our attitudes of superiority and oppression.
May we broaden our vision and widen our tents
    so that plurality and diversity determine who we are:
    people called and committed to a world united in justice and peace,
        now and forever. Amen.

470   *For Watch Night*

Lord Jesus, you asked your disciples to watch with you
    for one brief hour of prayer.
Bless our midnight songs of praise,
    that in these solemn moments
    we may know your presence
    and be awake to your glory. Amen.

471   *Witnessing by One's Life*

Dear Jesus, help us to spread your fragrance everywhere we go.
Flood our souls with your spirit and life.
Penetrate and possess our whole being so utterly
    that our lives may only be a radiance of yours.
Let us thus praise you in the way you love best
    by shining on those around us.
Let us preach you without preaching,
    not by words, but by our example,
    by the catching force,
    the sympathetic influence of what we do,
    the evident fullness of the love our hearts bear to you. Amen.

472   *For Our Witness to the World*
Fill us with your love so that we may gladly speak for you,
     work for you, and live our whole life for you,
          until all the nations of the earth join with us in endless praise;
through Jesus Christ our Lord. Amen.

473   *To Witness to the World*
Living God, whose love is freely given to good and bad alike;
     help us to show the world that it is not ourselves we trust but you.
Then our failures will not turn others against you
     but enable them to see more clearly
     how completely full of love you are,
          so that they may come to you in faith themselves;
through Jesus Christ our Lord. Amen.

474   *World Mission*
Eternal God, Creator of all, Savior of all, Lord of all, we thank you that
your love and power encompass all things and all people. As the universal
Creator, the whole universe is in your hands: there is no part of this earth
that does not belong to you. As our Savior and Lord, there are no people
beyond your redeeming love.

We thank you that in all countries there are witnesses to your gospel, bearing testimony through their words and actions to the good news of Jesus
Christ. We thank you for your church in each place, for your Spirit equip-
ping it with gifts and empowering your people to proclaim the good news
of Jesus Christ. We thank you for Christian partnership across continents
and national boundaries, for those who have responded to your call to serve
the church in a land that is not their own.

Grant that we may be worthy of this great company of saints, ready to
witness and serve in the name of our Lord Christ. Amen.

475   *True Worth*
Living God, as all our achievements, without your love, amount to nothing, help us to put your love first and to strive for it more than anything
else, so that everything we do may be given its true worth, to build up the
church, transform the world, and glorify your name; through Jesus Christ
our Lord. Amen.

CONSECRATION AND COMMITMENT

Prayer involves not only speaking but the living of a life of faithfulness to God. Prayers of consecration and commitment give expression to a people's intention to participate actively in fulfilling God's purposes. They are ways of praying that God's will be done on earth through God's people as it is in heaven.

476

Christ be with me, Christ within me,
Christ behind me, Christ before me,
  Christ beside me, Christ to win me,
  Christ to comfort and restore me,
Christ beneath me, Christ above me,
Christ in quiet, Christ in danger,
  Christ in hearts of all that love me,
  Christ in mouth of friend and stranger.

477

God to enfold me, God to surround me,
God in my speaking, God in my thinking.
  God in my sleeping, God in my waking,
  God in my watching, God in my hoping.
God in my life, God in my lips,
God in my soul, God in my heart.
  God in my suffering, God in my slumber,
  God in my ever-living soul, God in my eternity.

478

Christ, you demand that if we belong to you,
  the whole of our nature must be remade.
It is not sufficient to deal with one or two sins
  or to add one or two new duties.
We must be born again.
Respectable lives, that avoid scandalous sins
  and practice what others may judge generous giving,
  are not enough.
For you demand conversion, the total offering of our souls and bodies,
  all that we are and all that we have.
Only then can you use us to make the new world which is your will.
Only then shall we understand
  how constantly you are making all things new,
  recreating them in the original pattern that God willed for them.

479

I will follow you, Jesus, and I will give you all,
  for by your strength I will follow you in everything.

480

O God, we are your children and you love us.
So deep is your love that nothing we have done, or thought to do,
    shall take away the peace you give.
So strong is your love that no passing trouble
    shall tear us from your arms.
So precious is your love that all our life
    shall be lived in your service—
    and yours shall be the glory,
        through Jesus Christ our Lord. Amen.

481

We offer to God our skills and our service, our lives and our worship:

O God, you have given us life and health and strength and in Jesus Christ
you have given us a savior and a friend. For the love that made you enter
our world in Jesus to share our joys and sorrows and to die for our sin:
Loving God,
    receive the gift of our love.
For the forgiveness you promise to all who confess their sins and trust in
his sacrifice on the cross: Loving God,
    receive the gift of our penitence.
For the hope of eternal life we have in Christ because you raised him from
the dead: Loving God,
    receive the gift of our lives.
For the blessing of friendship and the satisfaction of working together, for
the stretching of mind and the exercise of body: Loving God,
    receive the gift of our worship.

Holy, holy, holy Lord, God of power and might:
heaven and earth are full of your glory.
Hosanna in the highest. Amen.

482

In the light of your love shining through the life of Jesus, O God,
    we offer ourselves to you.
In the light of the world's need for people who can truly love,
    we offer ourselves to you.
In the light of our own failure in the past to live unselfishly,
    we offer ourselves to you.
We put body, mind, and soul at the disposal of your love.
    Use us as you will to meet the needs of your family on earth.
Mold our lives
    so that the love and power of Christ may work through us.
Renew the life of this congregation
    so that Christ may be seen more clearly in our midst.

483
Lord, we are willing to face the challenge of mission and discipleship,
    even when this means the personal sacrifice
    of energy, time, and possessions.
You called us and now we come,
    you commanded us and now we go,
    you taught us your will and now we obey.
And, as you promised, we know that we will not be alone
    in our journey of faith and mission,
    for you are always with us.

484
Lord, we thank you that you chose to be one with us
    in the waters of baptism.
We ask that our baptism may make us one with you.
We are baptized into your death:
    may we die to what is selfish, impious, faithless,
    cowardly, and unworthy of your calling.
We are baptized into your resurrection:
    may we carry the unwavering hope of eternal life within us
    and live this present life as those who have tasted the life to come.
We are baptized into your Spirit:
    may there be no halt to our growth to maturity
    through his indwelling.
We are baptized into your church:
    Lord, may we never disown
    those who are our brothers and sisters in the faith
    but seek always that unity and compassion
    by which your family is to be recognized.
Lord, in whom we are baptized:
    keep us faithful in the wilderness;
    keep us brave at the cross;
    keep us joyous in the resurrection.
For your name's sake. Amen.

🍷 PRAYER FOR ILLUMINATION

The prayer for illumination seeks the assistance of the Holy Spirit in properly understanding God's word as read and proclaimed. It is spoken before the reading of the first scripture lesson. There is no need for a separate prayer relating specifically to the sermon.

485

Eternal God, in the reading of the scripture, may your word be heard;
in the meditations of our hearts, may your word be known;
and in the faithfulness of our lives, may your word be shown. Amen.

486

Almighty God, you have revealed yourself to us as one God;
give us grace to continue steadfast in the living of our faith
and constant in our worship of you,
for you live and reign, one God, now and forever. Amen.

487

Spirit of truth, open to us the scriptures,
speaking your holy word
and meeting us in the living Christ.

488

Guide us, O Lord, by your Word and Holy Spirit,
that in your light we may see light,
in your truth find freedom,
and in your will discover peace;
through Jesus Christ our Lord. Amen.

BEFORE A SERMON

489

Let the words of my mouth and the meditation of our hearts be always
acceptable in your sight, O Lord, our strength and our redeemer. Amen.

490

Take my lips, O Lord, and speak through them.
Take our minds and think with them.
Take our hearts and set them on fire;
through Jesus Christ our Lord. Amen.

$\mathcal{OS}$CRIPTURE READING

Each scripture reading may be introduced by a phrase that emphasizes the unique significance of the Holy Scriptures for the church. The scriptures are God's gift to the people through which God speaks. It is appropriate to express affirming gratitude for God's grace at the close of each reading.

491   *The Public Reading of the Bible*
Each scripture reading may be introduced by saying:
Hear the word of God. A reading from _____
Or:
Listen for the word of God in _____

The Old Testament or Epistle reading may conclude with the words:
The word of the Lord.
Thanks be to God.

The Epistle reading may also conclude with the words:
Here ends the Epistle lesson.

The Gospel reading may be introduced by saying:
Listen to the Gospel of Jesus Christ according to _____

The Gospel reading may conclude with the words:
The Gospel of the Lord.
Praise to you, Lord Jesus Christ.
Or:
This is the good news.
Praise to you, O Christ.

$\mathcal{A}$FFIRMATION OF FAITH

One appropriate response to the hearing and proclaiming of God's word is for the congregation to unite in an affirmation of faith. This may be accomplished by singing an appropriate hymn or by using a statement of faith from scripture or from the resources of the church. The affirmation of faith may be appropriately used in earlier portions of the service as the people identify who they are.

492   *Preamble to the Design for the Christian Church (Disciples of Christ)*
As members of the Christian Church,
We confess that Jesus is the Christ,
    the Son of the living God,
    and proclaim him Lord and Savior of the world.
In Christ's name and by his grace
    we accept our mission of witness
    and service to all people.
We rejoice in God,
    maker of heaven and earth,
    and in the covenant of love
    which binds us to God and one another.
Through baptism into Christ
    we enter into newness of life
    and are made one with the whole people of God.
In the communion of the Holy Spirit,
    we are joined together in discipleship
    and in obedience to Christ.
At the table of the Lord
    we celebrate with thanksgiving
    the saving acts and presence of Christ.
Within the universal church,
    we receive the gift of ministry
    and the light of scripture.
In the bonds of Christian faith
    we yield ourselves to God
    that we may serve the One
    whose kingdom has no end.
Blessing, glory, and honor
    be to God forever. Amen.

493   *United Church of Christ Statement of Faith*
We believe in you, O God, Eternal Spirit,
God of our Savior Jesus Christ and our God,
and to your deeds we testify.
    You call the worlds into being,
        create persons in your own image
        and set before each one the ways of life and death.
    You seek in holy love to save all people from aimlessness and sin.
    You judge people and nations by your righteous will
        declared through prophets and apostles.
    In Jesus Christ, the man of Nazareth, our crucified and risen Savior,
        you have come to us
        and shared our common lot,
        conquering sin and death
        and reconciling the world to yourself.

You bestow upon us your Holy Spirit,
    creating and renewing the church of Jesus Christ,
    binding in covenant faithful people of all ages,
    tongues and races.
You call us into your church
    to accept the cost and joy of discipleship,
    to be your servants in the service of others,
    to proclaim the gospel to all the world,
    to resist the powers of evil,
    to share in Christ's baptism and eat at his table,
    to join him in his passion and victory.
You promise to all who trust you
    forgiveness of sins and fullness of grace,
    courage in the struggle for justice and peace,
    your presence in trial and rejoicing,
    and eternal life in your realm which has no end.
Blessing and honor, glory and power be unto you. Amen.

494   *The Apostles' Creed*
I believe in God, the Father almighty,
    creator of heaven and earth.
I believe in Jesus Christ, God's only Son, our Lord.
    who was conceived by the Holy Spirit,
    born of the Virgin Mary.
    suffered under Pontius Pilate,
    was crucified, died, and was buried;
    he descended to the dead.
    On the third day he rose again.
    He ascended into heaven,
    he is seated at the right hand of the Father,
    and he will come again to judge the living and the dead.
I believe in the Holy Spirit,
    the holy catholic church,
    the communion of saints,
    the forgiveness of sins,
    the resurrection of the body,
    and the life everlasting. Amen.

495   *The Nicene Creed*
We believe in one God,
    the Father, the Almighty,
    maker of heaven and earth,
    of all that is, seen and unseen.

We believe in one Lord, Jesus Christ,
    the only Son of God,
    eternally begotten of the Father,
    God from God, Light from Light,
    true God from true God,
    begotten, not made,
    of one Being with the Father;
    through him all things were made.
    For us and for our salvation
        he came down from heaven,
        was incarnate of the Holy Spirit and the Virgin Mary
        and became truly human.
        For our sake he was crucified under Pontius Pilate;
        he suffered death and was buried.
        On the third day he rose again
        in accordance with the Scriptures;
        he ascended into heaven
        and is seated at the right hand of the Father.
        He will come again in glory to judge the living and the dead,
        and his kingdom will have no end.

We believe in the Holy Spirit, the Lord, the giver of life,
    who proceeds from the Father and the Son,
    who with the Father and the Son is worshiped and glorified,
    who has spoken through the prophets.

We believe in one holy catholic and apostolic church.
We acknowledge one baptism for the forgiveness of sins.
We look for the resurrection of the dead,
    and the life of the world to come. Amen.

496   *A Scriptural Affirmation*
We believe in one body, the church,
    one Holy Spirit,
    one hope to which we are called,
    one Lord Jesus,
    one faith,
    one baptism,
    one God and Father of all,
        who is over all and through all and in all.   (BASED ON EPHESIANS 4)

497   *An Affirmation of God's Grace*
We believe in God who saved us
    not because of good things we have done,
    but because of God's mercy.

God saved us by the washing of rebirth,
and renewal by the Holy Spirit,
whom God poured out on us generously
through Jesus Christ our Savior;
so that justified by his grace
we might become heirs with the hope of eternal life.
This is a trustworthy saying.   (BASED ON TITUS 3)

 INVITATION TO PRESENT GIFTS

The invitation to present gifts is an opportunity extended to present oneself as a living sacrifice to God through tangible expressions of one's life. It is appropriate for the offertory to be regarded as the first action of communion and be offered from behind the communion table. If bread and wine are included in the offering, it is appropriate for the offertory prayers to make reference to them. In some situations one elder may pray the offertory prayer and the other elder the communion prayer. In any case the emphasis is upon the presentation of the people to God through their gifts.

498
Give as you are able, in accord with how God has blessed you.
(DEUTERONOMY 16:17, ALT.)

499
The psalmist said:
Behold, God is my helper;
God is the upholder of my life.
With a freewill offering I will sacrifice to you;
I will give thanks to your name, O God, for it is good.
For you have delivered me from every trouble.   (PSALM 54:4, 6–7A, ADAPT.)

500
Bring the full tithe into the storehouse, so that there may be food in my house, and thus put me to the test, says the LORD of hosts; see if I will not open the windows of heaven for you and pour down for you an overflowing blessing.   (MALACHI 3:10)

501

Let your light so shine before people,
    that they may see your good works
    and give glory to God who is in heaven.   (Matthew 5:16, adapt.)

502

When you are offering your gift at the altar, if you remember that your brother or sister has something against you, leave your gift there before the altar and go; first be reconciled to your brother or sister, and then come and offer your gift.   (Matthew 5:23–24)

503

Freely you have received, freely give, remembering the words the Lord Jesus himself said: It is more blessed to give than to receive.

(Matthew 10:8; Acts 20:35, adapt.)

504

What, then, will anyone gain by winning the whole world and forfeiting one's life? Or what can anyone offer in exchange for one's life?

(Matthew 16:26, adapt.)

505

Let us make an offering to God, remembering Jesus' words: "From everyone to whom much has been given, much will be required; and from the one to whom much has been entrusted, even more will be demanded."

(Luke 12:48)

506

Remember the words of Jesus:
    It is more blessed to give than to receive.   (Acts 20:35, alt.)

507

Whatever your task, do it wholeheartedly, as to God:
    in teaching, give all you have;
    in speaking, stir to the depths;
    in giving, share liberally;
    in helping, do so cheerfully.
Contribute to the needs of God's people,
    and practice hospitality.   (Based on Colossians 3:23; Romans 12:7–10, 13)

508

Remember this: Whoever sows sparingly will also reap sparingly, and whoever sows generously will also reap generously. Each of you must give as you have made up your mind, not reluctantly or under compulsion, for God loves a cheerful giver.   (2 Corinthians 9:6–7, alt.)

509

All people shall give as they are able,
      according to the blessings God has given them.

510

As forgiven and reconciled people,
      let us offer ourselves and our gifts to God.

511

To receive food and drink from Christ's table and withhold it from others
is blasphemous. In Christ God freely gives. Through Christ may we share
from our abundance.

512

What an abundance of gifts we have to offer:
      musical talent, the melody of laughter,
      the use of our hands in cooking and repairs,
      the use of our minds in problem solving,
      curiosity, compassion, patience, urgency,
      spiritual reservoirs, financial resources,
      obedience, and courage to act.
All these gifts, and others which bear our personal marks,
      are symbolized in our offering for the work of the church.
Let us commit ourselves in service as we worship God with our offerings.

513

God calls upon us to love one another as God loves us.
Even as God has abundantly blessed us with good things,
      let us bless others through gifts that show we care.

514

Let us with gladness
      present the offerings of our life and labor
      to the Lord.

515

As we prepare to gather around the table of the Lord,
      let us share in God's generous hospitality
      to feed those who are dismissed from the world's tables,
      that they may no longer feel alone and be hungry.

516

As we give today, may we do so in love, in joy,
      in prayer, in thanksgiving, and in unselfishness.

517

God has shown us the meaning of generosity in the beautiful diversity of creation, in the overflowing love of Jesus Christ, and in the never-ending gift of the Holy Spirit! God has abundantly blessed us and called us to be a community that blesses others through the sharing of our love, our talents, and our material possessions. Let us rejoice now in what we have been given and in what is ours to give as we receive our morning offering.

518

The amazing gift of one
　　who fully embodied God's intention for humanity
　　prompts us to make a grateful response.
In Christ we have known a love that will not let us go.
Through an offering let us share this love
　　in our community and to the ends of the earth.

519

Let us make an offering to God for the ministries of the church.

(🏆) OFFERTORY PRAYERS

If bread and wine are included in the offering, it is appropriate for the offertory prayers to make reference to them. In some situations one elder may pray the offertory prayer and the other elder the communion prayer. In any case the emphasis is upon the presentation of the people to God through their gifts.

520

Lord, forgive our fears that stifle our stewardship.
Forgive our giving in and our giving up
　　instead of giving ourselves to Christ's mission of love.
Remind us that our hope is in standing up and risking,
Help us to remember, O Lord, that
　　the stewardship question is not really,
　　"How much will we give?"
The stewardship question is,
　　"How will we spend what we have been given?"
We pray it will be faithfully and cheerfully.

521

Yours, Lord, is the greatness,
the power, glory, and splendor and the majesty:
everything in heaven and on earth is yours.
Everything comes from you:
and of your own do we give you.　　　　　　　(1 CHRONICLES 29:11A, 14B, ALT.)

522

O God, use our offerings of money, time, and talents
>to enliven your church,
>to enhearten a world prone to discouragement,
>to enable a spreading of the love of Christ.

May all our gifts and our giving be acceptable in your sight.
In the name of Jesus Christ we pray. Amen.

523

We dedicate this money, Lord, for the work of the church,
>and ask you to use all that we have and are in your service.

524

God, we present these offerings that they may be used to extend your liberating reign. With them, we offer our varied ministries in the days ahead, that each of us may be part of your answer to the cries of the world. Amen.

525

What we have we bring:
our good intentions, our unknown motives,
our uncertainties about life, our grasp of truth,
our time, our uneasiness with what is.
We offer this in the midst of what remains unspoken
and affirm that it is received. Amen.

526

Accept our lives, O God, as well as our gifts.
Let the spirit in which we give them be your Spirit.
Let the use that is made of them be your use. Amen.

527

Gracious God, with thanks we offer the gifts of our hands and the fruits of our labors. Accept them as expressions of our response to the life and love you have given us.

528

God, we know that bread for ourselves is a material question. Bread for our sisters and brothers is a spiritual question. May these gifts reflect the spiritual dimensions of our lives. May they be used to renew the spirits of our brothers and sisters throughout your world. Amen.

529

All things come from you, O God,
>and with gratitude we return to you what is yours.

You created all that is, and with love formed us in your image.
When our love failed, your love remained steadfast.

You gave your only Son, Jesus Christ, to be our Savior.
All that we are, and all that we have, is a trust from you.
And so, in gratitude for all your gifts,
>we offer you ourselves, and all that we have,
>in union with Christ's offering for us.
By your Holy Spirit make us one with Christ,
>one with each other, and one in ministry to all the world,
>>through Jesus Christ our Savior. Amen.

530

We come with no great gifts to offer.
We are ordinary men and women,
>**some more gifted than others,**
>**some with greater capacity for love,**
>**some more in need of being loved.**
Yet what we have we bring to you
>to make your love felt in the loneliness of other people's lives,
>in their fear, their grief, and their pain.
Forgive us for having failed;
>**forgive us when we fail again;**
>**and though we are not worthy,**
>**your light will shine through our lives**
>**and others will see your glory in us,**
>**and honor you forever.**

531

We shall love the Lord our God with all our heart,
>with all our soul, with all our mind, and with all our strength,
>and we shall love our neighbor as ourself.
We make these offerings as a pledge of our love and loyalty;
>**to God, to each other, and to all our fellow human beings.**
We commit ourselves to live in love
>**and to be everyone's loyal servants,**
>**in the name of Christ our Servant Lord. Amen.**

532

With gratitude and praise we offer ourselves,
>with our talents and treasure, to God who has given us life.
We offer ourselves to be God's messengers;
>**to let people know that God is with them;**
>**to save them from despair and to give them hope;**
>**to save them from fear and give them confidence;**
>**to save them from death and to give them life,**
in the name of Jesus Christ our living, reigning Lord. Amen.

533

Eternal God, we bring you these gifts because we know that our life and all human life rightfully belong to you and that everything we have we hold in trust from you. We praise you for everything you have done for the world in Jesus Christ. Help us, through him, to make our own offering complete by living in obedience to you. Amen.

534

Lord God, we bring to you the ordinary things of life—
    food and drink and money—
    and with them we bring ourselves.
Take us, and our gifts of money, to do your work in the world.
Take this food and drink from our tables
    and feed us from your table with your love.
Accept the praise we offer; through Jesus Christ our Lord. Amen.

535

We offer to you, O God,
    the gift of our hands and the loyalty of our hearts.
Accept us with our gifts, we pray, in Jesus' name. Amen.

536

In our offering, O God,
    we proclaim our work and our worship are one;
    we proclaim that life is undivided.

537

Let our material gifts make possible
    spiritual ministries of reconciliation
    and love-restored community. Amen.

538

Loving God, the eyes of all look to you,
    and you give them their food in due season.
You open your hand,
    satisfying the desire of every living thing.
Accept and bless our open and bountiful hands
    as we share with all your creation
    food for the hungry and drink for those who thirst.

(BASED ON PSALM 145:15–16)

539

O God, having the same mind among us as we have in Christ Jesus,
    bless this offering of our lives
    that we may humbly serve others as Christ has ministered to us,
    compassionately reconcile as we have been reconciled,
    gladly witness as Christ has proclaimed good news to us.
Empty us that we may be filled with your generous spirit. Amen.

540

As joint workers with you, O God,
    we offer you the fruits of our labor
    that you may bless them for your service
    and us in our calling. Amen.

541

Transforming God,
take these expressions of our labor and turn them into
    hope for the weary,
    liberation for the oppressed,
    power for those who are dispossessed;
take us flawed creatures and manifest in us
    your love that knows no end,
    your faith that can do all things,
    your service that spares no cost,
    your patient endurance that hopes to the last. Amen.

542

O God, before whom at creation the morning stars sang together,
    and at the birth of whose Son angels praised you,
    singing "Glory to God in the highest":
may our offerings be a true sacrifice of praise,
    helping speed the time of peace on earth,
    and goodwill among all your people.

543

Upon this table of blessing, O God,
    we place the gifts of our lives:
        bread, the staff of life,
        wine, the joy of hearts,
        money, the fruit of our labors.
In your goodness receive these offerings
    to strengthen all who receive them.

544

Money, bread, and cup: these we offer you, O God.
By your Spirit, transform them into a life-giving cup,
    life-giving bread, life-giving money,
    that you may restore your people to life.

545

Creator God, receive these tokens of our praise
    and re-create our hearts in love
    that we may with our whole being
    serve you gladly with all that we have.

546

You shower us with your goodness every day, O God.
With grateful hearts we bring your these gifts.
Transform them into outpourings of peace and justice
    to reconcile all peoples to one another and to you.

547

Upon this sacred table, O God,
    we place food and drink and money.
Consecrate them all to your holy purpose.
As we drink may we know your salvation.
In breaking bread may we know Christ's presence.
Through the offering of our money may we know that
    life is sacred and is to be spent in grateful service.

548

Giver of life, receive all we offer you this day.
Let the Spirit you bestow on your church
    continue to work in the world
    through the hearts of all who believe.
We ask this in the name of Jesus Christ the Lord.

549

Eternal God, you have made our Savior Jesus Christ
    the head of all creation.
Receive all we offer you this day
    and renew us in his risen life,
    in the name of Jesus Christ the Lord.

550

Holy God, accept all we offer you this day.
May we who are reconciled at this table
    bring wholeness to our broken world.
We ask this in the name of Jesus Christ the Lord.

551

God of power, the glory of your works fills us with wonder and awe.
Accept our offering this day,
    and help us to live in peace and harmony with all your creation,
    for the sake of Jesus Christ our Lord.

552

God of constant love, in this holy meal
    you renew the covenant made once with us in baptism.
As you are faithful in all things
    may we, in our offering, be faithful to our calling.
We ask this in the name of Jesus Christ our Lord.

553

Holy God, in this holy meal we renew our baptismal covenant.
Help us, through our offering this day,
    to renounce all things that draw us from your love.
This we ask in the name of Jesus Christ our Lord.

554

God of faithfulness, in every age
    you call men and women to make known your love.
May we who celebrate this holy meal today
    be so strengthened in the ministries to which we are called,
    that we may always witness to your holy name.
This we pray in the name of Jesus Christ the Lord.

555

Almighty God, accept the joyful offering of your church,
    and grant that your Son may shine in us
    as the light that lightens every nation.
We ask this in the name of the same Jesus Christ our Lord.

556

Almighty God, accept all we offer you this day,
    and give us generous hearts
    to serve you in all who claim our help.
We ask this in the name of Jesus Christ our Lord.

557

God of our salvation, accept all we offer you this day.
May we learn to bear witness to the gospel of your Son
    both in word and deed.
This we ask in the name of Jesus Christ our Lord.

558

Living God, accept all we offer you this day,
    and grant that we may find the presence of your Son in the church,
    in each other, and in the poor and wounded victims of the world,
    for whom he gave his life, Jesus Christ your Son, our Lord.

559

In response, we bring our tithes and offerings
    to be used in the service of Christ.

560

O God, you have filled our cups to overflowing.
Take from the overflowing goodness
    which spills out on your table in this offering,
    and fill the cups of those who are empty.

561
Take these gifts, our Lord,
    as symbols of our whole love for you
    and transform with them the whole lives
    of those for whom they are used.

562
Creator God, we offer you these gifts with
    eyes open to human need;
    ears tuned to every cry of despair;
    hearts sympathetic to the plight of others;
    feet ready to go out of the way to help;
    and hands ready to reach out and share.

563
What good is our faith if it is only words?
We assume responsibility
    for the words we have spoken for the world through our offerings.
We bring our gifts as true symbols of our lives and our faith.

564
We dare to come before your table.
As we come, we have not forgotten
    to set the table with the symbols of our lives.
We bring our gifts as tokens of love for your word and your love for us.

565
God of all holiness, we bring this money to you.
If it represents no sacrifice,
    but merely a superstitious habit or a tiresome formality,
    then awaken us to our fault.
If it represents an act of love and a genuine sacrifice,
    then keep us from pride,
And increase our ability to give even ourselves to your will. Amen.

566
We offer to you these gifts which you have given us;
    this bread, this wine, this money.
With them we offer ourselves, our lives, and our work,
    to become through your Holy Spirit
    a reasonable, holy, and lively sacrifice.
So may we and all your people become channels of your love;
    through the same Christ our Lord. Amen.

567

We offer to you, Lord, our money.
We offer to you, Lord, ourselves.
We offer to you the work of the world
    in this neighborhood and beyond.
Grant that men and women may work with joy and dignity.
Grant that children may have bread with laughter.
And grant that we may reflect in our work and in our lives
    the community we have found in the sharing of the loaf,
    and the presence we have known in the breaking of the bread. Amen.

568

There is no way, O God, that we can repay you
    for what you have done for us in Jesus Christ,
    or for what you continue to do for us day by day.
Our gifts are but the tokens of children to a parent,
    to say, "We love you, God." Amen.

569

We acknowledge our baptism, O God,
    and the call to become members of Christ's body.
Accept our gifts, that others may be led into your way.
Help us to arrange our priorities
    that we may seek first the reign of God on earth.

570

We offer but a portion of the bounty you bestow, O God.
Receive our gifts as we seek to walk in your way.
Where justice is sought, use these gifts to bring Christ's liberating word.
Where there is pain, may they bring the healing of Christ's love.

571

Accept the gifts that we offer, O God,
    as we go seeking reconciliation with our brothers and sisters.
In them we seek to love you with all our hearts, souls, and minds.
May the reconciliation we pursue
    reflect our love for neighbor as ourselves.
We pray in the name of the Christ
    who allows us to present ourselves blameless before you.

572

We know, O God, that words without actions are less than complete.
As we confess Jesus as our Savior, we commit our lives to your care.
Enable us to serve you with boldness,
    enlivened by the promise of your unending presence.
Accept the gifts that we offer as signs of our devotion.
May they announce to your people that your will shall be done.

573
We gather about your table, O Christ,
    and there partake of bread and the fruit of the vine.
As bread is broken, nourish us to go forth and serve others.
As the cup is passed, give us new life to proclaim equality and mercy.
Accept the gifts that we offer as response to your atoning sacrifice
    and use them to teach others of your reconciling love.

574
O God, you give us tasks to perform.
    You equip us with strengths and abilities beyond what we deserve.
In Christ you call us to faithfulness,
    to exercise obedience, to be deliberate in our discipline.
We come now offering to you the results of our labors.
    Use them as a means to further your work in Christ's name.

575
Most giving and forgiving God, you provide for our every need.
    You open our lips to offer you praise.
    You strengthen our hands to respond to Christ's call.
With hearts, hands, and voices renewed by your Spirit,
    we place now before you our commitment to serve.
Use us in ways that will benefit others,
    and accept what we offer as a sign of our faith.

576
Blessed are you, Lord, God of all creation.
    Through your goodness we have this bread to offer,
    which earth has given and human hands have made;
    may it become for us the bread of life.
Blessed are you, Lord, God of all creation.
    Through your goodness we have this wine to offer,
    fruit of the vine and work of human hands;
    may it become for us our spiritual drink.
Blessed are you, Lord, God of all creation.
    Through your goodness we have this money to offer,
    the result of our human work and effort;
    may you bless its use for the good of your church,
through Jesus Christ, your Son, our Lord.

577
O God, the source of all good things, we bring to you our gifts.
Enable us, with our earthly things,
    to give you the love of our hearts and the service of our lives;
    through Jesus Christ, your Son, our Lord.

578

Almighty and ever blessed God,
     you in your great goodness give us always
     more than we desire or dare to ask.
Give us your Spirit of thankfulness and love
     that we may always be more willing to give than to receive,
     and so rule our hearts that all we have may be used for your service,
     and we ourselves be consecrated to you;
through Jesus Christ, your Son, our Lord.

579

Lord of all goodness, all things come from you,
     and of them we give to you.
Therefore, our God, accept us, your servants, and these our offerings
     which we bring in devotion to your holy name,
and give us grace evermore to serve you with gladness of heart;
     through Jesus Christ, your Son, our Lord.

580

Guard us, our God, from the wrong use of money:
     from selfishness, carelessness, or waste;
     and from that obsessive love of money that is a root of all evils.
Enable us to be good stewards of what is entrusted to us;
     to give or spend or save according to your will;
     so that neither poverty nor wealth
     may hinder our discipleship,
     harm our neighbors, or destroy our life;
through Jesus Christ our Lord.

ADVENT

581

God of all the earth and of the universe,
     although our offerings are sums of substance,
     we ourselves are the gifts you desire.
Unfold our hopes, open us up to service, use us well.
Magnify our giving as we rejoice in your gracious presence among us.
In the name of the one who was born Immanuel. Amen.

CHRISTMAS

582

Thank you, God of love, for the promise of this season.
We are grateful for the generosity aroused in us
     by Christ's coming into the world.
May these gifts represent a new spirit of joyous sharing among us,
     for the sake of all your children everywhere. Amen.

583
Eternal God of redemption,
 you bless your creation and it springs forth with beauty.
You judge your people with righteousness and new life abounds.
We bring you now the fruits of our labors.
Bless the work of our hands,
 so that what we do reflects the radiance of your love.
Fill us with your Holy Spirit,
 so that what we say proclaims to all people the new hope in Jesus.

584
Grant us, O God, such love and wonder that with shepherds and wise men
and pilgrims unknown we may hearken to the singing of the angels, that
following the guiding of the star we may come to the manger and adore
the holy child, and with our gifts, with our lives, worship him. And let us
say: **Amen.**

EPIPHANY

585
Loving and receptive God, creator of a Bethlehem birth and sustainer of
the whole human family, we come to you seeking to be wise women and
wise men. Like the gifts of those travelers long ago, may our gifts be a sign
that wisdom is marked by an offering of self and substance to the Christ,
in whose name we pray. Amen.

586
As Jesus offered water changed to wine that his friends might rejoice, we
offer these gifts, O God. With your grace may they be transformed into
food and water, justice and peace. We give them that the world may rejoice
in your work and presence. Amen.

587
Source of life and Bringer of light to the nations, you provide for all our
needs. We bring your gifts in response to your goodness. We thank you for
sending Christ into our midst. Use what we offer, to enlighten all people to
the truth of his salvation, and bless all our endeavors as we seek faithfully
in Christ's name to do your will.

588
Help us to remember that the first act of worship offered to the newborn
Christ was that of giving. When they had opened their treasures they presented to him gifts: gold, frankincense, and myrrh. Receive and bless our
offerings, bless us as we bring them, and use them for the extension of
your kingdom in the world. Through Christ our Lord. Amen.

PALM SUNDAY

589

Gracious God, as the faithful disciples of your Son spread their garments in the way and covered it with branches, so may we lay at his feet all that we have and are, and bless you, in whose name and by whose mercy he came. Amen.

EASTER

590

As Christ was offered in obedience to you, O God,
  so we offer ourselves and our gifts to be used in your service.
As you took Christ's sacrifice and filled it with your life and power,
  so use our gifts and transform our lives,
  that we may be the living presence of your reign on earth,
  now and always. Amen.

591

Wonderful, amazing God, we thank you that you have raised Jesus Christ from the dead, bringing us the promise of new life. With the dawning of this new day, may we awake to new opportunities to love and serve you and witness to Christ whom you have raised. Use us, and our gifts, to your glory. In Jesus' name we pray. Amen.

PENTECOST

592

Lord our God, send down upon us your Holy Spirit, we pray you, to cleanse our hearts, to hallow our gifts, and to make perfect the offering of ourselves to you; through Jesus Christ, your Son, our Lord.

593

With many voices we praise you, O God; in different ways we serve you. Take our diversity and mold it into a common theme of thanksgiving. Weave these gifts that we bring into a whole cloth of service that will blanket the world with your love as we announce with one accord your truth which sets us free.

594

As Christ did breathe on his disciples that they may receive the Holy Spirit, breathe on us, O Breath of God, kindling the devotion of our lips and inflaming the coals of our wills; that we may dedicate our selves wholeheartedly to you with these gifts we bring. Take them and us for use in your renewing your world.

$\mathscr{C}$HE LORD'S SUPPER

(Y) *INVITATION TO COMMUNE*

The invitation to commune serves both to make it clear who is welcome to share in the meal and to make clear the purpose of the meal. The emphasis is upon communion with God and with one another in thankful remembrance of Christ who dwells with his people. Since Christ regards us as worthy to eat with him, the emphasis is more upon God's grace than our unworthiness.

In accordance with the proposed orders of service in this book, the invitation to the table may precede the receiving and dedicating of the offering, which may include the elements for the holy meal.

595

Let us come to the table of communion,
    not because we must, but because we may.
Let us sit together in humility and thanksgiving
    rather than in pride or possessiveness.
Let us confess, not that we are righteous,
    but that we love our Lord Jesus Christ
    and desire to remember him.
Let us come, not that we are strong,
    but that we are needy;
not that we have any claim on Christ,
    but that he invites us to receive his grace
    and experience his presence.
Let us worthily partake,
    that he may be made known to us in the breaking of bread.

596

This table is open to all who confess Jesus as the Christ
    and seek to follow Christ's way.
Come to this sacred table,
    not because you must, but because you may.
Come not because you are fulfilled,
    but because in your emptiness
    you stand in need of God's mercy and assurance.
Come not to express an opinion,
    but to seek a presence and to pray for a spirit.
Come to this table, then, sisters and brothers, as you are.
Partake and share.

It is spread for you and me,
> that we might again know that God has come to us,
> shared our common lot,
> and invited us to join the people of God's new age.

597

This is the table of the Lord.
Come, not because you are strong,
> but because you are weak.

Come, not because any goodness of your own gives you a right to come,
> but because you need mercy and help;

Come, because you love the Lord a little
> and would like to love him more.

Come, because the Lord loves you
> and gives himself for you.

Let this bread and wine be for you the token and pledge
> of the grace of the Lord Jesus Christ, the love of God,
> and the communion of the Holy Spirit,
> all meant for you if you will receive them in humble faith.

O taste and see that God is good.

598

This is the Lord's table and Christ invites you to share his meal.
> Christ recognizes you and looks upon you with favor.
> Christ befriends you and wants you within his circle.

Count yourself among Christ's disciples
> by partaking in this feast of fellowship.

599

In the name of the living God,
in the name of the victorious Christ,
in the name of the mysterious Spirit,
> come to the table where bread is broken and wine poured out.

Receive the life of God,
> share the victory of Christ
> and enter into the mystery of the Spirit.

600

God in Christ breaks down the walls
> that make us strangers to ourselves
> and divide us from one another.

We are the body of Christ.
Around this table, we enact our faith.
The body broken is restored to wholeness;
> lifeblood poured out brings healing to our world.

601

This is the joyful feast of the people of God!
They will come from east and west, and from north and south,
    and sit at table in the kingdom of God.
According to Luke, when our risen Lord was at table with his disciples,
    he took bread, blessed, broke it, and gave it to them.
Then their eyes were opened and they recognized him.
This is the Lord's table.
Our Savior invites all those who trust him
    to share the feast which he has prepared.
O taste and see that the Lord is good.

(BASED ON LUKE 13:29, 24:30–31; PSALM 34:8A)

602

Ordinary bread made by ordinary people
    is holy when we take and eat and remember.
Ordinary grapes taken by ordinary people and made into ordinary wine
    are holy when we hold the wine to our lips and drink and remember.
This bread…remember his body was given for us.
This wine…remember his blood was poured out for us.
Bread and wine, from ordinary to holy…
Remember.

603

Jesus said: I am the bread of life.
Whoever comes to me will never be hungry,
    and whoever believes in me will never be thirsty.
No one who comes to me will I drive away.
Because there is one bread, we who are many are one body,
    for we all partake of the one bread.
So, whether you eat or drink, or whatever you do,
    do everything for the glory of God.

(JOHN 6:35, 37B, ALT.; 1 CORINTHIANS 10:17, 31)

604

Jesus said: I am the bread of life.
    You who come to me shall not hunger;
    you who believe in me shall never thirst.
In company with all who hunger for spiritual food,
    we come to this table to know the risen Christ
    in the sharing of this life-giving bread.

605

Christ invites to this table
    all who profess the Christian faith,
    who endeavor to be at peace with their neighbors,
    and who seek the mercy of God.

606

Sharing a meal with Christ we know we are accepted and reconciled.
Communing with Christ we encounter a transforming friendship.
Let us enter into the joy of our Lord.

607

We have gathered in the name of Jesus, our Savior and living Lord. We recall how Jesus made himself known to his friends in the breaking of bread, and how their hearts were set ablaze as they talked and communed with him. May our hearts rejoice and our tongues be filled with praise as we come to meet him here.

608

Let us in union with the whole church
    join with Christ to eat and drink with him.
May the bread we eat be to us the very bread of life.
    May the cup we share be to us God's wine of salvation.
Let us celebrate that Christ is alive and in our midst.

609

Even as Jesus called his disciples, one by one—by name,
    so the risen Christ calls each of you, one by one—by name,
    to come and share about this table in a community of love.
Join him, not because you are good, but because Christ wants you.
Eat and drink with Christ within the universal fellowship
    of those who are loved without reservation—just as they are.

610

Jesus broke bread with all sorts of people throughout his life: with sinners, with the self-righteous, with hungry crowds, and, most often, with his disciples. It was in the breaking of bread that the travelers to Emmaus recognized him. When the first Christians gathered on the Lord's Day to share in a meal of Christ's remembrance, they spoke of it as "the breaking of the bread." With all God's faithful, let us now break bread together in communion with Christ and with one another.

☙ *COMMUNION PRAYERS*

At the present time there is a diversity of views as to what shape the communion prayers should take within Disciples congregations. Commonly one or two brief prayers are given by elders. More recently there has been a movement to give a fuller expression in keeping with the most ancient patterns of Christian worship. These seek to assure a more adequate expression of communion's meaning and a greater participation by the people.

There is a growing consensus that the basic form of the communion prayer is one of thanksgiving to God. It is a table grace, relatively brief, which fits the occasion for which it is offered. The prayer needs to express the heart of what is intended in this sharing together with Christ.

Although there are limits to what can be expressed within any one prayer, it is important that these elements be central to the prayers:

1. Thanking God for creation and God's active participation in the life of the world.

2. Remembering God's acts of salvation in Jesus Christ: his birth, life, death, resurrection, and promise of coming; and his institution of this special meal of remembrance.

3. Calling upon the Holy Spirit to draw the people into the presence of the risen Christ so that they may be fed, joined in the communion of saints to all God's people and to the risen Christ, and be sent to serve as faithful disciples.

The following resources reflect the diversity of practices among present-day Disciples.

611   *Dialogue*
The Lord be with you;
And also with you.
Lift up your hearts.
We lift them up to the Lord.
Let us give thanks to the Lord.
It is right to give God thanks and praise.

612   *Dialogue, Preface, and Sanctus*
Lift up your hearts.
We lift them to the Lord.
Let us give thanks to the Lord our God.
It is right to give God thanks and praise.
It is not only right, it is our duty and our joy,
    at all times and in all places, to give you thanks and praise,
    holy Father, heavenly King, almighty and eternal God,
    through Jesus Christ, your only Son, our Lord.
Therefore with angels and archangels,
    and with all the company of heaven,
    we proclaim your great and glorious name,
    forever praising you and saying
Holy, holy, holy Lord,
God of power and might,
Heaven and earth are full of your glory.
Hosanna in the highest.

613

For the bread:
We give thanks to you, O God,
    that from the earth you cause the grain to come
    for the making of bread.
We praise you for Christ, the bread of life,
    whose body was broken for us.
By your Holy Spirit sanctify us and this loaf,
    that the bread which we break may be to us
    the communion of the body of Christ,
    and that we may be made one in him.
As of old you fed your people in the wilderness,
    so feed us now that we may live to your praise;
through Jesus Christ our Lord. Amen.

For the cup:
We give thanks to you, O God,
    that you cause the vine to yield fruit.
We bless you for Christ, the true vine,
    whose blood was poured out for us.
By your Holy Spirit sanctify us and this wine,
    that the cup which we bless may be to us
    the communion of the blood of Christ,
    and that through abiding in him
    we may bear fruit that shall last.
As we share the sufferings of Christ, so give us grace
    that we may know the power of his resurrection;
through Jesus Christ our Lord. Amen.

614

Everlasting God, we join with your church in all times and places
    to thank you for creating us in your image,
    caring for us who are only human.
When we marred your image through sin,
    you mercifully did not hold it against us,
    but gave of yourself sacrificially in Christ Jesus
    that we may become like him.
Formed into the body of Christ we praise you
    for restoring us to the joy of your salvation.
Nourished by holy food and drink from Christ's table,
    strengthen us by your Spirit to present ourselves to the world
    as living sacrifices, holy and acceptable to you. Amen.

615

Creator God, we bless you for making all things
  and pronouncing them good.
We thank you that when we have misused your gifts,
  you have not left us alone, but sought us out in Jesus Christ.
The bread which we break and the cup which we drink
  reminds us that Christ, though crucified, lives.
By the gift of your Holy Spirit make Christ known again to us
  that we may take fresh hope and live in his presence each day. Amen.

616

Holy God, we thank you
  for calling us into existence by your word;
  for speaking your words of demand and grace
    through teachers and prophets;
  for promising that your words shall be written on our hearts.
We marvel with gratitude
  that your Word became flesh and lived among us in Jesus;
  that he suffered as we suffer to be with us and die for us;
  that you raised him from the dead in victory over death and sin.
Holding the glad word of your good news in our minds,
  may your Spirit transform this bread and cup
  into signs of Christ's living presence
  and engrave upon our hearts the life-transforming image of Christ.
With all companions of Christ's way in every time and place
  we praise your holy name. Amen.

617

Christ Jesus, our Living Bread, we praise your mercy in the memorial of
your love. As we keep in mind your life, death, and resurrection, let our
eucharistic banquet enable us to share with one another the goodness and
love you have showered upon us. We ask this in your name. Amen.

618

God of love, send your Holy Spirit to be with us
  as we remember Jesus, your divine love in human form.
May we, by faith, feast on his body and blood
  which he freely sacrificed on the cross for his friends.
Make us to be his body in the life of the world.
Through the same Jesus Christ, with you and the Holy Spirit,
  one God forever and ever. Amen.

619

May this sacrament, Lord Jesus Christ,
    bring life to us and pardon for our sins,
    to us for whom you suffered your passion.
For our sake you drank gall
    to kill in us the bitterness that is the Enemy's.
For our sake you drank sour wine
    to strengthen what is weak in us.
For our sake you were spat upon
    to bathe us in the dew of immortality.
You were struck with a frail reed
    to strengthen what is frail in us
    and give us life for all eternity.
You were crowned with thorns
    to crown those who believe in you
    with that evergreen garland, your charity.
You were wrapped in a shroud
    to clothe us in your all-enfolding strength.
You were laid in a new grave
    to give us new grace in ages likewise new.

620

As the Holy Spirit strengthens your church,
    may this, your blessed bread,
    which is now broken, bring life to us.
May we be living signs of the charity
    we share with one another.
May this, your holy cup,
    poured out for all, be our salvation.
We pray that we who drink from the one cup
    may be faithful signs of your love.

621

Holy Source of all goodness,
    we give you thanks and praise
    for your dwelling among us in Christ Jesus.
We marvel at the one who
    opened wide his arms for us on the cross
    and put an end to death by dying for us,
    creating a new and holy people.
As we eat and drink these holy gifts of bread and wine
    may they be to us a living memorial of Christ's sacrifice.
By your Holy Spirit make Christ known to us
    that we may join the mighty host of all believers
    in growing into his likeness,
    looking to the day when we shall all be one
    in the fullness of your reign.

622
Met at this table in the name of Christ, the lamb who was sacrificed,
    let us think of every member of the worldwide church
        who meets as we do,
    to proclaim the same faith, though in diverse ways,
    to meet the same God and to promise the same devotion.
Let us pray for the unity of the church.

Silence

Met at this table in the name of Christ,
    let us think of every member of the human family
    meeting at family tables everywhere in the world.
Some of these tables are full of good things;
    others are empty.
Some give expression to creative love;
    others only aggravate bitterness and hatred.
Let us also think of those who have no family table
    but are left alone, rejected, or have lost themselves.
Let us pray for the peace and communion of the whole human race,
    and for the wholeness of every human being
    in loving relationship with God and neighbor.

Silence

Holy Friend, in the deep center of the being of each one of us,
    where we know the frightening truth about ourselves
        and cannot evade your challenge;
    keep making your demands on us,
    on your church, and on all humankind,
    until we have followed Christ to the end
    and come with him into the fulfillment of your purpose in creation.

623
Holy God, for creating the world
    and breathing into us the breath of life,
    we offer you our thankful praise.
For redeeming us through Jesus Christ,
    forgiving our sins and offering new life forever,
    we offer you our thankful praise.
For strengthening us by your Holy Spirit
    who lives within us, close as breath itself,
    we offer you our thankful praise.

Eternal God, as we gather around this table,
    set with bread and the fruit of the vine,
we remember that on the night he was betrayed
    the Lord Jesus took bread,
and when he had given thanks,
    he broke it and gave it to the disciples, saying:

"Take, eat, this is my body given for you.
    Do this in remembrance of me."
In the same way after supper, he took the cup, saying:
"This cup is the new covenant sealed by my blood,
    poured out for you and for many for the forgiveness of sins.
Do this as often as you drink it in remembrance of me."
Merciful God, by your Word and Holy Spirit,
    bless these gifts and your people
    that we may receive Christ's body and blood given for us.

ELDER 1: With great joy, O God, we give you thanks for this loaf
    wherein are gathered all the times
    when you have given us our daily bread.
Again we are hungry, in body and soul,
    and earnestly desire that you feed us.
As our bodies are strengthened by this bread,
    so may our inner selves be nourished by our Savior Jesus Christ
who comes to us in this earthly sign, and in whose name we pray.

ELDER 2: We give you thanks, O God, for this cup of blessing.
Here we remember the constancy of our thirst, and
    the overflowing abundance of water and wine that comes from you.
By your Holy Spirit be present as we drink from this cup,
    the sign of our Savior's blood poured out for us.
As our bodies are refreshed by the fruit of the vine,
    so may our spirits be replenished
    by the very life of Jesus Christ, in whose name we pray. Amen.
Amen.

624
ELDER 1: God, you are the source of life
    and the one who gives us everything.
Today we bring you these gifts
    of money, bread, and communion wine
    as our sacrifice of thanksgiving
    and of our lives given back to you.
Help us in all that we think, say, and do
    to honor you and serve all who are in need.
Through Jesus Christ, who showed us
    that it is more blessed to give than to receive. Amen.

ELDER 2: Dear God, we come to this table
    to remember our Lord and Savior Jesus Christ.
He lived among us full of grace and truth.
He forgave sinners and healed the sick.
He spoke the good news of your coming world of justice and peace.

Willingly he went to the cross,
    freely giving his life for the sins of the world.
At your right hand he lives forever, praying for the life of the world.
For all that Jesus does for us,
    we praise you, God, now and forever. Amen.

Holy, holy, holy Lord, God of power and might,
heaven and earth are full of your glory.
Hosanna in the highest.
Blessed is he who comes in the name of the Lord.
Hosanna in the highest.

Or:

Holy, holy, holy, Lord God of Hosts!
Heaven and earth are full of thee!
Heaven and earth are praising thee,
O Lord most high!

God of power, by your Word and Holy Spirit
    bless these gifts and the church as we offer them to you,
    that Jesus' own words may be fulfilled:
        My body given for you.
        My blood of the covenant poured out for you.

As we receive this holy meal, forgive our sins,
    renew in us the power of our baptism,
    and strengthen us for our ministry in the world.
Use us, we pray, for the restoration of the earth
    and the healing of the nations,
    until the coming of your holy commonwealth.
All this we ask in the name of our Savior Jesus Christ. Amen.

☙ WORDS OF INSTITUTION

625
For I received from the Lord what I also handed on to you,
that the Lord Jesus on the night when he was betrayed
    took a loaf of bread, and when he had given thanks,
    he broke it and said,
"This is my body that is for you. Do this in remembrance of me."

In the same way he took the cup also, after supper, saying,
"This cup is the new covenant in my blood.
    Do this, as often as you drink it, in remembrance of me."
For as often as you eat this bread and drink the cup,
    you proclaim the Lord's death until he comes.   (1 CORINTHIANS 11:23–26)

626

While they were eating, Jesus took a loaf of bread,
    and after blessing it he broke it,
    gave it to the disciples, and said,
"Take, eat; this is my body."

Then he took a cup,
    and after giving thanks he gave it to them, saying,
"Drink from it, all of you; for this is my blood of the covenant,
    which is poured out for many for the forgiveness of sins.
I tell you, I will never again drink of this fruit of the vine
    until that day when I drink it new with you
    in my Father's kingdom."   (MATTHEW 26:26–29)

627

Jesus took the bread and broke it, saying,
    "It is my body, broken for you.
    Go on doing this to recall my presence with you."
You shall eat bread and you shall praise the Lord your God.

He took the cup, saying,
    "This means the new relationship
    established by the shedding of my blood.
    Go on doing this, whenever you drink it,
    to recall my presence with you."
So he lets his glory be seen among us
    and we believe and share his undying life.

🍷 BREAKING THE BREAD

The risen Christ was known to the disciples in the breaking of bread. The breaking of the bread and the pouring of the wine are vivid reminders of Christ's sacrifice that the world may be made one with God. In dramatic fashion this reenactment is a reminder to all believers of the style of life that Christ's discipleship requires. The breaking of bread also signifies the oneness of the body of Christ in whose life every member shares.

628

The bread that we break,
    is it not a sharing in the body of Christ?
Because there is one bread,
    we who are many are one body,
    for we all partake of the one bread.   (1 CORINTHIANS 10:16B—17)
The wine that we drink,
    is it not a sharing in the blood of Christ?

The cup that we bless
   is the communion in the blood of Christ.   (BASED ON 1 CORINTHIANS 10:16A)
Optional:
As the bread that we break
   was scattered over the mountains
   and when brought together became one,
so let your church be brought together
   from the ends of the earth into your kingdom;
   for yours is the glory and the power
through Jesus Christ for evermore.   (DIDACHE 9:4 [2ND CENTURY])

629
At the breaking of the bread:
Jesus said, "I am the bread of life:
   those who come to me will never grow hungry,
   and those who believe in me will never be thirsty."
Lord, give us this bread for ever. Amen.

At the taking of the wine:
Jesus said, "I am the true vine…
   remain in me, and I will remain in you."
Amen.

630
At the breaking of the bread
The bread that we break:
is a sharing in the body of Christ. Amen.

At the sharing of the wine
The cup of thanksgiving for which we give thanks:
is a sharing in the blood of Christ. Amen.

631
At the breaking of the bread
We break the bread and eat:
to share in the body of Christ.
So we who eat are one:
for we share one bread.

At the sharing of the wine
We give thanks for the cup and drink:
to share in the blood of Christ. Amen.

632
When we break the bread,
   it is a sharing in the body of Christ.
When we bless the cup,
   it is a sharing in the blood of Christ.
The gifts of God for the people of God.

�Ⓨ WORDS OF ADMINISTRATION

The words of administration are spoken to the communicants as they receive the bread and wine. They emphasize the personal meaning of these elements for the recipients. It is appropriate that, as each person serves another person in the pew, these words be spoken and the given response be, in turn, spoken to the recipient.

The various forms reflect the variety of expressions found in the early church.

633
The body of Christ, given for you. **Amen.**
The blood of Christ, given for you. **Amen.**

634
Take and eat,
    this is the body of Christ, broken for you. **Amen!**
Take and drink,
    this is the cup of the new covenant, poured out for you. **Amen!**

635
The body of Christ, the bread of heaven. **Amen!**
The blood of Christ, the cup of salvation. **Amen!**

636
The body of Christ, the living bread. **Amen!**
The blood of Christ, the saving cup. **Amen!**

637
Eat this, for it is the body of Christ, broken for you. **Amen!**
Drink this, for it is the blood of Christ, shed for you. **Amen!**

638
The bread of heaven in Christ Jesus.
The cup of salvation in Christ Jesus.

639
Through the broken bread we participate in the body of Christ.
Through the cup of blessing we participate in the new life Christ gives.

640
Receive this bread as the token that Jesus loved you and died for you. **Amen.**
Take this wine, and let Christ cleanse you and fill you with his love. **Amen.**

ⓨ ACCLAMATION OF CHRIST

641

Your death, O Lord, we commemorate. **Amen.**
Your glory as our risen Lord, we now celebrate. **Amen.**
Your return as Lord in glory, together we await. **Amen.**

642

Your death, O Lord, we commemorate.
Your resurrection we confess.
Your final coming we await.
Glory be to you, O Christ.
Christ has died.
Christ is risen.
Christ will come again.

ⓨ CLOSING COMMUNION PRAYER OF THANKSGIVING

It is appropriate to offer a prayer of thanks at the close of the Lord's supper. It may take the form of a hymn or prayer or the two combined. It is an opportunity for all the people to bless God for this gift that constitutes them as a people within Christ's fellowship.

643

O God, we thank you for uniting us by baptism in the body of Christ
    and by this meal filling us with joy and hope.
Grant that in the days ahead
    our lips which have sung your praises
        may speak the truth;
    our eyes which have seen your love
        may look with compassion on the needs of the world;
    our hands which have held this loaf and cup
        may be active in your service.
We ask it in the name of Jesus Christ. Amen.

644

Creating God, may the life of our Savior Jesus Christ,
    which we have received at this table,
        give us the energy and vitality that we need.
Help us use this new life in all that we do and say
    so that the new world of justice and joy will come.
Through Jesus Christ we pray. Amen.

645

Gracious God, may the power of this sacrament
    take hold of our lives and inspire us to live boldly,
    that all things now and in time to come
    will be conformed to your eternal will.
Through Jesus Christ we pray. Amen.

646

Loving God, we thank you that you have fed us in this sacrament,
    united us with Christ,
    and given us a foretaste of the heavenly banquet
    in your eternal kingdom.
Send us out in the power of your Spirit
    to live and work to your praise and glory. Amen.

647

Most gracious God, we praise you for what you have given
    and for what you have promised us here.
You have made us one with all your people in heaven and on earth.
You have fed us with the bread of life, and renewed us for your service.
Now we give ourselves to you; and we ask that our daily living
        may be part of the life of your kingdom,
    and that our love may be your love
        reaching out into the life of the world;
through Jesus Christ our Lord. Amen.

648

Lord God, we have received your word and have tasted your truth:
    Jesus Christ, the Son of your love, *the Prince of Peace.*
We pray that he may guide us
    and that we may live with each other in his wisdom and love *and peace*
    and so grow in the faith that the future is his,
    today, every day, forever.

649

Loving God in Jesus Christ,
    with gratitude for your holy nourishment about this table,
we dedicate:
        our lips to be the hopeful voice of Christ to the despairing;
        our hands to reach out in Christ's name to heal the broken;
        our feet to walk with Christ to visit those who are shunned;
        our bodies to be Christ's living sacrifice to break the power of death.
Take us. Empower us. Use us. Amen.

650

Almighty and loving God,
      we marvel at the privilege of eating at Christ's table.
Made one with Christ in the fellowship of this meal,
      we know ourselves to be at one with all your people everywhere.
Help us to express Christ's hospitality toward all we meet. Amen.

651

We have received from your hand, O God, bread from the earth to fortify
our hearts and wine to gladden our spirits. May these signs of Christ's
presence fill our lives with such gratitude that we are impelled to spread
the joy wherever we go.

652

Almighty God, we give you thanks for the gift of our Savior's presence
      in the simplicity and splendor of this holy meal.
Unite us with all who are fed by Christ's body and blood
      that we may faithfully proclaim the good news of your love,
      that your universal church may be a rainbow of hope
            in an uncertain world;
through Jesus Christ our Redeemer. Amen.

653

Bountiful God, we give you thanks
      that you have refreshed us at your table
      by granting us the presence of Christ.
Strengthen our faith, increase our love for one another,
      and send us forth into the world in courage and peace,
      rejoicing in the power of the Holy Spirit. Amen.

654

Eternal God, you have called your people
      from east and west and north and south
      to eat at the table of Jesus Christ.
We thank you for Christ's presence
      and for the spiritual food of Christ's body and blood.
By the power of your Holy Spirit,
      keep us faithful to your will.
Go with us to the streets, to our homes,
      and to our places of labor and leisure
      that whether we are gathered or scattered,
      we may be the servant church of the servant Christ,
      in whose name we rejoice to pray. Amen.

655

We thank you, God, for inviting us to this table
    where we have known the presence of Christ
    and have received all Christ's gifts.
Strengthen our faith,
    increase our love for one another,
    and let us show forth your praise in our lives;
through Jesus Christ our Savior. Amen.

656

We give you thanks, O Father,
    for the life and knowledge that you have made known to us
    through your Son Jesus.
Yours is the glory forever and ever.
As this broken bread was scattered upon the mountains,
    and being gathered together became one,
so may your church be gathered together
    from the ends of the earth
    into your kingdom;
for yours is the glory and the power,
    through Jesus Christ, forever and ever. Amen.

657

Most gentle God, you have fed us this day with your holy word and life-
giving bread. May we continue to discern your calls in life, family, community, and in the movements of our hearts. May we always be among
those who worship you in spirit and in truth. We ask this through the intercession of all those who gave their lives that others may have bread and
a better quality of life. Amen.

658

God our help, we thank you for this supper
    shared in the Spirit with your servant Jesus,
    who makes us new and strong, who brings life eternal.
We praise you for giving us all good gifts,
    and pledge ourselves to serve you,
    even as in Christ you have served us. Amen.

659

O God, by coming to your table
    we receive more gifts than we deserve.
We give thanks for Jesus Christ, through whom we receive life
    and in whom we are bound in covenant.
Renew us so we may willingly serve as Christ served. Amen.

660

Almighty God, we thank you for feeding us
    with the body and blood of your Son Jesus Christ.
Through him we offer you our souls and bodies
    to be a living sacrifice.
Send us out in the power of your Spirit
    to live and work to your praise and glory. Amen.

661

We have remembered our Lord Jesus through the breaking of bread and
sharing of the cup. He has been made known to us in our midst. Let us,
then, greet him with the hospitality of our hearts.
Welcome, Christ, our sovereign and savior.
Welcome, Christ, our friend and companion.
Welcome, Christ, our teacher and guide.
Welcome, Christ, our strength and solace.
Abide daily in Christ, that Christ may abide daily with you.

662

With grateful hearts we praise you, O God,
    for your great goodness in the gift of Christ.
Through sacred memory Christ has come to us and fed us at his table.
Strengthen us by your grace to fellowship with Christ each day.
Stir us to share Christ's cross in daily sacrificial service. Amen.

663

Lord God, your lavish faithfulness puts us to shame.
You have never given up on us,
    even though our history is one of unfaithfulness and discouragement.
You have raised the dead to life in your Son,
    and are raising us to new life
    each time we set aside ourselves for someone else.
Having broken bread and shared
    the Body and Blood—the New Life of Jesus,
    we praise you and bless your name for your faithfulness and mercy.
In Jesus' name we pray forever and ever. Amen.

664

We marvel, O God, that you love us before we love you.
By your Spirit, help us to do unto others as you have done unto us;
    feeding others as you have first fed us;
    blessing others as you have first blessed us;
    giving to others as you have first given to us. Amen.

665

We thank you, God, for the assurance in bread and wine that Christ shall be with us at the last. Grant that by your Spirit we may stand firm in our faith, be courageous and strong. Let all that we do be done in love. Amen.

666

We bless you, merciful God, for the knowledge in Christ that you share our sufferings. Grant that we in turn, may comfort those who are in any affliction with the same comfort with which we ourselves are comforted. Amen.

667

O God of light, we thank you for the brightness of your countenance shining in the face of Jesus. As we depart from this table, may Christ's light so shine through us that others may see our good works and give you glory. Amen.

668

In remembering Christ, O God, we recall the moment when we personally confessed Jesus as the Christ to begin our walk of discipleship. Grateful for his redeeming presence, we ask your continuing spirit. Let us boldly cast aside every care and follow him. Amen.

669

Grateful, O God, that you do not hold our sin against us, let us not forget your love as we leave this table. Grant that in each living moment we shall consider ourselves dead to sin and alive in Christ. Amen.

670

Through bread and cup we rejoice, O God, in Christ's sacrificial love.
Grant within our depths the life-transforming knowledge that
    nothing can separate us from your love.
Help us to witness to that unbreakable love in word and deed. Amen.

671

We are grateful, O God,
    for the promise in Christ of a new creation.
Even as we join with your Spirit in recreating our own lives,
    help us to share in recreating the world about us.
Where there is futility, let there be hope;
    where there is decay, renewal. Amen.

672

We marvel, gracious God, that Jesus lived and died and was raised from the dead. With gratitude we affirm that nothing shall separate us from that love—not tribulation or distress or power or sword. We are more than conquerors through him who loved us. Amen.

673

Holy God, you come to us in bread and wine, that we may become more like you. With grateful hearts we ask that we may not be conformed to this world, but transformed, by the renewal of our minds. Help us to discern your will—to do what is good and acceptable and complete.

674

You come to set our spirits aglow, O God. For this we are grateful. Send us from this table to be genuine in our love and constant in our prayers. Grant that we may not flag in zeal, but rejoice in hope. Let our love be genuine. Amen.

675

We thank you, God for renewing our faith,
    strengthening our hope, and kindling our love.
Through the power of the living Christ, at work in us,
    grant that we shall walk in newness of life. Amen.

676

We are grateful, loving God, that through communion
    you knit us together into one body—the body of Christ.
Having gifts that differ according to the grace given to us,
    help us use them to build up one another in love—
    serving as Christ's hands and feet in the world. Amen.

677

What a fellowship is ours about the Lord's table, O God!
Filled with your Spirit, let us
    rejoice with those who rejoice,
    weep with those who weep—
    living in harmony with one another.
So far as it depends on upon us,
    help us to live peaceably with all. Amen.

678

At the foot of the cross, O God, we behold the Suffering Servant who gave his life as a sacrifice for many. For this we are deeply grateful. Empower us by Christ's spirit to serve rather than be served—to lose ourselves in loving care for others. Amen.

679

We love you, gracious God, because you have first loved us. About Christ's table we know this afresh. Grant that our whole lives, through the power of the Spirit, may be lived in grateful response to your love. Help us to love you with our whole hearts and our neighbors as ourselves. Amen.

680

Once more confronted by Christ through bread and cup, O God,
    we marvel that you save us solely by your grace.
Continue to nurture us by your merciful Spirit,
    that we may be faithful in our discipleship—
    loving as Christ loves in openness toward all. Amen.

681

We have eaten the bread. We have drunk the cup. We have discerned Christ's body. We are grateful, loving God, for your love. Help us now, in life and service, to proclaim the Lord's death until he comes. Amen.

682

In holy communion we have gratefully discerned, loving God, that we are one body in Christ. In common kinship we sense that if one member suffers, all suffer together; if one member is honored, all rejoice together. Help us to express our oneness with your larger family wherever life takes us. Amen.

683

Gratefully we have remembered Jesus Christ, who died for our sins and who was raised on the third day in accordance with the scriptures. Take our lives, Creator God, and transform them into living testimonies of your word, that the world may believe you sent him. Amen.

684

You have created us, O God, in the image of the one whom we have remembered about this table. With grateful hearts we ask your continuing Spirit to upbuild us ever more perfectly into that likeness. Help us together to become that new humanity in Jesus Christ. Amen.

The passing of the peace is a sign that those in the community of faith are reconciled in love to one another. It may be expressed as a verbal exchange or by gesture. More than a friendly greeting, it expresses the shalom of God that dwells among God's people. Throughout Christian history it has been placed in various parts of the service.

685
The peace of the Lord be always with you.
And also with you.
The minister may then invite the members of the congregation to greet one another with a sign of peace and with words such as those above or:
Christ is our peace:
Let us live in his love.

686
This is God's house, a place of peace,
    a place where we befriend one another in the name of Christ.
We enter strangers. We leave as friends.
Let us greet one another as a sign of God's peace and Christ's friendship.
May the peace of Christ be with each of you.
And also with you.

CLOSING WORDS

Worship closes with a charge to live the life experienced in worship. It frequently includes an expression of God's blessing upon the people as they go their separate ways. The dismissal is a churchly way of saying "good-bye"—that is, "God be with you." As a dismissal, it is addressed to the worshipers; as prayer, it is addressed to God. Often an apostolic benediction is included. Sometimes an ascription of praise serves to emphasize that the whole of worship is to the glory of God. This final section moves from congregational dismissal through prayers of blessing—both scriptural and general—to miscellaneous closing prayers and concluding ascriptions of glory to God.

Other appropriate closing words than the ones given here may be found within the services of worship found in earlier sections of this book.

687
Go. Serve the Lord. You are free.

688
May God give us new visions,
    to take advantage of new possibilities,
    to go out and reach new people.
May the Holy Spirit empower us to do this work.

689
Serve your God with patience and passion.
Be deliberate in enacting your faith.
Be steadfast in celebrating the Spirit's power.
And may peace be your way in the world.

690
Be strong and courageous,
    be careful to observe God's commandments—
    remember them, speak of them, obey them.
Do not be fearful, do not be discouraged;
    and the Lord your God be with you wherever you go.

691
At the word of Christ,
    and by the authority given to him in heaven and on earth,
go and make disciples of all people,
    in the name of the Father, of the Son and of the Holy Spirit;
and the presence of Christ be with you everywhere and always.

692
We who have shared food and drink as evidence of God's presence go out now to come to grips with a world in which many are still hungry. We get up from this table to share God's abundance with all. Go and bless those who are hungry. May they be satisfied.

693
We go forth as the people of shalom
    to heal the brokenness and bring justice and liberty to all the world.
May the peace of God be with you.
    And with you. Amen.

694
Go live as people of God,
    in the name of Jesus and by the power of the Holy Spirit.

695
Go into the world, shouting through your lives the self-giving love of Jesus Christ, who became poor for our sakes. Through the power of the Spirit and the love of God, may you serve others as though serving Christ.

696

God came down to us like the sun at morning,
  wounded to the heart by our helplessness.
Let us proceed in God's strength
  to love and serve one another.

697

Go forth into the world,
  rejoicing in the power of the Holy Spirit.
Go and join Christ in the world,
  healing and speaking words of freedom,
  revealing the sacred in the very midst of life,
  through the ever-flowing grace of God.

698

Go into the days ahead with strength in the spirit
  and confidence in Christ.
Grow within these days to rely on the love of God
  and the fellowship of faith.
Peace be within us and among us.

699

May the vital and spirited Word come to life on our lips,
  give definition to our deeds, return praise to God,
  and speak deep within.

700

People of God by grace,
  followers of Christ by choice,
  partners of the Spirit by faith,
  serve your Creator all your days.

701

The Spirit of God is upon us.
God has anointed us to bear good news to the afflicted,
  to bind up the brokenhearted,
  to proclaim freedom to the captives,
  to open the prisons of those who are bound.
  Amen and amen.
Greet one another with the shalom of Jesus the Christ,
  who seeks peace in broken relationships,
  who seeks healing in alienated persons,
  who seeks justice in oppressive structures.
Share this shalom by saying,
"May the peace of Christ be yours today."

702

As Jesus sent the disciples out into the countryside
    to preach and to heal, so Christ sends us out
    to speak words of hope and to heal human hurts today.
We accept this mission to be God's people in the world.
Go on your way, rejoicing in the presence of God's Spirit,
    and in the power of the gospel of love and hope.
For yours is the glory, O God, now and forever! Amen.

703

God sends us into the world,
    to accept the cost
    and to discover the joy of discipleship.
Therefore, go—carrying with you
    the peace of Christ,
    the love of God,
    and the encouragement of the Holy Spirit,
    in trial and rejoicing.

704

God, who transforms us from death to life and who gives us a new heart,
    send you into the city to bring hope and to build *koinonia*.

705

Go out in the power of the risen Christ. Alleluia!
Thanks be to God. Alleluia!

706

Go forth in Christ's name and in Christ's spirit.
Pursue righteousness, godliness,
    faith, love, endurance, gentleness.
Fight the good fight of the faith.
Take hold of the eternal life,
    to which you were called
    and for which you made the good confession
    in the presence of many witnesses.
Go now in peace,
    carrying the vision of a new heaven and a new earth.
Know that God is with us!

707

Go now, remembering what we have done here.
Go now, remembering what God has done for us.
Go now, into the world where apathy and halfheartedness
    are dominant, where love too often is hard to find.

Go now, walking with each other
    and working with each other in the spirit of love.
Be awake, be alert, be alive to the needs around you
    and to the glory of God in Jesus Christ.
And may God's peace and joy be with us always.

708

God plants a song of praise in our hearts. The God who is praiseworthy sends us forth to raise the voice of praise in the earth. We go forth this day, strengthened by our own musical heritage. We commit our lives to be the instruments for God's praise.

709

In this place your healing has begun.
Now begins the healing of the world.
Go in peace.

710

Go now; make peace with your God in the secrecy of your heart, that you might make peace with your neighbor in the service of the world.

711

The common has been made holy;
    the body has been remembered;
    reconciliation has been represented.
The world is waiting.
Go in peace, and in all that you do,
    do it for love,
    and by the Spirit of Jesus who is Lord.

712

Take courage; be confident and strong;
    go where you must go, do what you must do.
Shed tears, endure sorrow, live with loneliness.
Put your hope in the risen Christ,
    who leads us through death to resurrection and eternal joy.

713

Go forth, praying and working with all Christians
    for the visible unity of the church in the way Christ chooses,
that people and nations may be led to love, serve,
    and praise God more and more forever.

714

Go forth in the name of Christ.
Thanks be to God.

715
Go in peace to love and serve the Lord.
Thanks be to God.

716
Feed the hungry. Clothe the poor. Help the needy.
Visit the sick. Comfort the bereaved. Speak to the lonely.
For as you do it to the least of your brothers and sisters,
    you do it to Christ.

717
As the earth keeps turning, hurtling through space,
    and night falls and day breaks from land to land,
let us remember people—
    waking, sleeping, being born, and dying—
    one world, one humanity.
Let us go from here in peace.

718
Go in peace. Go in joy. Go in love. Go in faith. Go in hope.
For the Author of peace, joy, love, faith, and hope goes with you.

719
Christ is your shepherd, and in his presence
    all your deepest needs are met, your joy restored.
Into the chalice of your lives he pours mercy until it overflows.
Go now in peace, knowing that all the days of your life
    you dwell in the presence of the Eternal.   (BASED ON PSALM 23)

720
Let us go forth into the new seasons of our lives.
We go forth into growing and changing and living.
Let us go with caring awareness for the world and all that is in it.
We go to discover the needs and opportunities around us.
Let us go forth in peace and be led out in joy.
We go in God's continuing presence,
    with the power to love and the strength to serve.

721
O Like a rock, God is under our feet.
M Like a roof, God is over our heads.
O Like the horizon, God is beyond us.
M Like water in a pitcher, God is within us and in the pouring out of us.
O Like a pebble in the sea, we are in God.
A Let us go out and change our world as God has changed our lives.

Open our hearts & minds to God's
    transforming Spirit as we offer our worship & praise.

ADVENT

722

Return now to the places of work and leisure,
 of tension and release,
 of demand and achievement.
We will return, glorifying and praising God
 for all that we have heard and seen.
God's peace and goodwill go with you all.
Thanks be to God. Amen.

723

Go forth into the world to share the song:
 "Glory to God in the highest!"
God is alive in us and in our world.
God rules over all time and space.
Let all the earth hear of God's salvation:
 "Peace on earth, goodwill to all people."
God calls us away from evil to do good.
God invites us to be saints and deliverers.
Go in confidence, for God is with you,
 offering grace, mercy, and peace.
We are not alone; we are not afraid.
We are renewed; thanks be to God!
Amen. **Amen.**

CHRISTMAS

724

The Word has become flesh and dwelt among us.
Let Christ's light shine in the darkest corner of your life.
Let Christ's love shine in the darkest corners of our world.
God is with us. Alleluia. Amen.

725

Go into the world with joy and peace and be men and women of goodwill.
For it has pleased God to send his Son into our midst and to give us a
merry Christmas.

EPIPHANY

726

Go in peace—and take peace—into the world of human need.
 You are the body of Christ and members of one another.
Serve and honor one another, that you may be strengthened
 to be Christ's body in the world.

727

Go into the world. You are the body of Christ.
God grant you the eyes of Christ to perceive human need,
    Christ's hands to heal, and Christ's heart to love,
through the dynamic energy of the Holy Spirit.

728

Go into the world doing what the Lord requires:
    living with kindness and justice,
      walking your path humbly, with God.
Then you will find yourselves blessed.
Know that yours is the kingdom of heaven,
    yours the strength and mercy of God,
      yours all the blessings given to God's beloved children.

729

There is a people sent from God whose name is Hope.
**And the people named Hope shall bear witness to the light;
    despair shall not overcome us.**
There is a people sent from God whose name is Love.
**And the people named Love shall bear witness to the light;
    hatred shall not overwhelm us.**
There is a people sent from God whose name is Life.
**And the people named Life shall bear witness to the light;
    death shall not overpower us.**

LENT

730

Go forth to live as covenant people this week,
    for God is everywhere present and available.
**We would be led in God's ways,
    devoting ourselves to self-examination and growth.**
Reenter the everyday world, where Jesus walked,
    learning from the example lived among us.
**We dare to walk in the power of Christ's resurrection,
    claiming our baptism as God's beloved children.**
Rejoice in the Spirit's empowering gifts,
    for God will enable your ministry.
**Thanks be to God for opportunities
    to make a difference in the world!**

731

A new day is dawning when God's promises
    will be renewed in the risen Christ.
**All of us will know God,
    from the least of us to the greatest.**

We are people of the covenant,
>   in touch with the Eternal in our midst.
> **God has acted in Christ to save us,**
>   **that we might live as children of God.**
> Go forth as followers and servants,
>   among all who are being drawn to Christ.
> **We take the risks of faith,**
>   **rejoicing in our discipleship.**

Passion / Palm Sunday

732

Go forth in celebration,
> **asserting the Presence among us.**
> **Christ is here as promised.**
> Go forth in reflectiveness,
> **remembering how quickly we change.**
> **We reject tomorrow the one whom we embrace today.**
> Go forth in joy,
> **knowing that God is with us.**
> **The suffering is not in vain.**

Maundy Thursday

733

We have prayed and broken bread;
>   we have been forgiven and fed.
> **Praise God for the bread of heaven**
>   **and the cup of salvation.**
> Now we go out to face life's temptations and demands,
>   knowing we cannot stand alone against them.
> **We are united with Christ and one another**
>   **in a covenant that equips us for life.**
> God blesses us with gifts and freedom
>   and empowers our service.
> **We go forth in confidence to face life's riches**
>   **and undertake our servanthood.**

Easter

734

Go forth into the world,
>   just as God sent Christ into the world.
> Take with you the peace of Christ,
>   greater than the peace this world gives.
> And the Spirit will teach you the truth about God,
>   that you may know the joy of Christ in all its fullness.

735

Go into the world, with God's new song of love in your hearts.
Forgive others, as you are forgiven.
Open your hearts to the coming of God's Spirit.
And may the peace of God which exceeds all understanding
    keep your hearts and minds through Jesus our risen Christ.

736

Let us go and meet the world
    which God loves
    and for which Christ died.
Let us proclaim that
    God is worthy of our trust
    and Christ of our discipleship.
Let us live as heirs of Christ
    and as the people of God
    in the midst of God's world.

737

The feast is ended, the world is waiting; go, in peace.
Go in peace to love and serve the world,
    and give thanks to God
    for all that is accomplished in us
    through Jesus Christ our Lord.

738

Go to the world.
God is there before you.
Christ has fought and conquered there.
Eternity has broken into time—
the future is secure!

739

Receive now the blessed promise of Easter:
    Every night shall be broken by dawn,
    and every tear shall spring from joy;
    every step shall become a dance,
    and every word shall carry a song.

740

Christ walks with us in newness of life;
    go forth in confidence and joy!
**We are the hands and feet of Jesus,
    carrying God's love and forgiveness to others.**

We are the only scriptures some will read.
Jesus will be known by our deeds.
In awe and obedience we accept our tasks,
with humble sincerity and truth.
Let everything that breathes praise God,
who equips us for our ministry.
We praise God, not with boasting or sham,
but with honest delight in our mission, in Christ.

☙ SCRIPTURAL BLESSING

741

May God bless you and keep you.
May God's face shine upon you and be gracious to you.
May God look upon you with kindness and give you peace.

(Numbers 6:24–26, ADAPT.)

742

Be strong and of good courage; do not fear;
for it is God who goes with you,
and God will never fail you nor forsake you.
Go in peace. Amen.   (Deuteronomy 31:6, ADAPT.)

743

Go in peace and let your light shine before the world,
so that all may see your goodness
and give praise to your heavenly Father.   (Based on Matthew 5:16)

744

By the tender mercy of our God,
may the dawn from on high break upon us,
to give light to those who sit in darkness
and in the shadow of death,
to guide our feet into the way of peace.   (Luke 1:78–79, ALT.)

745

Receive Christ's own blessing:
Peace I leave with you;
my peace I give to you.
I do not give to you as the world gives.
Do not let your hearts be troubled,
and do not let them be afraid.

746

And now I commend you to God and to the message of God's grace,
   a message that is able to build you up
   and to give you the inheritance among all who are sanctified.

(ACTS 20:32, ALT.)

747

May the God of steadfastness and encouragement
   grant you to live in harmony with one another,
   in accordance with Christ Jesus,
so that together you may with one voice
   glorify the God and Father of our Lord Jesus Christ.   (ROMANS 15:5–6)

748

May the God of hope fill you with all joy and peace in believing,
   so that you may abound in hope by the power of the Holy Spirit.

(ROMANS 15:13)

749

The God of peace be with all of you. Amen.   (ROMANS 15:33)

750

May the God who said, "Let light shine out of darkness,"
   shine in our hearts to give us
the light of the knowledge of the glory of God
   in the face of Jesus Christ.   (2 CORINTHIANS 4:6, ADAPT.)

751

May God provide you with every blessing in abundance,
   so that by always having enough of everything,
   you may share abundantly in every good work.   (2 CORINTHIANS 9:8, ALT.)

752

The grace of the Lord Jesus Christ,
   the love of God,
   and the communion of the Holy Spirit
   be with all of you.   (2 CORINTHIANS 13:13)

753

The Spirit produces in human life fruits such as these:
   love, joy, peace, patience, kindness,
   generosity, fidelity, tolerance, and self-control.
If our lives are centered in the Spirit,
   let us be guided by the Spirit.   (GALATIANS 5:22–23, 25, PHILLIPS, ADAPT.)

754

Peace be to the whole community, and love with faith,
>from God the Father and the Lord Jesus Christ.
Grace be with all who have an undying love
>for our Lord Jesus Christ.   (Ephesians 6:23–24)

755

May your love abound more and more
>in knowledge and depth of insight,
so that you may be able to discern what is best,
>and may be pure and blameless until the day of Christ,
filled with the fruit of righteousness that comes through Jesus Christ—
>to the glory and praise of God.   (Philippians 1:9–11, NIV, adapt.)

756

Rejoice in the Lord always; again I will say, Rejoice.
Let your gentleness be known to everyone.
The Lord is near. Do not worry about anything,
>but in everything by prayer and supplication with thanksgiving
>let your requests be made known to God.
And the peace of God, which surpasses all understanding,
>will guard your hearts and your minds in Christ Jesus.   (Philippians 4:4–7)

757

May you be filled with the knowledge of God's will
>in all spiritual wisdom and understanding,
so that you may lead lives worthy of the Lord,
>fully pleasing to God,
as you bear fruit in every good work
>and as you grow in the knowledge of God.   (Colossians 1:9b–10, alt.)

758

Go out into the world in peace.
Whatever you do, in word or deed,
>do everything in the name of the Lord Jesus,
>giving thanks to God through him.   (Colossians 3:17, alt.)

759

Now may our God make you increase and abound in love
>for one another and for all people,
and establish your hearts unblamable in holiness.

>(1 Thessalonians 3:12–13, adapt.)

760

Go in peace, be very courageous, hold on to what is good,
    do not return evil for evil, encourage the fainthearted,
support the weak, help the afflicted, honor all people,
    love and serve the Lord, rejoicing in the power of the Holy Spirit;
and the grace of our Lord Jesus Christ be with you.

(BASED ON 1 THESSALONIANS 5:13–22, 28)

761

The very God of peace sanctify you wholly,
    and preserve you blameless
    until the coming of our Lord Jesus Christ.   (1 THESSALONIANS 5:23, ADAPT.)

762

May God make you worthy of your high calling;
    may God fulfill in you every good resolve and work of faith,
so that the name of our Lord Jesus
    may be glorified in you, and you in him,
    according to the grace of our God and the Lord Jesus Christ.

(2 THESSALONIANS 1:11B–12, ALT.)

763

Now may our Lord Jesus Christ and God our Father,
    who loved us and through grace
    gave us eternal comfort and good hope,
comfort your hearts and strengthen them
    in every good work and word.   (2 THESSALONIANS 2:16–17, ALT.)

764

Now may the very Lord of peace
    give you peace at all times in all ways.
The Lord be with all of you.   (2 THESSALONIANS 3:16, ALT.)

765

Grace, mercy, and peace
    from God the Father and Christ Jesus our Lord.   (1 TIMOTHY 1:2)

766

Grace and peace
    from God the Father and Christ Jesus our Savior.   (TITUS 1:4)

767

Now may the God of peace
　　who brought again from the dead our Savior Jesus,
　　the great Shepherd of the sheep,
　　by the blood of the eternal covenant,
equip you with everything good that you may do God's will,
　　working in you that which is pleasing in God's sight;
　　through Jesus Christ, to whom be glory forever and ever. Amen.

(HEBREWS 13:20–21, ALT.)

768

Live in harmony with one another.
Be sympathetic and loving,
compassionate and humble.
Do not repay evil with evil,
or insult with insult.
Instead, repay with a blessing,
for to this you have been called
that you may inherit God's blessing.

(BASED ON 1 PETER 3:8–9)

769

May grace and peace be yours in abundance
　　in the knowledge of God and of Jesus our Lord.

(2 PETER 1:2)

770

May we continue to grow in the grace and knowledge
　　of our Lord and Savior Jesus Christ,
to whom be glory both now and to the day of eternity. Amen.

(2 PETER 3:18, ALT.)

771

Keep yourselves in the love of God;
look forward to the mercy of our Lord Jesus Christ
　　that leads to eternal life.

(JUDE 21)

CHRISTMAS

772

Holy One, now let your servant go in peace;
　　your word has been fulfilled:
My own eyes have seen the salvation
　　which you have prepared in the presence of all people.
　　a light to reveal you to the nations;
　　and the glory of your people Israel.

(LUKE 2:29–31, ALT.)

☿ *GENERAL BLESSING*

773

May you be blessed with a wealth of wisdom.
May you worship as God intends.
May the gifts that we give be the gifts we receive:
    goodness and mercy, generosity and peace,
    now and forever. Amen.

774

May the God of Eve and her offspring,
    the God of Sarah, Rebecca, and Rachel,
    and God of Mary and all who love her,
bless you, protect you, and grant you peace,
    now and forever. Amen.

775

May the road rise to meet you,
may the wind be always at your back,
may the sun shine warm upon your face,
may the rains fall soft upon your fields,
and until we meet again,
may God hold you in the palm of his hand. Amen.

776

May God look upon you with kindness, and give you peace.
May the God of all consolation bless you in every way
    and grant you peace all the days of your life. Amen.

777

God bless you.
Christ love you.
The Holy Spirit fill you.
Amen.

778

The blessing of God, who creates life,
    be upon you as you celebrate life.
The blessing of God, who restores life,
    be upon you as you seek new life.
The blessing of God, who sanctifies life,
    be upon you as you give life to others. Amen.

779
The blessing of God,
    who has promised to come into our lives,
    be with you today.
The blessing of God,
    whose love ransoms us from all captivity,
    be with you forever.
The blessing of God,
    whose breath brings new beginnings,
    send you forth into the world
    to create a new day for the good of all. Amen.

780
The blessing of God,
    who creates life out of death,
    be with you today.
The blessing of God,
    who suffers with the sin of this world
    and blesses all humankind with grace,
    be with you always.
The blessing of God,
    who sanctifies our transformations and turnings,
    be with you
    as you reveal the power of God's love to save. Amen.

781
May God our Creator breathe into you
    new life and a whole new meaning.
May the Spirit of God breathe into you
    a new spirit and a new understanding.
May the Wisdom of God breathe into you
    new hope and a new awareness.
And may all who hear the Word of God
    be blessed forever. Amen.

782
The blessing of the God of Sarah and of Abraham,
    the blessing of the Son, born of the woman Mary,
    the blessing of the Holy Spirit who broods over us
    be with you all. Amen.

783

With wisdom and understanding,
    with justice and mercy,
      with courage and commitment,
        may we be blessed, this day and every day,
         by the God who has loved us all into life.
Give us life according to your promise.
Give us life according to your justice.
Give us life according to your word, we pray!
Blessed be God forever!
Blessed be God forever!
Let the people say: **Amen!**

784

May the God of all goodness bless you.
May Christ share with you his loving kindness.
May the Holy Spirit fill you with peace. Amen.

785

May the presence of God the Creator give you strength;
May the presence of God the Redeemer give you peace;
May the presence of God the Sustainer give you comfort.
May the presence of God the Sanctifier give you love. Amen.

786

May the blessing of God, fountain of living water,
    flow within us as a river of life.
May we drink deep of her wisdom.
May we never thirst again.
May we go through life refreshing many,
    as a sign of healing for all;
through the One who is Life eternal. Amen.

787

Blessed are you, Mother of all life.
Blessed be your name, forever and ever.
Blessed are you, Father and Creator.
Blessed be your name, forever and ever.
Blessed are you, Sanctifier of life.
Blessed be your name, forever and ever.
The blessing of God, Source of our salvation, be with you always.
Blessed be God's holy name, forever and ever.

788

God has breathed the breath of life with you.
    Blessed be God, and God's blessing be upon you.

God has saved us from sin and death through grace.
   Blessed be God, and God's blessing be upon you.
God has empowered us to serve others in Christ's name.
   Blessed be God, and God's blessing be upon you. Amen.

789

May God bless us, embrace us, and send us forth
   renewed, refreshed, revitalized.
May we live each day in the name of Love,
   and include all in our circle of love,
   and treat all with a spirit of love,
   through the Spirit who is Love. Amen.

790

The blessing of God, the Creator of life,
   be upon you always.
The blessing of God, the Redeemer of the world,
   be in your words and deeds.
The blessing of God, the Sanctifier of life,
   be with all, now and evermore.
So be it. Alleluia! Amen.

791

The grace of our Savior Jesus Christ,
   the love of God,
   and the communion of the Holy Spirit be with you all. Amen.

Go forth in the power of the Holy Spirit!
Proclaim the gospel throughout the earth!
Serve God with gladness, in deeds of justice and mercy!
We are sent in the name and with the power of Jesus Christ!
Thanks be to God!

792

Go forth in peace.
The grace of the Lord Jesus Christ,
   and the love of God,
   and the communion of the Holy Spirit
   be with you all. Amen.

793

The God of all grace,
   who has called us to eternal glory in Christ,
establish you and strengthen you
   by the power of the Holy Spirit,
that you may live in grace and peace.

794

God bless you, brothers and sisters.
May Christ keep us in the faith
    until the day we shall appear before his presence.

795

God be your comfort, your strength;
God be your hope and support;
God be your light and your way;
    and the blessing of God—
        Creator, Redeemer and Giver of life—
        remain with you now and forever. Amen.

796

The grace of God, deeper than our imagination;
the strength of Christ, stronger than our need;
and the communion of the Holy Spirit, richer than our togetherness;
guide and sustain us today and in all our tomorrows. Amen.

797

We have worshiped God together.
    Now we go our separate ways.
May the spirit which has blessed us here
    be your spirit in each day that comes! Amen.

798

May the great Ruler of all high places,
    God of many names,
touch you with a wind that keeps you strong,
    for all the days to come. Amen.

799

The blessing of God Almighty:
    the Creator, the Redeemer, and the Sanctifier,
be with you all. Amen.

800

God's peace go with you into the worlds in which you live;
    be nurtured by the time of gathering,
    be faithful in the time apart.
Love and serve each other in the name of the faithful God,
    who calls us to be God's people;
and the blessing of God,
    Creator, Redeemer, and Sanctifier,
    be with us always. Amen.

801

Go into God's world with joy, and peace,
    and love, and hope in your hearts;
and the blessing of almighty God,
    Creator, Redeemer, and Sustainer,
    be with you all.

802

May the one who was a carpenter in Nazareth
    and constructor of the universe
build you up in your inner lives
    until you achieve the stature God intended for you. Amen.

803

The Lord bless you and keep you in all your ways,
    and make light to shine around you and within.
The Lord hear you in every time of need,
    and watch over you and give you peace.

804

May God, who through the water of baptism
    has raised us from sin into newness of life,
make you holy and worthy to be united with Christ forever. Amen.

805

Go, serve the Lord, rejoicing in hope;
    and the blessing of God go with you all.

806

We have celebrated together—
    now let us go to serve our Lord.
We will go. We will serve.
The blessing of God go with you all.
Thanks be to God. Amen.

807

Go now, enjoy the riches of creation,
    share God's gifts with all humankind,
    and use wisely all that God has put into your care.
The grace of the Lord Jesus Christ, and the love of God,
    and fellowship in the Holy Spirit be with you all. Amen.

808

Go now, enjoy the goodness of God;
    and the blessing of God Almighty,
the Father, the Son, and the Holy Spirit,
    be upon you and remain with you forever. Amen.

809

The blessing of God who created you, be with you this *day/night*.
Blessed be God.
The blessing of God who redeemed you be with you always.
Blessed be God's holy name.
The blessing of God who sanctifies you be with you, now and forever.
Blessed be God, our Creator, Redeemer, and Sanctifier,
    throughout all ages. Alleluia! Amen.

810

O Lord Jesus,
    stretch forth your wounded hands in blessing over your people,
to heal and to restore,
    and to draw us to yourself and to one another in love. Amen.

811

The peace of God, which surpasses all understanding,
    keep your hearts and minds
    in the knowledge and love of God
    and of Jesus Christ
and the blessing of God Almighty
    remain with you always. Amen.

812

The blessing of God,
    who created both darkness and light,
    be with you today,
    that your life may be illumined by divine Wisdom.
The blessing of God,
    who loves you and restores you to wholeness,
    be with you always,
    that you may love others in Christ's name.
The blessing of God,
    who sanctifies the breath of your living,
    inspire your words and actions, thoughts, and feelings,
    that you may be the messenger of God's blessing
    in this world today. Amen.

813

The blessing of God,
    whose love creates new life
    and whose fire burns away our impurities,
    be with you in your journey of life.
The blessing of God,
    whose love has the power to transform our living
    from old habits into new hope,
    be with you always.

The blessing of God,
 whose Spirit blesses our spirit with wisdom and vision,
 embolden you to proclaim
 the good news of God's love to all. Amen.

814

May the love of the Lord Jesus draw us to himself;
 may the power of the Lord Jesus strengthen us in his service;
 may the joy of the Lord Jesus fill our souls;
and may the blessing of God Almighty,
 the Father, the Son, and the Holy Ghost,
 be with you and abide with you always. Amen.

ADVENT

815

Christ, the Sun of Righteousness, shine upon you and scatter the darkness from before your path; and the blessing of God Almighty, the Father, the Son, and the Holy Ghost, be with you and abide with you always. Amen.

CHRISTMAS

816

Christ, who by his incarnation gathered into one all things earthly and heavenly, fill you with his joy and peace, and the blessing of God Almighty, the Father, the Son, and the Holy Ghost, be with you and abide with you always. Amen.

817

May Christ the Son of God gladden your hearts by his coming to dwell among us, and bring you his peace; and the blessing of God Almighty, the Father, the Son, and the Holy Ghost, be with you and abide with you always. Amen.

818

The blessing of God,
 whose love created light and darkness, mystery and wonder,
 be with you this day.
The blessing of God,
 whose love entered this world vulnerable, naked, and helpless,
 be with you always.
The blessing of God,
 whose love burns in your heart, transforming your living,
 send you into the world
 to be the incarnation of God's love for others. Amen.

EPIPHANY

819

May Christ the Son of God be manifest to you that your lives may be a light to the world; and the blessing of God Almighty, the Father, the Son, and the Holy Ghost, be with you and abide with you always. Amen.

LENT

820

Christ give you grace to grow in holiness, to deny yourselves, take up your cross, and follow him, and the blessing of God Almighty, the Father, the Son, and the Holy Ghost, be with you and abide with you always. Amen.

821

Christ give you strength to overcome all temptation, to deny yourself, and to take up your cross and follow him; and the blessing of God Almighty, the Father, the Son, and the Holy Ghost, be with you and abide with you always. Amen.

EASTER

822

God, who through the resurrection of our Lord Jesus Christ has given us the victory, give you joy and peace in your faith; and the blessing of God Almighty, the Father, the Son, and the Holy Ghost, be with you and abide with you always. Amen.

PENTECOST

823

The Spirit of truth lead you into all truth, give you grace to confess that Jesus Christ is Lord, and to proclaim the word and works of God; and the blessing of God Almighty, the Father, the Son, and the Holy Ghost, be with you and abide with you always. Amen.

824

God stir up within you the gift of the Spirit, that you may confess Jesus Christ as Lord and proclaim the joy of the everlasting gospel wherever you may be; and the blessing of God Almighty, the Father, the Son, and the Holy Ghost, be with you and abide with you always. Amen.

℗ CLOSING PRAYERS

825
Grant, O Lord,
    that what has been said with our lips we may believe in our hearts,
    and that what we believe in our hearts we may practice in our lives;
through Jesus Christ our Lord. Amen.

826
To your care and protection, O Lord, we now commit ourselves.
Of your goodness forgive us; with your love inspire us.
By your Spirit guide us; and in your mercy keep us, now and always.

827
Deep peace of the running wave to you.
Deep peace of the flowing air to you.
Deep peace of the quiet earth to you.
Deep peace of the shining stars to you.
Deep peace of the Son of Peace to you.

828
Creator God, you have given us every reason to learn and promote the
wisdom of lives lived in harmony with creation. May we, your servants,
increasingly serve. May we, your servants, increasingly come to love your
creation as we also increasingly come to love you, through Christ our Lord.
Amen.

829
O God, in whom we were conceived and given birth, give us now the rock-
like strength to stand firm in our commitment to you when others chase
after false gods. Amen.

830
God Almighty, we offer you our souls and bodies,
    to be a living sacrifice through Jesus Christ our Lord.
Send us out into the world in the power of your Spirit
    to live and work to your praise and glory. Amen.

831
Send us forth, Master,
    as those convinced of a life worth living,
    as those committed to open handed self-giving,
    as those concerned about sharing wholeness.

Let us be light
  salt
  bread
  in a dark, tasteless, hungry world.
Hallelujah. Amen.

832

May God take your hands, and work through them,
  take your lips, and speak through them,
  take your minds, and think through them,
  take your hearts, and set them on fire with love;
by the power of Christ who goes with you. Amen.

833

We give you thanks, Gentle One who has touched our soul.
You have loved us from the moment of our first awakening
  and have held us in joy and in grief.
Stay with us, we pray.
Grace us with your presence
  and with it the fullness of our own humanity.
Help us claim our strength and need,
  our awesomeness and fragile beauty,
that encouraged by the truth we might work
  to restore compassion to the human family
  and renew the face of the earth. Amen.

834

O Risen One, you gave your word, saying:
  "You will be given power when the Holy Spirit comes upon you,
  and you will be my witnesses even to the ends of the earth."
Come, Spirit, now, we pray.

May the power of the Holy Spirit come upon us.
May the wisdom of godly women encourage us.
May the cloud of witnesses accompany us,
  and may we witness to the ends of the earth. Amen.

835

And now the God of justice who calls us to account for our lives,
and the God of compassion who forgives us and grants us the joy of grace,
be and remain with us this day, this week, and evermore. Amen.

836

May our Lord Jesus Christ be near to defend you,
  within to refresh you,
  around to preserve you,
  beneath to support you,
  before to guide you,
  above to bless you.
May he give health.
May he give wholeness.
May he give peace. Amen.

837

God be in our head, and in our understanding.
God be in our eyes, and in our looking.
God be in our mouth, and in our speaking.
God be in our heart, and in our thinking.
God be at our end, and at our departing.

838

O Lord, support us all the day long, until the shadows lengthen and the evening comes, and the busy world is hushed, and the fever of life is over, and our work is done. Then, Lord, in your mercy grant us a safe lodging, and a holy rest, and peace at the last; through Jesus Christ our Lord.

839

May the power of the love of Christ
  work in the hearts of all who hear;
may the power of the love of Christ
  fire many to go and tell;
may the power of the love of Christ
  uphold all who serve,
that by the same power the peoples of the earth
  may be blessed to be at one with each other.

840

May we live the Mystery, and love the Mystery,
  and be caught up and held secure in the Mystery,
    whose wisdom exceeds all human knowledge,
    whose ways surpass all understanding,
    whose blessing fulfills our every hope,
  now and forever. Amen.

841

May God direct our going forth by making a way through the waters.
May she journey with us in fire and cloud on our exodus from exile.
May she shorten our wilderness wandering
    and bring us to the promised land of freedom for all. Amen.

842

May the God who existed before the creation itself come presently into
your hearts and abide there always, that you may be forever young in your
spirits and have life everlasting, through Jesus Christ our Lord. Amen.

843

O Amazing God, you come into our ordinary lives
    and set a holy table among us,
        filling our plates with the bread of life
    and our cups with salvation.
Send us out, O God, with tenderheartedness
    to touch an ordinary everyday world
    with the promise of your holiness.

844

Now may God, who has sat at table with us,
    continue with us wherever we go
    and sit at table with us always.
Through Jesus Christ our Lord. Amen.

845

May wisdom herself take root in you,
    grow strong and tall within you;
May she touch what is old and dead
    and make you beautiful and fragrant like cedars and olive trees;
May she spread out her branches and shelter you;
    and as the tree of life sustains and heals you,
    so may your fruits and leaves be a source of life for the world.

846

O God, as you have brought us together to think the thoughts of Christ,
send us forth to do the deeds of Christ. Let the affections of our hearts and
the deeds of our hands proclaim our devotion to you and our love for one
another.

847

Deliver us, O God, from any hesitation to take a stand for justice.
May we never run from our responsibility to you.
In you, O God,we find the strength to confront the forces of evil,
    the courage to stand firm and speak your truth
    no matter what the cost.

You are our way, our truth, our life, our integrity forever.
Holy are you, O Blessed, Indwelling, now and forever. Amen.

848

O Holy One of Blessing, you call us into mission in a multitude of ways.
Some of us travel around the earth,
    some of us tend your gardens and your vineyards nearer home.
Be with us all as we struggle to do the ministry of your making, and
    may we always stay in touch with the power you place within us
    and the peace that your word proclaims.
May we be there for one another,
    and take the time to celebrate time even as it celebrates us.
Glory and praise to you, Shaddai, now and forever. Amen.

849

Lead us from death to life,
    from falsehood to truth.
Lead us from despair to hope,
    from fear to trust.
Lead us from hate to love,
    from war to peace.
Let peace fill our heart, our world, our universe. Amen.

850

You have shown us, O God, what is good.
Enable us, we pray, to act justly, to love mercy,
    and to walk humbly with you. Amen.

851

O Creator and Mighty God, you have promised
    strength for the weak, rest for the laborers,
    light for the way, grace for the trials,
    help from above, unfailing sympathy, undying love.
O Creator and Mighty God,
    help us to continue in your promise. Amen.

852

O God, send us out into the world in peace.
Help us to hold fast to that which is good.
Help us not to return evil for evil.
Help us to support the faint-hearted.
Help us to uphold the weak.
Help us to honor all people.
O God, help us so to live, for Jesus' sake. Amen.

853

Lord, you have called us to serve you.
Grant that we may walk in your presence:
   your love in our hearts,
   your truth in our minds,
   your strength in our wills;
until, at the end of our journey,
   we know the joy of our homecoming
   and the welcome of your embrace,
through Jesus Christ our Lord. Amen.

854

O Christ, our only Savior,
   so dwell within us that we may go forth
   with the light of hope in our eyes
      and the fire of inspiration on our lips,
   your word on our tongues,
      and your love in our hearts. Amen.

855

May the grace of our Lord Jesus Christ
   protect us from killing one another;
and may God's love fill our lives
   with a peace that extends its hand to others
   in true reconciliation and friendship.

856

May God make you steadfast in faith,
   joyful in hope, and untiring in love
all the days of your life.

857

May the brokenness of our Lord Jesus Christ
and the Calvary love of God
and the fellowship of the Holy Spirit
   be with us all.

858

Nothing can separate us from the love of God.
Wherever we go, or whatever we do, or whatever befalls us,
   the Eternal God is our refuge,
   and underneath are God's everlasting arms. Amen.

859
The God of all grace,
    who has called you to Christian faith and service,
strengthen you with the Holy Spirit,
    and keep you faithful to Christ all your days. Amen.

860
May God, the source and giver of love,
    fill you with all joy and peace,
that in Christ your love may be complete. Amen.

861
Now may you continue to grow in the grace and knowledge of our Lord
Jesus Christ, feeding on his Word, breathing in his Spirit, walking in his
light, resting on his promises. Amen.

862
May Christ's Spirit dwell within you, his word abide in you,
    his will guide you, his joy strengthen you
    as you give him your lives in loving service. Amen.

863
The peace of God go with you this day,
    reigning within you, and in your families.
God's peace will make a difference in our lives,
    in all our relationships. Amen.
Walk in confident friendship with Christ,
    who suffers and rejoices with you.
Christ's presence will transform and strengthen us,
    wherever our journeys take us this week.
Live by the Spirit,
    acknowledging God's rule in your hearts and in your actions.
We welcome the fires of the Holy Spirit,
    the refreshing wind of God's surprising grace. Amen.

864
The God of hope in whom you place your trust,
    fill you with all joy and peace
so that you may overflow with hope;
    through the power of the Holy Spirit.

ADVENT

865
May Christ, whose second coming in power and great glory we await, make
you steadfast in faith, joyful in hope, and constant in love. Amen.

866

May the One who comes become in us
    love-made-visible to all. Amen.

867

O Son of God, our Savior, today we await your coming,
    and tomorrow we shall see your glory.
Reveal the good news to all of us who long for your arrival.
Come, Love incarnate, do not delay.
Come, Lord Jesus! Amen.

868

May the power of the Most High,
    the lowliness of Jesus Christ,
    and the overshadowing of the Holy Spirit,
    give you peace, and love, and everlasting joy.

CHRISTMAS

869

May faith in God uphold you;
    may the hope of God overarch you;
    may the love of God surround you.
Light of the world: through our tears of sorrow,
    our tears of joy, our shared tears,
    we see refracted the many colors of your creation,
    the mingled colors of your promise: light of the world.

870

May God, who in the Word made flesh joined heaven to earth and earth to
heaven, give you peace and favor.

871

Now may God, who brightened the night skies over Bethlehem and filled
shepherds' hearts with mysteries and transformed a stable into a thing of
immortal beauty, brighten your skies, fill your hearts with mystery, and
transform your lives forever, in the name of the Father, and the Son, and
the Holy Spirit. Amen.

872

Sisters and brothers,
    let us claim the freedom Christ gives us
    by his self-giving on the cross.
May he enable us to serve together
    in faith, hope, and love.

Go in peace and serve the Lord.
Thanks be to God.

May the God of love who shared his love
    strengthen us in our love for others.
May the Son who shared his life
    grant us grace that we might share our life.
And may the Holy Spirit dwelling in us
    empower us to be only and always for others.
Amen.

Holy Week

873
Now may God, who sustained our Lord Jesus in the hour of his trial,
    undergird you with faith and hope and love,
    in this hour and throughout this holy week,
in the name of the Father, Son, and Holy Ghost. Amen.

Easter

874
We praise you, O Resurrected Hope,
    for exceeding our expectations,
    for breaking to bits the narrow scope of our finite comprehension.
Who could have guessed
    you would talk with us on our journey into meaning,
    instead of sending us out on our own to find the promised land?
May we never lose sight
    of that empty tomb that symbolizes resurrection,
    never forget that only the dead are capable of rising.
Take the bread of our limited experience
      and break it to our advantage,
    revealing a vision of healing
      and hope for all who come home to God.
For this we pray, this day and always. Amen.

Pentecost

875
You are God's servants gifted with dreams and vision.
Upon you rests the grace of God like flames of fire.
Love and serve the Lord in the strength of the Spirit.
May the deep peace of Christ be with you,
    the strong arms of God sustain you, and
    the power of the Holy Spirit strengthen you in every way. Amen.

876

May God, who sent the Holy Spirit as a flame of fire that rested upon the heads of the disciples, burn out all evil from your hearts, and make them shine with the pure light of God's presence. Amen.

877

May Almighty God, who enlightened the minds of the disciples by pouring out upon them the Holy Spirit, make you rich with abundant blessing, that you may abound more and more in that Spirit forever. Amen.

☥ *ASCRIPTIONS OF GLORY TO GOD*

878

Blessed be you, Lord,
>   God of tenderness and compassion,
>   rich in kindness and faithfulness,
>   who keeps us in your love forever!   (EXODUS 34:6–7, ADAPT.)

879

The Lord our God is a God of mercy.
To God be glory forever!   (BASED ON DEUTERONOMY 4:31)

880

Blessed be the Lord, the God of Israel,
>   who alone does wondrous things.
Blessed be his glorious name forever;
>   may his glory fill the whole earth.
>   Amen and Amen.   (PSALM 72:18–19)

881

Blessed be you, Lord,
>   God of the humble and help of the oppressed!
Blessed be you, Lord,
>   support of the weak and refuge of the forsaken!
Blessed be you, Lord,
>   savior of the despairing—to you be eternal glory!   (BASED ON JUDITH 9:11)

882

To the God of all wisdom and knowledge
>   whose judgments are unsearchable
>   and paths beyond understanding,
be glory forever and ever. Amen.   (BASED ON ROMANS 11:33, 36B)

883

Source, Guide, and Goal of all that is—
    to God be glory forever! Amen.   (ROMANS 11:36, JERUSALEM, ALT.)

884

Now to God who is able to strengthen you,
    according to the gospel and the proclamation of Jesus Christ,
    according to the revelation of the mystery that was
    kept secret for long ages but now is disclosed,
to the only wise God, through Jesus Christ,
    be glory forever and ever. Amen.   (ROMANS 16:25, 27, ALT.)

885

The one who began a good work in you will continue to complete it,
    until the day of Christ Jesus.
Blessed be the God and Father of our Lord Jesus Christ,
    who has blessed us in Christ with every spiritual blessing.
                                    (PHILIPPIANS 1:6 AND EPHESIANS 1:3, ADAPT.)

886

Now to the One who by the power at work within us
    is able to accomplish abundantly
    far more than all we can ask or imagine,
to God be glory in the church and in Christ Jesus,
    to all generations, forever and ever. Amen.   (EPHESIANS 3:20–21, ALT.)

887

Now to the one God be glory in the church and in Christ Jesus
    to all generations, forever and ever. Amen.   (EPHESIANS 3:21, ALT.)

888

To the Sovereign of the ages,
    immortal, invisible, the only God,
be honor and glory forever and ever. Amen.   (1 TIMOTHY 1:17, ALT.)

889

To the blessed and only Sovereign,
to the King of kings and Lord of lords,
    who alone is immortal,
    whose home is unapproachable light,
    whom no one has ever seen nor can see,
to him be honor and everlasting power!   (1 TIMOTHY 6:15–16, ADAPT.)

890

May God be glorified in all things through Jesus Christ.
It is this one to whom belongs the glory and the power
>forever and ever. Amen.   (1 PETER 4:11, ADAPT.)

891

Now to the one who is able to keep you from falling,
>and to make you stand without blemish
>in the presence of God's glory with rejoicing,
to the only God our Savior,
>through Jesus Christ our Lord,
>be glory, majesty, power, and authority,
>before all time and now and forever. Amen.   (JUDE 24–25, ALT.)

892

To Jesus Christ, who loves us and freed us from our sins by his blood,
>and made us to be a kingdom, priests serving his God and Father,
to him be glory and dominion forever and ever. Amen.   (REVELATION 1:5–6, ALT.)

893

Worthy is the Lamb that was slaughtered
>to receive power and wealth and wisdom and might
>and honor and glory and blessing!
To the one seated on the throne and to the Lamb
>be blessing and honor and glory and might
>forever and ever!   (REVELATION 5:12, 13B)

894

Glory be to you, O God,
>Father, Son, and Holy Spirit.
You have power, wisdom, and majesty:
>receive from us honor, glory, worship, and blessing.
Great and marvelous are your works,
>just and true are your ways.
Blessing and honor and glory and power
>be to him who reigns upon the throne, and to the Lamb,
through the one eternal Spirit, now and forever. Amen.

>(BASED ON REVELATION 5:12, 13B; 15:13B)

895

Blessing and glory and wisdom and thanksgiving
>and honor and power and might
>be to our God forever and ever! Amen.   (REVELATION 7:12)

896

To the God of all grace,
>who has called us into his eternal glory in Christ,
>belong glory and power forever and ever. Amen.

897

To God who has the power
>to make us strong in the gospel
>to proclaim Jesus Christ,
to God be glory forever and ever. Amen.

898

Now to the One who has power to make your standing sure,
>according to the gospel—
to God who alone is wise,
>through Jesus Christ, be glory for endless ages. Amen.

899

To God the Creator, who loved us first
>and gave this world to be our home;
to God the Redeemer, who loves us
>and by dying and rising pioneered the way of freedom;
to God the Sanctifier, who spreads the divine love in our hearts,
>be praise and glory for all time and for eternity. Amen.

900

To God the Father,
>who loved us and made us accepted in the Beloved:
To God the Son,
>who loved us and loosed us from our sins by his own blood:
To God the Holy Spirit,
>who sheds the love of God abroad in our hearts:
To the one true God,
>be all love and all glory for time and for eternity. Amen.

901

All praise to you, Eternal Spirit,
>Source of life and Savior of the world.
With faithful people of every generation, we praise you;
>through Jesus Christ, with you and the Holy Spirit
>one God forever and ever. Amen.

902

Now to God, who conceives our very being,
>midwifes us into faith in Christ,
>searches for us diligently when we are lost,
>and shelters us as under the wings of the she-eagle—
to her be all glory, honor and praise, now and forevermore. Amen.

903

You, O God, are mighty forever.
You cause the wind to blow and the rain to fall.
You sustain the living, give life to the dead,
    support the falling, loose those who are bound,
    and keep your faith with those who sleep in the dust.
Who is like unto you, O God of mighty acts?

904

Great, O God, is your kingdom, your power, and your glory;
    great are your works, your wonders, and your praises;
    great also is your wisdom, your goodness, your justice, your mercy;
    and for all these we do bless you,
    and will magnify your holy name forever and ever.

905

Yes, Lord, you are the God of all.
Yes, Lord, you are the King of all.
Yes, Lord, you are the Almighty.
Yes, Lord, you are the Governor of all.
Yes, Lord, you are the Savior of all.
Yes, Lord, you are the Judge of all.
Yes, Lord, you are the Life-giver of all.
Yes, Lord, you are the Keeper of all.
Yes, Lord, you are the Nourisher of all.

906

To God be glory;
to the angels, honor;
to Satan, confusion;
to the cross, reference;
to the church, exaltation;
to the departed, quickening;
to the penitent, acceptance;
to the sick and infirm, recovery and healing;
and to the four quarters of the world, great peace and tranquility;
and on us who are weak and sinful,
    may the compassion and mercies of our God come,
    and may they overshadow us continually. Amen.

907

Great is the Lord and worthy of all praise:
Amen! Praise and glory and wisdom,
    thanksgiving and honor, power and might,
    be to our God forever and ever! Amen.

INDEXES

Ⓘ NDEX OF SOURCES AND ACKNOWLEDGMENTS

I. General Services of Worship

6-10   Lord's Day Service I adapted from Colbert S. Cartwright, *Candles of Grace*, © 1992 Chalice Press.

11-14   Lord's Day Service II from *Thankful Praise*, © 1987 Chalice Press.

15-17   Daily Morning Worship: first call to worship and prayers of thanksgiving and intercession from *Daily Prayer*, © 1987 The Westminster Press, pp. 61, 281, 58.

18-20   Daily Evening Worship: first call to worship and blessing from *Daily Prayer*, © 1987 The Westminster Press, pp. 53, 203. Opening prayer from the liturgy of evening prayer, Syria, 4th century. Prayer of commendation from *Gates of Prayer*, © 1975 Central Conference of American Rabbis, p. 35, used by permission.

20-21   First additional resource from *Canticles and Gathering Prayers* by John Mossi, songs by Suzanne Toolan, © 1989 Saint Mary's Press (Winona, MN), p. 90. Used by permission of the publisher. All Rights Reserved.

21   First prayer from Augustine, bishop of Hippo, 4th-5th century. Second prayer excerpted from *Lord Hear Our Prayer* by Thomas McNally and William G.Storey, © 1978 by Ave Maria Press, Notre Dame IN 46556, p. 50. Used by permission of the publisher.

22   Prayer adapted from "Am Abend, da es Kuhle war" in J. S. Bach's *St. Matthew Passion*.

22-24   By Colbert S. Cartwright.

25   First congregational covenant from *Baptism and Belonging*, © 1991 Chalice Press, p. 101. Second congregational covenant by Colbert S. Cartwright. Third congregational covenant used by permission of the Consultation on Church Union.

26-32   Christian Baptism: baptismal collect from *With All God's People* by John Carden, vol. 2, © 1989 World Council of Churches, p. 105. Renunciation of evil and confession of faith and the baptismal blessing ("The Holy Spirit abide...") adapted from *The Alternative Service Book 1980*, Cambridge University Press, pp. 105, 233. © 1980 The Central Board of Finance of the Church of England. Used by permission. Alternate confession of faith by Ruth C. Duck. Statement of purpose and welcome by Colbert S. Cartwright. Prayer from *Baptism and Belonging*, © 1991 Chalice Press, p. 44. First post-baptismal prayer adapted by permission from *Book of Worship: United Church of Christ*, © 1986 United Church

of Christ Office for Church Life and Leadership, p. 143f. Second post-baptismal prayer ("Merciful God...") from *Holy Baptism and Services for the Renewal of Baptism*, © 1985 The Westminster Press, p. 42.

32-33   Service of Confirmation adapted from *United Reformed Church Service Book*, ©1989 Oxford University Press, p. 41ff.

34-42   Christian Marriage I adapted from *Book of Common Worship*,©1993 Westminster/John Knox Press, pp. 841-51.

42-45   Christian Marriage II uses resources from Colbert S. Cartwright, Marilyn T. Fraser, O. I. Cricket Harrison, and Stanley D. Wright. © 1997 Chalice Press.

46-47   Wedding Anniversary litany from *Canticles and Gathering Prayers* by John Mossi, songs by Suzanne Toolan, © 1989 Saint Mary's Press (Winona, MN), p. 86f. Used by permission of the publisher. All Rights Reserved.

47-48   Blessing of Friendship by O. I. Cricket Harrison.

49-56   Prayer Service for Healing developed by Colbert S. Cartwright, drawing on a variety of sources. Prayer of thanksgiving from *Book of Worship: United Church of Christ*, © 1986 United Church of Christ Office for Church Life and Leadership, p. 319.

56-58   Prayer for Christian Healing in Home or Hospital adapted from *Worship the Lord* by James R. Esther and Donald J. Bruggink, Wm. B. Eerdmans Publishing Co., p. 40ff. © 1987 The Reformed Church in America.

59-61   The Committal: prayer ("God of heaven and earth...") from *The Alternative Service Book 1980*, Cambridge University Press, p. 936. © 1980 The Central Board of Finance of the Church of England. Used by permission. First closing prayer ("God of all life...") by O. I. Cricket Harrison. Second closing prayer ("O Lord, support us...") from *The Book of Common Prayer*, 1979, p. 833. Third closing prayer ("God grant..."): ancient Celtic benediction.

61-69   Service of Grateful Memory developed by Colbert S. Cartwright, drawing on a variety of sources. Last opening prayer ("O God of grace and glory...") from *The Book of Common Prayer*, 1979, p. 493. First two prayers of illumination from *Worship the Lord* by James R. Esther and Donald J. Bruggink, Wm. B. Eerdmans Publishing Co., p. 43. © 1987 The Reformed Church in America. Third prayer of illumination ("Holy One...") by O. I. Cricket Harrison.

69-70   Additional Resources: first greeting from *Litanies and Other Prayers for the Common Lectionary, Year A* by Everett Tilson and Phyllis Cole, © 1992 Abingdon Press, p. 163.
Second greeting by O. I. Cricket Harrison.
Prayer ("Are we to mourn...") adapted from *My God, My Glory* by Eric Milner-White, © 1954 SPCK, p. 61.

70-72   For a Stillborn or Newly Born Child: greeting from *The United Methodist Book of Worship*, © 1992 UMPH, p. 161.
Prayer by Colbert S. Cartwright.

72-73   For a Child developed by Colbert S. Cartwright and O. I. Cricket Harrison. Committal from *Book of Common Worship*, © 1993 Westminster/John Knox Press, p. 945.

73-74   After a Suicide: prayers from *Patterns and Prayers for Christian Worship*, © 1991 Oxford University Press, p. 165.

74-76   In the Face of Sudden Tragedy: opening prayer from *Be Our Freedom, Lord*, © 1981 Terry Falla, p. 308.
Committal prayer from *The United Methodist Book of Worship*, © 1992 UMPH, p. 163f.

II. Ecumenical Services of Worship

79-84   Service for the Sacrament of the Lord's Supper used by permission of the Consultation on Church Union.

84-86   Martin Luther King, Jr., Day service developed by Colbert S. Cartwright.

Greeting by O. I. Cricket Harrison.

86-90   Ecumenical Celebration of Thanksgiving developed by Colbert S. Cartwright, drawing on a variety of sources.

III. Worship Services for the Christian Year

93-96   Lighting the Candles of Advent developed by O. I. Cricket Harrison.

96-97   Hanging of the Greens adapted from *The United Methodist Book of Worship*, © 1992 UMPH, pp. 258-60.

98-100   Festival of Nine Lessons and Carols adapted from traditional resources by Colbert S. Cartwright.

100-04   A Celebration of Candlelight Communion on Christmas Eve: call to worship by John W. Howell in *Touch Holiness*, © 1990 Pilgrim Press, p. 21.
Light of joy litany adapted from *The Taizé Office*.
Service of communion adapted from *Flames of the Spirit*, © 1985 Pilgrim Press, pp. 19, 21-22.

104-06   Epiphany: second call to worship from *Prayers of Our Hearts*, © 1991 by Vienna Cobb Anderson, p. 3. Used with permission of The Crossroad Publishing Company, New York.
First opening prayer from *Book of Common Worship*, © 1993 Westminster/John Knox Press, p. 191f.
Second opening prayer ("Almighty God...") from *With All God's People* by John Carden, vol. 1, © 1989 World Council of Churches, p. 340.
Confession of sin by O. I. Cricket Harrison.
Intercession for church and world from *We Pray to the Lord* by Richard Mazziotta (Ave Maria Press), p. 43.
Offertory prayer from *Words of Worship* by Glen E. Rainsley, © 1990 Pilgrim Press, p. 112.
Blessing from *An Australian Prayer Book* (AIO Press), p. 151 alt. © Anglican

Church of Australia Trust Corporation. Reproduced with permission.

107-09   Ash Wednesday: prayer from *The Alternative Service Book 1980*, Cambridge University Press, p. 499. © 1980 The Central Board of Finance of the Church of England. Used by permission.
Prayer over the ashes adapted from *The Book of Common Prayer, 1979*.
Act of penitence and reconciliation adapted from *Prayers of the Faithful* published by The Liturgical Press, Collegeville, Minnesota, p. 73. © 1977 The Order of St. Benedict, Inc. Used with permission.
Benediction by O. I. Cricket Harrison.

110-11   First Lenten prayer ("winter's robe...") by O. I. Cricket Harrison.
Second Lenten prayer from *With All God's People* by John Carden, vol. 2, © 1989 World Council of Churches, p. 29.
Third Lenten prayer from *Daily Prayer*, © 1987 The Westminster Press, p. 141.

111-14   Passion/Palm Sunday: purpose of gathering adapted from *Saint Andrew Bible Missal*, © 1982 William J. Hirten Co., p. 266.
Prayer ("Triumphant God...") by Colbert S. Cartwright.
First additional resource from *Bread in the Desert* by Pierre Talec, © 1973 Newman Press, p. 61.
Second additional resource from *Words of Worship* by Glen E. Rainsley, © 1990 Pilgrim Press, p. 44.

114-17   Holy Week: Monday through Thursday prayers by O. I. Cricket Harrison.
Wednesday call to worship from *New Companion to the Breviary with Seasonal*

Supplement, © 1988 by the Carmelites of Indianapolis. Reprinted by permission of the publisher.

Friday prayer from *Book of Divine Services,* vol. 1 (Presbyterian Church in Cameroon, 1984), p. 174.

Saturday prayer by Colbert S. Cartwright.

118-21   Holy Thursday with Tenebrae developed by Colbert S. Cartwright.

121-25   Holy Thursday: Remembering the Upper Room service developed by Colbert S. Cartwright.

Greeting from the *Book of Alternative Services* of the Anglican Church of Canada, © 1985 by the General Synod of the Anglican Church of Canada, p. 421. Used with permission.

Additional resource from *A Christian's Prayer Book,* © 1972 Franciscan Herald Press, p. 221.

125-29   Good Friday service developed by Colbert S. Cartwright, drawing on a variety of sources.

The reproaches (abbreviated from nine to four) from *Book of Common Worship,* © 1993 Westminster/John Knox Press, pp. 288-91.

130-43   The Easter Vigil is based on ancient texts and contemporary editions used throughout the church.

Reaffirmation of baptismal vows from *Liturgical Year,* © 1992 Westminster/John Knox Press, pp. 197, 200.

First subsequent prayer ("Almighty God, we thank you...") from the *Book of Alternative Services* of the Anglican Church of Canada, © 1985 by the General Synod of the Anglican Church of Canada, p. 161. Used with permission.

Second subsequent prayer ("Eternal God, you have declared...") from *The Alternative Service Book 1980,* Cambridge University Press, p. 278. © 1980 The Central Board of Finance of the Church of England. Used by permission.

Service of bread and cup: dismissal and blessing from *Liturgical Year,* © 1992 Westminster/John Knox Press, p. 202.

143-47   Easter: second call to worship from *Prayers of Our Hearts,* © 1991 by Vienna Cobb Anderson, p. 4. Used with permis-

sion of The Crossroad Publishing Company, New York.

Opening prayers by Colbert S. Cartwright.

Prayer of confession by Michael Perry, © 1986 Hope Publishing Company.

Prayer of the people from *Prayers of the Faithful* published by The Liturgical Press, Collegeville, Minnesota, p. 100. © 1977 The Order of St. Benedict, Inc. Used with permission.

Offertory prayer from *When We Gather, Year A,* by James G. Kirk, p. 71. © 1983 The Geneva Press.

Communion prayer from *New Prayers for Worship* by Alan Gaunt, © 1972 John Paul Press, p. 11.

First dismissal from *With All God's People* by John Carden, vol. 2, © 1989 World Council of Churches, p. 42.

148-50   Pentecost: call to worship from *Daily Prayer,* © 1987 The Westminster Press, p. 182.

Opening prayer by O. I. Cricket Harrison.

A prayer of confession by Michael Perry, © 1986 Hope Publishing Company.

A Pentecost litany of affirmation adapted with permission from *Psalter Hymnal,* p. 1028. © 1987 CRC Publications, Grand Rapids MI 49560. All rights reserved.

First offertory prayer by Don E. Saliers, from *The United Methodist Book of Worship,* © 1992 UMPH, #408.

Second offertory prayer from *Book of Divine Services,* vol. 1 (Presbyterian Church in Cameroon, 1984), p. 249.

Dismissal from *Prayers of Our Hearts,* © 1991 by Vienna Cobb Anderson, p. 211. Used with permission of The Crossroad Publishing Company, New York.

150   Trinity Sunday prayer by Michael Perry, © 1986 Hope Publishing Company.

150-51   The Festival of Christ the Cosmic Ruler: first item from *Litanies and Other Prayers for the Common Lectionary, Year A* by Everett Tilson and Phyllis Cole, © 1992 Abingdon Press, p. 175.

Second item adapted from *The Daily Office Revised* by Ronald C. D. Jasper, © 1978 SPCK, p. 110.

IV. Worship on Special Sundays

155-57   The New Year: "God of all times..." by O. I. Cricket Harrison.

"Come, that God may strengthen..." adapted from Psalm 29:11, Isaiah 32:16–17, Leviticus 26:6, Matthew 5:9, and Luke 2:14.

"Everlasting God of all the years..." by Colbert S. Cartwright.

"Eternal God, you have placed..." reprinted from *Lutheran Book of Worship,*

p. 41, alt., © 1978, by permission of Augsburg Fortress.

"Our God, your throne..." by Arlene Martin Mark.

"This day wilt Thou..." from Jewish daily service for the new year.

"The New Year is a time..." from *Litanies and Other Prayers for the Common Lectionary, Year C* by Everett Tilson and Phyllis Cole, © 1994 Abingdon Press, p. 178.

"Loving God, there is nothing..." from *God-With-Us* by Miriam Therese Winter, © 1979 Abingdon Press, p. 34, alt.

157-60   Week of Prayer for Christian Unity: "How very good and pleasant..." adapted from Psalm 133:1; Ephesians 2:19; Acts 17:28; Revelation 7:9, 12.
"God of love and unity..." from *Prayers for Today's Church*, © 1972 R. H. L. Williams. Used by permission of Kingsway Communications, Eastbourne, UK.
"O God, you are the giver..." from *In Spirit and In Truth*, © 1991 World Council of Churches, p. 20.
"We grieve that the church..." adapted with permission from *Psalter Hymnal*, p. 1028. © 1987 CRC Publications, Grand Rapids MI 49560. All rights reserved.
"We pray, O God..." adapted from *Book of Divine Services*, vol. 1 (Presbyterian Church in Cameroon, 1984), p. 405.
"Creating God, from the waters..." by O. I. Cricket Harrison.
"The unity of the church..." from the 1989 COCU Sunday worship at Northview Christian Church (Disciples of Christ), Kokomo, Indiana. © 1997 Chalice Press.

161-62   Week of Compassion: "Compassionate God..." from *Bread for the Journey*, © 1981 Pilgrim Press, p. 38.
"Gracious God, you have given..." adapted from *The Daily Office Revised* by Ronald C. D. Jasper, © 1978 SPCK, p. 109.
"O God, just as the disciples..." reprinted from *I Believe in the Resurrection of the Body* by Rubem A. Alves, © 1986 Fortress Press.

162   Celebrations Honoring Scouting: resource by Mark Trotter, from *The United Methodist Book of Worship*, © 1992 UMPH, #436.

163-64   Stewardship Sunday: "O God, creator of us all..." adapted from *People Praying* by Cowie, © 1972 St. Andrew Press, p. 13.
Litany by O. I. Cricket Harrison.

164-66   Earth Stewardship Sunday: "The earth is the Lord's..." from *New Parish Prayers*, © 1982 Hodder and Stoughton, p. 69.
"O God, the only source..." © Timothy Dudley-Smith, used by permission.
"Most provident God..." from *New Companion to the Breviary with Seasonal Supplement*, © 1988 by the Carmelites of Indianapolis, p. 28. Reprinted by permission of the publisher.
"Lord Jesus Christ..." by Maureen Edwards in *Oceans of Prayer*, © 1991, p. 63. Reproduced with the permission of the National Christian Education Council, UK.
Concluding litany: prayer by Walter Rauschenbusch; words in bold from the hymn "Many and Great, O God" by Joseph R. Renville, c. 1846, paraphrased by Philip Frazier, 1929.

166-68   Mother's Day: litany from *WomanWord* by Miriam Therese Winter, p. 284ff. © 1990 Medican Mission Sisters. Used with permission of The Crossroad Publishing Company, New York.
First prayer ("O God of grace and love...") by Christopher Idle from *Prayers for Today's Church*, © 1972 R. H. L. Williams. Used by permission of Kingsway Communications, Eastbourne, UK.
Second prayer ("O God, the true mother...") by Leslie D. Weatherhead from *New Parish Prayers*, © 1982 Hodder and Stoughton, p. 51.

169-71   Christian Family Week: "O holy and loving God..." from *Come, Let Us Worship God* by David M. Currie, © 1977 The Westminster Press, p. 11, alt.
"God, father and mother..." adapted from *Patterns and Prayers for Christian Worship*, © 1991 Oxford University Press, p. 47.
"God, our Mother..." by O. I. Cricket Harrison.
"Loving God..." from *Bible Praying* by Michael Perry, © 1992 HarperCollins Publishers Ltd., #294.
"God of infinite love..." from *New Prayers for Worship* by Alan Gaunt, © 1972 John Paul Press, p. 11.

171-72   Memorial Day/Remembrance: first two prayers from *Prayers for the People* ed. by Michael Perry, © 1992 HarperCollins Publishers Ltd., #29.27 (alt.) and #29.29.
Litany ("Memories are joyful...") adapted from *Prayers of the Faithful* published by The Liturgical Press, Collegeville, Minnesota, p. 200. © 1977 The Order of St. Benedict, Inc. Used with permission.

172-73   Father's Day resource from *Book of Blessings*, © 1987 United States Catholic Conference, Washington DC.

173-75   National Observance: "Almighty God, giver of all..." and "O Judge of the Nations..." adapted from *The Book of Common Prayer*, 1979.
"We have come to sing..." from *Litanies and Other Prayers for the Common Lectionary, Year A* by Everett Tilson and Phyllis Cole, © 1992 Abingdon Press, p. 167.
"We pray for this nation..." adapted from *People Praying* by Cowie, © 1972 St. Andrew Press, p. 37.
"You gather us together..." from *New Companion to the Breviary with Seasonal Supplement*, © 1988 by the Carmelites of Indianapolis, p. 86. Reprinted by permission of the publisher.
"Come, Lord God..." from *Bible Praying* by Michael Perry, © 1992 HarperCollins Publishers Ltd., #244.

175-76   Labor Day: "Bring yourselves..." from *Litanies and Other Prayers for the Common Lectionary, Year A* by Everett Tilson and Phyllis Cole, © 1992 Abingdon Press, p. 127.

"We praise you, O God…" by Colbert S. Cartwright.

"May the Lord give us…" from *We Celebrate* (Ave Maria Press), p. 152.

"God of the rough-worn hands…" by O. I. Cricket Harrison.

177 Reconciliation: "Gracious God, you show us…" by Rosemary C. Mitchell from *Birthings and Blessings*, p. 45. © 1991 by Rosemary Catalano Mitchell and Gail Anderson Ricciuti. Used with permission of The Crossroad Publishing Company, New York.

"O God, we are one…" by Andre Dumas, in *With All God's People* by John Carden, vol. 1, © 1989 World Council of Churches, p. 92.

178-79 World Communion Sunday: first litany adapted by Colbert S. Cartwright.

Second litany by O. I. Cricket Harrison.

180-82 All Saints: "Rejoice in the Lord…" from *With All God's People* by John Carden, vol. 2, © 1989 World Council of Churches, p. 55.

"Since we are surrounded…" adapted by Colbert S. Cartwright from Hebrews 12:1–2; 1 Corinthians 1:2–3, 9; Revelation 19:1.

"We give thanks to you…" reprinted from *Lutheran Book of Worship*, p. 46, © 1978, by permission of Augsburg Fortress.

"Eternal God, make us this day…" from William Barclay, *A Barclay Prayer Book* (Valley Forge PA: Trinity Press International, 1990), p. 176.

"May God, who has given…" from *Book of Occasional Services*, p. 27, alt. © Church Pension Fund. Used by permission.

182-85 Thanksgiving: "O give thanks to God…" adapted by Colbert S. Cartwright from Psalm 107:1, 8–9; 67:5; 136:25–26.

"Let us gather together…" from *Touch Holiness*, © 1990 Pilgrim Press, p. 101.

"O God, as our Father…" by Michael Perry, © 1986 Hope Publishing Company.

"Let us give thanks…" from *The Book of Common Prayer*, 1979.

"O God, we give you thanks…" by William Barclay, alt.

185-86 National Bible Week: "Almighty and most merciful…" by Sir George Adam Smith (1856-1942), principal of the University of Aberdeen, Scotland. Reprinted from *The Communion of Saints* (Wm. B. Eerdmans Publishing Co., 1990).

"Lord, grant us…" adapted from *My God, My Glory* by Eric Milner-White, © 1954 SPCK, p. 87.

"Thank you, Lord, for the Bible…" from *Prayers for Today's Church*, © 1972 R. H. L. Williams. Used by permission of Kingsway Communications, Eastbourne, UK.

186-87 AIDS Sunday: litany by Colbert S. Cartwright.

188-91 Peace/Shalom Sunday: "We remember all…" (by Jan S. Pickard), "Show forth your power…" and "God of power and of the poor…" from *Oceans of Prayer*, © 1991, pp. 45, 37, 62. Reproduced with the permission of the National Christian Education Council, UK.

"Lord Jesus, in a dark hour…" from *The Daily Office Revised* by Ronald C. D. Jasper, © 1978 SPCK, p. 122f.

"Remember, O God…" from *The Kingdom, the Power, and the Glory* (Oxford University Press, date undetermined), alt.

"Let us pray for the world…" from *With All God's People* by John Carden, vol. 1, © 1989 World Council of Churches, p. 219.

191-92 Mission Sunday: "Give thanks to the Lord…" by Michael Perry, © 1986 Hope Publishing Company.

"We are one worldwide family…" by Elizabeth Bellamy in *Oceans of Prayer*, © 1991, p. 79. Reproduced with the permission of the National Christian Education Council, UK.

192-94 Heritage Sunday: "God, whom we gather to worship…" from *Come, Let Us Worship God* by David M. Currie, p. 22, alt. © 1977 The Westminster Press.

"Lord God, we thank you…" from *Prayers for the People*, ed. by Michael Perry, © 1992 HarperCollins Publishers Ltd.

"We pray to you…" from *More Than Words* by Janet Schaffran and Pat Kozak, p. 42. First ed. © 1986, second rev. ed. © 1988, by Pat Kozak, CSJ, and Janet Schaffran, CDP. Used with permission of The Crossroad Publishing Company, New York.

"Living God…" by Gaspard Mensah, Togo, in *Oceans of Prayer*, © 1991, p. 15. Reproduced with the permission of the National Christian Education Council, UK.

For a church anniversary from *Bible Praying* by Michael Perry, © 1992 HarperCollins Publishers Ltd., #39.

V. Special Worship Occasions in the Life of the Church

197-99   Installation of a Minister developed by Colbert S. Cartwright.
Opening prayer adapted from *A House of Private Prayer* by Leslie D. Weatherhead, © 1958 Hodder and Stoughton.

200-02   Installation of a Minister on a Multiple Staff developed by O. I. Cricket Harrison and David Troxler. © 1997 Chalice Press.
Pledge of loyalty adapted from "Covenant for Installation of a pastor" by Dennis R. Knight in *Flames of the Spirit*, © 1985 Pilgrim Press.

203-05   Recognition, Commissioning, or Ordination of Elders developed by Colbert S. Cartwright.

205-07   Recognition of the Diaconate developed by Colbert S. Cartwright.

207-08   A General Installation by James C. Suggs. © 1997 Chalice Press.

208-10   Installation of Officers developed by Colbert S. Cartwright.

210   A prayer of blessing for church officers from *The Oxford Book of Prayer*, © 1985 Oxford University Press, p. 218.

211   Installation of Church School Teachers developed by Colbert S. Cartwright and O. I. Cricket Harrison.

212-13   Installation or Recognition of Persons in Music Ministries developed by O. I. Cricket Harrison and David P. Polk. © 1997 Chalice Press.

213-14   Commissioning to Mission developed by Colbert S. Cartwright.

214-15   Welcome to New Members: first reading by Colbert S. Cartwright from *Chalice Hymnal* #341, © 1995 Chalice Press. Second reading from *Book of Worship: United Church of Christ*, © 1986 United Church of Christ Office for Church Life and Leadership, p. 163.

215-16   Presentation of Bible to Young Readers by Colbert S. Cartwright.

216   Commissioning Youth for Camp and Conference from Altoona Christian Church, Altoona, Iowa. © 1997 Chalice Press.

217   Beginning of a New School Year: source untraced.
Honoring Graduates from First Christian Church, Fort Dodge, Iowa. © 1997 Chalice Press.

218   For an Engaged Couple from *Book of Blessings*, © 1987 United States Catholic Conference, Washington DC.
For Those Who Intend to Enter Christian Service by O. I. Cricket Harrison.
At a Minister's Sabbatical from Webster Groves Christian Church, St. Louis, Missouri. © 1997 Chalice Press.

219   Upon Retirement: source untraced.

219-20   Farewell to a Member or Minister: litany from *Be Our Freedom, Lord*, © 1981 Terry Falla, p. 300.
Farewell benediction by O. I. Cricket Harrison.

220-21   A Dialogue of Confession and Forgiveness by J. Dale Suggs. © 1997 Chalice Press.

222   Before a Committee Meeting: first prayer by O. I. Cricket Harrison.
Second prayer by John I. Searle in *Prayers for Today's Church*, © 1972 R. H. L. Williams, #216. Used by permission of Kingsway Communications, Eastbourne, UK.
Opening a Church Gathering by Colbert S. Cartwright.

223   At a Convention/Conference from *Prayers for the People*, ed. by Michael Perry, © 1992 HarperCollins Publishers Ltd., #19.56.
Where There Is Division in the Church: source untraced.

223-24   For God's Blessing on a Home: first prayer from *With All God's People* by John Carden, vol. 1, © 1989 World Council of Churches, p. 114.
Second prayer from St. Stephen's Wallbrook, London.

224   After Childbirth: first prayer by Colbert S. Cartwright.
Second prayer by Michael Botting in *New Parish Prayers*, © 1982 Hodder and Stoughton, p. 222.
After a Difficult Birth: prayer by O. I. Cricket Harrison.

225   For Parents of a Stillborn Child or at the Death of a Newly Born Child: prayer from *Book of Common Worship*, © 1993 Westminster/John Knox Press, p. 993.
Prayer for One Who Has Been Molested: first prayer from *Prayers of Our Hearts*, © 1991 by Vienna Cobb Anderson, p. 22. Used with permission of The Crossroad Publishing Company, New York.
Second prayer by O. I. Cricket Harrison.

226   For Those in a Coma or Unable to Communicate, and When a Life-Support System Is Withdrawn: prayers from *Book of Common Worship*, © 1993 Westminster/John Knox Press, p. 992, 993.
Dedication of a Church Building from *Prayers for the People* ed. by Michael Perry, © 1992 HarperCollins Publishers Ltd., #20.29.

227-31   Rededication of a Church Sanctuary developed by Colbert S. Cartwright.
Act of rededication and blessing adapted from the *Book of Common Order of the Church of Scotland*, © 1959 Oxford University Press, pp. 207, 204.

231-32   Dedication Prayer for Educational Spaces, and Dedication Prayer for a Fellowship Hall by O. I. Cricket Harrison.

232-33   Dedication of an Organ or Other Musical Instruments from *The United Methodist Book of Worship*, © 1992 UMPH, p. 606f.

233-34   Consecration of Special Gifts to the Church: developed by Colbert S. Cartwright.

VI. Worship Resources

(The items in Section VI are identified by number rather than by page.)

65   By Colbert S. Cartwright.

66   From *New Companion to the Breviary with Seasonal Supplement*, © 1988 by the Carmelites of Indianapolis, p. 115. Reprinted by permission of the publisher.

67   By Keith Watkins.

68   By O. I. Cricket Harrison.

69-70   By Colbert S. Cartwright, adapted from the Preamble to the Design for the Christian Church (Disciples of Christ).

71   By Ann Asper Wilson in *Worship: Inclusive Language Resources*, © 1977 United Church of Christ Office for Church Life and Leadership.

72   By Colbert S. Cartwright.

73   By Ruth Duck in *Touch Holiness*, © 1990 Pilgrim Press, p. 97.

74   From *Birthings and Blessings*, p. 45. © 1991 by Rosemary Catalano Mitchell and Gail Anderson Ricciuti. Used with permission of The Crossroad Publishing Company, New York.

75   By O. I. Cricket Harrison.

76   By Mary Elizabeth Moore.

77   Source untraced.

78-79   From *Book of Worship: United Church of Christ*, © 1986 United Church of Christ Office for Church Life and Leadership, pp. 110, 119.

80   Adapted from *Come, Let Us Worship God* by David M. Currie, © 1977 The Westminster Press, p. 25.

81   From *Bible Praying* by Michael Perry, © 1992 HarperCollins Publishers Ltd., #163.

82   Adapted from *New Prayers for Worship* by Alan Gaunt, © 1972 John Paul Press, p. 1.

83   By O. I. Cricket Harrison.

84   Traditional.

85   By Colbert S. Cartwright.

86   Adapted from *Christian Worship: A Service Book*, ed. by G. Edwin Osborn, © 1953 Bethany Press (now Chalice Press), #110. Based on Zechariah 8:16; Amos 5:24; Isaiah 1:17, 56:1.

87   By Ruth Duck, paraphrasing 1 John 4:19, in *Flames of the Spirit*, © 1985 Pilgrim Press, p. 67.

88   By Colbert S. Cartwright.

89   Adapted by Colbert S. Cartwright from William Temple.

90   Adapted by O. I. Cricket Harrison from Jeremiah 9:23-24.

91   By Rosemary C. Mitchell from *Birthings and Blessings*. © 1991 by Rosemary Catalano Mitchell and Gail Anderson Ricciuti. Used with permission of The Crossroad Publishing Company, New York.

92   Adapted from *Litanies and Other Prayers for the Common Lectionary, Year C* by Everett Tilson and Phyllis Cole, © 1994 Abingdon Press, p. 34.

93   By Elsa Tamez, Mexico, in *Women's Prayer Services*, © 1987 Twenty-Third Publications, p. 20, alt.

94   Adapted from *The Underground Mass Book*, © 1968 Helicon Press, p. 45.

95   "Be a Sojourner," reprinted by permission of Susan Gregg-Schroeder.

96-97   Adapted from *New Life: A Book of Prayers* by Margaret Cropper, © 1945 Longmans, Green and Co., pp. 82, 86.

98-99   By O. I. Cricket Harrison.

100-02   From *In Spirit and In Truth*, © 1991 World Council of Churches, pp. 5-7.

103   From *More Than Words*, p. 38. First ed. © 1986, second rev. ed. © 1988, by Pat Kozak, CSJ, and Janet Schaffran, CDP. Used with permission of The Crossroad Publishing Company, New York.

104   From *Bread for the Journey*, © 1981 Pilgrim Press, p. 55.

105   From *Birthings and Blessings*. © 1991 by Rosemary Catalano Mitchell and Gail Anderson Ricciuti. Used with permission of The Crossroad Publishing Company, New York.

106   From *Whispers of God* by Lavon Bayler, © 1987 Pilgrim Press, p. 27.

107   By Ruth Duck in *Bread for the Journey*, © 1981 Pilgrim Press, p. 51.

108   By Jann C. Weaver in *Flames of the Spirit*, © 1985 Pilgrim Press, p. 67.

109   By O. I. Cricket Harrison, based on Psalm 85:8-9.

110   By Ruth Duck in *Bread for the Journey*, © 1981 Pilgrim Press, p. 54.

111   From *Touch Holiness*, © 1990 Pilgrim Press, p. 96.

112   From *Litanies and Other Prayers for the Common Lectionary, Year B* by Everett Tilson and Phyllis Cole, © 1993 Abingdon Press, p. 134.

113   By O. I. Cricket Harrison, based on Psalm 89:1.

114   Source untraced.

115   Originally by Gerhard Tersteegen, 1729; composite translation.

116   From *Daily Prayer*, © 1987 The Westminster Press, p. 105, based on Revelation 22:20.

117   By Rosemary C. Mitchell in *Birthings and Blessings*. © 1991 by Rosemary Catalano Mitchell and Gail Anderson Ricciuti. Used with permission of The Crossroad Publishing Company, New York.

118   By Ruth Duck in *Bread for the Journey*, © 1981 Pilgrim Press, p. 23.

119   By Colbert S. Cartwright.

120   From *Prayers of Our Hearts*, © 1991 by Vienna Cobb Anderson, p. 3. Used with permission of The Crossroad Publishing Company, New York.

121   From *Fresh Winds of the Spirit* by Lavon Bayler, © 1986 Pilgrim Press, p. 11.

122-23   From *Whispers of God* by Lavon Bayler, © 1987 Pilgrim Press, pp. 12, 16.

124   From *With All God's People* by John Carden, vol. 2, © 1989 World Council of Churches, p. 14.

125   By O. I. Cricket Harrison, based on 1 John 4:8–9.

126   By O. I. Cricket Harrison.

127   "O Come, All Ye Faithful" by John Francis Wade, 1743; composite translation.

128   From *Prayers of Our Hearts*, © 1991 by Vienna Cobb Anderson, p. 3. Used with permission of The Crossroad Publishing Company, New York.

129   From *Whispers of God* by Lavon Bayler, © 1987 Pilgrim Press, p. 25.

130   By O. I. Cricket Harrison.

131   From *Litanies and Other Prayers for the Common Lectionary, Year C* by Everett Tilson and Phyllis Cole, © 1994 Abingdon Press, p. 58.

132   From *Birthings and Blessings*, p. 114. © 1991 by Rosemary Catalano Mitchell and Gail Anderson Ricciuti. Used with permission of The Crossroad Publishing Company, New York.

133   By Ruth Duck in *Touch Holiness*, © 1990 Pilgrim Press, p. 59.

134   From *Litanies and Other Prayers for the Common Lectionary, Year B* by Everett Tilson and Phyllis Cole, © 1993 Abingdon Press, p. 74.

135   From *Touch Holiness*, © 1990 Pilgrim Press, p. 59.

136   From *More Than Words*, p. 158. First ed. © 1986, second rev. ed. © 1988, by Pat Kozak, CSJ, and Janet Schaffran, CDP. Used with permission of The Crossroad Publishing Company, New York.

137   From *In His Name* by George Appleton, © 1978 Lutterworth, p. 48, alt.

138   From *With All God's People* by John Carden, vol. 2, © 1989 World Council of Churches, p. 39.

139   From *Daily Prayer*, © 1987 The Westminster Press, p. 156.

140   From *Church Family Worship*, © 1986 Hodder and Stoughton, #241.

142   Source untraced.

143   By O. I. Cricket Harrison.

144   Adapted from *New Parish Prayers*, © 1982 Hodder and Stoughton, #19.

145-46 From *More Than Words*, pp. 85, 38. First ed. © 1986, second rev. ed. © 1988, by Pat Kozak, CSJ, and Janet Schaffran, CDP. Used with permission of The Crossroad Publishing Company, New York.

153   Gregorian Sacramentary, 6th century.

154   From *Lutheran Book of Worship*, p. 47, © 1978, by permission of Augsburg Fortress.

155   From *The Alternative Service Book 1980*, Cambridge University Press, p. 733. © 1980 The Central Board of Finance of the Church of England. Used by permission.

156   By Colbert S. Cartwright.

157   From *Contemporary Prayers for Public Worship*, © 1967 SCM Press, p. 23.

158   By Ruth Duck in *Bread for the Journey*, © 1981 Pilgrim Press, p. 31.

159   By C. N. R. Wallwork in *A Book of Vestry Prayers*, © 1976 Epworth Press, p. 71.

160   From a Syrian Clementine liturgy.

161   By Hugh Thomas in *Oceans of Prayer*, © 1991, p. 55, alt. Reproduced with the permission of the National Christian Education Council, UK.

162   Adapted from *People Praying* by Cowie, © 1972 St. Andrew Press, p. 18.

163   Adapted by Colbert S. Cartwright from William Temple.

164-65 From *New Prayers for Worship* by Alan Gaunt, © 1972 John Paul Press, pp. 8, 9.

166   By C. N. R. Wallwork in *A Book of Vestry Prayers*, © 1976 Epworth Press, p. 62, alt.

167   By Karl Barth.

168-69 By O. I. Cricket Harrison.

170-72 By Colbert S. Cartwright.

173-80 By O. I. Cricket Harrison.

181-82 By Colbert S. Cartwright.

183   By John Johnson.

184-86 By Colbert S. Cartwright.

187   From *Book of Worship Aids* ed. by LeRoy Koopman (Palm Springs, FL: Sunday Publications, 1976), p. 39.

188   By John Johnson.

189   From *Every Day We Will Bless You* by Katherine and Michael Kinnamon, © 1990 CBP Press (now Chalice Press), p. 39.

190   From *Book of Worship: United Church of Christ*, © 1986 United Church of Christ Office for Church Life and Leadership, p. 111.

191   From *1987 United Methodist Clergywomen's Consultation Resource Book*, p. 61.

192   By Ruth Duck in *Bread for the Journey*, © 1981 Pilgrim Press, p. 62.

193   By Ronald J. Allen and Linda McKiernan-Allen. © 1997 Chalice Press.

194   From *Be Our Freedom, Lord*, © 1981 Terry Falla, p. 38.

195   Adapted from *Hear Our Prayer* by Roy Pearson (McGraw-Hill, 1961), p. 17.

196   From *Church Family Worship*, © 1986 Hodder and Stoughton, #176, alt.

197   From *Come, Let Us Worship God* by David M. Currie, © 1977 The Westminster Press, p. 61.

198   From *More Than Words*, p. 39, alt. First ed. © 1986, second rev. ed. © 1988, by Pat Kozak, CSJ, and Janet Schaffran, CDP. Used with permission of The Crossroad Publishing Company, New York.

199   From the *Book of Common Worship: The Presbyterian Church in Canada, 1991*, p. 49. © The Presbyterian Church in Canada, used by permission.

200   By Neil Dixon in *Companion to the Lectionary*, vol. 3 (publisher untraced).

201   By Alcuin, 8th century.

202   From *Flames of the Spirit*, © 1985 Pilgrim Press, p. 68.

203   From *Handbook for the Christian Year*, © 1986 Abingdon Press, p. 58.

204-05   From *Saint Andrew Bible Missal*, © 1982 William J. Hirten Co., pp. 76, 101.

206   Prayer from New Guinea, in *With All God's People* by John Carden, vol. 2, © 1989 World Council of Churches, p. 13.

207   By O. I. Cricket Harrison.

208   By Huub Oosterhuis in *A Christian's Prayer Book*, © 1972 Franciscan Herald Press, p. 51, alt.

209   From *Daily Prayer*, © 1987 The Westminster Press, p. 86.

210   From *Congregational Worshipbook*, © 1978, 1990 Henry David Gray, p. 58.

211   By Harry Emerson Fosdick.

212   From *WomanPrayer WomanSong* by Miriam Therese Winter, p. 74. © 1987 Medical Mission Sisters. Used with permission of The Crossroad Publishing Company, New York.

213   From *Saint Andrew Bible Missal*, © 1982 William J. Hirten Co., p. 134.

214   From *Patterns and Prayers for Christian Worship*, © 1991 Oxford University Press, p. 43.

215   From *Saint Andrew Bible Missal*, © 1982 William J. Hirten Co., p. 198, alt.

216   By O. I. Cricket Harrison.

217   By Colbert S. Cartwright.

218   Source untraced.

219   From *New Prayers for Worship* by Alan Gaunt, © 1972 John Paul Press, p. 8.

220   From *Bible Praying* by Michael Perry, © 1992 HarperCollins Publishers Ltd., #368.

221   Developed by Colbert S. Cartwright.

222   From the *United Reformed Church Service Book*, © 1989 Oxford University Press, p. 5.

223   From *Contemporary Prayers for Public Worship*, © 1967 SCM Press, p. 17.

224   From *Prayers for Use in Church* by J. W. G. Masterton, © 1970 St. Andrew Press, p. 17.

225   From the *Book of Common Worship: The Presbyterian Church in Canada, 1991*, p. 27. © The Presbyterian Church in Canada, used by permission.

226   By O. I. Cricket Harrison.

227   By Ephraim of Syria, 4th century.

228   From *Contemporary Prayers for Public Worship*, © 1967 SCM Press, p. 111.

229   From *Daily Prayer*, © 1987 The Westminster Press, p. 297.

230   Adapted from *A Christian's Prayer Book*, © 1972 Franciscan Herald Press, p. 64.

231   From *Church Family Worship*, © 1986 Hodder and Stoughton, #216.

232   From *Patterns and Prayers for Christian Worship*, © 1991 Oxford University Press, p. 51, alt.

233   By Neil Dixon in *Companion to the Lectionary*, vol. 3 (publisher untraced), p. 88, alt.

234   By Thomas Ken, 17th century.

235   Adapted by Gilbert H. Vieira, © 1989 UMPH.

236   By David W. Romig in *Birthings and Blessings*, p. 64. © 1991 by Rosemary Catalano Mitchell and Gail Anderson Ricciuti. Used with permission of The Crossroad Publishing Company, New York.

237   By Michael Perry, © 1986 Hope Publishing Company.

238   By Ruth Duck in *Touch Holiness*, © 1990 Pilgrim Press, p. 235.

239   By O. I. Cricket Harrison.

240   By Anne Knighton in *Oceans of Prayer*, © 1991, p. 11. Reproduced with the permission of the National Christian Education Council, UK.

241   From the Alternate Eucharistic Liturgy of the Church of South Africa.

242   By John Platts in *Oceans of Prayer*, © 1991, p. 13. Reproduced with the permission of the National Christian Education Council, UK.

243   From *Bible Praying* by Michael Perry, © 1992 HarperCollins Publishers Ltd., #271, alt. (based on Psalm 23).

244   From *The Daily Office Revised* by Ronald C. D. Jasper, © 1978 SPCK, p. 129.

245   From *Prayers for the People* ed. by Michael Perry, © 1992 HarperCollins Publishers Ltd., #24.44.

246   From *The Book of Common Prayer, 1979.*

247   From *Prayers for the People* ed. by Michael Perry, © 1992 HarperCollins Publishers Ltd., #10.37.

248   By Mary E. Morgan in *Oceans of Prayer*, © 1991, p. 57. Reproduced with the permission of the National Christian Education Council, UK.

249   By Walter Rauschenbush, alt.

250   Prayer of the Waldensian Church, in *With All God's People* by John Carden, vol. 1, © 1989 World Council of Churches, p. 317.

251   From *Canticles and Gathering Prayers* by John Mossi, songs by Suzanne Toolan, © 1989 Saint Mary's Press (Winona, MN), p. 35. Used by permission of the publisher. All Rights Reserved.

252   From *Church Family Worship*, © 1986 Hodder and Stoughton, #282.

253   By Rosemary Wass in *Oceans of Prayer*, © 1991, p. 58. Reproduced with the permission of the National Christian Education Council, UK.

254   From *Prayers of Our Hearts*, © 1991 by Vienna Cobb Anderson, p. 11. Used with permission of The Crossroad Publishing Company, New York.

255   By Neil Dixon in *Companion to the Lectionary*, vol. 3 (publisher untraced), p. 37.

256-57   From *More Than Words*, pp. 40, 39. First ed. © 1986, second rev. ed. © 1988, by Pat Kozak, CSJ, and Janet Schaffran, CDP. Used with permission of The Crossroad Publishing Company, New York.

258   From the *Book of Common Worship: The Presbyterian Church in Canada, 1991*, p. 49. © The Presbyterian Church in Canada, used by permission.

259   By Ronald J. Allen and Linda McKiernan-Allen. © 1997 Chalice Press.

260   By Alida Millhan in *Living in Community*, © 1977 United Church of Christ Office for Church Life and Leadership, p. 17.

261   From *New Parish Prayers*, © 1982 Hodder and Stoughton, #72, alt.

262   From *New Companion to the Breviary with Seasonal Supplement*, p. 154. © 1988 by the Carmelites of Indianapolis. Reprinted by permission of the publisher.

263   From *Daily Prayer*, © 1987 The Westminster Press, p. 300.

264   By O. I. Cricket Harrison.

265-66 By Frank Colquhoun in *New Parish Prayers*, © 1982 Hodder and Stoughton, pp. 55, 59.

267   By Kate Johnson in *Oceans of Prayer*, © 1991, p. 12. Reproduced with the permission of the National Christian Education Council, UK.

268   From *Patterns and Prayers for Christian Worship*, © 1991 Oxford University Press, p. 52.

269   "A Litany of Praise" from *Book of Worship*, p. 59, by Church of the Brethren. © 1964 Brethren Press, Elgin IL 60120. Used by permission.

270   From the *Book of Common Worship: The Presbyterian Church in Canada, 1991*, p. 51. © The Presbyterian Church in Canada, used by permission.

271   From *The Book of Common Prayer*, 1979, p. 79.

272   From *Prayers for the People* ed. by Michael Perry, © 1992 HarperCollins Publishers Ltd., #11.14.

273   From *Searching for Shalom*, p. 62. © 1991 Ann Weems. Used by permission of Westminster John Knox Press.

274   From *The Book of Common Prayer*, 1979, p. 234.

275-76 By Diego Frisch (Uruguay) and Bernie Colorado (The Philippines) in *Oceans of Prayer*, © 1991, pp. 62, 84. Reproduced with the permission of the National Christian Education Council, UK.

277   By Michael Perry, © 1986 Hope Publishing Company, based on 1 Corinthians 13.

278-79 From *Contemporary Prayers for Public Worship*, © 1967 SCM Press, p. 41, alt.

280-81 By Neil Dixon in *Companion to the Lectionary*, vol. 3 (publisher untraced), p.54, 68.

282   By O. I. Cricket Harrison.

283-86 From *New Prayers for Worship* by Alan Gaunt, © 1972 John Paul Press, pp. 3, 8, 15, 16.

287   By Ruth Duck in *Bread for the Journey*, © 1981 Pilgrim Press, p. 60.

288   By William Barclay.

289   From *Every Day We Will Bless You* by Katherine and Michael Kinnamon, © 1990 CBP Press (now Chalice Press), p. 44.

290   Source untraced.

291   From *Contemporary Prayers for Public Worship*, © 1967 SCM Press.

292   By Michael J. O'Donnell in *The United Methodist Book of Worship*, © 1992 UMPH, #491.

293   From *The Daily Office Revised* by Ronald C. D. Jasper, © 1978 SPCK, p. 128.

294   From *Daily Prayer*, © 1987 The Westminster Press, p. 196.

295   From *Be Our Freedom, Lord*, © 1981 Terry Falla, p. 100, alt.

296   From *An Australian Prayer Book* (AIO Press), p. 39. © Anglican Church of Australia Trust Corporation. Reproduced with permission.

297   From *Book of Worship: United Church of Christ*, © 1986 United Church of Christ Office for Church Life and Leadership, p. 101.

298   From *The Sacrament of the Lord's Supper*, © 1984 Consultation on Church Union, p. 4.

299   From *Jesus Christ—the Life of the World*, p. 6. © World Council of Churches.

300-01 From the *Book of Common Worship: The Presbyterian Church in Canada, 1991*, p. 27, 56. © The Presbyterian Church in Canada, used by permission.

302-03 From *Book of Worship: United Church of Christ*, © 1986 United Church of Christ Office for Church Life and Leadership, p. 63f.

304   From *Patterns and Prayers for Christian Worship*, © 1991 Oxford University Press, p. 53.

305   From *Prayers of Our Hearts*, © 1991 by Vienna Cobb Anderson, p. 107. Used with permission of The Crossroad Publishing Company, New York.

309   From *The Sacrament of the Lord's Supper*, © 1984 Consultation on Church Union.

311-13 From *Book of Worship: United Church of Christ*, © 1986 United Church of Christ Office for Church Life and Leadership, pp. 82, 38, 102.

314   From *New Prayers for Worship* by Alan Gaunt, © 1972 John Paul Press, p. 4, alt.

315   From *Contemporary Worship Resources for Special Days*, p. 37. Reprinted by permission from CSS Publishing Co., P.O. Box 4503, Lima OH 45802.

316   From *Living in Community*, © 1977 United Church of Christ Office for Church Life and Leadership, p. 46.

317   From *Patterns and Prayers for Christian Worship*, © 1991 Oxford University Press, p. 28.

318   From *Bread for the Journey*, © 1981 Pilgrim Press, p. 21.

319   From *Homiletics*, Oct.-Dec. 1992, alt.

320   By Michael Perry, © 1986 Hope Publishing Company.

321   From *Prayers of the Faithful* published by The Liturgical Press, Collegeville, Minnesota, p. 73, alt. © 1977 The Order of St. Benedict, Inc. Used with permission.

322   From *Book of Worship: United Church of Christ*, © 1986 United Church of Christ Office for Church Life and Leadership, pp. 181-83.

323   From *Words of Worship* by Glen E. Rainsley, © 1990 Pilgrim Press, p. 40.

324 By Michael Perry, © 1986 Hope Publishing Company.
325 From *Bread for the Journey*, © 1981 Pilgrim Press, p. 45.
326 By Michael Perry, © 1986 Hope Publishing Company.
327 From *Church Family Worship*, © 1986 Hodder and Stoughton, #310.
328 By Neil Dixon in *Companion to the Lectionary*, vol. 3 (publisher untraced), p. 116f., alt.
329 Adapted from *Prayers for Use in Church* by J. W. G. Masterton, © 1970 St. Andrew Press, p. 49.
330 By Maureen Edwards in *Oceans of Prayer*, © 1991, p. 86. Reproduced with the permission of the National Christian Education Council, UK.
331 From *Prayers for the People* ed. by Michael Perry, © 1992 HarperCollins Publishers Ltd., #17.62.
332 From *New Prayers for Worship* by Alan Gaunt, © 1972 John Paul Press, p. 21.
333 By William Barclay.
334 By Augustine, bishop of Hippo, 4th-5th century.
335 From *Searching for Shalom*, p. 60. © 1991 Ann Weems. Used by permission of Westminster John Knox Press.
336 By Thomas Aquinas, 13th century.
337 From *Risking Obedience*, prayer handbook of the Uniting Church, Australia.
338 From *Bible Praying* by Michael Perry, © 1992 HarperCollins Publishers Ltd., #295.
339 From *WomanWord* by Miriam Therese Winter, p. 141. © 1990 Medican Mission Sisters. Used with permission of The Crossroad Publishing Company, New York.
340 By John Kingsnorth in *New Parish Prayers*, © 1982 Hodder and Stoughton, p. 172.
341 By Michael Shaw and Paul Inwood in *With All God's People*, vol. 2, © 1989 World Council of Churches, p. 49.
342 From Claremont School of Theology.
343 Adapted from *People Praying* by Cowie, © 1972 St. Andrew Press, p. 165.
344 From *New Prayers for Worship* by Alan Gaunt, © 1972 John Paul Press, p. 12.
345 By Alan Gaunt in *Prayers for the People* ed. by Michael Perry, © 1992 HarperCollins Publishers Ltd., #19.70.
346 From *Church Family Worship*, © 1986 Hodder and Stoughton, #175.
347 From *With All God's People* by John Carden, vol. 1, © 1989 World Council of Churches, p. 217.
348 From *Gates of Prayer*, © 1975 Central Conference of American Rabbis, p. 540f., used by permission.
349 By Dorothy Nolte in *Birthings and Blessings*, p. 164. © 1991 by Rosemary Catalano Mitchell and Gail Anderson Ricciuti. Used with permission of The Crossroad Publishing Company, New York.
350 From the *Book of Services and Prayers* (Independent Press, 1959), p. 190, alt.
351 By William Barclay, adapted.
352 From the Taizé community.
353 By Colbert S. Cartwright.
354-55 From *In Spirit and In Truth*, © 1991 World Council of Churches, pp. 21, 22.
356 From *Intercessions for the Christian People*, published by The Liturgical Press, Collegeville, Minnesota, p. 16. © 1992 The Order of St. Benedict, Inc. Used with permission.
357 By Colbert S. Cartwright.
358 From *The Book of Common Prayer*, 1979, alt.
359 From the *Book of Common Worship: The Presbyterian Church in Canada, 1991*, p. 68. © The Presbyterian Church in Canada, used by permission.
360 Adapted from *Prayers for Use in Church* by J. W. G. Masterton, © 1970 St. Andrew Press, p. 63.
361 From *The Daily Office Revised* by Ronald C. D. Jasper, © 1978 SPCK, p. 121, alt.
362 From *Bible Praying* by Michael Perry, © 1992 HarperCollins Publishers Ltd., #242.
363 By George Appleton in *With All God's People* by John Carden, vol. 2, © 1989 World Council of Churches, p. 35, alt.
364-65 From *Be Our Freedom, Lord*, © 1981 Terry Falla, p. 139, alt., p. 144.
366 From *Prayers for Today's Church*, © 1972 R. H. L. Williams, #204. Used by permission of Kingsway Communications, Eastbourne, UK.
367 From *We Celebrate* (Ave Maria Press), p. 126, alt.
368 From *Prayers for the People* ed. by Michael Perry, © 1992 HarperCollins Publishers Ltd., #1.25.
369-70 From *New Prayers for Worship* by Alan Gaunt, © 1972 John Paul Press, pp. 23, 26.
371 From *Litanies and Other Prayers for the Common Lectionary, Year C* by Everett Tilson and Phyllis Cole, © 1994 Abingdon Press, p. 109.
372 From *Lord Hear Our Prayer* by Thomas McNally and William G. Storey, © 1978 by Ave Maria Press, Notre Dame IN 46556, p. 268, alt. Used by permission of the publisher.
373 From *Contemporary Prayers for Public Worship*, © 1967 SCM Press, p. 52, alt.
374 From *The Daily Office Revised* by Ronald C. D. Jasper, © 1978 SPCK, p. 108, alt.
375 Litany of the Holy Spirit from the Taizé community.
376 From "An Act of Intercession for the Whole Church of Christ" in *A Suggested Use for Pentecost, Christian Unity Sunday* by North American Provisional Committee of the World Council of Churches, no date (circa 1945). Final prayer from the Liturgy of St. Mark (reprinted in *The Book of Prayers for Church and Home*, Christian Education Press, Philadelphia, 1962).
377 Adapted from *The Worshipbook*, © 1970 The Westminster Press.

378   From *My God, My Glory* by Eric Milner-White, © 1954 SPCK, p. 87, alt.

379   From *God-With-Us* by Miriam Therese Winter, © 1979 Abingdon Press, p. 93.

380   From *Litanies for Living* by Kay Smallzried, © 1964 Oxford University Press, p. 39.

381   From *Jesus Christ—the Life of the World*, © World Council of Churches, p. 34.

382   From *Book of Occasional Services*, p. 149. © 1979 Church Pension Fund. Used by permission.

383   By Colbert S. Cartwright.

384   From *Intercessions for the Christian People*, published by The Liturgical Press, Collegeville, Minnesota, alt. © 1992 The Order of St. Benedict, Inc. Used with permission.

385   From *Blessings for God's People* by Thomas G. Simons, © Ave Maria Press, Notre Dame IN 46556, p. 57, alt. Used by permission of the publisher.

386   Adapted from *Prayers for Use in Church* by J. W. G. Masterton, © 1970 St. Andrew Press, p. 71.

387   From *With All God's People* by John Carden, vol. 2, © 1989 World Council of Churches, p.41.

388   From *Intercessions for the Christian People*, published by The Liturgical Press, Collegeville, Minnesota, p. 106. © 1992 The Order of St. Benedict, Inc. Used with permission.

389   From *Prayers of Our Hearts*, © 1991 by Vienna Cobb Anderson, p. 46. Used with permission of The Crossroad Publishing Company, New York.

390   From *Prayers for Today's Church*, © 1972 R. H. L. Williams, #147, alt. Used by permission of Kingsway Communications, Eastbourne, UK.

391   From *Prayers of Our Hearts*, © 1991 by Vienna Cobb Anderson, p. 71. Used with permission of The Crossroad Publishing Company, New York.

392   Anonymous, from Russia.

393   From *The Book of Common Prayer*, 1979, p. 823.

394   By Stanley Pritchard in *New Parish Prayers*, © 1982 Hodder and Stoughton, p. 30, alt.

395   By Leslie Weatherhead in *New Parish Prayers*, © 1982 Hodder and Stoughton, #53, alt.

396   From *Prayers of Our Hearts*, © 1991 by Vienna Cobb Anderson, p. 62. Used with permission of The Crossroad Publishing Company, New York.

397   By Thomas Chalmers (Scotland), 19th century.

398   From *Prayers for the People* ed. by Michael Perry, © 1992 HarperCollins Publishers Ltd., #5.29.

399   By A. R. McKinstry (adapted) in *Prayers for Today* by N. W. Goodacre, © Mowbray Publishing Co., p. 15.

400   From *Prayers for the People* ed. by Michael Perry, © 1992 HarperCollins Publishers Ltd., #18.67.

401   From *New Prayers for Worship* by Alan Gaunt, © 1972 John Paul Press, p. 30.

402   From *The Iona Community Worship Book*, © 1991 Wild Goose Publications, Iona Community, Glasgow G51 3UU, Scotland, UK.

403   From *Church Family Worship*, © 1986 Hodder and Stoughton, #. 824.

404   By Jan S. Pickard in *Oceans of Prayer*, © 1991, p. 40. Reproduced with the permission of the National Christian Education Council, UK.

405-07   © Timothy Dudley-Smith, used by permission.

408-09   From *The Book of Common Prayer*, 1979, p. 824.

410   By Michael Botting in *Prayers for the People* ed. by Michael Perry, © 1992 HarperCollins Publishers Ltd., #10.29.

411   A 10th-century African hymn.

412   Adapted from *Letters and Papers from Prison* by Dietrich Bonhoeffer, enlarged edition © 1971 Macmillan Co.

413   Copyright Anglican Church of Australia Trust Corporation. From the text of *An Australian Prayer Book*, p. 94. Published by AIO Press. Reproduced with permission.

414   Reprinted from *Lutheran Book of Worship*, p. 46, © 1978, by permission of Augsburg Fortress.

415   Reprinted from *Prayers for Public Worship* by Carl Uehling, p. 136, © 1972 by Fortress Press.

416   From *Prayers for Today's Church*, © 1972 R. H. L. Williams, #276. Used by permission of Kingsway Communications, Eastbourne, UK.

417   Adapted from *The Worshipbook*, © 1970 The Westminster Press.

418   From *The Alternative Service Book 1980*, Cambridge University Press, p. 504. © 1980 The Central Board of Finance of the Church of England. Used by permission.

419   Reprinted from *Lutheran Book of Worship*, p. 42, © 1978, by permission of Augsburg Fortress.

420   By Susan Williams in *Prayers for the People* ed. by Michael Perry, © 1992 HarperCollins Publishers Ltd., #6.50.

421   From *We Celebrate* (Ave Maria Press), p. 119.

422   By Ulrich Zwingli, 16th century.

423   By Michael Botting in *New Parish Prayers*, © 1982 Hodder and Stoughton, p. 198, alt.

424   From *The Book of Common Prayer*, 1979, p. 101.

425   From *Prayers for the People* ed. by Michael Perry, © 1992 HarperCollins Publishers Ltd., #4.34.

426   From *Prayers of Our Hearts*, © 1991 by Vienna Cobb Anderson, p. 25. Used with permission of The Crossroad Publishing Company, New York.

427   By Rajah Jacob (Sri Lanka) in *Oceans of Prayer*, © 1991, p. 63. Reproduced with the permission of the National Christian Education Council, UK.

428-29   From *Prayers for the People* ed. by Michael Perry, © 1992 HarperCollins Publishers Ltd., #29.40, #18.39

430-31   By Christopher Idle, Ian Bunting in *Prayers for Today's Church,* © 1972 R. H. L. Williams, #263, #7. Used by permission of Kingsway Communications, Eastbourne, UK.

432   From *Prayers for the People* ed. by Michael Perry, © 1992 HarperCollins Publishers Ltd., #12.22.

433   From *WomanWisdom* by Miriam Therese Winter, p. 338. © 1991 Medical Mission Sisters. Used with permission of The Crossroad Publishing Company, New York.

434   From *Prayers for the People* ed. by Michael Perry, © 1992 HarperCollins Publishers Ltd., #18.34.

435   From *Church Family Worship,* © 1986 Hodder and Stoughton, #760.

436   From *Prayers for the People* ed. by Michael Perry, © 1992 HarperCollins Publishers Ltd., #5.37.

437   Reprinted from *Prayers for Public Worship* by Carl Uehling, p. 140, © 1972 by Fortress Press.

438   By W. A. Hampson in *Prayers for Today's Church,* © 1972 R. H. L. Williams. Used by permission of Kingsway Communications, Eastbourne, UK.

439-41   From *Prayers for the People* ed. by Michael Perry, © 1992 HarperCollins Publishers Ltd., #29.61, #17.49, #1.28.

442   From *Church Family Worship,* © 1986 Hodder and Stoughton, #747.

443   By Michael Perry, © 1986 Hope Publishing Company.

444   By Susan Williams in *Prayers for the People* ed. by Michael Perry, © 1992 HarperCollins Publishers Ltd., #6.49.

445   Adapted from *New Parish Prayers,* © 1982 Hodder and Stoughton, p. 184.

446   By C. N. R. Wallwork in *A Book of Vestry Prayers,* © 1976 Epworth Press, p. 66.

447   From *Prayers for Today's Church,* © 1972 R. H. L. Williams, #326. Used by permission of Kingsway Communications, Eastbourne, UK.

448   By W. Temple Bourne in *New Parish Prayers,* © 1982 Hodder and Stoughton, p. 127.

449   From *Prayers for the People* ed. by Michael Perry, © 1992 HarperCollins Publishers Ltd., #19.54.

450   By Patricia Mitchell in *Prayers for Today's Church,* © 1972 R. H. L. Williams, #355, alt. Used by permission of Kingsway Communications, Eastbourne, UK.

451   From *Bible Praying* by Michael Perry, © 1992 HarperCollins Publishers Ltd., #30, based on Isaiah 66.

452   From *Prayers for the People* ed. by Michael Perry, © 1992 HarperCollins Publishers Ltd., #18.28.

453   From *WomanWisdom* by Miriam Therese Winter, p. 213. © 1991 Medical Mission Sisters. Used with permission of The Crossroad Publishing Company, New York.

454   From *With All God's People* by John Carden, vol. 1, © 1989 World Council of Churches, p. 65.

455   By Paul B. Robinson in *Book of Worship: United Church of Christ,* © 1986 United Church of Christ Office for Church Life and Leadership, p. 541.

456   By John Chrysostom, 4th century.

457   By Elizabeth Goudge in *Prayers for the People* ed. by Michael Perry, © 1992 HarperCollins Publishers Ltd., #18.49.

458   By Keith Watkins.

459   From *With All God's People* by John Carden, vol. 1, © 1989 World Council of Churches, p. 340.

460   From *Prayers for the People* ed. by Michael Perry, © 1992 HarperCollins Publishers Ltd., #17.68.

461   By Timothy Dudley-Smith in *Prayers for the People* ed. by Michael Perry, © 1992 HarperCollins Publishers Ltd., #17.42.

462   By Brother Roger of Taizé and Mother Teresa of Calcutta.

463   From *WomanWisdom* by Miriam Therese Winter, p. 239. © 1991 Medical Mission Sisters. Used with permission of The Crossroad Publishing Company, New York.

464   By Brother Roger of Taizé.

465   From *Prayers for the People* ed. by Michael Perry, © 1992 HarperCollins Publishers Ltd., #18.68.

466   Adapted from *The Worshipbook,* © 1970 The Westminster Press.

467   From *Prayers for the People* ed. by Michael Perry, © 1992 HarperCollins Publishers Ltd., #14.29.

468   A prayer from China, in *With All God's People* by John Carden, vol. 1, © 1989 World Council of Churches, p. 44.

469   From *WomanWisdom* by Miriam Therese Winter, p. 104. © 1991 Medical Mission Sisters. Used with permission of The Crossroad Publishing Company, New York.

470   By C. N. R. Wallwork in *A Book of Vestry Prayers,* © 1976 Epworth Press, p. 94.

471   From a prayer by John Henry Newman as adapted by Mother Teresa of Calcutta.

472   By Alan Gaunt in *Prayers for the People* ed. by Michael Perry, © 1992 HarperCollins Publishers Ltd., #17.59.

473   From *New Prayers for Worship* by Alan Gaunt, © 1972 John Paul Press, p. 15.

474   From *Patterns and Prayers for Christian Worship,* © 1991 Oxford University Press, p. 62.

475   From *New Prayers for Worship* by Alan Gaunt, © 1972 John Paul Press, p. 13.

476   Ireland, 5th century, translated by Cecil Frances Alexander.

477   An ancient Celtic prayer.

478   From *In His Name* by George Appleton, © 1978 Lutterworth, p. 39, alt.

479   Congolese baptismal hymn.

480-81   From *Prayers for the People* ed. by Michael Perry, © 1992 HarperCollins

Publishers Ltd., #15.39, #20.53 (alt.).

482 Adapted from *People Praying* by Cowie, © 1972 St. Andrew Press, p. 154.

483 By Bernie Colorado (The Philippines) in *Oceans of Prayer*, © 1991, p. 88, alt. Reproduced with the permission of the National Christian Education Council, UK.

484 Adapted from *Praise God*, © 1980 Baptist Union, p. 16.

485-86 From *Book of Worship: United Church of Christ*, © 1986 United Church of Christ Office for Church Life and Leadership, p. 114.

487 By Colbert S. Cartwright.

488 From *Worship the Lord* by James R. Esther and Donald J. Bruggink, Wm. B. Eerdmans Publishing Co., p. 5. © 1987 The Reformed Church in America.

490 From *Prayers, Thanksgivings, and Litanies*, p. 73. © 1973 Church Pension Fund. Used by permission.

492 From the Preamble to the Design for the Christian Church (Disciples of Christ).

493 Used by permission of The United Church of Christ.

509-10 Traditional.

511 By Colbert S. Cartwright.

512 By Laura A. Loving in *Book of Worship: United Church of Christ*, © 1986 United Church of Christ Office for Church Life and Leadership, p. 550.

513 By Colbert S. Cartwright.

514 Traditional.

515 By Colbert S. Cartwright.

516 Anonymous.

517 From *Touch Holiness*, © 1990 Pilgrim Press, p. 213.

518 Adapted from *Whispers of God* by Lavon Bayler, © 1987 Pilgrim Press, p. 8.

519 By Colbert S. Cartwright.

520 From *Searching for Shalom*, p. 64. © 1991 Ann Weems. Used by permission of Westminster John Knox Press.

522 From *Words of Worship* by Glen E. Rainsley, © 1990 Pilgrim Press, p. 118.

523 Traditional.

524 Jerry W. Paul in *Worship: Inclusive Language Resources*, © 1977 United Church of Christ Office for Church Life and Leadership.

525 By William A. Hulteen, Jr., in *Book of Worship: United Church of Christ*, © 1986 United Church of Christ Office for Church Life and Leadership, p. 551f.

526-28 From *Worship: Inclusive Language Resources*, © 1977 United Church of Christ Office for Church Life and Leadership.

529 By Hoyt L. Hickman in *The Worship Resources of the United Methodist Hymnal*, © 1989 UMPH, p. 51, alt.

530-32 From *New Prayers for Worship* by Alan Gaunt, © 1972 John Paul Press, p. 9, alt.

533-34 From *Contemporary Prayers for Public Worship*, © 1967 SCM Press, pp. 69, 71.

535 Attributed to W. Earl Ledden.

536-37 From *Prayer in Corporate Worship* by Anne Neufield Rupp, © 1981 Faith and Life Press, p. 31.

538 By Colbert S. Cartwright, based on Psalm 145:15–16.

539-41 By Colbert S. Cartwright.

542 By G. Edwin Osborn in *Christian Worship: A Service Book*, © 1953 Bethany Press (now Chalice Press), #957, alt.

543-47 By Colbert S. Cartwright.

548-58 From the *Book of Alternative Services* of the Anglican Church of Canada, © 1985 by the General Synod of the Anglican Church of Canada, pp. 346, 364, 380, 382, 386 (alt.), 393 (alt.), 396 (alt.), 401, 402, 402, 414. Used with permission.

559 Attributed to Norman E. Jacobs.

560-61 By Ronald J. Allen and Linda McKiernan-Allen. © 1997 Chalice Press.

562 By Colbert S. Cartwright.

563-64 From *The Congregation at Worship* by L. Jim Anthis, © 1983 Christian Board of Publication, p. 37.

565 From *Be Our Freedom, Lord*, © 1981 Terry Falla, p. 156, alt.

566 From the West Indies, in *Latest Anglican Liturgies*, © 1985 SPCK, p. 170, alt.

567 From *Be Our Freedom, Lord*, © 1981 Terry Falla, p. 162.

568 From *Lost in Wonder, Love and Praise* by John Killinger, © 1986 Angel Books, p. 77.

569-74 From *When We Gather, Year A*, by James G. Kirk, pp. 33, 39, 43, 87, 117, 119. © 1983 The Geneva Press.

575 From *When We Gather, Year B*, by James G. Kirk, p. 63. © 1984 The Geneva Press.

576-79 From *Book of Divine Services*, vol. 1 (Presbyterian Church in Cameroon, 1984), pp. 54, 128, 133, 284.

580 By Christopher Idle in *New Parish Prayers*, © 1982 Hodder and Stoughton, p. 107, alt.

581 From *Words of Worship* by Glen E. Rainsley, © 1990 Pilgrim Press, p. 111.

582 From *Flames of the Spirit*, © 1985 Pilgrim Press, p. 20.

583 From *When We Gather, Year B*, by James G. Kirk, p. 29. © 1984 The Geneva Press.

584 Source untraced.

585 From *Words of Worship* by Glen E. Rainsley, © 1990 Pilgrim Press, p. 112.

586 From *All the Seasons of Mercy*, © 1987 Diane Karay, p. 129. Used by permission of Westminster John Knox Press.

587 From *When We Gather, Year B*, by James G. Kirk, p. 23. © 1984 The Geneva Press.

588 From *Prayer in Corporate Worship* by Anne Neufield Rupp, © 1981 Faith and Life Press, p. 30.

589 From *Prayers and Other Resources for Public Worship*, © 1976 Abingdon Press, p. 84.

590 From *Bread for the Journey*, © 1981 Pilgrim Press, p. 48.

591 From *Flames of the Spirit*, © 1985 Pilgrim Press, p. 43.

592 From *Book of Divine Services*, vol. 1 (Presbyterian Church in Cameroon, 1984), p. 249.

593 From *When We Gather, Year A*, by James G. Kirk, p. 83. © 1983 The Geneva Press.

594	By Colbert S. Cartwright.
595	A traditional invitation, as found in *Christian Worship: A Service Book*, ed. by G. Edwin Osborn, © 1953 Bethany Press (now Chalice Press), p. 26.
596	Adapted from a traditional invitation to the table.
597	From the *Book of Common Worship: The Presbyterian Church in Canada, 1991*, p. 76. © The Presbyterian Church in Canada, used by permission.
598	By Colbert S. Cartwright.
599	From *New Prayers for Worship* by Alan Gaunt, © 1972 John Paul Press, p. 3.
600	From *Touch Holiness*, © 1990 Pilgrim Press, p. 146.
601	From the *Book of Common Worship: The Presbyterian Church in Canada, 1991*, p. 34. © The Presbyterian Church in Canada, used by permission.
602	From *Searching for Shalom*, p. 82. © 1991 Ann Weems. Used by permission of Westminster John Knox Press.
604-05	From *Book of Worship: United Church of Christ*, © 1986 United Church of Christ Office for Church Life and Leadership, pp. 68, 66.
606	By Colbert S. Cartwright.
607	Patrick Goodland, © 1986 Hope Publishing Company.
608-10	By Colbert S. Cartwright.
611-12	Traditional.
613	From *United Reformed Church Service Book*, © 1989 Oxford University Press, p. 27f.
614-16	By Colbert S. Cartwright.
617	From *New Companion to the Breviary with Seasonal Supplement*, © 1988 by the Carmelites of Indianapolis, p. 308. Reprinted by permission of the publisher.
618	By Keith Watkins.
619	From The Apocryphal Acts of Thomas, 3rd century.
620	From *Bread Blessed and Broken* (Paulist Press, 1974), p. 141.
621	By Colbert S. Cartwright.
622	From *New Prayers for Worship* by Alan Gaunt, © 1972 John Paul Press, p. 6, alt.
623-24	From *Celebrate with Thanksgiving* by Keith Watkins, © 1991 Chalice Press, pp. 81-83, 94f.
627	From *New Prayers for Worship* by Alan Gaunt, © 1972 John Paul Press, p. 12.
629	By Michael Perry, © 1986 Hope Publishing Company.
630-32	Based on 1 Corinthians 10:16–17.
641	From *With All God's People* by John Carden, vol. 1, © 1989 World Council of Churches, p. 61.
642	Traditional.
643	From *Thankful Praise*, © 1987 Chalice Press, p. 55.
644-45	From *Celebrate with Thanksgiving* by Keith Watkins, © 1991 Chalice Press, pp. 81, 84.
646	From the *Book of Common Worship: The Presbyterian Church in Canada, 1991*, p. 112. © The Presbyterian Church in Canada, used by permission.
647	From *United Reformed Church Service Book*, © 1989 Oxford University Press, p. 20.
648	From *New Prayers for Worship* by Alan Gaunt, © 1972 John Paul Press, p. 31.
649-51	By Colbert S. Cartwright.
652	From *Book of Worship: United Church of Christ*, © 1986 United Church of Christ Office for Church Life and Leadership, p. 52.
653	From *The Sacrament of the Lord's Supper*, © 1984 Consultation on Church Union, p. 6.
654-55	From *Book of Worship: United Church of Christ*, © 1986 United Church of Christ Office for Church Life and Leadership, pp. 74, 88.
656	Adapted from the Didache, 2nd century.
657	From *New Companion to the Breviary with Seasonal Supplement*, © 1988 by the Carmelites of Indianapolis, p. 80. Reprinted by permission of the publisher.
658	From *The Sacrament of the Lord's Supper*, © 1984 Consultation on Church Union, p. 7.
659	From *Book of Worship: United Church of Christ*, © 1986 United Church of Christ Office for Church Life and Leadership, p. 196.
660	From *The Alternative Service Book 1980*, Cambridge University Press, p. 145. © 1980 The Central Board of Finance of the Church of England. Used by permission.
661	By Colbert S. Cartwright, based on an early-medieval English post-communion litany.
662	By Colbert S. Cartwright.
663	From *More Parish Liturgies* by Thomas Boyer, © 1973 Paulist Press. Used by permission of Paulist Press.
664-84	By Colbert S. Cartwright.
685	Traditional.
686	By Rosemary C. Mitchell in *Birthings and Blessings*, p. 115. © 1991 by Rosemary Catalano Mitchell and Gail Anderson Ricciuti. Used with permission of The Crossroad Publishing Company, New York.
687	Anonymous.
688	By Josef Cereunak (Czechoslovakia) in *Oceans of Prayer*, © 1991, p. 87. Reproduced with the permission of the National Christian Education Council, UK.
689	By Glen E. Rainsley in *Touch Holiness*, © 1990 Pilgrim Press, p. 241.
690-91	From *Bible Praying* by Michael Perry, © 1992 HarperCollins Publishers Ltd., #409, #443.
692	By Colbert S. Cartwright.
693	From *The Congregation at Worship* by L. Jim Anthis, © 1983 Christian Board of Publication, p. 45.
694	Traditional.
695	By Ruth Duck in *Bread for the Journey*, © 1981 Pilgrim Press, p. 67.
696	From Asia Youth Assembly, in *With All God's People* by John Carden, vol. 1, © 1989 World Council of Churches, p. 199.

697 By Ruth Duck in *Bread for the Journey,* © 1981 Pilgrim Press, p. 32.

698-99 From *Words of Worship* by Glen E. Rainsley, © 1990 Pilgrim Press, pp. 147, 148.

700 From *Words of Worship* by Glen E. Rainsley, © 1990 Pilgrim Press, p. 151.

701-02 From *Bread for the Journey,* © 1981 Pilgrim Press, p. 67f.

703 By Ruth Duck in *Women's Prayer Services,* © 1987 Twenty-Third Publications, p. 45.

704 From *Prayers of Our Hearts,* © 1991 by Vienna Cobb Anderson, p. 215. Used with permission of The Crossroad Publishing Company, New York.

705 From Wales, in *Latest Anglican Liturgies,* © 1985 SPCK, p. 79.

706 From *Worship: Inclusive Language Resources,* © 1977 United Church of Christ Office for Church Life and Leadership.

707 By Nancy Rosenberger Faus in *We Gather Together,* p. 56. © 1979 Brethren Press, Elgin IL 60120. Used by permission.

708 From *Every Pastor's Worship Planning Book* by Gary R. Shiplett, p. 119. © 1983 Meriwether Publishing Ltd. Used by permission.

709-10 From *Litanies and Other Prayers for the Common Lectionary, Year B* by Everett Tilson and Phyllis Cole, © 1993 Abingdon Press, pp. 121, 60.

711-12 From *Praise God,* © 1980 Baptist Union, p. 128, 166.

713 Adapted from *United Reformed Church Service Book,* © 1989 Oxford University Press, p. 119.

714-15 From the *Book of Alternative Services* of the Anglican Church of Canada, © 1985 by the General Synod of the Anglican Church of Canada, p. 215. Used with permission.

716 From *Book of Worship Aids* ed. by LeRoy Koopman (Palm Springs, FL: Sunday Publications, 1976), p. 74, alt.

717 From *Jesus Christ—the Life of the World,* © World Council of Churches, p. 102.

718 Anonymous.

719 From *All the Seasons of Mercy,* © 1987 Diane Karay, p. 134, alt. Used by permission of Westminster John Knox Press.

720 By Mary Ann Neeval in *Bread for the Journey,* © 1981 Pilgrim Press.

721 From *Touch Holiness,* © 1990 Pilgrim Press, p. 242.

722 From *Contemporary Prayers for Public Worship,* © 1967 SCM Press, p. 90.

723 From *Whispers of God* by Lavon Bayler, © 1987 Pilgrim Press, p. 13.

724 By Ruth Duck in *Bread for the Journey,* © 1981 Pilgrim Press, p. 26.

725 From *Lost in Wonder, Love and Praise* by John Killinger, © 1986 Angel Books, p. 197.

726-27 By Ruth Duck in *Bread for the Journey,* © 1981 Pilgrim Press, p. 32.

728 From *All the Seasons of Mercy,* © 1987

Diane Karay, p. 132. Used by permission of Westminster John Knox Press.

729 From *Litanies and Other Prayers for the Common Lectionary, Year B* by Everett Tilson and Phyllis Cole, © 1993 Abingdon Press, p. 32.

730-31 From *Whispers of God* by Lavon Bayler, © 1987 Pilgrim Press, pp. 48, 56.

732 From *Bread for the Journey,* © 1981 Pilgrim Press, p. 40.

733 From *Whispers of God* by Lavon Bayler, © 1987 Pilgrim Press, p. 68.

734-35 By Ruth Duck in *Bread for the Journey,* © 1981 Pilgrim Press, p. 49.

736 From *Book of Worship: United Church of Christ,* © 1986 United Church of Christ Office for Church Life and Leadership, p. 126.

737-38 From *New Prayers for Worship* by Alan Gaunt, © 1972 John Paul Press, p. 14.

739-40 From *Whispers of God* by Lavon Bayler, © 1987 Pilgrim Press, p. 76.

773-74 From *WomanWisdom* by Miriam Therese Winter, pp. 88 (alt.), 72 (alt.). © 1991 Medical Mission Sisters. Used with permission of The Crossroad Publishing Company, New York.

775 Traditional Gaelic blessing.

776-77 Traditional.

778-80 From *Prayers of Our Hearts,* © 1991 by Vienna Cobb Anderson, pp. 210, 208, 209. Used with permission of The Crossroad Publishing Company, New York.

781 From *WomanWisdom* by Miriam Therese Winter, p. 35, alt. © 1991 Medical Mission Sisters. Used with permission of The Crossroad Publishing Company, New York.

782 By Lois Wilson in *Jesus Christ—the Life of the World,* p. 102. © World Council of Churches.

783 From *WomanWisdom* by Miriam Therese Winter, p. 172. © 1991 Medical Mission Sisters. Used with permission of The Crossroad Publishing Company, New York.

784 By Colbert S. Cartwright.

785 From *1987 United Methodist Clergywomen's Consultation Resource Book,* p. 67.

786 From *WomanPrayer WomanSong* by Miriam Therese Winter. © 1987 Medical Mission Sisters. Used with permission of The Crossroad Publishing Company, New York.

787-88 From *Prayers of Our Hearts,* © 1991 by Vienna Cobb Anderson, pp. 213, 216. Used with permission of The Crossroad Publishing Company, New York.

789 From *WomanPrayer WomanSong* by Miriam Therese Winter, p. 192. © 1987 Medical Mission Sisters. Used with permission of The Crossroad Publishing Company, New York.

790 Adapted from *Prayers of Our Hearts,* © 1991 by Vienna Cobb Anderson, p. 207. Used with permission of The Crossroad Publishing Company, New York.

791-94 From *The United Methodist Book of Worship,* © 1992 UMPH, pp. 660, 39, 94, 284.

795   From *Prayers for the People* ed. by Michael Perry, © 1992 HarperCollins Publishers Ltd., #23.67.

796   By Roger D. Knight in *Book of Worship: United Church of Christ*, © 1986 United Church of Christ Office for Church Life and Leadership, p. 114.

797   By Elizabeth A. Hambrick-Stowe in *Worship: Inclusive Language Resources*, © 1977 United Church of Christ Office for Church Life and Leadership.

798   Adapted from the 1982 Convocation of Lower Sioux, The Episcopal Church Dioceses of Minnesota and North Dakota, Order for Celebrating Holy Eucharist.

799   From *Book of Worship: United Church of Christ*, © 1986 United Church of Christ Office for Church Life and Leadership, p. 54.

800   From *Book of Worship: United Church of Christ*, © 1986 United Church of Christ Office for Church Life and Leadership, p. 117.

801   From *Patterns and Prayers for Christian Worship*, © 1991 Oxford University Press, p. 90.

802   By G. Edwin Osborn in *Christian Worship: A Service Book*, © 1953 Bethany Press (now Chalice Press), #1132, alt.

803   From *Let Us Worship God* by Hubert L. Simpson, ©1929 James Clark and Co., Ltd.

804   From *Book of Occasional Services*, p. 24. © Church Pension Fund. Used by permission.

805-08   From *Prayers for Contemporary Worship* (in the Church of Scotland), © 1977 St. Andrew Press, pp. 89-91.

809   From *Prayers of Our Hearts*, © 1991 by Vienna Cobb Anderson, p. 207. Used with permission of The Crossroad Publishing Company, New York.

810   From the Middle East, in *With All God's People* by John Carden, vol. 1, © 1989 World Council of Churches, p. 9, alt.

811   Based on Philippians 4:7.

812-13   From *Prayers of Our Hearts*, © 1991 by Vienna Cobb Anderson, pp. 209, 211. Used with permission of The Crossroad Publishing Company, New York.

814   By William Temple.

815-16   From *The Alternative Service Book 1980*, Cambridge University Press, p. 159. © 1980 The Central Board of Finance of the Church of England. Used by permission.

817   From *An Australian Prayer Book* (AIO Press), p. 151. © Anglican Church of Australia Trust Corporation. Reproduced with permission.

818   From *Prayers of Our Hearts*, © 1991 by Vienna Cobb Anderson, p. 208. Used with permission of The Crossroad Publishing Company, New York.

819   From *An Australian Prayer Book* (AIO Press), p. 151. © Anglican Church of Australia Trust Corporation. Reproduced with permission.

820   From *The Alternative Service Book 1980*, Cambridge University Press, p. 159. © 1980 The Central Board of Finance of the Church of England. Used by permission.

821   From *An Australian Prayer Book* (AIO Press), p. 152. © Anglican Church of Australia Trust Corporation. Reproduced with permission.

822-23   From *The Alternative Service Book 1980*, Cambridge University Press, p. 160. © 1980 The Central Board of Finance of the Church of England. Used by permission.

824   From *An Australian Prayer Book* (AIO Press), p. 152. © Anglican Church of Australia Trust Corporation. Reproduced with permission.

825   By John Hunter (Scotland), 19th century, alt.

826   From *New Parish Prayers*, © 1982 Hodder and Stoughton, p. 11.

827   Traditional Celtic blessing.

828   Source untraced.

829   From *Prayer in Corporate Worship* by Anne Neufield Rupp, © 1981 Faith and Life Press, p. 25.

830   From *The Alternative Service Book 1980*, Cambridge University Press, p. 173. © 1980 The Central Board of Finance of the Church of England. Used by permission.

831   From *Prayer in Corporate Worship* by Anne Neufield Rupp, © 1981 Faith and Life Press, p. 26.

832   From *Responsive Service Book* by Stephen F. Winward, © 1965 Hodder and Stoughton, p. 68, alt.

833   From *More Than Words*, p. 56. First ed. © 1986, second rev. ed. © 1988, by Pat Kozak, CSJ, and Janet Schaffran, CDP. Used with permission of The Crossroad Publishing Company, New York.

834   From *WomanPrayer WomanSong* by Miriam Therese Winter, p. 106. © 1987 Medical Mission Sisters. Used with permission of The Crossroad Publishing Company, New York.

835   From *Worship: Inclusive Language Resources*, © 1977 United Church of Christ Office for Church Life and Leadership.

836   From the *Book of Common Worship: The Presbyterian Church in Canada, 1991*, p. 200. © The Presbyterian Church in Canada, used by permission.

837   Sarum Liturgy, 13th century, alt.

838   Attributed to John Henry Newman, 19th century.

839   From *Danger! People at Prayer!* (1972, no publisher indicated), reprinted in *Praise God*, © 1980 Baptist Union, p. 120.

840-41   From *WomanWisdom* by Miriam Therese Winter, pp. 64 (alt.), 161. © 1991 Medical Mission Sisters. Used with permission of The Crossroad Publishing Company, New York.

842   From *Lost in Wonder, Love and Praise* by John Killinger, © 1986 Angel Books, p. 189.

843   From *Searching for Shalom*, p. 81. © 1991 Ann Weems. Used by permission of Westminster John Knox Press.

844 From *Lost in Wonder, Love and Praise* by John Killinger, © 1986 Angel Books, p. 193.

845 By Alison Geary in *Oceans of Prayer*, © 1991, p. 100. Reproduced with the permission of the National Christian Education Council, UK.

846 From *Litanies and Other Prayers for the Common Lectionary, Year B* by Everett Tilson and Phyllis Cole, © 1993 Abingdon Press, p. 87.

847-48 From *WomanWord* by Miriam Therese Winter, pp. 141, 226. © 1990 Medican Mission Sisters. Used with permission of The Crossroad Publishing Company, New York.

849 From *Jesus Christ—the Life of the World*, p. 103. © World Council of Churches.

850-51 From *With All God's People* by John Carden, vol. 1, © 1989 World Council of Churches, pp. 48, 327.

852 From *With All God's People* by John Carden, vol. 2, © 1989 World Council of Churches, p. 92.

853 From New Zealand, in *Latest Anglican Liturgies*, © 1985 SPCK, p. 224.

854 From *Prayers for the City of God* by G. C. Binyon, © 1927 Longmans, Green and Co., used by permission of Addison Wesley Longman Ltd.

855 From the Christian Conference of Asia, in *With All God's People* by John Carden, vol. 1, © 1989 World Council of Churches, p. 204.

856 From *Saint Andrew Bible Missal*, © 1982 William J. Hirten Co., p. 65.

857 From *With All God's People* by John Carden, vol. 1, © 1989 World Council of Churches, p. 299.

858 From *Celebrations for Today* by Stephen W. Burgess and James D. Righter, © 1977 Abingdon Press, p. 61.

859-60 From *United Reformed Church Service Book*, ©1989 Oxford University Press, pp. 46, 59.

861-62 From *A Pastor's Worship Resource* ed. by James R. Spruce, © 1988 Beacon Hill Press of Kansas City, p. 182.

863 From *Flames of the Spirit*, © 1985 Pilgrim Press, p. 94.

864 From *Bible Praying* by Michael Perry, © 1992 HarperCollins Publishers Ltd., #453.

865 From *Book of Occasional Services*, p. 20. © Church Pension Fund. Used by permission.

866-67 From *God-With-Us* by Miriam Therese Winter, © 1979 Abingdon Press, pp. 15, 23.

868 From *The Order of Divine Service for Public Worship* by W. E. Orchard, © 1925 Oxford University Press, p. 73.

869 By Jan S. Pickard in *Oceans of Prayer*, © 1991, p. 100. Reproduced with the permission of the National Christian Education Council, UK.

870 Adapted from *Book of Occasional Services*, p. 21. © Church Pension Fund. Used by permission.

871 From *Lost in Wonder, Love and Praise* by John Killinger, © 1986 Angel Books, p. 198.

872 From *With All God's People* by John Carden, vol. 2, © 1989 World Council of Churches, p. 35.

873 From *Lost in Wonder, Love and Praise* by John Killinger, © 1986 Angel Books, p. 198.

874 From *WomanWord* by Miriam Therese Winter, p. 168. © 1990 Medican Mission Sisters. Used with permission of The Crossroad Publishing Company, New York.

875 From *All the Seasons of Mercy*, © 1987 Diane Karay, p. 133. Used by permission of Westminster John Knox Press.

876-77 Adapted from *Book of Occasional Services*, p. 25. © Church Pension Fund. Used by permission.

896 From *Contemporary Prayers for Public Worship*, © 1967 SCM Press, p. 64.

897 From *Bible Praying* by Michael Perry, © 1992 HarperCollins Publishers Ltd., #383, alt.

898 From *Prayers for Use in Church* by J. W. G. Masterton, © 1970 St. Andrew Press, p. 120.

899 By Jim Cotter in *Prayers for the People* ed. by Michael Perry, © 1992 HarperCollins Publishers Ltd., #10.43.

900 By Thomas Ken, 17th century.

901 By Keith Watkins.

902 By O. I. Cricket Harrison.

903 Adapted from a 1st-century daily Jewish liturgy.

904 By George Wither in *Daily Prayer*, © 1941 Oxford University Press, p. 80, alt.

905 From the *Anaphora* of Dioscorus, 5th century.

906 A prayer from the old Syriac, used by Christians in Turkey, Iran, and South India, reprinted in *With All God's People* by John Carden, vol. 1, © 1989 World Council of Churches, p. 29.

907 From *Prayers for the People* ed. by Michael Perry, © 1992 HarperCollins Publishers Ltd., #13.38.

SCRIPTURE INDEX

Numbers in Roman type refer to pages in the first five sections of the book.
Numbers in *italics* refer to individual items in Section VI beginning on p. 237.

$\mathcal{S}$UBJECT INDEX

Numbers in Roman type refer to pages in the first five sections of the book.
Numbers in *italics* refer to individual items in Section VI beginning on p. 237.